# Black Americans

## A Statistical Sourcebook & Guide to Government Data

# 2008 Edition

# Black Americans

## A Statistical Sourcebook & Guide to Government Data

## 2008 Edition

**American Profiles Series**

Woodside, California

Books from Information Publications

### State & Municipal Profiles Series
*Almanac of the 50 States*

*California Cities, Towns & Counties*       *Connecticut Municipal Profiles*

*Florida Cities, Towns & Counties*       *Massachusetts Municipal Profiles*

*The New Jersey Municipal Data Book*   *North Carolina Cities, Towns & Counties*

### American Profiles Series
*Asian Americans: A Statistical Sourcebook and Guide to Government Data*

*Black Americans: A Statistical Sourcebook and Guide to Government Data*

*Hispanic Americans: A Statistical Sourcebook and Guide to Government Data*

### Essential Topics Series
*Energy, Transportation & the Environment:*
*A Statistical Sourcebook and Guide to Government Data*

Black Americans: A Statistical Sourcebook and Guide to Government Data, 2008
ISBN 978-0-929960-49-4

**©2008 Information Publications, Inc.**
Printed in the United States of America

Information Publications, Inc.
2995 Woodside Rd., Suite 400-182
Woodside, CA  94062-2446

www.informationpublications.com
info@informationpublications.com

Toll Free Phone 877.544.INFO (4636)
Toll Free Fax 877.544.4635

Direct Dial Phone 650.568.6170
Direct Dial Fax 650.568.6150

# Table of Contents

# Detailed Table of Contents

## Chapter 2: Vital Statistics and Health 41

## Chapter 3: Education       113

## Chapter 6: Labor, Employment & Unemployment     247

## Chapter 7: Earnings, Income, Poverty & Wealth                    285

# Introduction

**{ip}**
American
Profiles
Series

The 2008 edition of *Black Americans: A Statistical Sourcebook and Guide to Government Data* is the 19th edition of this annual reference publication. It is part of Information Publications' **American Profiles** series, which also includes *Asian Americans: A Statistical Sourcebook and Guide to Government Data* and *Hispanic Americans: A Statistical Sourcebook and Guide to Government Data*. While some information on Black Americans is provided in a variety of other reference sources, *Black Americans: A Statistical Sourcebook and Guide to Government Data* is a single-volume statistical reference devoted entirely to this important segment of the population.

The overall goal of *Black Americans* is to bring together a variety of diverse information into a single volume and present it in a clear, comprehensible format. It is not intended as a detailed research tool, but rather as a ready reference source that provides a statistical overview and guide to government data on Black Americans.

*Black Americans* contains an extensive collection of tables providing information on a wide variety of topics. With a few exceptions, each table presents data on the Black population, the White population, and a total for Americans of all races and ethnic groups. The purpose of this approach is not to advance a specific perspective about Black Americans, but to provide a context within which the tabular data can be more fully understood and evaluated.

Presenting data by race and ethnicity puts any publisher at risk of having its motives questioned. While some may view the presentation of such data with suspicion, or perceive a hidden agenda, Information Publications' intent is merely to serve as a reportorial resource, providing access to federal government information. This collection of sometimes difficult to find and hard to understand information serves students, business persons, reporters, social scientists, researchers, and others who need basic data about Black Americans.

The use of the term 'Black' requires some explanation, as it can be controversial. Black Americans have used a number of terms to name themselves, and in many circles, 'African-American' has replaced 'Black' as the preferred term. 'Black' is used here only because it is the word currently used by the federal government in gathering data. Federal usage has changed over the years, and as it continues to change, those changes will be reflected here.

Whether or not someone is identified as Black can also be a sensitive issue. For federal data-collection and statistical reporting purposes, being Black is based solely on self-identification: Black persons are those who say they are

Black (or, in some surveys, African-American or Afro-American).

The federal government considers 'Black' to be a racial group, similar to 'White', or 'Asian'. However, Hispanic origin is not counted as a racial group. For almost all federal data collection programs, persons may be of any race *and* also of Hispanic origin. There are some exceptions, such as the US Department of Education and the Centers for Disease Control, which count Hispanics separately from non-Hispanic Blacks and non-Hispanic Whites for some (but not necessarily all) types of data. As a general guideline, the majority of persons identifying themselves as Hispanic as well as a racial category for federal data collection purposes identify themselves as White, although there are persons who identify as both Black and Hispanic.

### Organization

The main portion of this book has been divided into eight chapters:

| | |
|---|---|
| Chapter 1: | Demographics & Social Characteristics |
| Chapter 2: | Vital Statistics & Health |
| Chapter 3: | Education |
| Chapter 4: | Government & Elections |
| Chapter 5: | Crime, Law Enforcement & Corrections |
| Chapter 6: | Labor, Employment & Unemployment |
| Chapter 7: | Earnings, Income, Poverty & Wealth |
| Chapter 8: | Special Topics |

The tables in each chapter present a comprehensive review of available federal government statistical information on the Black population. Each table presents pertinent information from the source or sources in a clear, comprehensible fashion. The information selected for presentation was chosen for its broad scope and general appeal for a diverse group of readers.

## The Sources

All of the information in **Black Americans** is either collected directly or re-published by US Government sources. Most of the federal information is from the US Bureau of the Census. Without question, the Census Bureau is the largest data-gathering organization in the nation. It collects information on an exceptionally broad range of topics, not only for its own use and for the use of Congress and the Executive Branch, but also for other federal agencies and departments. The reach of the Census Bureau is wider than most people realize. It encompasses the decennial Census of Population, the Current Population Survey, the Annual Housing Survey, and the American Community Survey. In cooperation with other agencies, the Bureau produces the Consumer Expenditure Survey, the National Crime Survey, the National Family Growth Survey, and many other surveys. The Census Bureau's role in so much of the federal government's data collection adds uniformity to the statistical information published by different agencies and makes the data easier to understand and use. In addition, because of the sheer volume of data it collects, many private data collectors have adopted some of its procedures and terminology, enhancing compatibility between private and public data.

Observant readers will note that the source of many tables found here is a Census Bureau publication, the *Statistical Abstract of the United States*. There are several reasons for this. First, due to budgetary constraints and the huge amount of data collected, much of the information presented in the *Abstract* has never been previously published, or has only been published in part. Second, the *Abstract* presents data that is accessible to many different types of readers. As the preeminent federal data publisher, the Census Bureau has access to a wealth of raw data that it can aggregate and break down by details such as age, sex, race, or geographic region, using its own parameters for publication. Some data has only been published in very fine detail, and the *Abstract* provides an overview that is more accessible to more casual readers.

## Types of Information

Data presented here is divided into two categories:

The first is complete count data. For example, questions asked of all Americans by the Census Bureau in its decennial census attempt a complete count of a given universe.

The second type of data is survey information. When surveying the entire population would be impractical or impossible, a subset of a population is drawn to represent the entire population or universe. Data on housing units and money income are some of the items in this book based on this type of survey information. Of course, survey information is only as good as the survey itself, so the reader should always consider the accuracy and methods used by the original source. Survey methodology is not discussed here: interested readers should consult the original source materials for a detailed explanation of survey methodology. A full reference to each source appears in every table. Readers should also note that most data collected by government agencies (except for the short form of the Decennial Census) is based on a sample, and that data based on small numbers of individuals is considered statistically unreliable and not presented in the results. In these cases, a note appears in the table.

## The Tables

This section details how the tables have been prepared and presented. Table titles are the first source of valuable information. For example:

> ### Table 2.02:  Fertility, Births, and Birth Rates
> ### by Age of the Mother, 1990–2006

The table number contains the chapter number to the left of the decimal and the location of the table within the chapter to the right of the decimal. Thus Table 2.02 is the second table in Chapter 2. In general, information in tables and across each chapter is presented with the oldest, most general information first, followed by newer, more specific information.

The table title first presents the general topic of the table, followed by the detail presented about the general topic (e.g., the data is presented by age, sex, state of residence, marital status, etc.), and the years for which data is presented. In most cases, the tables retain the original terms used in the source material to make the book compatible with the original sources.

For most tables, the left-most column or columns show data for the Black population, the center column or columns show data for the White population, and the right-hand column or columns show data for all races.

Along the left margin of each table appears a column of line descriptors. Here, after a general heading, subgroups of the heading are shown. In general, counts and quantities appear first, followed by percentages, medians, means, rates, and per capita amounts.

Wherever available and appropriate, a time span of data is presented in order to provide readers with a historical context for the information. However, readers should be cautioned that the years selected have been chosen from no special knowledge of the subject, nor to make any specific point. The fact that there has been an increase or decrease in a given indicator for the period displayed does not mean that the same trend will continue, or that it represents the continuation of a historical trend, or even that which appears to be a trend within this period actually is one. Many apparent changes are merely the result of an agency's redefining its terms: for example, many Census programs have different specifications for Black: 'Black,' 'Black Alone,' 'non-Hispanic Black,' and 'Black Alone or in Combination.' Programs sometimes change the definition that they use, and this may give the appearance of a real change in the population when there was none. For this reason, readers are advised to use caution when comparing figures across different time periods.

## Table Notes

The bottom of each table contains three key paragraphs: Source, Notes, and Units. The **Source** paragraph lists the source of the data presented in the table. When more than one source was used, the sources are listed in the same order in which the data itself appears in the table. As all sources are government publications, the issuing agency is listed as the author. Citations provide the table number in the source from which the material was taken. An increasing number of sources are now available on the internet, and in many cases, only on the internet. For tables pulled exclusively from online sources, the URL is listed as the source, along with the date it was accessed.

The **Notes** paragraph includes pertinent facts about the data. One general note will apply to all tabular data: detail (subgroups) may not add to the total shown, due either to rounding or to the fact that only selected subgroups are displayed.

The final paragraph of a table, **Units**, identifies the units used, specifically stating that the quantity is millions of persons, thousands of workers, dollars per capita, etc. Readers are urged to pay special attention to the units when a median, mean, percent, rate, or a per capita amount is provided.

## Guide to Sources

*Black Americans* also presents a complete guide to sources. Sources are listed by chapter and sorted alphabetically by the name of the publication, with the issuing department or group appearing next. Each entry gives a description of the source, including how it was used in the present volume and what information it might present for further research, as well as the online location where the data or report can be accessed.

## The Glossary

This book contains definitions for any specialized terms that are needed to understand the data. The tables contain short, clear definitions with only as much background material as necessary to make a term understandable in a general sense. However, for many tables, when it is not possible to adequately define a term in the table notes, the glossary provides a full definition and serves as an important tool in using the tables.

Before drawing any conclusions from the data, it is absolutely vital to understand the meaning of all terms used in a table. Certain terms require some methodological background in order to accurately understand the material presented. The government not only has its own specialized, clearly-defined terms, but it also uses ordinary words in specialized ways. For example, there are real differences between a household and a family, a family and a married couple, the resident population and the civilian non-institutional population, a service industry and a service occupation, and an urban area and a metropolitan area.

Readers requiring detailed definitions and an understating of the technical and methodological detail should refer to the sources for more complete explanations.

## The Index

Most key terms from the tables have been indexed. Readers should note that the index provides table numbers as opposed to page numbers.

## A Suggestion on How to Use This Book

One way to use this book is by locating a subject of general interest in the **Table of Contents** and turning to that chapter. While the **Table of Contents** is detailed enough to narrow a search, and the index can speed access to specific items, sometimes paging through the dozen or so tables on a given topic uncovers unexpected information that can prove useful. It is just this type of serendipity that has lead to the inclusion of some of the information in this book, and sometimes an unexpected find can greatly enhance a research project.

## Disclaimer

*Black Americans: A Statistical Sourcebook and Guide to Government Data* contains thousands of pieces of information. Every reasonable precaution, along with a good deal of care, was taken in its preparation. Despite our efforts it is possible that some of the information contained in this book may not be accurate. Some errors may be due to errors in the original source materials, others may have been made by the compilers of this volume. An incorrect spelling may occur, a figure may be inverted, or similar mistakes may exist. The compilers, editors, typists, printers and others are all human, and in a work of this magnitude the possibility of error can never be fully eliminated.

The publisher is also aware that some users may apply the data in this book in various remunerative projects. Although we have taken reasonable, responsible measures to insure accuracy, we cannot take responsibility for liability or losses suffered by users of the data. No other guarantees are made or implied.

**The publisher assumes no liability for losses incurred by users, and warrants only that diligence and care were used in the production of this volume.**

## A Final Word

As this book is updated on an annual basis, questions, comments, and criticisms from users are vital to making informed editorial choices about succeeding editions. If you have a suggestion or comment, be assured that it will be both appreciated and carefully considered. If you should find an error here, please let us know so that it may be corrected. Our goal is to provide accurate, easy to use, statistical compendiums that serve our readers' needs. Your help enables us to do our job better. If you know how this book could become more useful to you, please contact us.

The Editors
Information Publications, Inc.
2995 Woodside Road, Suite 400-182
Woodside, CA 94062
www.informationpublications.com
info@informationpublications.com
Toll Free Phone: 877-544-4636
Toll Free Fax: 877-544-4635

# Data Tables

American
Profiles
Series

# Chapter 1

## Demographics and
## Social Characteristics

## Chapter One Highlights

This chapter provides information about the demographics and social characteristics of Black persons in the United States, including both the most current data available as well as comparisons of the Black population over time. For almost all tables, corresponding data is provided for the total population of the United States as well as for White persons. This allows for easy comparison between groups.

The chapter includes general population statistics for Black persons organized in a number of different ways, including by age (tables 1.02 and 1.10); sex (table 1.02); residence (tables 1.01, 1.02, 1.04, and 1.09); and educational attainment (table 1.10). In addition, population projections are provided up to the year 2100 (tables 1.07 and 1.08). Since the year 2000, the Black population has increased across the United States, and the latest data on births, deaths, and internal migration is also provided (table 1.03).

In addition, this chapter contains marriage statistics, both for the total population (table 1.12) and divided by gender (tables 1.13 and 1.14). Statistics on the increasing number of interracial marriages is also provided (table 1.15).

Also of note are the tables comparing characteristics such as marital status, residence, and age during 1985, 1990, and 2006. These tables are divided by statistics on households (tables 1.16–1.18) and statistics on family households (tables 1.19–1.21).

This chapter also provides statistics on minors (tables 1.19–1.23), in addition to data on childcare arrangements (table 1.26).

## Table 1.01: Resident Population and Median Age, 1790–2006

| | Black | | White | | All Races | |
|---|---|---|---|---|---|---|
| | **Total** | **Median Age** | **Total** | **Median Age** | **Total** | **Median Age** |
| 1790 (August 2) | 757 | NA | 3,172 | NA | 3,930 | NA |
| 1800 (August 4) | 1,002 | NA | 4,306 | 16.0 | 5,308 | NA |
| 1820 (August 7) | 1,772 | 17.2 | 7,867 | 16.5 | 9,638 | 16.7 |
| 1840 (June 1) | 2,874 | 17.3 | 14,196 | 17.9 | 17,069 | 17.8 |
| 1860 (June 1) | 4,442 | 17.7 | 26,923 | 19.7 | 31,443 | 19.4 |
| 1880 (June 1) | 6,581 | 18.0 | 43,403 | 21.4 | 50,156 | 20.9 |
| 1900 (June 1) | 8,834 | 19.4 | 66,809 | 23.4 | 75,995 | 22.9 |
| 1920 (January 1) | 10,463 | 22.3 | 94,821 | 25.6 | 105,711 | 25.3 |
| 1940 (April 1) | 12,866 | 25.3 | 118,215 | 29.5 | 131,669 | 29.0 |
| 1960 (April 1) | 18,872 | 23.5 | 158,832 | 30.3 | 179,323 | 29.5 |
| 1980 (April 1) | 26,683 | 24.9 | 194,713 | 30.9 | 226,546 | 30.0 |
| 1990 (April 1) | 29,986 | NA | 199,686 | NA | 248,710 | 32.8 |
| 1995 (July 1) | 33,141 | 29.2 | 218,085 | 35.3 | 262,755 | 34.3 |
| 2000 (April) | 35,705* | 30.0 | 228,107* | 36.6 | 281,425* | 35.3 |
| 2001 (July 1) | 36,247 | 30.3 | 230,290 | 36.9 | 284,797 | 35.6 |
| 2002 (July 1) | 36,746 | 30.5 | 232,647 | 37.1 | 288,369 | 35.7 |
| 2003 (July 1) | 37,099 | 30.6 | 234,196 | 37.3 | 290,810 | 35.9 |
| 2004 (July 1) | 37,502 | 30.8 | 236,058 | 37.5 | 293,655 | 36.0 |
| 2005 (July 1) | 37,909 | 30.9 | 237,855 | 37.6 | 296,410 | 36.2 |
| 2006 (July 1) | 38,343 | 31.0 | 239,746 | 37.8 | 299,398 | 36.4 |

**Source:** US Bureau of the Census, *Statistical Abstract of the United States, 1989*, table 21; *1990*, table 19; *1991*, tables 12 and 27; *1995*, table 22; *2000*, table 19; *2002*, table 15; *2003*, table 13; *2004-2005*, table 14; *2006*, table 14; *2007*, table 14; *2008*, table 8.

**Notes:** 'All Races' includes races not shown separately.
* Reflects changes to the Census 2000 population from the Count Question Resolution program and geographic program revisions.

**Units:** Population in thousands of persons; median age in years.

## Table 1.02: Resident Population by Age and Sex, 1980–2006

| | Black | White | All Races |
|---|---|---|---|
| **1980** | | | |
| *All people* | *26,683* | *194,713* | *226,546* |
| Under 5 years old | 2,459 | 13,414 | 16,348 |
| 16 years old and older | 18,425 | 149,121 | 171,196 |
| 65 years old and older | 2,092 | 23,162 | 25,549 |
| **1985** | | | |
| *All people* | *28,887* | *202,768* | *238,740* |
| Under 5 years old | 2,706 | 14,636 | 18,037 |
| 16 years old and older | 20,380 | 157,584 | 183,010 |
| 65 years old and older | 2,343 | 25,743 | 28,530 |
| **2000** | | | |
| *All people* | *35,705* | *228,107* | *281,425* |
| Under 5 years old | 2,926 | 14,657 | 19,176 |
| 5-13 years old | 5,924 | 28,381 | 37,026 |
| 14-17 years old | 2,426 | 12,523 | 16,093 |
| 18-24 years old | 3,943 | 21,197 | 27,141 |
| 65 years and older | 2,859 | 30,964 | 34,992 |
| 85 years old and older | 316 | 3,827 | 4,240 |
| **2006** | | | |
| *All people* | *38,343* | *239,746* | *299,398* |
| Under 5 years old | 3,073 | 15,549 | 20,418 |
| 5-13 years old | 5,528 | 27,519 | 36,078 |
| 14-17 years old | 2,763 | 13,167 | 17,240 |
| 18-24 years old | 4,377 | 22,831 | 29,455 |
| 65 years and older | 3,168 | 32,444 | 37,260 |
| 85 years old and older | 380 | 4,743 | 5,297 |

**Source:** US Bureau of the Census, *Statistical Abstract of the United States, 1985*, table 30; *1987*, table 20; *2008*, table 8.

**Notes:** 'All Races' includes races not shown separately.

**Units:** Population in thousands of persons.

## Table 1.03: Components of Population Change, 2000–2007

|                                 | Black      | White       | All Races   |
|---------------------------------|-----------:|------------:|------------:|
| Population on April 1, 2000     | 35,812,983 | 228,622,981 | 281,194,308 |
| + Births                        | 4,582,754  | 22,647,264  | 29,809,472  |
| – Deaths                        | 2,122,903  | 14,985,410  | 17,597,188  |
| + Net international migration    | 591,609    | 5,398,422   | 7,984,271   |
| Net Population Increase         | 3,051,581  | 13,060,390  | 20,196,555  |
| Population on July 1, 2007      | 38,756,452 | 241,166,890 | 301,621,157 |

**Source:**   US Bureau of the Census, Population Estimates Division, *Cumulative Estimates of the Components of Population Change by Race and Hispanic or Latino Origin for the United States: April 1, 2000 to July 1, 2007* (NC-EST2007-05).
US Bureau of the Census, Population Estimates Division, *Annual Estimates of the Population by Sex, Race and Hispanic or Latino Origin for the United States: April 1, 2000 to July 1, 2007* (NC-EST2007-03).

**Notes:**   'All Races' includes races not shown separately.
The sum of the components may not add to the total.

**Units:**   Population in number of persons.

## Table 1.04  Resident Population by State, 1970, 1980, 1990, and 2007

| | 1970 | | | 1980 | | |
|---|---|---|---|---|---|---|
| | Black | White | All Races | Black | White | All Races |
| Alabama | 903 | 2,534 | 3,444 | 996 | 2,873 | 3,894 |
| Alaska | 9 | 237 | 300 | 14 | 310 | 402 |
| Arizona | 53 | 1,605 | 1,771 | 75 | 2,241 | 2,718 |
| Arkansas | 352 | 1,566 | 1,923 | 374 | 1,890 | 2,286 |
| California | 1,400 | 17,761 | 19,953 | 1,819 | 18,031 | 23,668 |
| Colorado | 66 | 2,112 | 2,207 | 102 | 2,571 | 2,890 |
| Connecticut | 181 | 2,835 | 3,032 | 217 | 2,799 | 3,108 |
| Delaware | 78 | 466 | 548 | 96 | 488 | 594 |
| District of Columbia | 538 | 209 | 757 | 449 | 172 | 638 |
| Florida | 1,042 | 5,719 | 6,789 | 1,343 | 8,185 | 9,746 |
| Georgia | 1,187 | 3,391 | 4,590 | 1,465 | 3,947 | 5,463 |
| Hawaii | 8 | 298 | 769 | 17 | 319 | 965 |
| Idaho | 2 | 699 | 713 | 3 | 902 | 944 |
| Illinois | 1,426 | 9,600 | 11,114 | 1,675 | 9,233 | 11,427 |
| Indiana | 357 | 4,820 | 5,194 | 415 | 5,004 | 5,490 |
| Iowa | 33 | 2,783 | 2,824 | 42 | 2,839 | 2,914 |
| Kansas | 107 | 2,122 | 2,247 | 126 | 2,168 | 2,364 |
| Kentucky | 231 | 2,982 | 3,219 | 259 | 3,379 | 3,661 |
| Louisiana | 1,087 | 2,541 | 3,641 | 1,238 | 2,912 | 4,206 |
| Maine | 3 | 985 | 992 | 3 | 1,110 | 1,125 |
| Maryland | 699 | 3,195 | 3,922 | 958 | 3,159 | 4,217 |
| Massachusetts | 176 | 5,478 | 5,689 | 221 | 5,363 | 5,737 |
| Michigan | 991 | 7,833 | 8,875 | 1,199 | 7,872 | 9,262 |
| Minnesota | 35 | 3,736 | 3,805 | 53 | 3,936 | 4,076 |
| Mississippi | 816 | 1,393 | 2,217 | 887 | 1,615 | 2,521 |
| Missouri | 480 | 4,177 | 4,677 | 514 | 4,345 | 4,917 |

*(continued on next page)*

## Table 1.04: Resident Population by State, 1970, 1980, 1990, and 2007

| | **1970** | | | **1980** | | |
|---|---|---|---|---|---|---|
| | **Black** | **White** | **All Races** | **Black** | **White** | **All Races** |
| Montana | 2 | 663 | 694 | 2 | 740 | 787 |
| Nebraska | 40 | 1,433 | 1,483 | 48 | 1,490 | 1,570 |
| Nevada | 28 | 448 | 489 | 51 | 700 | 800 |
| New Hampshire | 3 | 733 | 738 | 4 | 910 | 921 |
| New Jersey | 770 | 6,350 | 7,168 | 925 | 6,127 | 7,365 |
| New Mexico | 20 | 916 | 1,016 | 24 | 978 | 1,303 |
| New York | 2,169 | 15,834 | 18,237 | 2,402 | 13,961 | 17,558 |
| North Carolina | 1,126 | 3,902 | 5,082 | 1,319 | 4,458 | 5,882 |
| North Dakota | 2 | 599 | 618 | 3 | 626 | 653 |
| Ohio | 970 | 9,647 | 10,652 | 1,077 | 9,597 | 10,798 |
| Oklahoma | 172 | 2,280 | 2,559 | 205 | 2,598 | 3,025 |
| Oregon | 26 | 2,032 | 2,091 | 37 | 2,491 | 2,633 |
| Pennsylvania | 1,017 | 10,738 | 11,794 | 1,047 | 10,652 | 11,864 |
| Rhode Island | 25 | 915 | 947 | 28 | 897 | 947 |
| South Carolina | 789 | 1,794 | 2,591 | 949 | 2,147 | 3,122 |
| South Dakota | 2 | 630 | 666 | 2 | 640 | 691 |
| Tennessee | 621 | 3,294 | 3,924 | 726 | 3,835 | 4,591 |
| Texas | 1,399 | 9,717 | 11,197 | 1,710 | 11,198 | 14,229 |
| Utah | 7 | 1,032 | 1,059 | 9 | 1,383 | 1,461 |
| Vermont | 1 | 443 | 444 | 1 | 507 | 511 |
| Virginia | 861 | 3,762 | 4,648 | 1,009 | 4,230 | 5,347 |
| Washington | 71 | 3,251 | 3,409 | 106 | 3,779 | 4,132 |
| West Virginia | 67 | 1,673 | 1,744 | 65 | 1,875 | 1,950 |
| Wisconsin | 128 | 4,259 | 4,418 | 183 | 4,443 | 4,706 |
| Wyoming | 3 | 323 | 332 | 3 | 446 | 470 |

*(continued on next page)*

## Table 1.04: Resident Population by State, 1970, 1980, 1990, and 2007

| | 1990 | | | 2007 | | |
|---|---|---|---|---|---|---|
| | Black | White | All Races | Black | White | All Races |
| Alabama | 1,021 | 2,976 | 4,041 | 1,224 | 3,287 | 4,628 |
| Alaska | 22 | 415 | 550 | 28 | 484 | 683 |
| Arizona | 111 | 2,963 | 3,665 | 252 | 5,513 | 6,339 |
| Arkansas | 374 | 1,945 | 2,351 | 448 | 2,293 | 2,835 |
| California | 2,209 | 20,524 | 29,760 | 2,450 | 28,082 | 36,553 |
| Colorado | 133 | 2,905 | 3,294 | 206 | 4,370 | 4,862 |
| Connecticut | 274 | 2,859 | 3,287 | 361 | 2,959 | 3,502 |
| Delaware | 112 | 535 | 666 | 180 | 644 | 865 |
| District of Columbia | 400 | 180 | 607 | 325 | 232 | 588 |
| Florida | 1,760 | 10,749 | 12,938 | 2,897 | 14,604 | 18,251 |
| Georgia | 1,747 | 4,600 | 6,478 | 2,864 | 6,259 | 9,545 |
| Hawaii | 27 | 370 | 1,108 | 37 | 374 | 1,283 |
| Idaho | 3 | 950 | 1,007 | 13 | 1,421 | 1,499 |
| Illinois | 1,694 | 8,953 | 11,431 | 1,927 | 10,177 | 12,853 |
| Indiana | 432 | 5,021 | 5,544 | 572 | 5,593 | 6,345 |
| Iowa | 48 | 2,683 | 2,777 | 77 | 2,820 | 2,988 |
| Kansas | 143 | 2,232 | 2,478 | 169 | 2,467 | 2,776 |
| Kentucky | 263 | 3,392 | 3,685 | 327 | 3,817 | 4,241 |
| Louisiana | 1,299 | 2,839 | 4,220 | 1,369 | 2,793 | 4,293 |
| Maine | 5 | 1,208 | 1,228 | 13 | 1,271 | 1,317 |
| Maryland | 1,190 | 3,394 | 4,781 | 1,655 | 3,571 | 5,618 |
| Massachusetts | 300 | 5,405 | 6,016 | 448 | 5,576 | 6,450 |
| Michigan | 1,292 | 7,756 | 9,295 | 1,442 | 8,175 | 10,072 |
| Minnesota | 95 | 4,130 | 4,375 | 233 | 4,640 | 5,198 |
| Mississippi | 915 | 1,633 | 2,573 | 1,087 | 1,771 | 2,919 |
| Missouri | 548 | 4,486 | 5,117 | 678 | 5,001 | 5,878 |
| Montana | 2 | 741 | 799 | 6 | 868 | 958 |
| Nebraska | 57 | 1,481 | 1,578 | 79 | 1,625 | 1,775 |
| Nevada | 79 | 1,013 | 1,202 | 204 | 2,087 | 2,565 |

*(continued on next page)*

## Table 1.04: Resident Population by State, 1970, 1980, 1990, and 2007

| | 1990 | | | 2007 | | |
|---|---|---|---|---|---|---|
| | Black | White | All Races | Black | White | All Races |
| New Hampshire | 7 | 1,087 | 1,109 | 16 | 1,258 | 1,316 |
| New Jersey | 1,037 | 6,130 | 7,730 | 1,260 | 6,624 | 8,686 |
| New Mexico | 30 | 1,146 | 1,515 | 56 | 1,664 | 1,970 |
| New York | 2,859 | 13,385 | 17,990 | 3,347 | 14,194 | 19,298 |
| North Carolina | 1,456 | 5,008 | 6,629 | 1,967 | 6,704 | 9,061 |
| North Dakota | 4 | 604 | 639 | 7 | 586 | 640 |
| Ohio | 1,155 | 9,522 | 10,847 | 1,378 | 9,731 | 11,467 |
| Oklahoma | 234 | 2,584 | 3,146 | 287 | 2,833 | 3,617 |
| Oregon | 46 | 2,637 | 2,842 | 74 | 3,383 | 3,747 |
| Pennsylvania | 1,090 | 10,520 | 11,882 | 1,338 | 10,640 | 12,433 |
| Rhode Island | 39 | 917 | 1,003 | 67 | 938 | 1,058 |
| South Carolina | 1,040 | 2,407 | 3,487 | 1,266 | 3,025 | 4,408 |
| South Dakota | 3 | 638 | 696 | 9 | 704 | 796 |
| Tennessee | 778 | 4,048 | 4,877 | 1,039 | 4,948 | 6,157 |
| Texas | 2,022 | 12,775 | 16,987 | 2,857 | 19,742 | 23,904 |
| Utah | 12 | 1,616 | 1,723 | 32 | 2,465 | 2,645 |
| Vermont | 2 | 555 | 563 | 5 | 599 | 621 |
| Virginia | 1,163 | 4,792 | 6,187 | 1,538 | 5,642 | 7,712 |
| Washington | 150 | 4,309 | 4,867 | 235 | 5,473 | 6,468 |
| West Virginia | 54 | 1,792 | 1,856 | 64 | 1,714 | 1,812 |
| Wisconsin | 245 | 4,513 | 4,892 | 337 | 5,034 | 5,602 |
| Wyoming | 4 | 427 | 454 | 6 | 492 | 523 |

Source:  US Bureau of the Census, *Statistical Abstract of the United States, 1972*, tables 12 and 30; *1991*, table 27.
US Bureau of the Census, Population Estimates Division, *Estimates of the Population by Race and Hispanic or Latino Origin for the United States and States: July 1, 2007* (table SC-EST2007-04).

Notes:  'All Races' includes races not shown separately.

Units:  Population in thousands of persons.

## Table 1.05: Population of Cities with 250,000 or More Inhabitants, 2000

| | Black | White | All Races |
|---|---|---|---|
| Albuquerque, NM | 13.9 | 321.2 | 448.6 |
| Anaheim, CA | 8.7 | 179.6 | 328.0 |
| Anchorage, AK | 15.2 | 188.0 | 260.3 |
| Arlington, TX | 45.7 | 225.4 | 333.0 |
| Atlanta, GA | 255.7 | 138.4 | 416.5 |
| Aurora, CO | 37.1 | 190.3 | 276.4 |
| Austin, TX | 66.0 | 429.1 | 656.6 |
| Baltimore, MD | 419.0 | 206.0 | 651.2 |
| Boston, MA | 149.2 | 320.9 | 589.1 |
| Buffalo, NY | 109.0 | 159.3 | 292.6 |
| Charlotte, NC | 177.0 | 315.1 | 540.8 |
| Chicago, IL | 1,065.0 | 1,215.3 | 2,896.0 |
| Cincinnati, OH | 142.2 | 175.5 | 331.3 |
| Cleveland, OH | 243.9 | 198.5 | 478.4 |
| Colorado Springs, CO | 23.7 | 291.1 | 360.9 |
| Columbus, OH | 174.1 | 483.3 | 711.5 |
| Corpus Christi, TX | 13.0 | 198.7 | 277.5 |
| Dallas, TX | 308.0 | 604.2 | 1,188.6 |
| Denver, CO | 61.6 | 362.2 | 554.6 |
| Detroit, MI | 775.8 | 116.6 | 951.3 |
| El Paso, TX | 17.6 | 413.1 | 563.7 |
| Fort Worth, TX | 108.3 | 319.2 | 534.7 |
| Fresno, CA | 35.8 | 214.6 | 427.7 |
| Honolulu, HI | 6.0 | 73.1 | 371.7 |
| Houston, TX | 494.5 | 962.6 | 1,953.6 |
| Indianapolis, IN | 199.4 | 540.2 | 781.9 |
| Jacksonville, FL | 213.5 | 474.3 | 735.6 |
| Kansas City, MO | 137.9 | 267.9 | 441.5 |
| Las Vegas, NV | 49.6 | 334.2 | 478.4 |
| Lexington-Fayette, KY | 35.1 | 211.1 | 260.5 |
| Long Beach, CA | 68.6 | 208.4 | 461.5 |
| Los Angeles, CA | 415.2 | 1,734.0 | 3,694.8 |
| Louisville, KY | 84.6 | 161.3 | 256.2 |
| Memphis, TN | 399.2 | 223.7 | 650.1 |
| Mesa, AZ | 10.0 | 323.7 | 396.4 |

*(continued on next page)*

## Table 1.05: Population of Cities with 250,000 or More Inhabitants, 2000

|  | Black | White | All Races |
|---|---|---|---|
| Miami, FL | 80.9 | 241.5 | 362.5 |
| Milwaukee, WI | 222.9 | 298.4 | 597.0 |
| Minneapolis, MN | 68.8 | 249.2 | 382.6 |
| Nashville-Davidson, TN | 146.2 | 359.6 | 545.5 |
| New Orleans, LA | 325.9 | 136.0 | 484.7 |
| New York, NY | 2,129.8 | 3,576.4 | 8,008.3 |
| Newark, NJ | 146.3 | 72.5 | 273.5 |
| Oakland, CA | 142.5 | 125.0 | 399.5 |
| Oklahoma City, OK | 77.8 | 346.2 | 506.1 |
| Omaha, NE | 51.9 | 305.7 | 390.0 |
| Philadelphia, PA | 655.8 | 683.3 | 1,517.6 |
| Phoenix, AZ | 67.4 | 938.9 | 1,321.0 |
| Pittsburgh, PA | 90.8 | 226.3 | 334.6 |
| Portland, OR | 35.1 | 412.2 | 529.1 |
| Raleigh, NC | 76.8 | 174.8 | 276.1 |
| Riverside, CA | 18.9 | 151.4 | 255.2 |
| Sacramento, CA | 63.0 | 196.5 | 407.0 |
| San Antonio, TX | 78.1 | 774.7 | 1,144.6 |
| San Diego, CA | 96.2 | 736.2 | 1,223.4 |
| San Francisco, CA | 60.5 | 385.7 | 776.7 |
| San Jose, CA | 31.3 | 425.0 | 894.9 |
| Santa Ana, CA | 5.7 | 144.4 | 338.0 |
| Seattle, WA | 47.5 | 394.9 | 563.4 |
| St. Louis, MO | 178.3 | 152.7 | 348.2 |
| St. Paul, MN | 33.6 | 192.4 | 287.2 |
| Tampa, FL | 79.1 | 194.9 | 303.4 |
| Toledo, OH | 73.9 | 220.3 | 313.6 |
| Tucson, AZ | 21.1 | 341.4 | 486.7 |
| Tulsa, OK | 60.8 | 275.5 | 393.0 |
| Virginia Beach, VA | 80.6 | 303.7 | 425.3 |
| Washington, DC | 343.3 | 176.1 | 572.1 |
| Wichita, KS | 39.3 | 258.9 | 344.3 |

**Source:** US Bureau of the Census, *Statistical Abstract of the United States, 2003*, table 32.

**Notes:** Population as of April 1, 2000. Data refers to boundaries in effect on January 1, 2000.

**Units:** Population in thousands of persons.

## Table 1.06: Population of the 50 Largest Metropolitan Statistical Areas, 2005

|  | Black | White | All Races |
|---|---|---|---|
| Atlanta, GA | 1,516 | 3,129 | 4,918 |
| Austin, TX | 114 | 1,244 | 1,453 |
| Baltimore, MD | 756 | 1,761 | 2,656 |
| Birmingham, AL | 307 | 762 | 1,090 |
| Boston, MA | 336 | 3,749 | 4,412 |
| Buffalo, NY | 141 | 969 | 1,148 |
| Charlotte, NC | 356 | 1,104 | 1,521 |
| Chicago, IL | 1,735 | 7,087 | 9,443 |
| Cincinnati, OH | 244 | 1,767 | 2,070 |
| Cleveland, OH | 423 | 1,635 | 2,126 |
| Columbus, OH | 241 | 1,386 | 1,709 |
| Dallas, TX | 829 | 4,604 | 5,819 |
| Denver, CO | 133 | 2,075 | 2,360 |
| Detroit, MI | 1,036 | 3,234 | 4,488 |
| Hartford, CT | 129 | 1,002 | 1,188 |
| Houston, TX | 889 | 4,005 | 5,280 |
| Indianapolis, IN | 240 | 1,349 | 1,641 |
| Jacksonville, FL | 281 | 910 | 1,248 |
| Kansas City, MO | 240 | 1,626 | 1,948 |
| Las Vegas, NV | 172 | 1,349 | 1,711 |
| Los Angeles, CA | 1,017 | 9,718 | 12,924 |
| Louisville, KY | 162 | 1,014 | 1,208 |
| Memphis, TN | 569 | 657 | 1,261 |
| Miami, FL | 1,132 | 4,090 | 5,422 |
| Milwaukee, WI | 249 | 1,195 | 1,513 |
| Minneapolis, MN | 198 | 2,707 | 3,143 |
| Nashville, TN | 217 | 1,156 | 1,423 |
| New Orleans, LA | 503 | 765 | 1,319 |
| New York, NY | 3,692 | 12,968 | 18,747 |

*(continued on next page)*

## Table 1.06: Population of the 50 Largest Metropolitan Statistical Areas, 2005

|                    | Black | White | All Races |
|--------------------|------:|------:|----------:|
| Oklahoma City, OK  | 124   | 914   | 1,157     |
| Orlando, FL        | 303   | 1,519 | 1,933     |
| Philadelphia, PA   | 1,220 | 4,276 | 5,823     |
| Phoenix, AZ        | 166   | 3,435 | 3,865     |
| Pittsburgh, PA     | 196   | 2,134 | 2,386     |
| Portland, OR       | 59    | 1,844 | 2,096     |
| Providence, RI     | 86    | 1,465 | 1,623     |
| Richmond, VA       | 359   | 771   | 1,176     |
| Riverside, CA      | 314   | 3,227 | 3,910     |
| Rochester, NY      | 119   | 882   | 1,039     |
| Sacramento, CA     | 153   | 1,553 | 2,042     |
| St. Louis, MO      | 506   | 2,185 | 2,779     |
| Salt Lake City, UT | 14    | 955   | 1,034     |
| San Antonio, TX    | 123   | 1,692 | 1,890     |
| San Diego, CA      | 163   | 2,340 | 2,933     |
| San Francisco, CA  | 383   | 2,681 | 4,153     |
| San Jose, CA       | 48    | 1,126 | 1,755     |
| Seattle, WA        | 175   | 2,531 | 3,203     |
| Tampa, FL          | 300   | 2,234 | 2,648     |
| Virginia Beach, VA | 523   | 1,033 | 1,647     |
| Washington, DC     | 1,389 | 3,269 | 5,215     |

**Source:** US Bureau of the Census, *Statistical Abstract of the United States, 2007*, table 27.

**Notes:** As of July 1, 2005. When a Metropolitan Statistical Area contains several cities (i.e., Los Angeles-Long Beach-Santa Ana, CA), only the primary city is shown here.

**Units:** Population in thousands of persons.

## Table 1.07: Population Projections, by Age, 2010 and 2015

| | Black | White | All Races |
|---|---|---|---|
| *Total population* | *42,927* | *252,850* | *322,366* |
| Under 5 years | 3,498 | 16,556 | 22,358 |
| 5 to 9 years | 3,347 | 16,114 | 21,623 |
| 10 to 14 years | 3,163 | 15,799 | 20,984 |
| 15 to 19 years | 3,043 | 15,341 | 20,243 |
| 20 to 24 years | 3,451 | 16,473 | 21,810 |
| 25 to 29 years | 3,413 | 16,890 | 22,195 |
| 30 to 34 years | 3,180 | 16,727 | 21,858 |
| 35 to 39 years | 2,880 | 15,758 | 20,543 |
| 40 to 44 years | 2,697 | 15,616 | 20,250 |
| 45 to 49 years | 2,685 | 16,473 | 20,926 |
| 50 to 54 years | 2,768 | 17,966 | 22,376 |
| 55 to 59 years | 2,546 | 17,637 | 21,649 |
| 60 to 64 years | 2,044 | 15,484 | 18,761 |
| 65 to 69 years | 1,518 | 13,125 | 15,621 |
| 70 to 74 years | 979 | 9,363 | 10,987 |
| 75 to 79 years | 688 | 6,641 | 7,761 |
| 80 to 84 years | 471 | 4,861 | 5,600 |
| 85 to 89 years | 303 | 3,404 | 3,857 |
| 90 to 94 years | 165 | 1,839 | 2,069 |
| 95 to 99 years | 68 | 636 | 723 |
| 100 years old and over | 22 | 147 | 173 |

Source: U.S. Bureau of the Census, *Statistical Abstract of the United States, 2007*, table 16.

Notes: 'All Races' includes other races not shown separately.
Population projections as of July 1 of the year shown.
Includes members of the armed forces service overseas.

Units: Total population in thousands of persons,.

## Table 1.08: Population Projections, 2010–2100

| | Black | White | All Races |
|---|---|---|---|
| 2010* | 40,454 | 244,995 | 308,936 |
| 2015 | 42,385 | 249,467 | 312,268 |
| 2020* | 45,365 | 260,629 | 335,805 |
| 2025 | 47,089 | 265,305 | 337,814 |
| 2030* | 50,442 | 275,731 | 363,584 |
| 2035 | 52,019 | 280,555 | 364,319 |
| 2040* | 55,876 | 289,690 | 391,946 |
| 2045 | 56,862 | 295,019 | 390,397 |
| 2050* | 61,361 | 302,626 | 419,854 |
| 2055 | 61,627 | 310,300 | 417,477 |
| 2060 | 64,055 | 318,752 | 432,010 |
| 2065 | 66,544 | 327,907 | 447,415 |
| 2070 | 69,096 | 337,719 | 463,639 |
| 2075 | 71,705 | 348,027 | 480,504 |
| 2080 | 74,367 | 358,664 | 497,829 |
| 2085 | 77,082 | 369,547 | 515,528 |
| 2090 | 79,852 | 380,674 | 533,605 |
| 2095 | 82,684 | 392,063 | 552,085 |
| 2100 | 85,579 | 403,696 | 570,954 |

**Source:** US Bureau of the Census, *Projections of the Resident Population by Race, Hispanic Origin, and Nativity, Middle Series, 1999 to 2100*, tables NP-T5-A to NP-T5-H.
\* US Bureau of the Census, *US Interim Projections by Age, Sex, Race, and Hispanic Origin, 2000-2050*, table 1a.

**Notes:** 'All Races' includes races not shown separately.
Population projections as of July 1 of the year shown. Includes members of the armed forces serving overseas.

**Units:** Total population in thousands of persons.

## Table 1.09: Nativity by State, 2006

| | Black | | White | | All Races | |
|---|---|---|---|---|---|---|
| | Native | % of Total | Native | % of Total | Native | % of Total |
| *United States* | 34,125,679 | 92.1% | 204,332,202 | 92.3% | 261,850,696 | 87.5% |
| Alabama | 1,198,685 | 99.1% | 3,174,238 | 98.0% | 4,468,981 | 97.2% |
| Alaska | 18,935 | 88.2% | 444,406 | 96.6% | 622,987 | 93.0% |
| Arizona | 187,735 | 90.3% | 4,157,300 | 87.7% | 5,237,235 | 84.9% |
| Arkansas | 435,627 | 99.5% | 2,162,042 | 97.9% | 2,703,526 | 96.2% |
| California | 2,129,220 | 94.2% | 17,879,839 | 82.0% | 26,555,482 | 72.8% |
| Colorado | 157,650 | 88.6% | 3,667,056 | 93.2% | 4,263,881 | 89.7% |
| Connecticut | 272,480 | 81.9% | 2,557,519 | 91.3% | 3,052,451 | 87.1% |
| Delaware | 163,848 | 92.7% | 586,400 | 95.3% | 784,754 | 91.9% |
| District of Columbia | 304,593 | 94.6% | 175,243 | 87.4% | 507,710 | 87.3% |
| Florida | 2,216,958 | 79.8% | 11,637,399 | 84.5% | 14,664,255 | 81.1% |
| Georgia | 2,659,499 | 95.2% | 5,504,103 | 94.6% | 8,504,351 | 90.8% |
| Hawaii | 26,735 | 95.3% | 315,687 | 93.5% | 1,075,336 | 83.7% |
| Idaho | 5,664 | 82.8% | 1,302,301 | 96.0% | 1,384,425 | 94.4% |
| Illinois | 1,844,027 | 97.1% | 8,271,761 | 91.2% | 11,058,370 | 86.2% |
| Indiana | 537,804 | 97.5% | 5,310,051 | 97.8% | 6,049,913 | 95.8% |
| Iowa | 61,432 | 91.3% | 2,723,360 | 98.2% | 2,869,786 | 96.2% |
| Kansas | 145,250 | 94.6% | 2,284,554 | 96.8% | 2,590,681 | 93.7% |
| Kentucky | 302,789 | 97.6% | 3,707,123 | 98.5% | 4,094,350 | 97.3% |
| Louisiana | 1,349,965 | 99.5% | 2,701,154 | 97.9% | 4,162,564 | 97.1% |
| Maine | 8,200 | 60.0% | 1,238,619 | 97.9% | 1,279,618 | 96.8% |
| Maryland | 1,466,499 | 90.3% | 3,216,774 | 93.5% | 4,932,570 | 87.8% |
| Massachusetts | 270,783 | 68.9% | 4,884,590 | 91.7% | 5,528,922 | 85.9% |
| Michigan | 1,401,938 | 98.3% | 7,688,382 | 95.8% | 9,496,992 | 94.1% |
| Minnesota | 166,488 | 72.9% | 4,424,661 | 97.5% | 4,827,865 | 93.4% |
| Mississippi | 1,083,601 | 99.7% | 1,727,997 | 98.8% | 2,859,496 | 98.2% |
| Missouri | 647,758 | 97.9% | 4,816,382 | 98.2% | 5,649,023 | 96.7% |
| Montana | 4,125 | 92.3% | 835,561 | 98.6% | 927,120 | 98.1% |

*(continued on next page)*

**Black Americans: A Statistical Sourcebook 2008**

## Table 1.09: Nativity by State, 2006

| | Black | | White | | All Races | |
|---|---|---|---|---|---|---|
| | Native | % of Total | Native | % of Total | Native | % of Total |
| *United States* | *34,125,679* | *92.1%* | *204,332,202* | *92.3%* | *261,850,696* | *87.5%* |
| Nebraska | 65,128 | 90.3% | 1,524,037 | 97.3% | 1,668,831 | 94.4% |
| Nevada | 171,413 | 93.6% | 1,585,894 | 86.3% | 2,019,615 | 80.9% |
| New Hampshire | 8,470 | 61.2% | 1,205,791 | 96.4% | 1,243,695 | 94.6% |
| New Jersey | 1,015,344 | 85.5% | 5,329,996 | 87.8% | 6,970,307 | 79.9% |
| New Mexico | 37,591 | 94.8% | 1,199,868 | 90.5% | 1,757,348 | 89.9% |
| New York | 2,201,373 | 73.6% | 11,247,022 | 87.8% | 15,127,221 | 78.4% |
| North Carolina | 1,853,152 | 97.9% | 5,993,066 | 96.3% | 8,242,307 | 93.1% |
| North Dakota | 4,245 | 70.8% | 571,992 | 98.8% | 622,489 | 97.9% |
| Ohio | 1,317,193 | 97.0% | 9,434,969 | 97.8% | 11,065,654 | 96.4% |
| Oklahoma | 253,238 | 96.2% | 2,620,411 | 97.1% | 3,403,225 | 95.1% |
| Oregon | 55,965 | 88.0% | 3,013,032 | 94.6% | 3,340,891 | 90.3% |
| Pennsylvania | 1,217,235 | 94.4% | 10,145,957 | 97.3% | 11,804,054 | 94.9% |
| Rhode Island | 36,598 | 67.3% | 820,362 | 93.0% | 933,220 | 87.4% |
| South Carolina | 1,230,130 | 99.4% | 2,811,361 | 96.7% | 4,145,231 | 95.9% |
| South Dakota | 4,163 | 79.1% | 675,650 | 99.1% | 765,067 | 97.8% |
| Tennessee | 992,372 | 98.1% | 4,667,461 | 97.6% | 5,802,287 | 96.1% |
| Texas | 2,589,731 | 95.3% | 14,477,609 | 88.2% | 19,767,116 | 84.1% |
| Utah | 17,674 | 77.7% | 2,161,197 | 95.1% | 2,339,563 | 91.7% |
| Vermont | 3,808 | 73.7% | 582,576 | 97.0% | 599,726 | 96.1% |
| Virginia | 1,420,473 | 94.9% | 5,114,928 | 94.5% | 6,869,099 | 89.9% |
| Washington | 181,143 | 83.1% | 4,823,508 | 93.7% | 5,602,009 | 87.6% |
| West Virginia | 57,021 | 97.2% | 1,711,133 | 99.4% | 1,796,522 | 98.8% |
| Wisconsin | 320,348 | 97.6% | 4,755,049 | 97.8% | 5,311,500 | 95.6% |

**Source:** US Bureau of the Census, *American Community Survey 2006*, tables B060014B, B06004B, and B06003.

**Notes:** Use caution when comparing this data to other Census data.

**Units:** Number of native-born residents; percent of total.

## Table 1.10: Age, Educational Attainment, and Residence, 1990

**1990**

| | Black | White | All Races |
|---|---|---|---|
| **Age** | | | |
| *Persons of all ages* | *30,332* | *206,853* | *245,992* |
| Under 18 years old | 10,012 | 51,400 | 64,144 |
| 18-24 years old | 3,568 | 20,767 | 25,311 |
| 25-44 years old | 9,498 | 67,925 | 80,435 |
| 45-64 years old | 4,766 | 40,281 | 46,536 |
| 65 years old and over | 2,487 | 26,479 | 29,566 |
| **Years of school completed** | | | |
| *All persons 25 years old and over* | *16,751* | *134,687* | *156,537* |
| Persons completing: | | | |
| 0-8 years of school | 2,701 | 14,131 | 17,590 |
| 1-3 years of high school | 2,968 | 14,080 | 17,462 |
| 4 years of high school | 6,239 | 52,449 | 60,119 |
| 1-3 years of college | 2,952 | 24,349 | 28,075 |
| 4 or more years of college | 1,891 | 29,676 | 33,291 |
| **Residence** | | | |
| Northeast | 5,282 | 43,650 | 50,520 |
| Midwest | 5,991 | 52,399 | 59,428 |
| South | 16,499 | 66,004 | 84,044 |
| West | 2,561 | 44,800 | 52,000 |
| Nonfarm | 30,276 | 202,339 | 241,374 |
| Farm | 56 | 4,515 | 4,618 |
| Inside metro areas | 25,402 | 158,087 | 191,169 |
| Outside metro areas | 4,930 | 48,766 | 54,824 |

Source: US Bureau of the Census, *Statistical Abstract of the United States, 1987*, table 39; *1990*, table 43. US Bureau of the Census, Current Population Reports: *Money Income of Households, Families and Persons in the United States, 1984* (Series P-60, #151), table 4; *1988 and 1989* (Series P-60, #171 & 172), tables 4, 20, and 29.

Notes: 'All Races' includes races not shown separately.

Units: Population in thousands of persons.

## Table 1.11: Age and Residence, 2006

|  | Black | White | All Races |
|---|---|---|---|
| **Age** |  |  |  |
| *Persons of all ages* | *37,306* | *237,619* | *296,450* |
| Under 18 years old | 11,315 | 56,205 | 73,727 |
| 18-24 years old | 4,067 | 22,152 | 28,405 |
| 25-34 years old | 5,230 | 31,152 | 39,868 |
| 35-44 years old | 5,307 | 34,108 | 42,762 |
| 45-54 years old | 5,091 | 35,577 | 43,461 |
| 55-59 years old | 1,903 | 15,238 | 18,221 |
| 60-64 years old | 1,309 | 11,916 | 13,970 |
| 65 years old and over | 3,085 | 31,270 | 36,035 |
| **Residence** |  |  |  |
| Northeast | 6,624 | 43,583 | 54,072 |
| Midwest | 6,641 | 55,780 | 65,411 |
| South | 20,667 | 66,345 | 107,902 |
| West | 3,374 | 56,147 | 69,065 |

**Source:**  US Bureau of the Census, Current Population Survey, *Annual Social and Economic Supplement, 2007*, poverty tables POV01 and POV41.

**Notes:**  'All Races' includes races not shown separately. 'White' as shown is equivalent to 'White alone' and 'Black' as shown is equivalent to 'Black alone.'

**Units:**  Population in thousands of persons.

## Table 1.12: Marital Status, Persons 15 Years Old and Older, 1990–2006

| | Black | | White | | All Races | |
|---|---|---|---|---|---|---|
| | Number | Percent | Number | Percent | Number | Percent |
| **1990** | | | | | | |
| *Total* | *21,914* | *100%* | *163,417* | *100%* | *191,793* | *100%* |
| Single, never married | 8,735 | 39.9 | 39,516 | 24.2 | 50,223 | 26.2 |
| Married, spouse present | 7,619 | 34.8 | 95,337 | 58.3 | 106,513 | 55.3 |
| Married, spouse absent | 1,683 | 7.7 | 4,191 | 2.6 | 6,118 | 3.2 |
| Widowed | 1,730 | 7.9 | 11,731 | 7.2 | 13,810 | 7.2 |
| Divorced | 2,146 | 9.8 | 12,643 | 7.7 | 15,128 | 7.9 |
| **2000** | | | | | | |
| *Total* | *25,855* | *100%* | *177,581* | *100%* | *213,773* | *100%* |
| Married, spouse present | 8,391 | 32.5 | 99,258 | 55.9 | 113,002 | 52.9 |
| Married, spouse absent | 430 | 1.7 | 1,971 | 1.1 | 2,730 | 1.3 |
| Widowed | 1,695 | 6.6 | 11,532 | 6.5 | 13,665 | 6.4 |
| Divorced | 2,778 | 10.7 | 16,547 | 9.3 | 19,881 | 9.3 |
| Separated | 1,307 | 5.1 | 2,976 | 1.7 | 4,479 | 2.1 |
| Never married | 11,253 | 43.5 | 45,297 | 25.5 | 60,016 | 28.1 |
| **2006** | | | | | | |
| *Total* | *27,680* | *100%* | *189,500* | *100%* | *233,039* | *100%* |
| Married, spouse present | 8,442 | 30.5 | 102,573 | 54.1 | 119,055 | 51.1 |
| Married, spouse absent | 526 | 1.9 | 2,837 | 1.5 | 3,785 | 1.6 |
| Widowed | 1,773 | 6.4 | 11,548 | 6.1 | 13,914 | 6.0 |
| Divorced | 3,127 | 11.3 | 18,573 | 9.8 | 22,806 | 9.8 |
| Separated | 1,352 | 4.9 | 3,298 | 1.7 | 4,963 | 2.1 |
| Never married | 12,460 | 45.0 | 50,672 | 26.7 | 68,515 | 29.4 |

Source:  US Bureau of the Census, Current Population Reports, *Marital Status and Living Arrangements: 1990* (Series P-20, #450), table 1.
US Bureau of the Census, Current Population Reports, *America's Families and Living Arrangements: 2000*, (Series P-20, #537), table A1; *2006*, table A1.

Notes:  'All Races' includes races not shown separately.
For 2006 data, 'Black' as shown is equivalent to 'Black Alone' and 'White' is equivalent to 'White Alone.'
Percents may not add to 100.

Units:  Number of persons 15 years old and older in thousands; percent of total.

## Table 1.13: Marital Status, Men 15 Years Old and Older, 1990–2006

| | Black | | White | | All Races | |
|---|---|---|---|---|---|---|
| | Number | Percent | Number | Percent | Number | Percent |
| **1990** | | | | | | |
| *Total* | *9,948* | *100%* | *78,908* | *100%* | *91,033* | *100%* |
| Single, never married | 4,319 | 43.4 | 22,078 | 28.0 | 27,422 | 30.1 |
| Married, spouse present | 3,862 | 38.8 | 47,700 | 60.4 | 52,924 | 58.1 |
| Married, spouse absent | 627 | 6.3 | 1,842 | 2.3 | 2,360 | 2.6 |
| Widowed | 338 | 3.4 | 1,930 | 2.4 | 2,282 | 2.5 |
| Divorced | 802 | 8.1 | 5,359 | 6.8 | 6,045 | 6.6 |
| **2000** | | | | | | |
| *Total* | *11,687* | *100%* | *86,443* | *100%* | *103,114* | *100%* |
| Married, spouse present | 4,294 | 36.7 | 49,672 | 57.5 | 56,501 | 54.8 |
| Married, spouse absent | 207 | 1.8 | 979 | 1.1 | 1,365 | 1.3 |
| Widowed | 328 | 2.8 | 2,196 | 2.5 | 2,604 | 2.5 |
| Divorced | 1,108 | 9.5 | 7,246 | 8.4 | 8,572 | 8.3 |
| Separated | 504 | 4.3 | 1,237 | 1.4 | 1,818 | 1.8 |
| Never married | 5,246 | 44.9 | 25,113 | 29.1 | 32,253 | 31.3 |
| **2006** | | | | | | |
| *Total* | *12,518* | *100%* | *92,889* | *100%* | *113,073* | *100%* |
| Married, spouse present | 4,331 | 34.6 | 51,354 | 55.3 | 59,528 | 52.6 |
| Married, spouse absent | 257 | 2.1 | 1,603 | 1.7 | 2,096 | 1.9 |
| Widowed | 336 | 2.7 | 2,181 | 2.3 | 2,624 | 2.3 |
| Divorced | 1,176 | 9.4 | 8,055 | 8.7 | 9,679 | 8.6 |
| Separated | 528 | 4.2 | 1,411 | 1.5 | 2,059 | 1.8 |
| Never married | 5,891 | 47.1 | 28,286 | 30.5 | 37,086 | 32.8 |

**Source:** US Bureau of the Census, Current Population Reports, *Marital Status and Living Arrangements: 1990* (Series P-20, #450), table 1.

US Bureau of the Census, Current Population Reports, *America's Families and Living Arrangements: 2000*, (Series P-20, #537), table A1; *2006*, table A1..

**Notes:** 'All Races' includes races not shown separately.

For 2006 data, 'Black' as shown is equivalent to 'Black Alone' and 'White' is equivalent to 'White Alone.'

Percents may not add to 100.

**Units:** Number of men 15 years old and older in thousands; percent of total.

## Table 1.14: Marital Status, Women 15 Years Old and Older, 1990–2006

| | Black | | White | | All Races | |
|---|---|---|---|---|---|---|
| | Number | Percent | Number | Percent | Number | Percent |
| **1990** | | | | | | |
| *Total* | *11,966* | *100%* | *84,508* | *100%* | *99,838* | *100%* |
| Single, never married | 4,416 | 36.9 | 17,438 | 20.6 | 22,718 | 22.8 |
| Married, spouse present | 3,757 | 31.4 | 47,637 | 56.4 | 53,256 | 53.3 |
| Married, spouse absent | 1,056 | 8.8 | 2,349 | 2.8 | 3,541 | 3.5 |
| Widowed | 1,392 | 11.6 | 9,800 | 11.6 | 11,477 | 11.5 |
| Divorced | 1,344 | 11.2 | 7,284 | 8.6 | 8,845 | 8.9 |
| **2000** | | | | | | |
| *Total* | *14,167* | *100%* | *91,138* | *100%* | *110,660* | *100%* |
| Married, spouse present | 4,097 | 28.9 | 49,586 | 54.4 | 56,501 | 51.1 |
| Married, spouse absent | 223 | 1.6 | 992 | 1.1 | 1,365 | 1.2 |
| Widowed | 1,367 | 9.6 | 9,336 | 10.2 | 11,061 | 10.0 |
| Divorced | 1,670 | 11.8 | 9,301 | 10.2 | 11,309 | 10.2 |
| Separated | 803 | 5.7 | 1,739 | 1.9 | 2,661 | 2.4 |
| Never married | 6,008 | 42.4 | 20,184 | 22.1 | 27,763 | 25.1 |
| **2006** | | | | | | |
| *Total* | *15,162* | *100%* | *96,611* | *100%* | *119,966* | *100%* |
| Married, spouse present | 4,112 | 27.1 | 51,219 | 53.0 | 59,528 | 49.6 |
| Married, spouse absent | 269 | 1.8 | 1,234 | 1.3 | 1,689 | 1.4 |
| Widowed | 1,437 | 9.5 | 9,368 | 9.7 | 11,290 | 9.4 |
| Divorced | 1,951 | 12.9 | 10,518 | 10.9 | 13,127 | 10.9 |
| Separated | 823 | 5.4 | 1,887 | 2.0 | 2,904 | 2.4 |
| Never married | 6,569 | 43.3 | 22,386 | 23.2 | 31,429 | 26.2 |

Source: US Bureau of the Census, Current Population Reports, *Marital Status and Living Arrangements: 1990* (Series P-20, #450), table 1.
US Bureau of the Census, Current Population Reports, *America's Families and Living Arrangements: 2000*, (Series P-20, #537), table A1; *2006*, table A1.

Notes: 'All Races' includes races not shown separately.
For 2006 data, 'Black' as shown is equivalent to 'Black Alone' and 'White' is equivalent to 'White Alone.'
Percents may not add to 100.

Units: Number of women 15 years old and older in thousands; percent of total.

## Table 1.15: Interracial Married Couples, 1980–2002

|      | Total | Black Husband, White Wife | White Husband, Black Wife | Black/ Other Race |
|------|-------|---------------------------|---------------------------|-------------------|
| 1980 | 651   | 122 | 45  | 34 |
| 1985 | 762   | 111 | 64  | 23 |
| 1990 | 964   | 150 | 61  | 33 |
| 1995 | 1,392 | 206 | 122 | 76 |
| 2000 | 1,464 | 268 | 95  | 50 |
| 2001 | 1,596 | 247 | 113 | 63 |
| 2002 | 1,674 | 279 | 116 | 57 |

**Source:** US Bureau of the Census, Current Population Report, *America's Families and Living Arrangements, 2003* (Series P20, *#553)*, table MS-3.

**Notes:** 'Black/Other Race' includes couples in which one partner is Black and the other partner is any race other than White or Black, such as American Indian, Japanese, Chinese, etc.

**Units:** Number of couples in thousands.

## Table 1.16: Selected Characteristics of Households, 1985

|  | Black | White | All Races |
|---|---|---|---|
| *Total households* | *9,480* | *75,328* | *86,789* |
| **By Marital status and sex of householder** | | | |
| Male householder | 4,665 | 53,868 | 60,025 |
| Married, wife present | 3,077 | 43,444 | 47,683 |
| Married, wife absent | 349 | 1,013 | 1,416 |
| Widowed | 211 | 1,386 | 1,620 |
| Divorced | 415 | 3,078 | 3,535 |
| Single, never married | 623 | 4,947 | 5,772 |
| Female householder | 4,815 | 21,461 | 26,763 |
| Married, wife present | 392 | 2,199 | 2,667 |
| Married, wife absent | 777 | 1,668 | 2,497 |
| Widowed | 1,271 | 8,304 | 9,728 |
| Divorced | 950 | 5,203 | 6,265 |
| Single, never married | 1,425 | 4,087 | 5,606 |
| **By Age of the householder** | | | |
| 15-24 years old | 669 | 4,626 | 5,438 |
| 25-34 years old | 2,470 | 17,010 | 20,013 |
| 35-44 years old | 1,947 | 15,024 | 17,481 |
| 45-54 years old | 1,488 | 10,792 | 12,628 |
| 55-64 years old | 1,350 | 11,471 | 13,073 |
| 65 years old and over | 1,556 | 16,406 | 18,155 |

*(continued on next page)*

## Table 1.16: Selected Characteristics of Households, 1985

|                                  | Black | White  | All Races |
|----------------------------------|-------|--------|-----------|
| **By Housing tenure**            |       |        |           |
| Own housing unit                 | 4,185 | 50,611 | 55,845    |
| Rent housing unit                | 5,295 | 24,667 | 30,943    |
| **By Size of the household**     |       |        |           |
| One person                       | 2,367 | 17,876 | 20,602    |
| Two persons                      | 2,391 | 24,558 | 27,289    |
| Three persons                    | 1,795 | 13,336 | 15,465    |
| Four persons                     | 1,441 | 11,795 | 13,631    |
| Five persons                     | 800   | 5,061  | 6,108     |
| Six persons                      | 370   | 1,819  | 2,299     |
| Seven or more persons            | 317   | 882    | 1,296     |
| Average persons per household    | 2.96  | 2.64   | 2.69      |
| **By Residence**                 |       |        |           |
| Northeast                        | 1,860 | 16,244 | 18,348    |
| Midwest                          | 1,863 | 19,599 | 21,697    |
| South                            | 4,924 | 24,283 | 29,581    |
| West                             | 834   | 15,202 | 17,163    |

Source:  US Bureau of the Census, Current Population Report, *Money Income of Households, Families, and Persons in the United States, March 1984* (Series P-60, *#151*), table 4; *March 1985 (Series P-20,* #411), table 22.

Notes:  'All Races' includes races not shown separately.

Units:  Number of households in thousands; average persons per household.

## Table 1.17: Selected Characteristics of Households, 1990

|  | Black | White | All Races |
|---|---|---|---|
| *Total households* | *10,486* | *80,163* | *93,347* |
| **By Marital status and type of Householder** | | | |
| Family households | 7,470 | 56,590 | 66,090 |
|   Married couple families | 3,750 | 46,981 | 52,317 |
|   Male householder, no wife present | 446 | 2,303 | 2,884 |
|   Female householder, no husband present | 3,275 | 7,306 | 10,890 |
| Non-family households | 3,015 | 23,573 | 27,257 |
|   Male householder | 1,313 | 9,951 | 11,606 |
|     Living alone | 1,084 | 7,718 | 9,049 |
|   Female householder | 1,702 | 13,622 | 15,651 |
|     Living alone | 1,525 | 12,161 | 13,950 |
| **By Age of the householder** | | | |
| 15-24 years old | 709 | 4,222 | 5,121 |
| 25-34 years old | 2,625 | 17,137 | 20,472 |
| 35-44 years old | 2,456 | 17,395 | 20,554 |
| 45-54 years old | 1,606 | 12,404 | 14,514 |
| 55-64 years old | 1,395 | 10,862 | 12,529 |
| 65 years old and over | 1,695 | 18,144 | 20,156 |
| **By Housing tenure** | | | |
| Own housing unit | 4,445 | 54,094 | 59,846 |
| Rent housing unit | 5,862 | 24,685 | 31,895 |

*(continued on next page)*

## Table 1.17: Selected Characteristics of Households, 1990

|  | Black | White | All Races |
|---|---|---|---|
| **By Size of the household** | | | |
| One person | 2,610 | 19,879 | 22,999 |
| Two persons | 2,721 | 26,714 | 30,114 |
| Three persons | 2,043 | 13,585 | 16,128 |
| Four persons | 1,550 | 12,399 | 14,456 |
| Five persons | 858 | 5,104 | 6,213 |
| Six persons | 412 | 1,615 | 2,143 |
| Seven or more persons | 293 | 877 | 1,295 |
| Average persons per household | 2.89 | 2.58 | 2.63 |
| **By Residence** | | | |
| Northeast | 1,866 | 16,773 | 19,127 |
| Midwest | 2,092 | 20,339 | 22,760 |
| South | 5,622 | 26,155 | 32,262 |
| West | 906 | 16,896 | 19,197 |
| Inside metropolitan areas | 8,816 | 61,155 | 72,331 |
| Outside metropolitan areas | 1,670 | 19,009 | 21,016 |
| Nonfarm | 10,464 | 78,556 | 91,710 |
| Farm | 21 | 1,608 | 1,637 |

Source:   US Bureau of the Census, Current Population Report, *Money Income of Households, Families and, Persons in the United States: 1988 and 1989 (Series P-60, #172),* table 1.

Notes:   'All Races' includes races not shown separately.

Units:   Number of households in thousands; average persons per household.

## Table 1.18: Selected Characteristics of Households, 2006

|  | Black | White | All Races |
|---|---|---|---|
| *All households* | *14,354* | *94,705* | *116,011* |
| **By Marital status and sex of householder** | | | |
| Family households | 9,272 | 64,091 | 78,425 |
| Married couple families | 4,358 | 50,729 | 58,945 |
| Male householder, no wife present | 864 | 3,806 | 5,063 |
| Female householder, no husband present | 4,050 | 9,556 | 14,416 |
| Non-family households | 5,081 | 30,614 | 37,587 |
| Male householder | 2,249 | 14,138 | 17,338 |
| Living alone | 1,881 | 10,993 | 13,528 |
| Female householder | 2,832 | 16,476 | 20,249 |
| Living alone | 2,586 | 14,286 | 17,604 |
| **By Age of householder** | | | |
| 15-24 years old | 1,106 | 5,108 | 6,662 |
| 25-34 years old | 2,806 | 15,095 | 19,435 |
| 35-44 years old | 3,078 | 18,021 | 22,779 |
| 45-54 years old | 3,113 | 19,641 | 24,140 |
| 55-64 years old | 2,074 | 16,191 | 19,266 |
| 65 years old and over | 2,176 | 20,649 | 23,729 |
| **By Size of household** | | | |
| One person | 4,467 | 25,280 | 31,132 |
| Two persons | 3,970 | 32,546 | 38,580 |
| Three persons | 2,624 | 14,888 | 18,808 |
| Four persons | 1,813 | 13,074 | 16,172 |
| Five persons | 864 | 5,794 | 7,202 |
| Six persons | 401 | 2,083 | 2,702 |
| Seven or more persons | 216 | 1,040 | 1,415 |
| Average persons per household | 2.56 | 2.53 | 2.56 |

*(continued on next page)*

## Table 1.18: Selected Characteristics of Households, 2006

|  | Black | White | All Races |
|---|---|---|---|
| *All households* | *14,354* | *94,705* | *116,011* |
| **By Residence** | | | |
| Northeast | 2,502 | 17,489 | 21,261 |
| Midwest | 2,680 | 22,903 | 26,508 |
| South | 7,860 | 33,054 | 42,587 |
| West | 1,312 | 21,259 | 25,656 |
| Inside metropolitan areas | 12,837 | 77,638 | 96,739 |
| Outside metropolitan areas | 1,517 | 17,067 | 19,272 |

Source:  US Bureau of the Census, *Current Population Reports: Annual Social and Economic Supplement 2007*, household income table HINC-01.

Notes:  'All Races' includes races not shown separately. 'White' as shown is equivalent to 'White alone' and 'Black' as shown is equivalent to 'Black alone.'

Units:  Number of households in thousands.

## Table 1.19: Selected Characteristics of Family Households, 1985

|  | Black | White | All Races |
|---|---|---|---|
| *Total families* | *6,778* | *54,400* | *62,706* |
| **By Type of family** | | | |
| Married couple families | 3,469 | 45,643 | 50,350 |
| Male householder, no wife present | 344 | 1,816 | 2,228 |
| Female householder, no husband present | 2,964 | 6,941 | 10,129 |
| **By Size of family** | | | |
| Two persons | 2,261 | 22,711 | 25,349 |
| Three persons | 1,730 | 12,743 | 14,804 |
| Four persons | 1,358 | 11,517 | 13,259 |
| Five persons | 762 | 4,894 | 5,894 |
| Six persons | 366 | 1,704 | 2,175 |
| Seven or more persons | 300 | 831 | 1,225 |
| Average per family | 3.60 | 3.16 | 3.23 |
| **By Number of related children under 18 years old** | | | |
| No children | 2,887 | 28,169 | 31,594 |
| One child | 1,579 | 11,174 | 13,108 |
| Two children | 1,330 | 9,937 | 11,645 |
| Three children | 612 | 3,695 | 4,486 |
| Four children | 223 | 1,049 | 1,329 |
| Five children | 97 | 261 | 373 |
| Six or more children | 50 | 115 | 171 |
| Average per family | 1.14 | 0.88 | 0.92 |
| Average per family with children | 1.99 | 1.83 | 1.85 |

*(continued on next page)*

## Table 1.19: Selected Characteristics of Family Households, 1985

|  | Black | White | All Races |
|---|---|---|---|
| **By Number of earners** | | | |
| No earners | 1,376 | 7,674 | 9,221 |
| One earner | 2,312 | 15,219 | 17,949 |
| Two earners | 2,237 | 23,303 | 26,160 |
| Three earners | 527 | 5,317 | 6,029 |
| Four earners or more | 218 | 2,263 | 2,570 |
| **By Housing tenure** | | | |
| Own housing unit | 3,271 | 40,865 | 45,015 |
| Rent housing unit | 3,508 | 13,535 | 17,691 |
| **By Residence** | | | |
| Northeast | 1,322 | 11,631 | 13,149 |
| Midwest | 1,345 | 14,309 | 15,839 |
| South | 3,561 | 17,953 | 21,781 |
| West | 550 | 10,507 | 11,938 |

Source: US Bureau of the Census, Current Population Reports, *Money Income of Households, Families, and Persons in the United States, 1984* (Series P-60, #151), table 21.
US Bureau of the Census, Current Population Reports, *Household & Family Characteristics, March 1985* (Series P-20, #437), tables 1 and 22.

Notes: 'All Races' includes races not shown separately.
'Number of earners' excludes families with members in the armed forces.

Units: Number of family households in thousands; average children and persons per family.

## Table 1.20: Selected Characteristics of Family Households, 1990

| | Black | White | All Races |
|---|---|---|---|
| *Total families* | *7,470* | *56,590* | *66,090* |
| **By Type of family** | | | |
| Married couple families | 3,750 | 46,981 | 52,317 |
| Male householder, no wife present | 446 | 2,303 | 2,884 |
| Female householder, no husband present | 3,275 | 7,306 | 10,890 |
| **By Size of family** | | | |
| Two persons | 2,574 | 24,438 | 27,606 |
| Three persons | 1,951 | 12,937 | 15,353 |
| Four persons | 1,478 | 12,048 | 14,036 |
| Five persons | 819 | 4,882 | 5,938 |
| Six persons | 371 | 1,505 | 1,997 |
| Seven or more persons | 276 | 781 | 1,170 |
| Average per family | 3.46 | 3.11 | 3.17 |
| **By Number of related children under 18 years old** | | | |
| No children | 3,093 | 29,872 | 33,801 |
| One child | 1,894 | 11,186 | 13,530 |
| Two children | 1,433 | 10,342 | 12,263 |
| Three children | 635 | 3,853 | 4,650 |
| Four children | 256 | 970 | 1,279 |
| Five children | 107 | 247 | 379 |
| Six or more children | 51 | 121 | 188 |
| Average per family | 1.09 | 0.86 | 0.89 |
| Average per family with children | 1.86 | 1.82 | 1.83 |

*(continued on next page)*

## Table 1.20: Selected Characteristics of Family Households, 1990

|  | Black | White | All Races |
|---|---|---|---|
| **By Number of earners** | | | |
| No earners | 1,396 | 7,816 | 9,439 |
| One earner | 2,601 | 14,970 | 18,146 |
| Two earners | 2,609 | 25,737 | 29,235 |
| Three earners | 659 | 5,832 | 6,724 |
| Four earners or more | 259 | 2,236 | 2,546 |
| **By Housing tenure** | | | |
| Own housing unit | 3,448 | 42,588 | 47,142 |
| Rent housing unit | 4,023 | 14,003 | 18,948 |
| **By Residence** | | | |
| Northeast | 1,279 | 11,837 | 13,494 |
| Midwest | 1,446 | 14,370 | 16,059 |
| South | 4,147 | 18,746 | 23,244 |
| West | 598 | 11,638 | 13,293 |
| Nonfarm | 7,453 | 55,225 | 64,701 |
| Farm | 17 | 1,365 | 1,390 |
| Inside metropolitan areas | 6,256 | 42,592 | 50,619 |
| Outside metropolitan areas | 1,215 | 13,999 | 15,471 |

Source:   US Bureau of the Census, Current Population Reports, *Money Income of Households, Families, and Persons in the United States: 1988 and 1989* (Series P-60, #172), tables 1, 13, and 18.
US Bureau of the Census, Current Population Reports, *Household & Family Characteristics: March 1990 and 1989* (Series P-20, #447), tables 1 and 2.

Notes:   'All Races' includes races not shown separately.
'Number of earners' excludes families with members in the armed forces.

Units:   Number of family households in thousands; average children and persons per family.

GARDNER HARVEY LIBRARY
Miami University-Middletown
Middletown, Ohio

## Table 1.21: Selected Characteristics of Family Households, 2006

|  | Black | White | All Races |
|---|---|---|---|
| *All families* | *9,274* | *64,120* | *78,454* |
| **By Type of family** | | | |
| Married couple families | 4,359 | 50,747 | 58,964 |
| Male householder, no wife present | 864 | 3,809 | 5,067 |
| Female householder, no husband present | 4,050 | 9,563 | 14,424 |
| **By Size of family** | | | |
| Two persons | 3,715 | 29,604 | 35,102 |
| Three persons | 2,448 | 13,919 | 17,566 |
| Four persons | 1,745 | 12,420 | 15,400 |
| Five persons | 799 | 5,413 | 6,718 |
| Six persons | 366 | 1,895 | 2,456 |
| Seven or more persons | 201 | 868 | 1,213 |
| **By Number of earners** | | | |
| No earner | 1,508 | 9,152 | 11,185 |
| One earner | 3,819 | 19,450 | 25,013 |
| Two earners | 3,223 | 28,423 | 33,808 |
| Three earners | 570 | 5,379 | 6,377 |
| Four earners or more | 154 | 1,715 | 2,070 |
| **By Residence** | | | |
| Northeast | 1,627 | 11,634 | 14,197 |
| Midwest | 1,698 | 15,350 | 17,706 |
| South | 5,149 | 22,778 | 29,142 |
| West | 801 | 14,358 | 17,409 |

Source: US Bureau of the Census, Current Population Reports, *Annual Social and Economic Supplement 2007*, family income table FINC-01.

Notes: 'All Races' includes races not shown separately. 'White' as shown is equivalent to 'White alone' and 'Black' as shown is equivalent to 'Black alone.'
'Number of earners' excludes families with members in the armed forces.

Units: Number of family households in thousands.

## Table 1.22: Family Structure and Living Arrangements, Children 17 and Under, 1990–2006

| | Black | | | White | | | All Races | | |
|---|---|---|---|---|---|---|---|---|---|
| | Married Parents | Mother Only | Father Only | Married Parents | Mother Only | Father Only | Married Parents | Mother Only | Father Only |
| 1990 | 38% | 51% | 4% | 81% | 15% | 3% | 73% | 22% | 3% |
| 1991 | 36 | 54 | 4 | 80 | 15 | 3 | 72 | 22 | 3 |
| 1992 | 36 | 54 | 3 | 79 | 16 | 3 | 71 | 23 | 3 |
| 1993 | 36 | 54 | 3 | 79 | 16 | 3 | 71 | 23 | 3 |
| 1994 | 33 | 53 | 4 | 79 | 16 | 3 | 69 | 23 | 3 |
| 1995 | 33 | 52 | 4 | 78 | 16 | 3 | 69 | 23 | 4 |
| 1996 | 33 | 53 | 4 | 77 | 16 | 4 | 68 | 24 | 4 |
| 1997 | 35 | 52 | 5 | 77 | 17 | 4 | 68 | 24 | 4 |
| 1998 | 36 | 51 | 4 | 76 | 16 | 5 | 68 | 23 | 4 |
| 1999 | 35 | 52 | 4 | 77 | 16 | 4 | 68 | 23 | 4 |
| 2000 | 38 | 49 | 4 | 77 | 16 | 4 | 69 | 22 | 4 |
| 2001 | 38 | 48 | 5 | 78 | 16 | 4 | 69 | 22 | 4 |
| 2002 | 38 | 48 | 5 | 77 | 16 | 4 | 69 | 23 | 5 |
| 2003 | 36 | 51 | 5 | 77 | 16 | 4 | 68 | 23 | 5 |
| 2004 | 35 | 50 | 6 | 77 | 16 | 4 | 68 | 23 | 5 |
| 2005 | 35 | 50 | 5 | 76 | 16 | 5 | 67 | 23 | 5 |
| 2006 | 35 | 51 | 5 | 76 | 16 | 5 | 67 | 23 | 5 |

**Source:**   US Census Bureau, *Current Population Survey, Families and Living Arrangements 2006*, table FAM1.A.

**Notes:**   For years 2003 and later, 'Black,' and 'White' as used here refer to persons who indicated only one racial identity within the racial categories presented. For 2002 and earlier, 'Black' and 'White' may also refer to persons who selected more than one racial category.

**Units:**   Percent of total family households for each category.

## Table 1.23: Living Arrangements of Children
### Under 18 Years of Age, 2000 and 2006

|  | Black Children | White Children | All Children |
|---|---|---|---|
| **2000** | | | |
| Living with both parents | 4,286 | 42,497 | 49,795 |
| Living with mother only | 5,596 | 9,765 | 16,162 |
| Living with father only | 484 | 2,427 | 3,058 |
| Living with neither parent | 1,046 | 1,752 | 2,981 |
| **2006** | | | |
| Living with both parents | 3,886 | 41,599 | 49,661 |
| Living with mother only | 5,743 | 10,090 | 17,161 |
| Living with father only | 540 | 2,603 | 3,458 |
| Living with neither parent | 1,056 | 2,040 | 3,383 |

Source: US Bureau of the Census, Current Population Report, *America's Families and Living Arrangements: 2000 (Series P-20, #537), table C2; 2006*, table C2.

Notes: 'All Children' includes children of races not shown separately.
For 2006 data, 'White' and 'Black' are equivalent to 'White Alone' and 'Black Alone,' respectively.

Units: Number of children in thousands.

## Table 1.24: Single Parents Living With Own Children Under 18 Years Old, 2000 and 2006

|  | Black | White | All Races |
|---|---|---|---|
| **2000** | | | |
| *Single Mothers* | | | |
| With own children under 18 | 3,060 | 6,216 | 9,681 |
| With own children under 12 | 2,484 | 4,558 | 7,337 |
| With own children under 6 | 1,459 | 2,519 | 4,115 |
| With own children under 3 | 846 | 1,396 | 2,319 |
| With own children under 1 | 307 | 499 | 824 |
| *Single Fathers* | | | |
| With own children under 18 | 335 | 1,622 | 2,044 |
| With own children under 12 | 225 | 1,145 | 1,441 |
| With own children under 6 | 138 | 647 | 819 |
| With own children under 3 | 95 | 393 | 511 |
| With own children under 1 | 38 | 152 | 196 |
| **2006** | | | |
| *Single Mothers* | | | |
| With own children under 18 | 3,143 | 6,628 | 10,404 |
| With own children under 12 | 2,322 | 4,661 | 7,438 |
| With own children under 6 | 1,390 | 2,678 | 4,350 |
| With own children under 3 | 739 | 1,551 | 2,467 |
| With own children under 1 | 256 | 515 | 830 |
| *Single Fathers* | | | |
| With own children under 18 | 415 | 1,914 | 2,501 |
| With own children under 12 | 307 | 1,252 | 1,683 |
| With own children under 6 | 180 | 691 | 952 |
| With own children under 3 | 111 | 411 | 575 |
| With own children under 1 | 45 | 165 | 227 |

**Source:**   US Bureau of the Census, Current Population Reports, *America's Families and Living Arrangements: 2000*, table FG-5; *2006*, table FG-5.

**Notes:**   'All Races' includes other races not shown separately. For 2006 data, 'White' and 'Black' as shown are equivalent to 'White Alone' and 'Black Alone', respectively.

**Units:**   Thousands of mothers or fathers.

**Table 1.25: Primary Child Care Arrangements Used for Preschoolers by Families With Employed Mothers: Spring 1999, Winter 2002, and Spring 2005**

| | Black Children | White Children | All Children |
|---|---|---|---|
| **Spring 1999** | | | |
| *All preschoolers with employed mothers* | *1,735* | *8,411* | *10,587* |
| Designated parent | 1.9% | 3.4% | 3.2% |
| Other parent | 13.9 | 20.4 | 19.3 |
| Grandparent | 26.5 | 19.4 | 21.7 |
| Other relative or sibling | 11.3 | 7.8 | 8.4 |
| Daycare center | 24.8 | 18.0 | 18.7 |
| Nursery/preschool | 3.1 | 4.1 | 4.0 |
| Head start | 1.2 | 0.2 | 0.4 |
| Family day care | 5.2 | 13.2 | 11.4 |
| Other non-relative | 8.2 | 10.2 | 9.7 |
| **Winter 2002** | | | |
| *All preschoolers with employed mothers* | *1,556* | *7,699* | *9,823* |
| Designated parent | 1.2% | 3.6% | 3.3% |
| Other parent | 14.0 | 19.0 | 18.2 |
| Sibling | 3.8 | 0.5 | 1.0 |
| Grandparent | 22.5 | 18.5 | 19.4 |
| Other relative | 9.3 | 4.6 | 5.4 |
| Daycare center | 21.5 | 18.6 | 19.0 |
| Nursery/preschool | 5.8 | 5.0 | 5.3 |
| Head start | 1.2 | 0.7 | 0.8 |
| Family day care | 7.9 | 9.5 | 9.2 |
| Other non-relative | 7.0 | 9.6 | 9.0 |

*(continued on next page)*

## Table 1.25: Primary Child Care Arrangements Used for Preschoolers by Families With Employed Mothers: Spring 1999, Winter 2002, and Spring 2005

|  | Black Children | White Children | All Children |
|---|---|---|---|
| **Spring 2005** | | | |
| *All preschoolers with employed mothers* | *1,840* | *8,739* | *11,334* |
| Designated parent | 3.2% | 4.9% | 4.6% |
| Other parent | 12.7 | 19.3 | 18.2 |
| Sibling | 3.7 | 1.1 | 1.5 |
| Grandparent | 20.3 | 20.2 | 20.5 |
| Other relative | 7.8 | 4.8 | 5.4 |
| Daycare center | 23.6 | 18.1 | 19.1 |
| Nursery/preschool | 5.5 | 5.2 | 5.3 |
| Head start | 2.0 | 0.5 | 0.8 |
| Family day care | 6.9 | 8.5 | 7.8 |
| Other non-relative | 6.9 | 9.5 | 9.0 |
| School | 5.2 | 2.2 | 2.6 |
| No regular arrangement | 7.0 | 11.4 | 10.5 |

**Source:** US Bureau of the Census, Current Population Reports, *Who's Minding the Kids? Child Care Arrangements: Spring 1999*, table 2B; *Winter 2002*, table 2B; *Spring 2005*, table 2B.

**Notes:** 'All Children' includes children of races not shown separately.
Because of multiple arrangements, numbers and percentages may exceed the total number of children. 'Designated parent' is selected in households where both parents are present to report child care arrangements for each child.

**Units:** Thousands of children living in family households; percent of total with specified child-care arrangement.

## Table 1.26: Average Weekly Child Care Expenditures of Families with Employed Mothers, Winter 2002 and Spring 2005

| | Black | White | All Races |
|---|---|---|---|
| **Winter 2002** | | | |
| *Families with children under 5 years* | 691 | 3,522 | 4,475 |
| Average weekly child care expenditures | $92 | $127 | $122 |
| Average monthly family income | $3,881 | $5,648 | $5,598 |
| Percent of family's monthly income spent on child care | 10.3% | 9.8% | 9.5% |
| Average monthly mother's income | $1,967 | $2,531 | $2,577 |
| Ratio of child care expenditures to mother's income | 20.4 | 21.8 | 20.5 |
| *Families with children 5 to 14 years* | 777 | 4,351 | 5,372 |
| Average weekly child care expenditures | $79 | $85 | $84 |
| Average monthly family income | $4,405 | $5,941 | $5,762 |
| Percent of family's monthly income spent on child care | 7.8% | 6.2% | 6.3% |
| Average monthly mother's income | $2,348 | $2,874 | $2,796 |
| Ratio of child care expenditures to mother's income | 14.6 | 12.8 | 13.0 |
| **Spring 2005** | | | |
| *Families with children under 5 years* | 693 | 3,565 | 4,599 |
| Average weekly child care expenditures | $114 | $129 | $128 |
| Average monthly family income | $4,488 | $6,880 | $6,482 |
| Percent of family's monthly income spent on child care | 11.0% | 8.2% | 8.6% |
| Average monthly mother's income | $2,326 | $3,418 | $3,199 |
| Ratio of child care expenditures to mother's income | 21.2 | 16.4 | 17.4 |
| *Families with children 5 to 14 years* | 765 | 4,279 | 5,379 |
| Average weekly child care expenditures | $96 | $94 | $97 |
| Average monthly family income | $4,191 | $8,443 | $7,749 |
| Percent of family's monthly income spent on child care | 9.9% | 4.8% | 5.4% |
| Average monthly mother's income | $2,497 | $4,108 | $3,803 |
| Ratio of child care expenditures to mother's income | 16.7 | 9.9 | 11.1 |

Source: US Bureau of the Census, Current Population Reports, *Who's Minding the Kids? Child Care Arrangements: Winter 2002*, table 6; *Spring 2005*, table 6.

Notes: 'All Races' includes races not shown separately. Race designation is based on race of mother.

Units: Families in thousands; monthly income; expenditures per week; percent of income, ratio of expenditures to income.

# Chapter 2

# Vital Statistics and Health

## Chapter Two Highlights

This chapter provides vital statistics and information about the health of Black persons in the United States, including both the most current data available as well as comparisons of the Black population over time. For almost all tables, corresponding data is provided for the total population of the United States as well as for White persons. This allows for easy comparison between groups.

This chapter includes information about birth rates (tables 2.02–2.04), as well as information about infant mortality and its causes (tables 2.08–2.10). Statistics on abortion are also included (table 2.12).

Information about children's health is provided, including data on health status (table 2.13), health care access (table 2.13), and vaccinations (table 2.14).

The chapter also contains statistics about death rates and causes of death, including heart disease (table 2.19) cancer (tables 2.21 and 2.31), motor vehicle accidents (table 2.22), homicide (table 2.23), and suicide (table 2.24). Data on HIV transmission and AIDS rates are also included (tables 2.26–2.28).

The chapter also contains statistics on a variety of physical conditions, such as injuries, migraines, and hearing and vision trouble (tables 2.32–2.35).

Also of note are statistics on body mass, including statistics about obese, overweight, and underweight persons (tables 2.41 and 2.42). Information is provided for adults, adolescents, and children (table 2.43). We have also included data on time spent engaging in leisure-time physical exercise (tables 2.44 and 2.45).

The chapter includes statistics on smoking, alcohol consumption, and other substances organized in a number of ways, including by sex (tables 2.47 and 2.48) and education (table 2.48).

We have also provided data on feelings of emotional distress in adults (table 2.50) and suicide attempts by teenagers (table 2.51).

The chapter contains statistics on health insurance coverage by type of coverage (tables 2.52–2.54) and statistics on persons lacking coverage (table 2.53). In addition, we have included data on heath care visits (table 2.55), including dental visits (table 2.56) and hospitalization rates (table 2.57).

## Table 2.01: Self-Assessment of Health, 1990–2006

|  | Black | White | All Races |
|---|---|---|---|
| **1990** | | | |
| Excellent | 31.1% | 42.1% | 40.5% |
| Very good | 25.3 | 29.0 | 28.5 |
| Good | 28.5 | 20.8 | 22.0 |
| Fair or poor | 15.1 | 8.1 | 8.9 |
| **1995** | | | |
| Fair or poor | 17.2% | 9.7% | 10.6% |
| **2000** | | | |
| Fair or poor | 14.6% | 8.2% | 9.0% |
| **2003** | | | |
| Fair or poor | 14.7% | 8.5% | 9.2% |
| **2005** | | | |
| Excellent | 29.9% | 36.8% | 35.8% |
| Very good | 27.5 | 31.5 | 31.0 |
| Good | 28.3 | 23.0 | 24.0 |
| Fair or poor | 14.3 | 8.6 | 9.2 |
| **2006** | | | |
| Excellent | 29.6% | 36.4% | 35.5% |
| Very good | 26.5 | 31.5 | 30.8 |
| Good | 29.4 | 23.4 | 24.4 |
| Fair | 11.2 | 6.7 | 7.2 |
| Poor | 3.2 | 2.0 | 2.1 |

**Source:** US Department of Health and Human Services, Centers for Disease Control and Prevention, National Center for Health Statistics, *Health, United States, 1988*, table 50; *1991*, table 61; *1992*, table 63; *2001*, table 58; *2002*, table 59; *2003*, table 57; *2004*, table 57; *2005*, table 60.

US Department of Health and Human Services, Centers for Disease Control and Prevention, *National Health Interview Survey: Summary Health Statistics, 2005*, table 2; *2006*, table 2.

**Notes:** 'All Races' includes races not shown separately.

Data is age-adjusted.

Data starting in 1997 is not strictly comparable with data for earlier years due to the 1997 questionnaire redesign.

**Units:** Percent of the population.

## Table 2.02: Fertility, Births, and Birth Rates, by Age of the Mother, 1990–2006

| | Black mothers | White mothers | All mothers |
|---|---|---|---|
| **1990** | | | |
| Births | NA | NA | NA |
| Fertility rate | 86.8 | 68.3 | 70.9 |
| *Birth rate per 1,000, by age group* | | | |
| 15-19 years old | 112.8 | 50.8 | 59.9 |
| 20-24 years old | 160.2 | 109.8 | 116.5 |
| 25-29 years old | 115.5 | 120.7 | 120.2 |
| 30-34 years old | 68.7 | 81.7 | 80.8 |
| 35-39 years old | 28.1 | 31.5 | 31.7 |
| 40-44 years old | 5.5 | 5.2 | 5.5 |
| **2000** | | | |
| Births | NA | NA | NA |
| Fertility rate | 70.0 | 65.3 | 65.9 |
| *Birth rate per 1,000, by age group* | | | |
| 15-19 years old | 77.4 | 43.2 | 47.7 |
| 20-24 years old | 141.3 | 106.6 | 109.7 |
| 25-29 years old | 100.3 | 116.7 | 113.5 |
| 30-34 years old | 65.4 | 94.6 | 91.2 |
| 35-39 years old | 31.5 | 40.2 | 39.7 |
| 40-44 years old | 7.2 | 7.9 | 8.0 |
| **2005** | | | |
| Births | 583,759 | 2,279,768 | 4,138,349 |
| Fertility rate | 67.2 | 58.3 | 66.7 |
| *Birth rate per 1,000, by age group* | | | |
| Total | 15.7 | 11.5 | 14.0 |
| 10-14 years old | 1.7 | 0.2 | 0.7 |
| 15-19 years old | 60.9 | 25.9 | 40.5 |
| 20-24 years old | 126.8 | 81.4 | 102.2 |
| 25-29 years old | 103.0 | 109.1 | 115.5 |
| 30-34 years old | 68.4 | 96.9 | 95.8 |
| 35-39 years old | 34.3 | 45.6 | 46.3 |
| 40-44 years old | 8.2 | 8.3 | 9.1 |
| 45-54 years old | 0.5 | 0.5 | 0.6 |

*(continued on next page)*

## Table 2.02: Fertility, Births, and Birth Rates, by Age of the Mother, 1990–2006

| | Black mothers | White mothers | All mothers |
|---|---|---|---|
| **2006 (Preliminary)** | | | |
| Births | 617,220 | 2,309,833 | 4,265,996 |
| Fertility rate | 70.6 | 59.5 | 68.5 |
| *Birth rate per 1,000, by age group* | | | |
| Total | 16.5 | 11.6 | 14.2 |
| 10-14 years old | 1.6 | 0.2 | 0.6 |
| 15-19 years old | 63.7 | 26.6 | 41.9 |
| 20-24 years old | 133.1 | 83.4 | 105.9 |
| 25-29 years old | 107.1 | 109.2 | 116.8 |
| 30-34 years old | 72.6 | 98.1 | 97.7 |
| 35-39 years old | 36.0 | 46.3 | 47.3 |
| 40-44 years old | 8.3 | 8.4 | 9.4 |
| 45-54 years old | 0.5 | 0.6 | 0.6 |

**Source:**  US Department of Health and Human Services, Centers for Disease Control and Prevention, *Births: Final Data for 2005*, tables 1 and 4.
US Department of Health and Human Services, Centers for Disease Control and Prevention, *Births: Preliminary Data for 2006*, tables 1 and 2.

**Notes:**  'All Races' includes races not shown separately.
Data based on race of the mother. Fertility rate is the total number of births, regardless of age of mother, per 1,000 women aged 15-44 years.

**Units:**  Live births in number of births; rates per 1,000 women.

## Table 2.03: Selected Characteristics of Live Births, 1980–2004

| | Black births | White births | All births |
|---|---|---|---|
| **1980** | | | |
| Birth weight under 2,500 grams | 12.69% | 5.72% | 6.84% |
| Birth weight under 1,500 grams | 2.48 | 0.90 | 1.15 |
| Mother under 18 years old | 12.5 | 4.5 | 5.8 |
| Mother 18-19 years old | 14.5 | 9.0 | 9.8 |
| Births to unmarried mothers | 56.1 | 11.2 | 18.4 |
| Mother with less than 12 years of school | 36.4 | 20.8 | 23.7 |
| Mother with 16 years or more of school | 6.2 | 15.5 | 14.0 |
| Prenatal care began in 1st trimester | 62.4 | 79.2 | 76.3 |
| Prenatal care began in 3rd trimester or no prenatal care | 8.9 | 4.3 | 5.1 |
| Twin births | 2.40 | 1.81 | 1.89 |
| **1990** | | | |
| Birth weight under 2,500 grams | 13.25% | 5.70% | 6.97% |
| Birth weight under 1,500 grams | 2.92 | 0.95 | 1.27 |
| Mother under 18 years old | 10.1 | 3.6 | 4.7 |
| Mother 18-19 years old | 13.0 | 7.3 | 8.1 |
| Births to unmarried mothers | 66.5 | 20.4 | 28.0 |
| Mother with less than 12 years of school | 30.2 | 22.4 | 23.8 |
| Mother with 16 years or more of school | 7.2 | 19.3 | 17.5 |
| Prenatal care began in 1st trimester | 60.6 | 79.2 | 75.8 |
| Prenatal care began in 3rd trimester or no prenatal care | 11.3 | 4.9 | 6.1 |
| Twin births | 2.65 | 2.21 | 2.26 |
| **2000** | | | |
| Birth weight under 2,500 grams | 12.99% | 6.55% | 7.57% |
| Birth weight under 1,500 grams | 3.07 | 1.14 | 1.43 |
| Mother under 18 years old | 7.8 | 3.5 | 4.1 |
| Mother 18-19 years old | 11.9 | 7.1 | 7.7 |
| Births to unmarried mothers | 68.5 | 27.1 | 33.2 |
| Mother with less than 12 years of school | 25.5 | 21.4 | 21.7 |
| Mother with 16 years or more of school | 11.7 | 26.3 | 24.7 |
| Prenatal care began in 1st trimester | 74.3 | 85.0 | 83.2 |
| Prenatal care began in 3rd trimester or no prenatal care | 6.7 | 3.3 | 3.9 |
| Twin births | 3.31 | 2.92 | 2.93 |

*(continued on next page)*

## Table 2.03: Selected Characteristics of Live Births, 1980–2004

|  | Black births | White births | All births |
|---|---|---|---|
| **2004** | | | |
| Birth weight under 2,500 grams | 13.44% | 7.07% | 8.08% |
| Birth weight under 1,500 grams | 3.07 | 1.20 | 1.48 |
| Mother under 18 years old | 6.4 | 3.0 | 3.4 |
| Mother 18-19 years old | 10.7 | 6.4 | 6.8 |
| Births to unmarried mothers | 68.8 | 30.5 | 35.8 |
| Mother with less than 12 years of school | 23.8 | 22.7 | 22.2 |
| Mother with 16 years or more of school | 13.7 | 28.0 | 26.9 |
| Prenatal care began in 1st trimester | 76.4 | 85.4 | 83.9 |
| Prenatal care began in 3rd trimester or no prenatal care | 5.7 | 3.2 | 3.6 |
| Twin births | 3.51 | 3.21 | 3.22 |

**Source:** US Department of Health and Human Services, Centers for Disease Control and Prevention, National Center for Health Statistics, *Health, United States, 2007*, tables 6, 7, 9, 10, 11, and 13.

**Notes:** Data based on race of the mother.

**Units:** Percent of all live births.

## Table 2.04: Birth Rates by Live Birth Order, 2005 and 2006

|  | Black mothers | White mothers | All mothers |
|---|---|---|---|
| **2005** | | | |
| *All live births* | *69.0* | *66.3* | *66.7* |
| First child | 26.6 | 26.3 | 26.5 |
| Second child | 19.9 | 21.7 | 21.5 |
| Third child | 12.1 | 11.4 | 11.3 |
| Fourth child | 5.7 | 4.4 | 4.5 |
| Fifth child | 2.5 | 1.5 | 1.6 |
| Sixth and Seventh child | 1.6 | 0.8 | 0.9 |
| Eighth child and over | 0.5 | 0.3 | 0.3 |
| **2006** | | | |
| *All live births* | *70.6* | *59.5* | *68.5* |
| First child | 27.5 | 24.8 | 27.4 |
| Second child | 20.2 | 19.8 | 21.9 |
| Third child | 12.3 | 9.5 | 11.6 |
| Fourth child and over | 10.6 | 5.4 | 7.7 |

Source: US Department of Health and Human Services, Centers for Disease Control and Prevention, Births: *Preliminary Data for 2006*, table 5.
US Department of Health and Human Services, Centers for Disease Control and Prevention, *Births: Final Data for 2005*, table 3.

Notes: Data based on race of the mother.
Data for 2006 is preliminary.

Units: Births per 1,000 women aged 15-44 years.

## Table 2.05: Nonmarital Childbearing, 1980–2005

| | Black women | White women | All women |
|---|---|---|---|
| **Live births per 1,000 to unmarried mothers** | | | |
| 1980 | 81.1 | 18.1 | 29.4 |
| 1985 | 77.0 | 22.5 | 32.8 |
| 1990 | 90.5 | 32.9 | 43.8 |
| 1995 | 74.5 | 37.0 | 44.3 |
| 2000 | 70.5 | 38.2 | 44.0 |
| 2001 | 68.2 | 38.5 | 43.8 |
| 2002 | 66.2 | 38.9 | 43.7 |
| 2003 | 66.3 | 40.4 | 44.9 |
| 2004 | 67.2 | 41.6 | 46.1 |
| 2005 | 67.8 | 43.0 | 47.5 |
| | | | |
| **Percent of live births to unmarried mothers** | | | |
| 1980 | 56.1% | 11.2% | 18.4% |
| 1985 | 61.2 | 14.7 | 22.0 |
| 1990 | 66.5 | 20.4 | 28.0 |
| 1995 | 69.9 | 25.3 | 32.2 |
| 2000 | 68.5 | 27.1 | 33.2 |
| 2001 | 68.4 | 27.7 | 33.5 |
| 2002 | 68.2 | 28.5 | 34.0 |
| 2003 | 68.2 | 29.4 | 34.6 |
| 2004 | 68.8 | 30.5 | 35.8 |
| 2005 | 69.3 | 31.7 | 36.9 |

**Source:**   US Department of Health and Human Services, Centers for Disease Control and Prevention, National Center for Health Statistics, *Health, United States, 2006*, table 10.
US Department of Health and Human Services, Centers for Disease Control and Prevention, National Vital Statistics Reports, *Births: Final Data for 2005*, table 18.

**Notes:**   'All women' includes women of races not shown separately.

**Units:**   Live births per 1,000 unmarried women 15-44 years of age.

## Table 2.06: Projected Fertility Rates, Women 10–49 years old, 2010

|  | Black women | White women | All women |
|---|---|---|---|
| Total fertility rate | 2,140 | 2,098 | 2,123 |
| *Birth rates by age* | | | |
| 10-14 years old | 3.5 | 0.9 | 1.3 |
| 15-19 years old | 95.6 | 54.3 | 60.2 |
| 20-24 years old | 137.1 | 112.6 | 115.8 |
| 25-29 years old | 95.5 | 118.5 | 115.7 |
| 30-34 years old | 63.4 | 90.0 | 87.8 |
| 35-39 years old | 28.9 | 36.6 | 36.7 |
| 40-44 years old | 6.0 | 7.1 | 7.3 |
| 45-49 years old | 0.3 | 0.3 | 0.3 |

**Source:**  US Bureau of the Census, *Statistical Abstract of the United States, 2006*, table 78.

**Notes:**  'All women' includes women of races not shown separately.
The total fertility rate is the number of births that 1,000 women would have in their lifetime if, at each year of age, they experienced the birth rates occurring in the specified year. Projections are based on middle fertility assumptions.

**Units:**  Total fertility rate and birth rate in births per 1,000 women.

## Table 2.07: Contraceptive Use for Women 15–44 Years of Age, by Method of Contraception, 1995 and 2002

|  | Black women | White women | All women |
|---|---|---|---|
| **1995** | | | |
| *All methods* | *62.3%* | *66.2%* | *64.2%* |
| Female sterilization | 39.9 | 24.5 | 27.8 |
| Male sterilization | 1.8* | 13.7 | 10.9 |
| Birth control pill | 23.7 | 28.7 | 27.0 |
| Intrauterine device | NA | 0.7 | 0.8 |
| Diaphragm | NA | 2.3 | 1.9 |
| Condom | 24.9 | 22.5 | 23.4 |
| **2002** | | | |
| *All methods* | *57.6%* | *64.6%* | *61.9%* |
| Female sterilization | 39.2 | 23.9 | 27.0 |
| Male sterilization | NA | 12.9 | 10.2 |
| Birth control pill | 23.1 | 34.9 | 31.0 |
| Intrauterine device | NA | 1.7 | 2.2 |
| Diaphragm | NA | NA | 0.6 |
| Condom | 29.6 | 21.7 | 23.8 |

**Source:** US Department of Health and Human Services, Centers for Disease Control and Prevention, National Center for Health Statistics, *Health, United States, 2007*, table 17.

**Notes:** 'All women' includes women of races not shown separately. 'Black' and 'White' include women who are not of Hispanic or Latino origin only. Data is based on household interviews of samples of women in the childbearing ages.
'NA' means that estimates are considered unreliable and are not shown.
* Indicates data with a relative standard error of 20-30%.

**Units:** Percent of women using contraception; individual methods as a percent of all women using some form of contraception.

## Table 2.08: Infant Mortality, Fetal Deaths, and Perinatal Mortality Rates, 1990–2004

|  | Black | White | All Races |
|---|---|---|---|
| **1990** | | | |
| Infant mortality rate | 18.0 | 7.6 | 9.2 |
| Neonatal mortality rates: | | | |
| Under 28 days | 11.6 | 4.8 | 5.8 |
| Under 7 days | 9.7 | 3.9 | 4.8 |
| Post-neonatal mortality rate | 6.4 | 2.8 | 3.4 |
| Fetal death rate | 13.3 | 6.4 | 7.5 |
| Late fetal death rate | 6.7 | 3.8 | 4.3 |
| Perinatal mortality rate | 16.4 | 7.7 | 9.1 |
| **2000** | | | |
| Infant mortality rate | 14.1 | 5.7 | 6.9 |
| Neonatal mortality rates: | | | |
| Under 28 days | 9.4 | 3.8 | 4.6 |
| Under 7 days | 7.6 | 3.0 | 3.7 |
| Post-neonatal mortality rate | 4.7 | 1.9 | 2.3 |
| Fetal death rate | 12.4 | 5.6 | 6.6 |
| Late fetal death rate | 5.4 | 2.9 | 3.3 |
| **2004** | | | |
| Infant mortality rate | 13.2 | 5.7 | 6.8 |
| Neonatal mortality rate | 8.9 | 3.8 | 4.5 |
| Post-neonatal mortality rate | 4.3 | 1.9 | 2.3 |

**Source:** US Department of Health and Human Services, Centers for Disease Control and Prevention, National Center for Health Statistics, *Health, United States, 2005*, table 19; *2007*, table 19.

**Notes:** 'All Races' includes races not shown separately.
Data based on race of the mother.
Infant mortality rate is the number of deaths of infants under one year; neonatal deaths occur within 28 days of birth; post-neonatal deaths occur 28 days to 11 months after birth; deaths within 7 days of birth are early neonatal deaths; fetal deaths are deaths of fetuses of more than 20 weeks gestation; late fetal deaths are deaths of fetuses of more than 28 weeks of gestation; perinatal mortality is the sum of late fetal deaths and infant deaths within the first 7 days of life.

**Units:** All rates per 1,000 live births, as shown.

## Table 2.09: Infant Mortality Rates, Leading Causes of Death, 2004 and 2005

|  | Black | White | All Races |
|---|---|---|---|
| **2004** | | | |
| *All causes* | *1,378.7* | *565.7* | *679.4* |
| Congenital malformations | 174.8 | 132.5 | 136.7 |
| Disorders related to short gestation and low birth rate | | 82.4 | 293.6 |
| Sudden infant death syndrome | 117.8 | 44.7 | 54.6 |
| Newborn affected by maternal complications of pregnancy | 104.2 | 31.1 | 41.7 |
| Newborn affected by complications of placenta, cord and membranes | 52.1 | 21.2 | 25.3 |
| **2005** | | | |
| *All causes* | *1,373.3* | *573.3* | *687.2* |
| Congenital malformations | 170.6 | 129.7 | 134.2 |
| Disorders related to short gestation and low birth rate | 299.1 | 81.2 | 113.9 |
| Sudden infant death syndrome | 104.7 | 46.2 | 53.9 |
| Newborn affected by maternal complications of pregnancy | 104.2 | 32.5 | 42.9 |
| Newborn affected by complications of placenta, cord and membranes | 23.1 | 13.0 | 14.1 |

Source: US Department of Health and Human Services, Centers for Disease Control and Prevention, National Vital Statistics Reports, *Deaths: Final Data for 2004*, table 31; *2005*, table 31.

Notes: 'All Races' includes races not shown separately.
Data based on race of mother.

Units: Deaths per 100,000 live births.

## Table 2.10:  Infant Mortality Rate, by State, 2002–2004

| | Black infants | White Infants | All infants |
|---|---|---|---|
| *United States* | *13.7* | *5.7* | *6.9* |
| Alabama | 13.5 | 6.7 | 8.8 |
| Alaska | * | 5.1 | 6.4 |
| Arizona | 11.1 | 6.0 | 6.6 |
| Arkansas | 13.2 | 7.6 | 8.5 |
| California | 11.3 | 4.6 | 5.3 |
| Colorado | 16.3 | 5.1 | 6.1 |
| Connecticut | 12.1 | 4.4 | 5.8 |
| Delaware | 15.0 | 7.1 | 8.9 |
| District of Columbia | 15.5 | *3.8 | 11.4 |
| Florida | 13.1 | 5.8 | 7.3 |
| Georgia | 13.6 | 6.3 | 8.7 |
| Hawaii | *15.0 | 4.6 | 6.9 |
| Idaho | * | 6.1 | 6.1 |
| Illinois | 15.5 | 5.9 | 7.5 |
| Indiana | 15.0 | 6.9 | 7.8 |
| Iowa | *10.4 | 5.1 | 5.4 |
| Kansas | 14.1 | 6.6 | 7.0 |
| Kentucky | 11.6 | 6.5 | 6.9 |
| Louisiana | 14.0 | 7.2 | 9.9 |
| Maine | * | 4.9 | 5.0 |
| Maryland | 13.6 | 5.5 | 8.1 |
| Massachusetts | 10.2 | 3.9 | 4.8 |
| Michigan | 16.8 | 6.2 | 8.1 |
| Minnesota | 8.7 | 4.4 | 4.9 |
| Mississippi | 14.7 | 6.9 | 10.3 |
| Missouri | 14.8 | 6.7 | 7.9 |
| Montana | * | 5.8 | 6.4 |
| Nebraska | 16.2 | 5.5 | 6.3 |
| Nevada | 13.0 | 5.8 | 6.0 |

*(continued on next page)*

**Black Americans: A Statistical Sourcebook 2008**

## Table 2.10: Infant Mortality Rate, by State, 2002–2004

| | Black infants | White Infants | All infants |
|---|---|---|---|
| *United States* | *13.7* | *5.7* | *6.9* |
| New Hampshire | * | 4.8 | 4.9 |
| New Jersey | 12.2 | 3.8 | 5.6 |
| New Mexico | * | 6.5 | 6.1 |
| New York | 11.7 | 4.7 | 6.1 |
| North Carolina | 15.4 | 6.1 | 8.4 |
| North Dakota | * | 5.9 | 6.5 |
| Ohio | 15.6 | 6.3 | 7.7 |
| Oklahoma | 13.8 | 7.5 | 8.0 |
| Oregon | *10.1 | 5.6 | 5.6 |
| Pennsylvania | 13.9 | 6.0 | 7.4 |
| Rhode Island | *11.6 | 5.4 | 6.4 |
| South Carolina | 14.4 | 6.2 | 9.0 |
| South Dakota | * | 5.8 | 7.1 |
| Tennessee | 17.3 | 7.0 | 9.0 |
| Texas | 12.2 | 5.9 | 6.4 |
| Utah | * | 4.8 | 5.3 |
| Vermont | * | 4.7 | 4.7 |
| Virginia | 13.9 | 5.8 | 7.5 |
| Washington | 9.2 | 5.1 | 5.6 |
| West Virginia | *13.6 | 7.7 | 8.0 |
| Wisconsin | 17.6 | 5.1 | 6.4 |
| Wyoming | * | 6.8 | 7.0 |

**Source:** US Department of Health and Human Services, Centers for Disease Control and Prevention, National Center for Health Statistics, *Health, United States, 2007*, table 23.

**Notes:** Infant deaths are defined as occurring prior to 1 year of age.
\* Estimates are considered unreliable. Rates preceded by an asterisk are based on fewer than 50 deaths. Rates not shown are based on fewer than 20 deaths.

**Units:** Infant deaths per 1,000 live births.

## Table 2.11: Maternal Mortality Rates, by Age of the Mother, 1970–2005

|  | Black mothers | White mothers | All mothers |
|---|---|---|---|
| **1970** |  |  |  |
| *Number of deaths* | *342* | *445* | *803* |
| *All ages, age-adjusted rate* | *65.5* | *14.4* | *21.5* |
| Under 20 years old | 32.3 | 13.8 | 18.9 |
| 20-24 years old | 41.9 | 8.4 | 13.0 |
| 25-29 years old | 65.2 | 11.1 | 17.0 |
| 30-34 years old | 117.8 | 18.7 | 31.6 |
| 35 years old and over | 207.5 | 59.3 | 81.9 |
| **1980** |  |  |  |
| *Number of deaths* | *127* | *193* | *334* |
| *All ages, age-adjusted rate* | *24.9* | *6.7* | *9.4* |
| Under 20 years old | 13.1 | 5.8 | 7.6 |
| 20-24 years old | 13.9 | 4.2 | 5.8 |
| 25-29 years old | 22.4 | 5.4 | 7.7 |
| 30-34 years old | 44.0 | 9.3 | 13.6 |
| 35 years old and over | 100.6 | 25.5 | 36.3 |
| **1990** |  |  |  |
| *Number of deaths* | *153* | *177* | *343* |
| *All ages, age-adjusted rate* | *21.7* | *5.1* | *7.6* |
| Under 20 years old | NA | NA | 7.5 |
| 20-24 years old | 14.7 | 3.9 | 6.1 |
| 25-29 years old | 14.9 | 4.8 | 6.0 |
| 30-34 years old | 44.2 | 5.0 | 9.5 |
| 35 years old and over | 79.7 | 12.6 | 20.7 |

*(continued on next page)*

## Table 2.11: Maternal Mortality Rates, by Age of the Mother, 1970–2005

|  | Black mothers | White mothers | All mothers |
|---|---|---|---|
| **2000** |  |  |  |
| *Number of deaths* | *137* | *240* | *396* |
| *All ages, age-adjusted rate* | *20.1* | *6.2* | *8.2* |
| Under 20 years old | NA | NA | NA |
| 20-24 years old | 15.3 | 5.6 | 7.4 |
| 25-29 years old | 21.8 | 5.9 | 7.9 |
| 30-34 years old | 34.8 | 7.1 | 10.0 |
| 35 years old and over | 62.8 | 18.0 | 22.7 |
| **2005** |  |  |  |
| *Number of deaths* | *231* | *360* | *623* |
| *All ages, age-adjusted rate* | *31.7* | *9.1* | *12.4* |
| Under 20 years old | * | * | 7.4 |
| 20-24 years old | 18.2 | 9.0 | 10.7 |
| 25-29 years old | 37.1 | 7.2 | 11.8 |
| 30-34 years old | 46.6 | 9.3 | 12.8 |
| 35 years old and over | 112.8 | 28.9 | 38.0 |

**Source:** US Department of Health and Human Services, Centers for Disease Control and Prevention, National Center for Health Statistics, *Health, United States, 2007*, table 43.

**Notes:** 'All mothers' includes mothers of races not shown separately.
Data for maternal mortality for complications of pregnancy, childbirth, and the puerperium.
Rates for women 35 years old and over computed by relating deaths to live births to women in this age group. Rates based on fewer than 20 deaths are considered unreliable and are not shown.

**Units:** Number of maternal deaths; deaths of mothers per 100,000 live births.

## Table 2.12: Abortions, 1973–2004

|      | Black women | White women | All women |
|------|-------------|-------------|-----------|
| 1973 | 42.0 | 32.6 | 19.6 |
| 1975 | 47.6 | 27.7 | 27.2 |
| 1980 | 54.3 | 33.2 | 35.9 |
| 1985 | 47.2 | 27.7 | 35.4 |
| 1987 | 50.0 | 26.7 | 35.6 |
| 1988 | 48.9 | 25.9 | 35.2 |
| 1989 | 49.6 | 25.2 | 34.6 |
| 1990 | 53.7 | 25.8 | 34.4 |
| 1991 | 50.2 | 24.6 | 33.9 |
| 1992 | 51.8 | 23.6 | 33.5 |
| 1993 | 55.2 | 23.1 | 33.4 |
| 1994 | 53.8 | 21.7 | 32.1 |
| 1995 | 53.1 | 20.3 | 31.1 |
| 1996 | 55.5 | 20.2 | 31.4 |
| 1997 | 54.3 | 19.4 | 30.6 |
| 1998 | 51.2 | 18.9 | 26.4 |
| 1999 | 52.9 | 17.7 | 25.6 |
| 2000 | 50.3 | 16.7 | 24.5 |
| 2001 | 49.1 | 16.5 | 24.6 |
| 2002 | 49.5 | 16.4 | 24.6 |
| 2003 | 49.1 | 16.5 | 24.1 |
| 2004 | 47.2 | 16.1 | 22.5 |

Source: US Department of Health and Human Services, Centers for Disease Control and Prevention, National Center for Health Statistics, *Health, United States, 2005*, table 16; *2006*, table 16. US Department of Health and Human Services, Centers for Disease Control and Prevention, *Morbidity and Mortality Weekly Report*, vol. 56, no. SS-9, "Abortion Surveillance–United States, 2004," table 9.

Notes: 'All women' includes women of races not shown separately. For 1989 and later, 'White' includes women of Hispanic ethnicity.
The following states did not report abortion data in the years given: Alaska (1998-2002), California (1998-2004), New Hampshire (1998-2004), Oklahoma (1998-1999), and West Virginia (2004-2004). Data for these years exclude those states.

Units: Abortions per 100 live births.

## Table 2.13: Health Status and Health Care Access
## for Children, 2005 and 2006

|  | Black children | White Children | All Children |
|---|---|---|---|
| **2005** | | | |
| **Respondent-assessed health status** | | | |
| All children under 18 | 11,152 | 56,761 | 73,376 |
| Excellent | 5,372 | 31,809 | 39,979 |
| Very good | 3,014 | 15,599 | 20,302 |
| Good | 2,390 | 8,280 | 11,539 |
| Fair/poor | 368 | 1,068 | 1,540 |
| **Selected measures of health care access** | | | |
| All children under 18 | 11,157 | 56,561 | 73,374 |
| Uninsured for health care | 972 | 5,204 | 6,763 |
| Unmet medical need | 222 | 1,170 | 1,513 |
| Delayed care due to cost | 329 | 2,190 | 2,715 |
| **2006** | | | |
| **Respondent-assessed health status** | | | |
| All children under 18 | 11,455 | 55,881 | 73,493 |
| Excellent | 5,378 | 30,773 | 39,501 |
| Very good | 3,105 | 15,878 | 20,621 |
| Good | 2,592 | 8,284 | 11,933 |
| Fair/poor | 378 | 912 | 1,398 |
| **Selected measures of health care access** | | | |
| All children under 18 | 11,496 | 55,866 | 73,492 |
| Uninsured for health care | 949 | 5,250 | 6,921 |
| Unmet medical need | 363 | 1,327 | 1,792 |
| Delayed care due to cost | 458 | 2,309 | 2,942 |

Source:  US Department of Health and Human Services, Centers for Disease Control and Prevention, *National Health Interview Survey: Summary Health Statistics for US Children, 2005,* tables 5 and 15; *2006,* tables 5 and 15.

Notes:  'All Children' includes races and ethnic groups not shown separately.

Units:  Number of children under 18 years of age in thousands.

## Table 2.14: Vaccinations of Children 19-35 Months of Age for Selected Diseases, 2000 and 2006

|  | Black | White | All Races |
|---|---|---|---|
| **2000** |  |  |  |
| Combined series (4:3:1:3) | 71% | 79% | 76% |
| DTP (4 doses or more) | 76 | 84 | 82 |
| Polio (3 doses or more) | 87 | 91 | 90 |
| Measles-containing | 88 | 92 | 91 |
| Hib (3 doses or more) | 93 | 95 | 93 |
| Hepatitis B (3 doses or more) | 89 | 91 | 90 |
| Varicella | 67 | 66 | 68 |
| **2006** |  |  |  |
| Combined series (4:3:1:3) | 74% | 78% | 77% |
| DTP (4 doses or more) | 81 | 87 | 85 |
| Polio (3 doses or more) | 91 | 93 | 93 |
| Measles-containing | 91 | 93 | 92 |
| Hib (3 doses or more) | 91 | 94 | 93 |
| Hepatitis B (3 doses or more) | 92 | 94 | 93 |
| Varicella | 89 | 89 | 89 |

**Source:** US Department of Health and Human Services, Centers for Disease Control and Prevention, National Center for Health Statistics, *Health, United States, 2007*, table 83.

**Notes:** 'All Races' includes races not shown separately. 'Black' excludes Black Hispanics, 'White' excludes White Hispanics.
Data excludes cases of residents of US Territories.
The 4:3:1:3 combined series consists of 4 doses of diphtheria-tetanus-pertussis (DTP) vaccine, 3 doses of polio vaccine, 1 dose of a measles-containing vaccine, and 3 doses of *Haemophilus influenza* type b (Hib) vaccine. DTP is the Diphtheria-tetanus-pertussis vaccine. Hib is the *Haemophilus influenza* type b (Hib) vaccine.

**Units:** Percent of children 19-35 months of age receiving vaccinations.

## Table 2.15: Life Expectancy at Birth, by Sex, Selected Years 1970–2005 and Projections

|  | Black | | White | | All Races | |
|---|---|---|---|---|---|---|
|  | **Male** | **Female** | **Male** | **Female** | **Male** | **Female** |
| 1970 | 60.0 | 68.3 | 68.0 | 75.6 | 67.1 | 74.7 |
| 1980 | 63.8 | 72.5 | 70.7 | 78.1 | 70.0 | 77.4 |
| 1990 | 64.5 | 73.6 | 72.7 | 79.4 | 71.8 | 78.8 |
| 2000 | 68.3 | 75.2 | 74.9 | 80.1 | 74.3 | 79.7 |
| 2001 | 68.6 | 75.5 | 75.0 | 80.2 | 74.4 | 79.8 |
| 2002 | 68.8 | 75.6 | 75.1 | 80.3 | 74.5 | 79.9 |
| 2003 | 69.2 | 76.1 | 75.4 | 80.5 | 74.8 | 80.1 |
| 2004 | 69.8 | 76.5 | 75.7 | 80.8 | 75.2 | 80.4 |
| 2005 | 69.5 | 76.5 | 75.7 | 80.8 | 75.2 | 80.4 |
| 2010 (projected) | 70.9 | 77.8 | 76.1 | 81.8 | 75.6 | 81.4 |
| 2015 (projected) | 71.9 | 78.9 | 78.0 | 83.8 | 76.2 | 82.2 |

**Source:** US Bureau of the Census, *Statistical Abstract of the United States, 2007*, table 98.
US Department of Health and Human Services, Centers for Disease Control and Prevention, National Center for Health Statistics, *Deaths: Final Data for 2005*, table 8.

**Notes:** 'All Races' includes races not shown separately.
Projections based on middle mortality assumptions.

**Units:** Life expectancy in years.

## Table 2.16: Life Expectancy, by Sex, by Age, 2005

|  | Black | | White | | All Races | |
|---|---|---|---|---|---|---|
|  | Male | Female | Male | Female | Male | Female |
| *At birth* | *69.5* | *76.5* | *75.7* | *80.8* | *75.2* | *80.4* |
| Age 5 | 65.7 | 72.5 | 71.3 | 76.3 | 70.8 | 76.0 |
| Age 10 | 60.8 | 67.6 | 66.3 | 71.3 | 65.9 | 71.0 |
| Age 15 | 55.9 | 62.7 | 61.4 | 66.4 | 61.0 | 66.1 |
| Age 20 | 51.2 | 57.8 | 56.6 | 61.5 | 56.2 | 61.2 |
| Age 25 | 46.8 | 53.0 | 52.0 | 56.6 | 51.6 | 56.4 |
| Age 30 | 42.3 | 48.2 | 47.3 | 51.8 | 47.0 | 51.5 |
| Age 35 | 37.9 | 43.5 | 42.6 | 46.9 | 42.3 | 46.7 |
| Age 40 | 33.4 | 38.9 | 38.0 | 42.2 | 37.7 | 41.9 |
| Age 45 | 29.2 | 34.4 | 33.5 | 37.5 | 33.2 | 37.3 |
| Age 50 | 25.2 | 30.2 | 29.1 | 32.9 | 28.9 | 32.7 |
| Age 55 | 21.6 | 26.2 | 24.9 | 28.4 | 24.8 | 28.3 |
| Age 60 | 18.2 | 22.3 | 20.9 | 24.1 | 20.8 | 24.0 |
| Age 65 | 15.2 | 18.7 | 17.2 | 20.0 | 17.2 | 20.0 |
| Age 70 | 12.4 | 15.3 | 13.8 | 16.2 | 13.8 | 16.3 |
| Age 75 | 10.0 | 12.3 | 10.7 | 12.8 | 10.8 | 12.8 |
| Age 80 | 7.9 | 9.7 | 8.1 | 9.7 | 8.2 | 9.7 |
| Age 90 | 4.8 | 5.7 | 4.4 | 5.1 | 4.4 | 5.2 |
| Age 100 | 2.9 | 3.2 | 2.3 | 2.5 | 2.3 | 2.6 |

**Source:** US Department of Health and Human Services, Centers for Disease Control and Prevention, National Center for Health Statistics, *Deaths: Final Data for 2005*, table 7.

**Notes:** 'All Races' includes races not shown separately.

**Units:** Life expectancy in years from time of estimate.

## Table 2.17: Death Rates, by Selected Causes of Death, 2003 and 2005

| | Black | White | All Races |
|---|---|---|---|
| **2003** | | | |
| Heart disease | | | |
| Men | 364.3 | 282.9 | 286.6 |
| Women | 253.8 | 185.4 | 190.3 |
| Cerebrovascular diseases | | | |
| Men | 79.5 | 51.7 | 54.1 |
| Women | 69.8 | 50.5 | 52.3 |
| Suicide | | | |
| Men | 9.2 | 19.6 | 18.0 |
| Women | 1.9 | 4.6 | 4.2 |
| HIV (human immunodeficiency virus) | | | |
| Men | 31.3 | 4.2 | 7.1 |
| Women | 12.8 | 0.9 | 2.4 |
| Malignant neoplasms | | | |
| Men | 308.8 | 230.1 | 233.3 |
| Women | 187.7 | 160.2 | 160.9 |
| **2005** | | | |
| Heart disease | | | |
| Men | 329.8 | 258.0 | 260.9 |
| Women | 228.3 | 168.2 | 172.3 |
| Cerebrovascular diseases | | | |
| Men | 70.5 | 44.7 | 46.9 |
| Women | 60.7 | 44.0 | 45.6 |
| Suicide | | | |
| Men | 9.2 | 19.6 | 18.0 |
| Women | 1.9 | 4.9 | 4.4 |
| HIV (human immunodeficiency virus) | | | |
| Men | 28.2 | 3.6 | 6.2 |
| Women | 12.0 | 0.8 | 2.3 |
| Malignant neoplasms | | | |
| Men | 293.7 | 222.3 | 225.1 |
| Women | 179.6 | 155.2 | 155.6 |

**Source:** US Department of Health and Human Services, Centers for Disease Control and Prevention, National Center for Health Statistics, *Health, United States, 2007*, tables 36-38, 42, and 46.

**Notes:** Age-adjusted rates for all ages.
'All Races' includes races not shown separately.

**Units:** Deaths per 100,000 population.

## Table 2.18: Death Rates, by Age and Sex, 1980–2005

| | Black | | White | | All Races | |
|---|---|---|---|---|---|---|
| | Male | Female | Male | Female | Male | Female |
| **1980** | | | | | | |
| *All ages, age-adjusted* | *1,697.8* | *1,033.3* | *1,317.6* | *796.1* | *1,348.1* | *817.9* |
| *All ages, crude* | *1,034.1* | *733.3* | *983.3* | *806.1* | *976.9* | *785.3* |
| Under 1 year old | 2,586.7 | 2,123.7 | 1,230.3 | 962.5 | 1,428.5 | 1,141.7 |
| 1-4 years old | 110.5 | 84.4 | 66.1 | 49.3 | 72.6 | 54.7 |
| 5-14 years old | 47.4 | 30.5 | 35.0 | 22.9 | 36.7 | 24.2 |
| 15-24 years old | 209.1 | 70.5 | 167.0 | 55.5 | 172.3 | 57.5 |
| 25-34 years old | 407.3 | 150.0 | 171.3 | 65.4 | 196.1 | 75.9 |
| 35-44 years old | 689.8 | 323.9 | 257.4 | 138.2 | 299.2 | 159.3 |
| 45-54 years old | 1,479.9 | 768.2 | 698.9 | 372.7 | 767.3 | 412.9 |
| 55-64 years old | 2,873.0 | 1,561.0 | 1,728.5 | 876.2 | 1,815.1 | 934.3 |
| 65-74 years old | 5,131.1 | 3,057.4 | 4,035.7 | 2,066.6 | 4,105.2 | 2,144.7 |
| 75-84 years old | 9,231.6 | 6,212.1 | 8,829.8 | 5,401.7 | 8,816.7 | 5,440.1 |
| 85 years old and over | 16,098.8 | 12,367.2 | 19,097.3 | 14,979.6 | 18,801.1 | 14,746.9 |
| **1990** | | | | | | |
| *All ages, age-adjusted* | *1,644.5* | *975.1* | *1,165.9* | *728.8* | *1,202.8* | *750.9* |
| *All ages, crude* | *1,008.0* | *747.9* | *930.9* | *846.9* | *918.4* | *812.0* |
| Under 1 year old | 2,112.4 | 1,735.5 | 896.1 | 690.0 | 1,082.8 | 855.7 |
| 1-4 years old | 85.8 | 67.6 | 45.9 | 36.1 | 52.4 | 41.0 |
| 5-14 years old | 41.2 | 27.5 | 26.4 | 17.9 | 28.5 | 19.3 |
| 15-24 years old | 252.2 | 68.7 | 131.3 | 45.9 | 147.4 | 49.0 |
| 25-34 years old | 430.8 | 159.5 | 176.1 | 61.5 | 204.3 | 74.2 |
| 35-44 years old | 699.6 | 298.6 | 268.2 | 117.4 | 310.4 | 137.9 |
| 45-54 years old | 1,261.0 | 639.4 | 548.7 | 309.3 | 610.3 | 342.7 |
| 55-64 years old | 2,618.4 | 1,452.6 | 1,467.2 | 822.7 | 1,553.4 | 878.8 |
| 65-74 years old | 4,946.1 | 2,865.7 | 3,397.7 | 1,923.5 | 3,491.5 | 1,991.2 |
| 75-84 years old | 9,129.5 | 5,688.3 | 7,844.9 | 4,839.1 | 7,888.6 | 4,883.1 |
| 85 years old and over | 16,954.9 | 13,309.5 | 18,268.3 | 14,400.6 | 18,056.6 | 14,274.3 |

*(continued on next page)*

## Table 2.18: Death Rates, by Age and Sex, 1980–2005

| | Black | | White | | All Races | |
|---|---|---|---|---|---|---|
| | **Male** | **Female** | **Male** | **Female** | **Male** | **Female** |
| **2000** | | | | | | |
| *All ages, age-adjusted* | *1,403.5* | *927.6* | *1,029.4* | *715.3* | *1,053.8* | *731.4* |
| *All ages, crude* | *834.1* | *733.0* | *887.8* | *912.3* | *853.0* | *855.0* |
| Under 1 year old | 1,567.6 | 1,279.8 | 667.6 | 550.5 | 806.5 | 663.4 |
| 1-4 years old | 54.5 | 45.3 | 32.6 | 25.5 | 35.9 | 28.7 |
| 5-14 years old | 28.2 | 20.0 | 19.8 | 14.1 | 20.9 | 15.0 |
| 15-24 years old | 181.4 | 58.3 | 105.8 | 41.1 | 114.9 | 43.1 |
| 25-34 years old | 261.0 | 121.8 | 124.1 | 55.1 | 138.6 | 63.5 |
| 35-44 years old | 453.0 | 271.9 | 233.6 | 125.7 | 255.2 | 143.2 |
| 45-54 years old | 1,017.7 | 588.3 | 496.9 | 281.4 | 542.8 | 312.5 |
| 55-64 years old | 2,080.1 | 1,227.2 | 1,163.3 | 730.9 | 1,230.7 | 772.2 |
| 65-74 years old | 4,253.5 | 2,689.6 | 2,905.7 | 1,868.3 | 2,979.6 | 1,921.2 |
| 75-84 years old | 8,486.0 | 5,696.5 | 6,933.1 | 4,785.3 | 6,972.6 | 4,814.7 |
| 85 years old and over | 16,791.0 | 13,941.3 | 17,716.4 | 14,890.7 | 17,501.4 | 14,719.2 |
| **2005** | | | | | | |
| *All ages, age-adjusted* | *1,252.9* | *845.7* | *933.2* | *666.5* | *951.1* | *677.6* |
| *All ages, crude* | *799.2* | *703.9* | *864.5* | *882.8* | *827.2* | *824.6* |
| Under 1 year old | 1,437.2 | 1,179.7 | 640.0 | 515.3 | 762.3 | 619.4 |
| 1-4 years old | 46.7 | 36.7 | 30.9 | 22.9 | 33.4 | 25.1 |
| 5-14 years old | 27.0 | 19.4 | 17.1 | 12.8 | 18.6 | 13.9 |
| 15-24 years old | 172.1 | 51.2 | 110.4 | 41.5 | 117.8 | 42.7 |
| 25-34 years old | 254.3 | 109.8 | 130.8 | 58.0 | 143.4 | 64.1 |
| 35-44 years old | 395.5 | 250.0 | 228.5 | 130.4 | 243.0 | 143.6 |
| 45-54 years old | 948.6 | 568.4 | 509.3 | 291.1 | 547.8 | 319.9 |
| 55-64 years old | 1,954.3 | 1,103.6 | 1,068.1 | 663.9 | 1,131.0 | 698.5 |
| 65-74 years old | 3,747.3 | 2,341.5 | 2,552.7 | 1,700.4 | 2,612.2 | 1,736.3 |
| 75-84 years old | 7,667.1 | 5,263.7 | 6,343.2 | 4,519.4 | 6,349.8 | 4,520.0 |
| 85 years old and over | 13,809.8 | 12,789.9 | 15,156.5 | 13,498.3 | 14,889.4 | 13,297.7 |

**Source:** US Department of Health and Human Services, Centers for Disease Control and Prevention, National Center for Health Statistics, *Health, United States, 2007*, table 35.

**Notes:** 'All Races' includes races not shown separately. 'All ages' includes ages not stated.

**Units:** Rates per 100,000 of population in specified age groups, as shown.

## Table 2.19: Death Rates for Heart Disease, 1980–2005

| | Black | | White | | All Races | |
|---|---|---|---|---|---|---|
| | Male | Female | Male | Female | Male | Female |
| **1980** | | | | | | |
| *All ages, age-adjusted rate* | *561.4* | *378.6* | *539.6* | *315.9* | *538.9* | *320.8* |
| *All ages, crude rate* | *301.0* | *249.7* | *384.0* | *319.2* | *368.6* | *305.1* |
| 45-54 years old | 433.4 | 202.4 | 269.8 | 71.2 | 282.6 | 84.5 |
| 55-64 years old | 987.2 | 530.1 | 730.6 | 248.1 | 746.8 | 272.1 |
| 65-74 years old | 1,847.2 | 1,210.3 | 1,729.7 | 796.7 | 1,728.0 | 828.6 |
| 75-84 years old | 3,578.8 | 2,707.2 | 3,883.2 | 2,493.6 | 3,834.3 | 2,497.0 |
| 85 years old and over | 6,819.5 | 5,796.5 | 8,958.0 | 7,501.6 | 8,752.7 | 7,350.5 |
| **1990** | | | | | | |
| *All ages, age-adjusted rate* | *485.4* | *327.5* | *409.2* | *250.9* | *412.4* | *257.0* |
| *All ages, crude rate* | *256.8* | *237.0* | *312.7* | *298.4* | *297.6* | *281.8* |
| 45-54 years old | 328.9 | 155.3 | 170.6 | 50.2 | 183.0 | 61.0 |
| 55-64 years old | 824.0 | 442.0 | 516.7 | 192.4 | 537.3 | 215.7 |
| 65-74 years old | 1,632.9 | 1,017.5 | 1,230.5 | 583.6 | 1,250.0 | 616.8 |
| 75-84 years old | 3,107.1 | 2,250.9 | 2,983.4 | 1,874.3 | 2,968.2 | 1,893.8 |
| 85 years old and over | 6,479.6 | 5,766.1 | 7,558.7 | 6,563.4 | 7,418.4 | 6,478.1 |
| **2000** | | | | | | |
| *All ages, age-adjusted rate* | *392.5* | *277.6* | *316.7* | *205.6* | *320.0* | *210.9* |
| *All ages, crude rate* | *211.1* | *212.6* | *265.8* | *274.5* | *249.8* | *255.3* |
| 45-54 years old | 247.2 | 125.0 | 130.7 | 40.9 | 140.2 | 49.8 |
| 55-64 years old | 631.2 | 332.8 | 351.8 | 141.3 | 371.7 | 159.3 |
| 65-74 years old | 1,268.8 | 815.2 | 877.8 | 445.2 | 898.3 | 474.0 |
| 75-84 years old | 2,597.6 | 1,913.1 | 2,247.0 | 1,452.4 | 2,248.1 | 1,475.1 |
| 85 years old and over | 5,633.5 | 5,298.7 | 6,560.8 | 5,801.4 | 6,430.0 | 5,720.9 |
| **2005** | | | | | | |
| *All ages, age-adjusted rate* | *329.8* | *228.3* | *258.0* | *168.2* | *260.9* | *172.3* |
| *All ages, crude rate* | *194.8* | *185.2* | *234.9* | *235.5* | *221.1* | *218.9* |
| 45-54 years old | 237.4 | 115.4 | 121.3 | 40.8 | 131.5 | 49.2 |
| 55-64 years old | 549.1 | 272.0 | 288.2 | 114.5 | 306.9 | 129.1 |
| 65-74 years old | 1,041.6 | 614.9 | 671.9 | 351.8 | 692.3 | 372.7 |
| 75-84 years old | 2,204.1 | 1,595.1 | 1,831.8 | 1,193.3 | 1,829.4 | 1,210.5 |
| 85 years old and over | 4,230.5 | 4,365.6 | 5,288.4 | 4,691.0 | 5,143.4 | 4,610.8 |

**Source:** US Department of Health and Human Services, Centers for Disease Control and Prevention, National Center for Health Statistics, *Health, United States, 2007*, table 36.

**Notes:** 'All Races' includes races not shown separately.

**Units:** Rate is the number of deaths per 100,000 resident population, by age group.

## Table 2.20:  Death Rates for Cerebrovascular Disease, by Sex and Age, 2000 and 2005

|  | Black | | White | | All Races | |
|---|---|---|---|---|---|---|
|  | **Male** | **Female** | **Male** | **Female** | **Male** | **Female** |
| **2000** | | | | | | |
| *All ages, age-adjusted* | *89.6* | *76.2* | *59.8* | *57.3* | *62.4* | *59.1* |
| *All ages, crude* | *46.1* | *58.3* | *48.4* | *76.9* | *46.9* | *71.8* |
| 45-54 years old | 49.5 | 38.1 | 13.6 | 11.2 | 17.5 | 14.5 |
| 55-64 years old | 115.4 | 76.4 | 39.7 | 30.2 | 47.2 | 35.3 |
| 65-74 years old | 268.5 | 190.9 | 133.8 | 107.3 | 145.0 | 115.1 |
| 75-84 years old | 659.2 | 549.2 | 480.0 | 434.2 | 490.8 | 442.1 |
| 85 years old and over | 1,458.8 | 1,556.5 | 1,490.7 | 1,646.7 | 1,484.3 | 1,632.0 |
| **2005** | | | | | | |
| *All ages, age-adjusted* | *70.5* | *60.7* | *44.7* | *44.0* | *46.9* | *45.6* |
| *All ages, crude* | *40.3* | *49.1* | *39.7* | *61.6* | *38.8* | *57.8* |
| 45-54 years old | 44.8 | 35.0 | 12.8 | 10.5 | 16.5 | 13.6 |
| 55-64 years old | 103.7 | 59.8 | 31.7 | 23.8 | 38.5 | 27.9 |
| 65-74 years old | 224.3 | 153.7 | 103.0 | 83.2 | 113.6 | 90.5 |
| 75-84 years old | 503.7 | 450.2 | 364.8 | 342.9 | 372.9 | 349.5 |
| 85 years old and over | 983.5 | 1,156.5 | 1,033.7 | 1,208.5 | 1,023.3 | 1,196.1 |

**Source:**  US Department of Health and Human Services, Centers for Disease Control and Prevention, National Center for Health Statistics, *Health, United States, 2007*, table 37.

**Notes:**  'All Races' includes races not shown separately.
Excludes deaths of nonresidents of the United States.

**Units:**  Rate is the number of deaths per 100,000 resident population.

## Table 2.21: Female Death Rates for Malignant Neoplasms of the Breast, Age, 1980–2005

|  | Black women | White women | All women |
|---|---|---|---|
| **1980** | | | |
| *All ages, age-adjusted rate* | *31.7* | *32.1* | *31.9* |
| *All ages, crude rate* | *22.9* | *32.3* | *30.6* |
| 35-44 years old | 24.1 | 17.3 | 17.9 |
| 45-54 years old | 52.7 | 48.1 | 48.1 |
| 55-64 years old | 79.9 | 81.3 | 80.5 |
| 65-74 years old | 84.3 | 103.7 | 101.1 |
| 75-84 years old | 114.1 | 128.4 | 126.4 |
| 85 years old and over | 149.9 | 171.7 | 169.3 |
| **1990** | | | |
| *All ages, age-adjusted rate* | *38.1* | *33.2* | *33.3* |
| *All ages, crude rate* | *29.0* | *35.9* | *34.0* |
| 35-44 years old | 25.8 | 17.1 | 17.8 |
| 45-54 years old | 60.5 | 44.3 | 45.4 |
| 55-64 years old | 93.1 | 78.5 | 78.6 |
| 65-74 years old | 112.2 | 113.3 | 111.7 |
| 75-84 years old | 140.5 | 148.2 | 146.3 |
| 85 years old and over | 201.5 | 198.0 | 196.8 |
| **2000** | | | |
| *All ages, age-adjusted rate* | *34.5* | *26.3* | *26.8* |
| *All ages, crude rate* | *27.9* | *30.7* | *29.2* |
| 35-44 years old | 20.9 | 11.3 | 12.4 |
| 45-54 years old | 51.5 | 31.2 | 33.0 |
| 55-64 years old | 80.9 | 57.9 | 59.3 |
| 65-74 years old | 98.6 | 89.3 | 88.3 |
| 75-84 years old | 139.8 | 130.2 | 128.9 |
| 85 years old and over | 238.7 | 205.5 | 205.7 |

*(continued on next page)*

## Table 2.21: Female Death Rates for Malignant Neoplasms of the Breast, Age, 1980–2005

|  | Black women | White women | All women |
|---|---|---|---|
| **2005** | | | |
| *All ages, age-adjusted rate* | 32.8 | 23.4 | 24.1 |
| *All ages, crude rate* | 28.4 | 28.3 | 27.3 |
| 35-44 years old | 20.2 | 10.2 | 11.3 |
| 45-54 years old | 50.0 | 26.2 | 28.7 |
| 55-64 years old | 81.1 | 52.4 | 54.5 |
| 65-74 years old | 96.2 | 79.3 | 79.2 |
| 75-84 years old | 126.6 | 120.7 | 119.2 |
| 85 years old and over | 201.8 | 179.1 | 177.9 |

Source: US Department of Health and Human Services, Centers for Disease Control and Prevention, National Center for Health Statistics, *Health, United States, 2007*, table 40.

Notes: 'All women' includes women of races not shown separately.
Data excludes deaths of nonresidents of the United States.
Age-adjusted rates may differ from those shown in previous editions of *Health, United States*.

Units: Rate is the number of deaths per 100,000 resident female population, by age group.

## Table 2.22: Death Rates for Motor Vehicle Accidents, by Sex and Age, 2000 and 2005

| | Black | | White | | All Races | |
|---|---|---|---|---|---|---|
| | Male | Female | Male | Female | Male | Female |
| **2000** | | | | | | |
| *All ages, age-adjusted* | *24.4* | *8.4* | *21.8* | *9.8* | *21.7* | *9.5* |
| *All ages, crude* | *22.5* | *8.2* | *21.6* | *10.0* | *21.3* | *9.7* |
| Under 1 year | 6.7 | * | 4.2 | 3.5 | 4.6 | 4.2 |
| 1-14 years old | 5.5 | 3.9 | 4.8 | 3.7 | 4.9 | 3.7 |
| 15-24 years old | 30.2 | 11.7 | 39.6 | 17.1 | 37.4 | 15.9 |
| 25-34 years old | 32.6 | 9.4 | 25.1 | 8.9 | 25.5 | 8.8 |
| 35-44 years old | 27.2 | 8.2 | 21.8 | 8.9 | 22.0 | 8.8 |
| 45-64 years old | 27.1 | 9.0 | 19.7 | 8.7 | 20.2 | 8.7 |
| 65 years old and over | 32.1 | 10.4 | 29.4 | 16.2 | 29.5 | 15.8 |
| **2005** | | | | | | |
| *All ages, age-adjusted* | *22.5* | *7.6* | *22.2* | *9.2* | *21.7* | *8.9* |
| *All ages, crude* | *21.2* | *7.5* | *22.3* | *9.5* | *21.7* | *9.1* |
| Under 1 year | * | 6.8 | 3.3 | 2.9 | 3.5 | 3.6 |
| 1-14 years old | 4.4 | 3.4 | 4.1 | 3.1 | 4.1 | 3.1 |
| 15-24 years old | 28.0 | 10.7 | 39.1 | 15.8 | 36.5 | 14.7 |
| 25-34 years old | 30.8 | 7.5 | 27.3 | 9.3 | 26.9 | 8.8 |
| 35-44 years old | 25.9 | 7.7 | 22.4 | 8.9 | 22.2 | 8.6 |
| 45-64 years old | 24.8 | 8.3 | 21.7 | 8.6 | 21.6 | 8.5 |
| 65 years old and over | 29.3 | 9.8 | 28.7 | 14.4 | 28.5 | 14.0 |

**Source:** US Department of Health and Human Services, Centers for Disease Control and Prevention, National Center for Health Statistics, *Health, United States, 2007*, table 44.

**Notes:** 'All Races' includes races not shown separately. Excludes deaths of nonresidents of the United States.
*Indicates data based on fewer than 20 deaths.
Age-adjusted rates may differ from those shown in previous editions of *Health, United States*.

**Units:** Rate is the number of deaths per 100,000 resident population.

## Table 2.23: Death Rates for Assault (Homicide), by Sex and Age, 2000 and 2005

| | Black | | White | | All Races | |
|---|---|---|---|---|---|---|
| | Male | Female | Male | Female | Male | Female |
| **2000** | | | | | | |
| All ages, age-adjusted | 35.4 | 7.1 | 5.2 | 2.1 | 9.0 | 2.8 |
| All ages, crude | 37.2 | 7.2 | 5.2 | 2.1 | 9.3 | 2.8 |
| Under 1 year | 23.3 | 22.2 | 8.2 | 5.0 | 10.4 | 7.9 |
| 1-14 years old | 3.1 | 2.7 | 1.2 | 0.8 | 1.5 | 1.1 |
| 15-24 years old | 85.3 | 10.7 | 9.9 | 2.7 | 20.9 | 3.9 |
| 25-44 years old | 55.8 | 11.0 | 7.4 | 2.9 | 13.3 | 4.0 |
| 45-64 years old | 21.9 | 4.5 | 4.1 | 1.8 | 6.0 | 2.1 |
| 65 years old and over | 12.8 | 3.5 | 2.5 | 1.6 | 3.3 | 1.8 |
| **2005** | | | | | | |
| All ages, age-adjusted | 37.3 | 6.1 | 5.3 | 1.9 | 9.6 | 2.5 |
| All ages, crude | 39.7 | 6.2 | 5.4 | 1.9 | 9.8 | 2.5 |
| Under 1 year | 15.9 | 12.6 | 6.7 | 5.5 | 8.2 | 6.6 |
| 1-14 years old | 3.9 | 2.3 | 1.0 | 0.8 | 1.4 | 1.1 |
| 15-24 years old | 84.1 | 8.8 | 10.6 | 2.3 | 22.0 | 3.4 |
| 25-44 years old | 63.4 | 9.3 | 8.0 | 2.8 | 14.9 | 3.7 |
| 45-64 years old | 22.3 | 4.9 | 4.3 | 1.5 | 6.2 | 1.9 |
| 65 years old and over | 11.9 | 2.9 | 2.2 | 1.6 | 3.0 | 1.7 |

Source: US Department of Health and Human Services, Centers for Disease Control and Prevention, National Center for Health Statistics, *Health, United States, 2007*, table 45.

Notes: 'All Races' includes races not shown separately.
Excludes deaths of nonresidents of the United States.
Age-adjusted rates may differ from those shown in previous editions of *Health, United States*.

Units: Rate is the number of deaths per 100,000 resident population.

## Table 2.24: Death Rates for Suicide, by Sex and Age, 2000 and 2005

|  | Black | | White | | All Races | |
|---|---|---|---|---|---|---|
|  | Male | Female | Male | Female | Male | Female |
| **2000** |  |  |  |  |  |  |
| *All ages, age-adjusted* | *10.0* | *1.8* | *19.1* | *4.3* | *17.7* | *4.0* |
| *All ages, crude* | *9.4* | *1.7* | *18.8* | *4.4* | *17.1* | *4.0* |
| 15-24 years old | 14.2 | 2.2 | 17.9 | 3.1 | 17.1 | 3.0 |
| 25-44 years old | 14.3 | 2.6 | 22.9 | 6.0 | 21.3 | 5.4 |
| 45-64 years old | 9.9 | 2.1 | 23.2 | 6.9 | 21.3 | 6.2 |
| 65 years old and over | 11.5 | 1.3 | 33.3 | 4.3 | 31.1 | 4.0 |
| **2005** |  |  |  |  |  |  |
| *All ages, age-adjusted* | *9.2* | *1.9* | *19.6* | *4.9* | *18.0* | *4.4* |
| *All ages, crude* | *8.7* | *1.8* | *19.7* | *5.0* | *17.7* | *4.5* |
| 15-24 years old | 11.5 | 1.7 | 17.3 | 3.7 | 16.2 | 3.5 |
| 25-44 years old | 13.7 | 2.8 | 23.5 | 6.5 | 21.6 | 5.8 |
| 45-64 years old | 9.4 | 2.5 | 26.6 | 8.1 | 24.0 | 7.2 |
| 65 years old and over | 10.2 | 1.4 | 32.1 | 4.2 | 29.5 | 4.0 |

Source:  US Department of Health and Human Services, Centers for Disease Control and Prevention, National Center for Health Statistics, *Health, United States, 2007*, table 46.

Notes:  'All Races' includes races not shown separately. Excludes deaths of nonresidents of the United States.
Age-adjusted rates may differ from those shown in previous editions of *Health, United States*.

Units:  Rate is the number of deaths per 100,000 resident population.

## Table 2.25: Death Rates for Firearm-Related Injuries, 2000 and 2005

|  | Black | | White | | All Races | |
|  | Male | Female | Male | Female | Male | Female |
|---|---|---|---|---|---|---|
| **2000** | | | | | | |
| *All ages* | *34.2* | *3.9* | *15.9* | *2.7* | *18.1* | *2.8* |
| 1-14 years | 1.8 | NA | 1.0 | NA | 1.1 | 0.3 |
| 15-24 years | 89.3 | 7.6 | 19.6 | 2.8 | 29.4 | 3.5 |
| 25-44 years | 54.1 | 6.5 | 18.0 | 3.9 | 22.0 | 4.2 |
| 45-64 years | 18.4 | 3.1 | 17.4 | 3.5 | 17.1 | 3.4 |
| 65 years and over | 13.8 | 1.3 | 28.2 | 2.4 | 26.4 | 2.2 |
| **2005** | | | | | | |
| *All ages* | *36.4* | *3.6* | *15.7* | *2.6* | *18.3* | *2.7* |
| 1-14 years | 2.1 | NA | 0.8 | NA | 1.0 | 0.4 |
| 15-24 years | 86.8 | 6.7 | 18.2 | 2.3 | 28.7 | 3.0 |
| 25-44 years | 63.6 | 6.0 | 17.9 | 3.7 | 23.1 | 3.9 |
| 45-64 years | 17.8 | 2.7 | 19.0 | 3.6 | 18.3 | 3.3 |
| 65 years and over | 13.6 | 1.3 | 27.1 | 2.3 | 25.1 | 2.1 |

Source: US Department of Health and Human Services, Centers for Disease Control and Prevention, National Center for Health Statistics, *Health, United States, 2007*, table 47.

Notes: 'All Races' includes races not shown separately. Data excludes residents of US Territories. NA = data not collected.
Age-adjusted rates may differ from those shown in previous editions of *Health, United States*.

Units: Death rate per 100,000 population.

## Table 2.26: AIDS (Acquired Immunodeficiency Syndrome) Cases, by Sex and Age, 1985–2005

|  | Black | White | All Races |
|---|---|---|---|
| **All years\*** | | | |
| Children under 13 years old | 5,631 | 1,613 | 9,101 |
| Persons over 13 years old | | | |
| Male | 278,917 | 346,533 | 761,723 |
| Female | 112,999 | 37,390 | 181,802 |
| **1985** | | | |
| Children under 13 years old | 87 | 26 | 131 |
| Persons over 13 years old | | | |
| Male | 1,710 | 4,746 | 7,504 |
| Female | 280 | 143 | 524 |
| **1990** | | | |
| Children under 13 years old | 390 | 157 | 725 |
| Persons over 13 years old | | | |
| Male | 10,239 | 20,825 | 36,179 |
| Female | 2,557 | 1,228 | 4,544 |
| **1995** | | | |
| Children under 13 years old | 483 | 117 | 745 |
| Persons over 13 years old | | | |
| Male | 20,833 | 26,028 | 56,689 |
| Female | 7,586 | 3,042 | 12,978 |
| **2000** | | | |
| Children under 13 years old | 122 | 32 | 189 |
| Persons over 13 years old | | | |
| Male | 13,082 | 11,314 | 30,135 |
| Female | 6,489 | 1,859 | 9,958 |
| **2001** | | | |
| Children under 13 years old | 111 | 30 | 170 |
| Persons over 13 years old | | | |
| Male | 13,764 | 11,054 | 30,663 |
| Female | 6,963 | 1,993 | 10,617 |

*(continued on next page)*

## Table 2.26:  AIDS (Acquired Immunodeficiency Syndrome) Cases, by Sex and Age, 1985–2005

| | Black | White | All Races |
|---|---|---|---|
| **2002** | | | |
| Children under 13 years old | 99 | 23 | 150 |
| Persons over 13 years old | | | |
| Male | 14,310 | 11,221 | 31,644 |
| Female | 7,339 | 1,930 | 10,951 |
| **2003** | | | |
| Children under 13 years old | 93 | 23 | 153 |
| Persons over 13 years old | | | |
| Male | 13,820 | 11,831 | 32,781 |
| Female | 7,373 | 1,923 | 11,297 |
| **2004** | | | |
| Children under 13 years old | 31 | 6 | 50 |
| Persons over 13 years old | | | |
| Male | 12,483 | 9,714 | 28,817 |
| Female | 7,108 | 1,800 | 10,656 |
| **2005** | | | |
| Children under 13 years old | 46 | 6 | 68 |
| Persons over 13 years old | | | |
| Male | 13,048 | 10,027 | 29,766 |
| Female | 7,093 | 1,747 | 10,774 |

**Source:** US Department of Health and Human Services, Centers for Disease Control and Prevention, National Center for Health Statistics, *Health, United States, 2004*, table 52; *2007*, table 52.

**Notes:** 'All Races' includes races not shown separately. 'Black' and 'White' exclude Hispanics. Data excludes residents of US Territories.
Historical data is revised on an ongoing basis.
* 'All years' includes cases prior to 1985. Data for all years has been updated through June 30, 2006, to include temporarily delayed case reports and may differ from previous editions of *Health, United States*.

**Units:** Number of cases known to the Centers for Disease Control.

## Table 2.27:  Estimated Number of AIDS (Acquired Immunodefiency Syndrome) Cases, by Transmission Category, 2000–2004

| | Black | White | All cases |
|---|---|---|---|
| **Cumulative** | | | |
| *All transmission categories* | *379,278* | *375,154* | *944,306* |
| Adults and Adolescents | 373,688 | 373,542 | NA |
| Male adult or adolescent | 267,235 | 337,771 | NA |
|   Male-to-male sexual contact | 111,764 | 256,079 | NA |
|   Injection drug use | 92,051 | 33,906 | NA |
|   Male-to-male sexual contact | | | |
|     and injection drug use | 22,565 | 30,624 | NA |
|   High-risk heterosexual contact | 36,473 | 9,344 | NA |
| Female adult or adolescent | 106,453 | 35,770 | NA |
|   Injection drug use | 42,875 | 15,566 | NA |
|   High-risk heterosexual contact | 60,354 | 17,888 | NA |
| Children under 13 | 5,590 | 1,612 | NA |
|   Perinatal | 5,440 | 1,253 | NA |
| **2000** | | | |
| *All transmission categories* | *19,510* | *11,378* | *39,513* |
| Adults and Adolescents | 19,417 | 11,367 | NA |
| Male adult or adolescent | 12,725 | 9,669 | NA |
|   Male-to-male sexual contact | 5,222 | 6,955 | NA |
|   Injection drug use | 3,890 | 1,243 | NA |
|   Male-to-male sexual contact | | | |
|     and injection drug use | 822 | 820 | NA |
|   High-risk heterosexual contact | 2,679 | 522 | NA |
| Female adult or adolescent | 6,692 | 1,698 | NA |
|   Injection drug use | 2,039 | 696 | NA |
|   High-risk heterosexual contact | 4,504 | 961 | NA |
| Children under 13 | 93 | 11 | NA |
|   Perinatal | 91 | 11 | NA |

*(continued on next page)*

## Table 2.27: Estimated Number of AIDS (Acquired Immunodefiency Syndrome) Cases, by Transmission Category, 2000–2004

| | Black | White | All cases |
|---|---|---|---|
| **2002** | | | |
| *All transmission categories* | *19,934* | *11,604* | *40,267* |
| Adults and Adolescents | 19,864 | 11,589 | NA |
| Male adult or adolescent | 13,050 | 9,869 | NA |
|   Male-to-male sexual contact | 5,749 | 7,115 | NA |
|   Injection drug use | 3,373 | 1,203 | NA |
|   Male-to-male sexual contact and injection drug use | 776 | 813 | NA |
|   High-risk heterosexual contact | 3,025 | 635 | NA |
| Female adult or adolescent | 6,814 | 1,720 | NA |
|   Injection drug use | 1,850 | 654 | NA |
|   High-risk heterosexual contact | 4,813 | 1,026 | NA |
| Children under 13 | 70 | 14 | NA |
|   Perinatal | 69 | 14 | NA |
| **2004** | | | |
| *All transmission categories* | *20,965* | *12,013* | *42,514* |
| Adults and Adolescents | 20,936 | 12,006 | NA |
| Male adult or adolescent | 13,499 | 10,138 | NA |
|   Male-to-male sexual contact | 6,294 | 7,358 | NA |
|   Injection drug use | 3,156 | 1,176 | NA |
|   Male-to-male sexual contact and injection drug use | 740 | 769 | NA |
|   High-risk heterosexual contact | 3,177 | 736 | NA |
| Female adult or adolescent | 7,437 | 1,868 | NA |
|   Injection drug use | 1,906 | 680 | NA |
|   High-risk heterosexual contact | 5,343 | 1,142 | NA |
| Children under 13 | 29 | 7 | NA |
|   Perinatal | 29 | 7 | NA |

**Source:** US Department of Health and Human Services, Centers for Disease Control and Prevention, Centers for Disease Control, *Cases of HIV Infection and AIDS in the United States, by Race/Ethnicity, 2000–2004*, table 4.

**Notes:** 'Cumulative' includes all cases with a diagnosis of AIDS since the beginning of the epidemic. 'High-risk heterosexual contact' includes heterosexual contact with a person who is HIV-positive, a male who engages in sex with other males, a person who injects drugs, has hemophelia or another coagulation disorder, or is a transplant or transfusion recipient. 'Other' includes hemophilia, blood transfusions, perinatal exposure (for adults), and other factors not identified. Totals are based on estimates, and may not equal the sum of the subgroups.

**Units:** Estimated cases of AIDS.

## Table 2.28: Death Rates for Human Immunodeficiency Virus (HIV) Infection, by Sex, 1987–2005

|      | Black | | White | | All Races | |
|------|------|--------|------|--------|------|--------|
|      | **Male** | **Female** | **Male** | **Female** | **Male** | **Female** |
| 1987 | 26.2 | 4.6  | 8.7  | 0.6 | 10.4 | 1.1 |
| 1990 | 46.3 | 10.1 | 15.7 | 1.1 | 18.5 | 2.2 |
| 1995 | 89.0 | 24.4 | 20.4 | 2.5 | 27.3 | 5.3 |
| 1997 | 40.9 | 13.7 | 5.9  | 1.0 | 9.6  | 2.6 |
| 1998 | 33.2 | 12.0 | 4.5  | 0.8 | 7.6  | 2.2 |
| 1999 | 36.1 | 13.1 | 4.9  | 1.0 | 8.2  | 2.5 |
| 2000 | 35.1 | 13.2 | 4.6  | 1.0 | 7.9  | 2.5 |
| 2001 | 33.8 | 13.4 | 4.4  | 0.9 | 7.5  | 2.5 |
| 2002 | 33.3 | 13.4 | 4.3  | 0.9 | 7.4  | 2.5 |
| 2003 | 31.3 | 12.8 | 4.2  | 0.9 | 7.1  | 2.4 |
| 2004 | 29.2 | 13.0 | 3.8  | 0.9 | 6.6  | 2.4 |
| 2005 | 28.2 | 12.0 | 3.6  | 0.8 | 6.2  | 2.3 |

Source:  US Department of Health and Human Services, Centers for Disease Control and Prevention, National Center for Health Statistics, *Health, United States, 2007*, table 42.

Notes:  'All Races' includes races not shown separately. Excludes residents of US Territories. Age-adjusted rates may differ from those shown in previous editions of *Health, United States*.

Units:  Number of deaths per 100,000 population known to the Centers for Disease Control.

## Table 2.29: Sexual Contact for People Ages 15-44, by Sex and Number of Lifetime Partners, 2002

| | Black | | White | | All Races | |
|---|---|---|---|---|---|---|
| | **Male** | **Female** | **Male** | **Female** | **Male** | **Female** |
| Total people | 6,940 | 8,250 | 38,738 | 39,498 | 61,147 | 61,561 |
| **By Number of partners** | | | | | | |
| *Any partners* | *91.8%* | *92.4%* | *90.3%* | *92.1%* | *90.3%* | *91.4%* |
| 1 | 5.8 | 12.4 | 13.4 | 21.0 | 12.8 | 22.5 |
| 2 | 5.9 | 8.4 | 8.3 | 10.6 | 8.1 | 10.8 |
| 3-6 | 24.1 | 44.8 | 27.1 | 32.1 | 27.5 | 32.6 |
| 7-14 | 22.2 | 18.0 | 19.2 | 18.2 | 19.3 | 16.3 |
| More than 15 | 33.8 | 8.8 | 22.3 | 10.2 | 22.6 | 9.2 |
| Median number of partners | 8.3 | 4.1 | 5.3 | 3.6 | 5.4 | 3.3 |

**Source:**  US Census Bureau, *Statistical Abstract of the United States: 2008*, table 91.

**Notes:**  Includes opposite-sex partners only. Same-sex contact was assessed using different questions, and results are not shown here.
Median number of partners excludes people who have have had no opposite-sex partners.
'All Races' includes races not shown here. 'White' and 'Black' exclude Hispanic.

**Units:**  Number of people age 15-44 in thousands; percent of total; median number of sexual partners.

## Table 2.30: Cancer Incidence Rates for Selected Sites, by Sex, 1990, 2000 and 2004

| | Black | | White | | All Races | |
|---|---|---|---|---|---|---|
| | Male | Female | Male | Female | Male | Female |
| **1990** | | | | | | |
| *All sites* | *685.3* | *403.4* | *590.5* | *421.0* | *583.7* | *410.9* |
| Lung/bronchus | 133.6 | 52.8 | 94.2 | 48.4 | 95.0 | 47.2 |
| Colon/rectum | 72.7 | 60.9 | 72.9 | 49.8 | 72.2 | 50.2 |
| Oral cavity/pharynx | 25.4 | 6.4 | 17.9 | 7.4 | 18.5 | 7.3 |
| Stomach | 21.5 | 9.9 | 12.8 | 5.7 | 14.6 | 6.7 |
| Pancreas | 19.3 | 12.9 | 12.7 | 9.8 | 13.0 | 10.0 |
| Urinary bladder | 19.6 | 8.6 | 40.7 | 9.9 | 37.2 | 9.5 |
| Non-Hodgkin's lymphoma | 17.4 | 10.2 | 23.7 | 15.4 | 22.6 | 14.5 |
| Leukemia | 16.0 | 8.4 | 17.9 | 10.2 | 17.1 | 9.8 |
| Prostate | 217.9 | NA | 168.3 | NA | 166.7 | NA |
| Breast | NA | 116.5 | NA | 134.2 | NA | 129.2 |
| Cervix uteri | NA | 16.4 | NA | 11.2 | NA | 11.9 |
| Corpus uteri | NA | 16.2 | NA | 26.0 | NA | 24.2 |
| Ovary | NA | 11.2 | NA | 16.4 | NA | 15.5 |
| **2000** | | | | | | |
| *All sites* | *692.6* | *394.6* | *565.7* | *428.6* | *560.5* | *411.1* |
| Lung/bronchus | 109.6 | 54.1 | 76.3 | 50.8 | 77.5 | 48.5 |
| Colon/rectum | 72.4 | 57.3 | 62.2 | 45.5 | 62.4 | 45.9 |
| Oral cavity/pharynx | 19.1 | 5.3 | 15.6 | 6.2 | 15.7 | 6.2 |
| Stomach | 18.4 | 8.6 | 10.7 | 5.0 | 12.5 | 6.1 |
| Pancreas | 18.1 | 12.7 | 12.6 | 9.6 | 12.8 | 9.8 |
| Urinary bladder | 19.9 | 7.7 | 40.7 | 9.9 | 36.7 | 9.0 |
| Non-Hodgkin's lymphoma | 17.5 | 11.8 | 24.7 | 16.8 | 23.4 | 15.8 |
| Leukemia | 13.3 | 9.2 | 17.3 | 10.6 | 16.3 | 9.9 |
| Prostate | 284.2 | NA | 173.0 | NA | 177.0 | NA |
| Breast | NA | 119.1 | NA | 140.6 | NA | 133.5 |
| Cervix uteri | NA | 10.6 | NA | 8.9 | NA | 8.8 |
| Corpus uteri | NA | 16.3 | NA | 25.2 | NA | 23.3 |
| Ovary | NA | 10.5 | NA | 15.0 | NA | 14.1 |

*(continued on next page)*

## Table 2.30: Cancer Incidence Rates for Selected Sites, by Sex, 1990, 2000 and 2004

|  | Black | | White | | All Races | |
|---|---|---|---|---|---|---|
|  | Male | Female | Male | Female | Male | Female |
| **2004** | | | | | | |
| *All sites* | *628.2* | *396.7* | *527.8* | *407.7* | *523.0* | *394.1* |
| Lung/bronchus | 98.4 | 55.9 | 68.1 | 48.8 | 69.3 | 47.2 |
| Colon/rectum | 70.9 | 51.6 | 54.0 | 39.7 | 54.8 | 40.7 |
| Oral cavity/pharynx | 15.6 | 5.8 | 15.0 | 5.9 | 14.7 | 5.9 |
| Stomach | 15.4 | 7.2 | 10.0 | 4.9 | 11.5 | 5.8 |
| Pancreas | 17.1 | 13.6 | 12.7 | 9.7 | 12.9 | 9.9 |
| Urinary bladder | 20.9 | 8.0 | 39.3 | 9.7 | 35.5 | 8.9 |
| Non-Hodgkin's lymphoma | 21.0 | 12.7 | 25.2 | 17.5 | 24.0 | 16.6 |
| Leukemia | 13.9 | 8.3 | 15.7 | 9.7 | 15.0 | 9.3 |
| Prostate | 233.9 | NA | 155.5 | NA | 159.3 | NA |
| Breast | NA | 118.8 | NA | 125.4 | NA | 121.0 |
| Cervix uteri | NA | 9.5 | NA | 7.6 | NA | 7.7 |
| Corpus uteri | NA | 18.2 | NA | 24.2 | NA | 22.9 |
| Ovary | NA | 10.1 | NA | 13.2 | NA | 12.6 |

**Source:** US Department of Health and Human Services, Centers for Disease Control and Prevention, National Center for Health Statistics, *Health, United States, 2007*, table 53.

**Notes:** 'All Races' includes races not shown separately.

**Units:** Number of new cases per 100,000 population.

## Table 2.31: Five-Year Relative Cancer Survival Rates
for Selected Cancer Sites, 1996–2003

| | Black | | White | |
|---|---|---|---|---|
| | **Male** | **Female** | **Male** | **Female** |
| *All cancer sites* | *59.2%* | *54.5%* | *66.6%* | *67.4%* |
| Oral cavity and pharynx | 35.0 | NA | 61.2 | NA |
| Esophagus | 9.4 | NA | 17.1 | NA |
| Stomach | 22.1 | NA | 20.4 | NA |
| Colon | 56.1 | 53.7 | 65.8 | 65.5 |
| Rectum | 57.1 | 59.6 | 65.7 | 67.3 |
| Pancreas | 3.2 | 5.8 | 5.3 | 4.4 |
| Lung and bronchus | 10.8 | 14.9 | 13.6 | 18.1 |
| Prostate gland | 95.3 | NA | 99.0 | NA |
| Urinary bladder | 68.3 | NA | 82.1 | NA |
| Non-Hodgkin's lymphoma | 52.1 | 61.1 | 62.8 | 67.1 |
| Leukemia | 40.6 | NA | 50.8 | NA |
| Melanoma | NA | 77.5 | NA | 94.1 |
| Breast | NA | 77.9 | NA | 90.3 |
| Cervix uteri | NA | 65.8 | NA | 74.3 |
| Corpus uteri | NA | 62.4 | NA | 86.9 |
| Ovary | NA | 37.5 | NA | 44.7 |

**Source:** US Department of Health and Human Services, Centers for Disease Control and Prevention, National Center for Health Statistics, *Health, United States, 2007*, table 54.

**Notes:** Data is based on the Surveillance, Epidemiology, and End Results program's population-based registries in Atlanta, Detroit, Seattle-Puget Sound, San Francisco-Oakland, Connecticut, Iowa, New Mexico, Utah, and Hawaii. Rates are based on follow-up of patients through 2004.

The five-year cancer relative survival rate is the ratio of the observed survival rate for the patient group to the expected survival rate for persons in the general population similar to the patient group with respect to age, sex, race, and calendar year of observation. It uses the survival rate five years after diagnoisis to estimate the chance of surviving cancer.

**Units:** Percent of patients surviving, relative to the expected survival rate of the general population.

## Table 2.32: Medical Injury and Poisoning Episodes, 2004 and 2006

| | Black | White | All Races |
|---|---|---|---|
| **2004** | | | |
| *All persons* | *35,765* | *234,601* | *288,252* |
| *All episodes* | *3,390* | *27,975* | *31,173* |
| Fall | 834 | 10,524 | 12,030 |
| Struck by person or object | 470 | 3,293 | 3,852 |
| Transportation | 622 | 2,843 | 3,690 |
| Over-exertion | 532 | 3,987 | 4,763 |
| Cutting / piercing instrument | *214 | 2,516 | 2,844 |
| Other causes | 642 | 4,551 | 5,619 |
| Poisoning | † | *261 | 375 |
| **2006** | | | |
| *All persons* | *37,779* | *235,531* | *293,756* |
| *All episodes* | *2,871* | *28,826* | *33,256* |
| Fall | 768 | 11,798 | 13,071 |
| Struck by person or object | 380 | 3,212 | 3,935 |
| Transportation | *293 | 2,963 | 3,396 |
| Over-exertion | 529 | 3,895 | 4,572 |
| Cutting / piercing instrument | † | 2,305 | 2,628 |
| Other causes | 750 | 4,016 | 5,018 |
| Poisoning | 0 | *636 | *636 |

Source:   US Department of Health and Human Services, Centers for Disease Control and Prevention, *Summary Health Statistics for the US Population: National Health Interview Survey, 2004*, tables 8 and 9; *2006*, tables 8 and 9.

Notes:   'All Races' includes races not shown separately.
Based on a question in survey that asked all respondents whether they had been poisoned and/or injured seriously enough in the past 3 months to seek medical advice or treatment.
* Estimates have a relative standard error between 30 and 50 percent, and should be used with caution.
† Estimates have a relative standard error over 50 percent, and are not reported.

Units:   Number of persons and incidents in thousands.

## Table 2.33: Injuries, by Selected Characteristics, 2004 and 2006

|  | Black | White | All Races |
|---|---|---|---|
| **2004** |  |  |  |
| *All episodes* | *3,390* | *27,975* | *33,173* |
| **By Activity engaged** |  |  |  |
| Driving | 519 | 1,839 | 2,534 |
| Working at paid job | 446 | 4,753 | 5,324 |
| Working around house or yard | *262 | 4,414 | 4,831 |
| Attending school | *165 | 791 | 1,069 |
| Sports | 557 | 4,432 | 5,103 |
| Leisure activities (non-sports) | 698 | 7,500 | 8,935 |
| **By Place of occurrence** |  |  |  |
| Home, inside | 785 | 7,218 | 8,567 |
| Home, outside | 605 | 5,772 | 6,701 |
| School/childcare center | 439 | 2,036 | 2,598 |
| Hospital | † | 450 | 554 |
| Street or highway | 695 | 3,481 | 4,449 |
| Recreational area | *264 | 3,638 | 4,003 |
| Industrial place | † | 1,676 | 1,766 |
| Service area | *146 | 1,112 | 1,314 |

*(continued on next page)*

## Table 2.33: Injuries, by Selected Characteristics, 2004 and 2006

|  | Black | White | All Races |
|---|---|---|---|
| **2006** | | | |
| *All episodes* | *2,871* | *28,826* | *33,256* |
| **By Activity engaged** | | | |
| Driving | † | 1,602 | 1,813 |
| Working at paid job | *396 | 4,000 | 4,661 |
| Working around house or yard | *289 | 4,768 | 5,170 |
| Attending school | † | *466 | 586 |
| Sports | 403 | 4,103 | 4,824 |
| Leisure activities (non-sports) | 751 | 7,105 | 8,287 |
| **By Place of occurrence** | | | |
| Home, inside | 900 | 8,976 | 10,248 |
| Home, outside | *332 | 5,795 | 6,521 |
| School/childcare center | *151 | 1,562 | 1,771 |
| Hospital | † | *795 | *854 |
| Street or highway | *413 | 3,231 | 3,818 |
| Recreational area | *507 | 3,357 | 4,105 |
| Industrial place | † | 1,645 | 1,769 |
| Service area | *270 | 1,176 | 1,538 |

Source: US Department of Health and Human Services, Centers for Disease Control and Prevention, *Summary Health Statistics for the US Population: National Health Interview Survey, 2004*, tables 8, 11 and 13; *2006*, tables 8, 11, and 13.

Notes: 'All Races' includes races not shown separately.
Based on a question in survey that asked all respondents whether they had been poisoned and/or injured seriously enough in the past 3 months to seek medical advice or treatment.
* Estimates have a relative standard error between 30 and 50 percent, and should be used with caution.
† Estimates have a relative standard error over 50 percent, and are not reported.

Units: Number of persons who had a medically-attended injury episode in thousands.

## Table 2.34: Migraines and Pain in the Neck,
## Lower Back, Face, and Jaw, 2006

|  | Black | White | All Races |
|---|---|---|---|
| *Total adults* | 26,223 | 179,456 | 220,267 |
| Migraine or severe headache | 4,236 | 26,977 | 33,099 |
| Neck pain | 2,769 | 27,487 | 32,002 |
| Lower back pain | 6,264 | 50,988 | 60,607 |
| Face or jaw pain | 872 | 8,471 | 9,893 |
| **Percent of total** | | | |
| Migraine or severe headache | 15.8% | 15.3% | 15.1% |
| Neck pain | 11.0 | 15.1 | 14.3 |
| Lower back pain | 24.3 | 28.2 | 27.4 |
| Face or jaw pain | 3.4 | 4.7 | 4.5 |

**Source:** US Department of Health and Human Services, Centers for Disease Control and Prevention, *National Health Interview Survey: Summary Health Statistics for US Adults, 2006,* tables 9 and 10.

**Notes:** Respondents were asked, in separate questions, whether during the past three months, they had experienced: a severe headache or migraine, meck pain, lower back pain, and facial or jaw pain. Respondents were instructed to report only pain that had lasted a whole day or more, and not fleeting or minor aches and pains. Respondents may have answered 'yes' to more than one question.

**Units:** Number of adults 18 years of age and older in thousands; percent of total.

## Table 2.35: Hearing Trouble, Vision Trouble, and Absence of Teeth, 2006

|  | Black | White | All Races |
|---|---|---|---|
| *Total adults* | *26,223* | *179,456* | *220,267* |
| Hearing trouble | 2,478 | 33,010 | 37,517 |
| Vision trouble | 2,500 | 17,517 | 21,211 |
| Absence of all natural teeth | 2,087 | 14,714 | 17,577 |
| **Percent of total** |  |  |  |
| Hearing trouble | 10.7% | 17.8% | 16.8% |
| Vision trouble | 10.4 | 9.5 | 9.5 |
| Absence of all natural teeth | 9.7 | 7.9 | 8.0 |

Source:   US Department of Health and Human Services, Centers for Disease Control and Prevention, *National Health Interview Survey: Summary Health Statistics for US Adults, 2006*,
tables 11 and 12.

Notes:   Respondents were asked, in separate questions, whether they had trouble hearing without
a hearing aid, whether they had trouble seeing without glasses or contact lenses, and
whether they had lost all of their upper and lower natural (permanent) teeth. Respondents may be represented in more than one column.

Units:   Number of adults 18 years of age and older in thousands; percent of total.

## Table 2.36: Limitation of Activity, 2004 and 2006

**Physical activities that are very difficult or cannot be done at all:**

|  | Black | White | All Races |
|---|---|---|---|
| **2004** | | | |
| *Any physical difficulty* | *17.6%* | *14.5%* | *14.7%* |
| Walk a quarter of a mile | 9.8 | 6.7 | 7.0 |
| Climb up to 10 steps without resting | 8.2 | 5.0 | 5.3 |
| Stand for 2 hours | 11.3 | 8.3 | 8.6 |
| Sit for 2 hours | 3.4 | 3.1 | 3.1 |
| Stoop, bend or kneel | 10.1 | 8.4 | 8.5 |
| Reach over one's head | 2.9 | 2.4 | 2.4 |
| Grasp or handle small objects | 2.1 | 1.8 | 1.8 |
| Lift or carry 10 pounds | 6.4 | 4.0 | 4.3 |
| Push or pull large objects | 8.4 | 6.3 | 6.5 |
| **2006** | | | |
| *Any physical difficulty* | *17.7%* | *14.3%* | *14.6%* |
| Walk a quarter of a mile | 9.3 | 7.0 | 7.1 |
| Climb up to 10 steps without resting | 8.3 | 5.2 | 5.4 |
| Stand for 2 hours | 10.3 | 8.4 | 8.6 |
| Sit for 2 hours | 3.7 | 3.2 | 3.2 |
| Stoop, bend or kneel | 10.4 | 8.6 | 8.7 |
| Reach over one's head | 3.0 | 2.7 | 2.6 |
| Grasp or handle small objects | 2.0 | 1.8 | 1.8 |
| Lift or carry 10 pounds | 6.6 | 4.2 | 4.4 |
| Push or pull large objects | 8.7 | 6.2 | 6.4 |

**Source:** US Department of Health and Human Services, Centers for Disease Control and Prevention, *National Health Interview Survey: Summary Health Statistics for US Adults, 2004*, table 19; *2006*, table 19.

**Notes:** 'All Races' includes races not shown separately.
'Heavy object' is defined as something as heavy as 10 pounds (such as a full bag of groceries).

**Units:** Percent of the population of 18 years of age and over.

## Table 2.37: Selected Characteristics of Persons With a Work Disability, 2005

|  | Black | White | All Races |
|---|---|---|---|
| **Persons with a work disability by age** | | | |
| *Total* | *3,620* | *14,828* | *19,656* |
| 16-24 years old | 434 | 1,154 | 1,709 |
| 25-34 years old | 520 | 1,771 | 2,475 |
| 35-44 years old | 705 | 2,823 | 3,764 |
| 45-54 years old | 1,009 | 4,058 | 5,382 |
| 55-64 years old | 952 | 5,022 | 6,327 |
| **Work Disabled as a percent of total population, by age** | | | |
| 16-24 years old | 8.2% | 4.1% | 4.7% |
| 25-34 years old | 10.3 | 5.8 | 6.4 |
| 35-44 years old | 13.3 | 8.2 | 8.7 |
| 45-54 years old | 20.8 | 11.8 | 12.9 |
| 55-64 years old | 32.7 | 20.1 | 21.4 |
| **Percent of work disabled:** | | | |
| Receiving Social Security Income | 31.4% | 35.5% | 34.1% |
| Receiving Food Stamps | 29.2 | 15.7 | 18.4 |
| Covered by Medicaid | 53.6 | 66.8 | 64.2 |
| Residing in public housing | 9.4 | 4.1 | 5.9 |
| Residing in subsidized housing | 6.9 | 3.3 | 3.9 |

**Source:** US Bureau of the Census, *Statistical Abstract of the United States, 2008*, table 541.

**Notes:** 'All Races' includes races not shown separately.
Covers the civilian noninstitutional population and members of the armed forces living off post or with members of their families on post.
Persons are classified as having a work disability if they (1) have a health problem or disability which prevents them from or which limits the kind or amount of work they can do; (2) have a service disability or ever retired or left a job for health reasons; (3) did not work in survey reference week or previous year because of long-term illness or disability; or, (4) are under age 65 and are covered by Medicare or receive Supplemental Security Income.

**Units:** Persons with a work disability in thousands of persons; work disabled as a percent of total population in percent; characteristics as a percent of the work disabled.

## Table 2.38: Work-Loss Days, 2004–2006

|  | Black | White | All Races |
|---|---|---|---|
| **2004** | | | |
| *All persons* | 224,602 | 178,552 | 215,191 |
| Bed days in the past 12 months | 107,598 | 728,668 | 872,431 |
| Days per person | 4.5 | 4.1 | 4.1 |
| *All employed persons* | 17,112 | 125,757 | 151,650 |
| Work-loss days in the past 12 months | 71,793 | 476,176 | 578,319 |
| Days per person | 4.3 | 3.8 | 3.9 |
| **2005** | | | |
| *All persons* | 24,817 | 180,477 | 217,774 |
| Bed days in the past 12 months | 146,197 | 810,240 | 1,001,761 |
| Days per person | 6.0 | 4.6 | 4.7 |
| *All employed persons* | 17,316 | 128,151 | 154,265 |
| Work-loss days in the past 12 months | 84,658 | 542,535 | 652,984 |
| Days per person | 5.0 | 4.3 | 4.3 |
| **2006** | | | |
| *All persons* | 26,223 | 179,456 | 220,267 |
| Bed days in the past 12 months | 126,750 | 852,537 | 1,022,637 |
| Days per person | 5.0 | 4.8 | 4.7 |
| *All employed persons* | 18,705 | 126,980 | 156,295 |
| Work-loss days in the past 12 months | 72,009 | 528,519 | 637,465 |
| Days per person | 3.9 | 4.2 | 4.1 |

Source: US Department of Health and Human Services, Centers for Disease Control and Prevention, *National Health Interview Survey: Summary Health Statistics for US Adults, 2004*, table 17; *2005*, table 17; *2006*, table 17.

Notes: 'All Races' includes races not shown separately.
Respondents were asked how many times in the last 12 months an injury or illness caused them to miss a day of work or had kept them in bed more than half a day.

Units: Number of persons and employed persons in thousands; average (mean) work-loss days and bed-days per person.

## Table 2.39: Learning Disabilities and Attention Deficit Hyperactivity Disorder for Children Age 3–17, 2005 and 2006

|  | Black | White | All Races |
|---|---|---|---|
| **2005** |  |  |  |
| *Total children* | *9,355* | *47,287* | *61,192* |
| Learning disability | 774 | 3,233 | 4,244 |
| ADHD | 634 | 3,123 | 3,998 |
| *Percent of total* |  |  |  |
| Learning disability | 8.2% | 6.8% | 6.9% |
| ADHD | 6.8 | 6.6 | 6.5 |
| **2006** |  |  |  |
| *Total children* | *9,571* | *46,885* | *61,354* |
| Learning disability | 739 | 3,736 | 4,748 |
| ADHD | 705 | 3,553 | 4,545 |
| *Percent of total* |  |  |  |
| Learning disability | 7.7% | 8.0% | 7.7% |
| ADHD | 7.4 | 7.6 | 7.4 |

Source:  US Census Bureau, *Statistical Abstract of the United States: 2008*, table 178.
US Department of Health and Human Services, Centers for Disease Control and Prevention, *National Health Interview Survey: Summary Health Statistics for US Children, 2006*, table 3.

Notes:  Questions measure whether children have been told by a doctor or school or health professional that they had a learning disorder or Attention Deficit Hyperactivity Disorder.

Units:  Number of children age 3-17 in thousands; percent of total.

## Table 2.40: Asthma in Children, 2005 and 2006

| | Black | White | All Races |
|---|---|---|---|
| **2005** | | | |
| *Total children under 18* | 11,152 | 56,761 | 73,376 |
| Ever told they had asthma | 1,949 | 6,558 | 9,287 |
| Still have asthma | 1,467 | 4,519 | 6,531 |
| *Percent of total* | | | |
| Ever told they had asthma | 17.5% | 11.6% | 12.7% |
| Still have asthma | 13.2 | 8.0 | 8.9 |
| **2006** | | | |
| *Total children under 18* | 11,455 | 55,881 | 73,493 |
| Ever told they had asthma | 1,921 | 7,100 | 9,876 |
| Still have asthma | 1,461 | 4,816 | 6,819 |
| *Percent of total* | | | |
| Ever told they had asthma | 16.9% | 12.8% | 13.6% |
| Still have asthma | 12.9 | 8.7 | 9.4 |

Source: US Department of Health and Human Services, Centers for Disease Control and Prevention, *National Health Interview Survey: Summary Health Statistics for US Children, 2005*, table 1; *2006*, table 1.

Notes: Respondents were asked if their child has ever been diagnosed with asthma by a doctor or other health professional, and if the child still has asthma.

Units: Number of children under 18 years old in thousands; percent of total.

## Table 2.41: Obese, Overweight, and Underweight Adults, 2005 and 2006

|  | Black | White | All Races |
|---|---|---|---|
| **2005** |  |  |  |
| *Total number* | *24,817* | *180,477* | *217,774* |
| Obese | 7,767 | 42,082 | 51,954 |
| Overweight | 8,311 | 61,787 | 73,623 |
| Healthy weight | 7,431 | 65,472 | 78,646 |
| Underweight | 259 | 3,411 | 4,189 |
| *Frequency* |  |  |  |
| Obese | 32.4% | 24.1% | 24.7% |
| Overweight | 35.4 | 35.5 | 35.4 |
| Healthy weight | 31.1 | 38.4 | 38.1 |
| Underweight | 1.1 | 2.0 | 2.1 |
| **2006** |  |  |  |
| *Total number* | *26,223* | *179,456* | *220,267* |
| Obese | 8,713 | 43,311 | 54,050 |
| Overweight | 8,657 | 60,240 | 73,285 |
| Healthy weight | 7,377 | 64,196 | 78,705 |
| Underweight | 339 | 2,763 | 3,618 |
| *Frequency* |  |  |  |
| Obese | 34.7% | 25.1% | 25.5% |
| Overweight | 34.4 | 35.1 | 34.9 |
| Healthy weight | 29.5 | 38.2 | 37.9 |
| Underweight | 1.5 | 1.7 | 1.8 |

Source: US Department of Health and Human Services, Centers for Disease Control and Prevention, *National Health Interview Survey: Summary Health Statistics for US Adults, 2005*, tables 30 and 31; *2006*, tables 30 and 31.

Notes: Weight categories are measured using the Body Mass Index (BMI), based on weight and height. 'Overweight' is indicated by a BMI of greater than or equal to 25.0 and less than 30.0. 'Obese' is indicated by at BMI over 30.0. 'Healthy weight' is indicated by a BMI between 18.5 and 25.0. 'Underweight' is indicated by a BMI less than 18.5.
'All Races' includes races not shown separately.

Units: Number of adults over 18 in thousands; percent of total.

## Table 2.42: Overweight, Obesity, and Healthy Weight Among Adults Ages 20 to 74, 1988–1994 and 2001–2004

|  | Black | | White | | All Races | |
|---|---|---|---|---|---|---|
|  | **Male** | **Female** | **Male** | **Female** | **Male** | **Female** |
| **1988–1994** | | | | | | |
| Overweight | 58.2% | 68.5% | 61.6% | 47.2% | 61.0% | 51.2% |
| Obese | 21.3 | 39.1 | 20.7 | 23.3 | 20.6 | 26.0 |
| Healthy Weight | 40.0 | 28.9 | 37.4 | 49.2 | 37.9 | 45.3 |
| **2001–2004** | | | | | | |
| Overweight | 66.8% | 79.5% | 71.1% | 57.1% | 70.7% | 61.4% |
| Obese | 31.2 | 51.6 | 31.0 | 31.5 | 30.2 | 34.0 |
| Healthy Weight | 31.3 | 18.9 | 27.8 | 40.2 | 28.1 | 36.2 |

**Source:**  US Department of Health and Human Services, Centers for Disease Control and Prevention, National Center for Health Statistics, *Health, United States, 2007*, table 74.

**Notes:**  Weight categories are measured using the Body Mass Index (BMI), based on weight and height. 'Overweight' is indicated by a BMI of greater than or equal to 25.0 and less than 30.0. 'Obese' is indicated by at BMI over 30.0. 'Healthy weight' is indicated by a BMI between 18.5 and 25.0. 'All Races' includes races not shown separately.
'All Races' includes races not shown separately.

**Units:**  Percent of total adults over ages 20 to 74 in the US.

## Table 2.43: Overweight Among Children and Adolescents 6-19 Years of Age, 1976–1980, 1988–1994, and 2001–2004

| | Black | | White | | All Races | |
|---|---|---|---|---|---|---|
| | **Boys** | **Girls** | **Boys** | **Girls** | **Boys** | **Girls** |
| **1976–1980** | | | | | | |
| 6-11 years of age | 6.8% | 11.2% | 6.1% | 5.2% | 6.6% | 6.4% |
| 12-19 years of age | 6.1 | 10.7 | 3.8 | 4.6 | 4.8 | 5.3 |
| **1988–1994** | | | | | | |
| 6-11 years of age | 12.3% | 17.0% | 10.7% | *9.8% | 11.6% | 11.0% |
| 12-19 years of age | 10.7 | 16.3 | 11.6 | 8.9 | 11.3 | 9.7 |
| **2001–2004** | | | | | | |
| 6-11 years of age | 17.2% | 24.8% | 16.9% | 15.6% | 18.7% | 16.3% |
| 12-19 years of age | 17.7 | 23.8 | 17.9 | 14.6 | 17.9 | 16.0 |

Source:   US Department of Health and Human Services, Centers for Disease Control and Prevention, National Center for Health Statistics, *Health, United States, 2007,* table 75.

Notes:   'Overweight' is defined as a Body Mass Index (BMI) at or above the sex and age-specific 95th percentile, based on 2000 CDC growth charts.
* Estimate has a relative standard error between 20 and 30 percent and is considered unreliable.

Units:   Percent of total children and adolescents in the US.

## Table 2.44: Leisure-Time Physical Exercise, by Frequency, 2005 and 2006

|  | Black | White | All Races |
|---|---|---|---|
| **2005** | | | |
| Total adults | 24,817 | 180,477 | 217,774 |
| *Frequency of vigorous leisure-time physical activity per week:* | | | |
| Never | 71.7% | 60.0% | 61.6% |
| Less than 1 | 2.0 | 2.5 | 2.5 |
| 1 or 2 | 8.6 | 12.4 | 11.9 |
| 3 or 4 | 9.3 | 13.9 | 13.2 |
| 5 or more | 8.5 | 11.2 | 10.8 |
| **2006** | | | |
| Total adults | 26,223 | 179,456 | 220,267 |
| *Frequency of vigorous leisure-time physical activity per week:* | | | |
| Never | 67.4% | 60.7% | 61.7% |
| Less than 1 | 1.9 | 2.7 | 2.6 |
| 1 or 2 | 10.6 | 11.9 | 11.6 |
| 3 or 4 | 11.6 | 13.4 | 13.1 |
| 5 or more | 8.6 | 11.3 | 11.0 |

**Source:** US Department of Health and Human Services, Centers for Disease Control and Prevention, *National Health Interview Survey: Summary Health Statistics for US Adults, 2005*, tables 28 and 29; *2006*, tables 28 and 29.

**Notes:** 'Activity' is defined as vigorous activity lasting at least 10 minutes that causes heavy sweating and large increases in breathing or heart rates.
'All Races' includes races not shown separately.

**Units:** Thousands of adults age 18 or over; percent of total.

## Table 2.45: Percent of Adults Engaging in Leisure-Time Physical Activity, Selected Years 1997–2005

|  | Black | White | All Races |
|---|---|---|---|
| **1997** | | | |
| No participation in physical activity | 38.2% | 27.6% | 29.5% |
| Participates in regular, sustained activity | 16.3 | 20.3 | 19.6 |
| Participates in regular, vigorous activity | 9.3 | 14.0 | 12.9 |
| **1998** | | | |
| No participation in physical activity | 33.8% | 26.7% | 28.7% |
| Participates in regular, sustained activity | 17.8 | 21.6 | 20.8 |
| Participates in regular, vigorous activity | 12.3 | 14.0 | 13.6 |
| **2000** | | | |
| Persons who are physically inactive | 34.8% | 24.2% | 27.6% |
| Persons with insufficient activity | 43.3 | 48.3 | 46.2 |
| Persons who meet recommended activity | 21.9 | 27.5 | 26.2 |
| **2003** | | | |
| Persons who are physically inactive | 32.7% | 20.9% | 24.3% |
| Persons not meeting recommended activity | 63.7 | 51.0 | 54.0 |
| Persons who meet recommended activity | 36.3 | 49.0 | 46.0 |
| **2005** | | | |
| Persons who are physically inactive | 32.8% | 21.4% | 25.1% |
| Persons not meeting recommended activity | 59.8 | 49.1 | 51.7 |
| Persons who meet recommended activity | 40.2 | 50.9 | 48.3 |

**Source:** US Bureau of the Census, *Statistical Abstract of the United States, 1999*, table 248; *2000*, table 232; *2002*, table 191; *2004*, table 195; *2008*, table 200.

**Notes:** 'All Races' includes races not shown separately.
'Recommended activity' is physical activity at least 30 minutes of activity 5 times per week, or 20 minutes of vigorous activity 3 times per week. 'Regular, sustained activity' is any type or intensity of activity that occurs 5 or more times per week and 30 minutes or more per occasion. 'Regular, vigorous activity' is rhythmic contraction of large muscle groups performed 3 times per week or more for at least 20 minutes per occasion.

**Units:** Percent of persons 18 years of age and over.

## Table 2.46: Smoking and Alcohol Consumption among Adults, 2006

|                      | Black   | White    | All Races |
|----------------------|---------|----------|-----------|
| *Total adults*       | *26,223* | *179,456* | *220,267* |
| **Smoking**          |         |          |           |
| All current smokers  | 21.8%   | 21.1%    | 20.8%     |
|   Everyday smokers | 16.4 | 17.1  | 16.5      |
|   Some day smokers | 5.4  | 4.1   | 4.2       |
| Former smokers       | 13.7    | 22.1     | 20.7      |
| Non-smokers          | 65.5    | 56.8     | 58.6      |
| **Alcohol**          |         |          |           |
| Lifetime abstainer   | 36.0%   | 22.3%    | 25.2%     |
| Former infrequent    | 9.6     | 7.6      | 7.9       |
| Former regular       | 6.3     | 6.3      | 6.2       |
| Current infrequent   | 12.8    | 12.2     | 12.4      |
| Current regular      | 34.8    | 51.1     | 47.9      |

**Source:** US Department of Health and Human Services, Centers for Disease Control and Prevention, *National Health Interview Survey: Summary Health Statistics for US Adults, 2006*, tables 24-27.

**Notes:** 'Current smokers' have smoked at least 100 cigarettes in their lifetime and curently smoke. 'Everyday smokers' are current smokers who smoke every day. 'Some day smokers' are current smokers who smoke on some days. 'Former smokers' have smoked at least 100 cigarettes in their lifetime, but currently do not smoke at all. 'Non-smokers' have smoked fewer than 100 cigarettes in their lifetime.

'Lifetime abstainers' have had fewer than 12 drinks in their lifetime. 'Former drinkers' have had at least 12 drinks in any one year and no drinks in the last year. 'Current infrequent drinkers' have had at least 12 drinks in their lifetime and fewer than 12 drinks in the past year. 'Current regular drinkers' have had at least 12 drinks in the past year. Drinkers whose frequency or amount of drinking was not known are not included.

**Units:** Thousands of adults 18 years or age and over; percent of total.

## Table 2.47: Current Cigarette Smoking by Persons 18 Years Old and Older, by Sex and Age, 2000 and 2005

| | Black | | White | | All Races | |
|---|---|---|---|---|---|---|
| | Male | Female | Male | Female | Male | Female |
| **2000** | | | | | | |
| *18 years old and over* | *25.7%* | *20.7%* | *25.4%* | *22.0%* | *25.2%* | *21.1%* |
| 18-24 years old | 20.9 | 14.2 | 30.4 | 28.5 | 28.1 | 24.9 |
| 25-34 years old | 23.2 | 15.5 | 29.7 | 24.9 | 28.9 | 22.3 |
| 35-44 years old | 30.7 | 30.2 | 30.6 | 26.6 | 30.2 | 26.2 |
| 45-64 years old | 32.2 | 25.6 | 25.8 | 21.4 | 26.4 | 21.7 |
| 65 years old and over | 14.2 | 10.2 | 9.8 | 9.1 | 10.2 | 9.3 |
| **2005** | | | | | | |
| *18 years old and over* | *25.9%* | *17.1%* | *23.3%* | *19.1%* | *23.4%* | *18.3%* |
| 18-24 years old | 21.6 | 14.2 | 29.7 | 22.6 | 28.0 | 20.7 |
| 25-34 years old | 29.8 | 16.9 | 27.7 | 23.1 | 27.7 | 21.5 |
| 35-44 years old | 23.3 | 19.0 | 26.3 | 22.2 | 26.0 | 21.3 |
| 45-64 years old | 32.4 | 21.0 | 24.5 | 18.9 | 25.2 | 18.8 |
| 65 years old and over | 16.8 | 10.0 | 7.9 | 8.4 | 8.9 | 8.3 |

**Source:** US Department of Health and Human Services, Centers for Disease Control and Prevention, National Center for Health Statistics, *Health, United States, 2007*, table 63.

**Notes:** 'All Races' includes races not shown separately.
Rates are age-adjusted.

**Units:** Percent of US civilian non-institutionalized population.

## Table 2.48: Current Cigarette Smoking by Persons 25 Years Old and Older, by Sex and Education, 2000 and 2005

|  | Black | White | All Races |
|---|---|---|---|
| **2000** |  |  |  |
| *Males* | *26.4%* | *24.7%* | *24.7%* |
| No high school diploma or GED | 38.2 | 38.2 | 36.0 |
| High school diploma or GED | 29.0 | 32.4 | 32.1 |
| Some college, no bachelor's degree | 19.9 | 23.5 | 23.3 |
| Bachelor's degree or higher | 14.6 | 11.3 | 11.6 |
| *Females* | *21.6%* | *21.0%* | *20.5%* |
| No high school diploma or GED | 31.1 | 28.4 | 27.1 |
| High school diploma or GED | 25.4 | 27.8 | 26.6 |
| Some college, no bachelor's degree | 20.4 | 21.1 | 20.4 |
| Bachelor's degree or higher | 10.8 | 10.2 | 10.1 |
| **2005** |  |  |  |
| *Males* | *26.5%* | *22.4%* | *22.7%* |
| No high school diploma or GED | 35.9 | 31.6 | 31.7 |
| High school diploma or GED | 30.1 | 30.0 | 29.9 |
| Some college, no bachelor's degree | 27.4 | 24.5 | 24.9 |
| Bachelor's degree or higher | 10.0 | 9.3 | 9.7 |
| *Females* | *17.5%* | *18.6%* | *18.0%* |
| No high school diploma or GED | 27.8 | 24.6 | 24.6 |
| High school diploma or GED | 18.2 | 25.9 | 24.1 |
| Some college, no bachelor's degree | 17.5 | 19.5 | 19.1 |
| Bachelor's degree or higher | *6.6 | 9.1 | 8.5 |

Source: US Department of Health and Human Services, Centers for Disease Control and Prevention, National Center for Health Statistics, *Health, United States, 2007*, table 64.

Notes: 'All Races' includes races not shown separately.
* Estimates have a relative standard error between 20 and 30 percent and are considered unreliable.

Units: Percent of total US civilian non-institutionalized population who are current smokers.

## Table 2.49: Use of Selected Substances by Persons 12 Years and Older, 2000 and 2005

|  | Black | White | All Races |
|---|---|---|---|
| **2000** | | | |
| Any illicit drug | 6.4% | 6.4% | 6.3% |
| Marijuana | 5.2 | 4.9 | 4.8 |
| Psychotherapeutic drug | 1.2 | 1.8 | 1.7 |
| Alcohol | 33.7 | 50.7 | 46.6 |
| Binge alcohol | 17.7 | 21.2 | 20.6 |
| Any tobacco | 26.7 | 31.0 | 29.3 |
| Cigarettes | 23.3 | 25.9 | 24.9 |
| Cigars | 5.1 | 5.0 | 4.8 |
| **2005** | | | |
| Any illicit drug | 9.7% | 8.1% | 8.1% |
| Marijuana | 7.6 | 6.1 | 6.0 |
| Psychotherapeutic drug | 1.8 | 2.8 | 2.6 |
| Alcohol | 40.8 | 56.5 | 51.8 |
| Binge alcohol | 20.3 | 23.4 | 22.7 |
| Any tobacco | 28.4 | 31.2 | 29.4 |
| Cigarettes | 24.5 | 26.0 | 24.9 |
| Cigars | 6.4 | 5.9 | 5.6 |

**Source:** US Department of Health and Human Services, Centers for Disease Control and Prevention, National Center for Health Statistics, *Health, United States, 2003*, tables 62 and 63; *2007*, table 66.

**Notes:** Data is based on household interviews with a sample of the civilian noninstitutional population.

'All Races' includes races not shown separately. Both 'Black' and 'White' exclude Hispanic persons.

Use of selected substances in the past month by person 12 years of age and over. 'Any illicit drug' includes marijuana/hashish, cocaine, heroin, hallucinogens, or any psychotherapeutic drug for nonmedical use. 'Psychotherapeutic drug' includes non-medical use of prescription-type pain relievers, tranquilizers, stimulants, or sedatives; does not include over-the-counter drugs. 'Binge Alcohol' refers to consuming five or more drinks on the same occasion at least once in the past month.

**Units:** Percent of population 12 years old and over using selected substances.

## Table 2.50: Feelings of Emotional Distress in Adults, 2006

|  | Black | White | All Races |
|---|---|---|---|
| *Sadness* |  |  |  |
| All or most of the time | 4.3% | 2.7% | 3.0% |
| Some of the time | 10.0 | 7.5 | 7.9 |
|  |  |  |  |
| *Hopelessness* |  |  |  |
| All or most of the time | 2.4% | 1.9% | 2.0% |
| Some of the time | 4.4 | 3.5 | 3.7 |
|  |  |  |  |
| *Worthlessness* |  |  |  |
| All or most of the time | 1.9% | 1.7% | 1.8% |
| Some of the time | 3.5 | 3.1 | 3.2 |
|  |  |  |  |
| *Everything is an effort* |  |  |  |
| All or most of the time | 7.5% | 4.8% | 5.1% |
| Some of the time | 9.3 | 8.1 | 8.3 |
|  |  |  |  |
| *Nervousness* |  |  |  |
| All or most of the time | 4.3% | 4.0% | 4.0% |
| Some of the time | 10.3 | 11.2 | 11.0 |
|  |  |  |  |
| *Restlessness* |  |  |  |
| All or most of the time | 5.7% | 5.7% | 5.6% |
| Some of the time | 11.3 | 11.4 | 11.3 |

Source: US Department of Health and Human Services, Centers for Disease Control and Prevention, *National Health Interview Survey: Summary Health Statistics for US Adults, 2006*, tables 14 and 16.

Notes: Respondents were asked, in separate questions, how often in the past 30 days they felt: so sad that nothing could cheer them up, hopeless, worthless, that everything was an effort, nervous, or restless. Respondents could choose from among five response categories: 'all of the time,' 'most of the time,' 'some of the time,' 'a little of the time,' or 'none of the time.' Here, 'all' and 'most' are combined, and 'some' is shown separately.

Units: Percent of adults 18 years of age or older.

## Table 2.51: Suicidal Ideation and Suicide Attempts Among Teenagers, by Sex, 1991–2005

| | Black | | White | | All Races | |
|---|---|---|---|---|---|---|
| | Male | Female | Male | Female | Male | Female |
| **Seriously considered suicide** | | | | | | |
| 1991 | 13.3% | 29.4% | 21.7% | 38.6% | 20.8% | 37.2% |
| 1993 | 15.4 | 24.5 | 19.1 | 29.7 | 18.8 | 29.6 |
| 1995 | 16.7 | 22.2 | 19.1 | 31.6 | 18.3 | 30.4 |
| 1997 | 10.6 | 22.0 | 14.4 | 26.1 | 15.1 | 27.1 |
| 1999 | 11.7 | 18.8 | 12.5 | 23.2 | 13.7 | 24.9 |
| 2001 | 9.2 | 17.2 | 14.9 | 24.2 | 14.2 | 23.6 |
| 2003 | 10.3 | 14.7 | 12.0 | 21.2 | 12.8 | 21.3 |
| 2005 | 7.0 | 17.1 | 12.4 | 21.5 | 12.0 | 21.8 |
| **Attempted suicide** | | | | | | |
| 1991 | 3.3% | 9.4% | 3.3% | 10.4% | 3.9% | 10.7% |
| 1993 | 5.4 | 11.2 | 4.4 | 11.3 | 5.0 | 12.5 |
| 1995 | 7.0 | 10.8 | 5.2 | 10.4 | 5.6 | 11.9 |
| 1997 | 5.6 | 9.0 | 3.2 | 10.3 | 4.5 | 11.6 |
| 1999 | 7.1 | 7.5 | 4.5 | 9.0 | 5.7 | 10.9 |
| 2001 | 7.5 | 9.8 | 5.3 | 10.3 | 6.2 | 11.2 |
| 2003 | 7.7 | 9.0 | 3.7 | 10.3 | 5.4 | 11.5 |
| 2005 | 5.2 | 9.8 | 5.2 | 9.3 | 6.0 | 10.8 |
| **Suicide attempt requiring medical attention** | | | | | | |
| 1991 | 0.4% | 2.9% | 1.0% | 2.3% | 1.0% | 2.5% |
| 1993 | 2.0 | 4.0 | 1.4 | 3.6 | 1.6 | 3.8 |
| 1995 | 2.8 | 3.6 | 2.1 | 2.9 | 2.2 | 3.4 |
| 1997 | 1.8 | 3.0 | 1.5 | 2.6 | 2.0 | 3.3 |
| 1999 | 3.4 | 2.4 | 1.6 | 2.3 | 2.1 | 3.1 |
| 2001 | 3.6 | 3.1 | 1.7 | 2.9 | 2.1 | 3.1 |
| 2003 | 5.2 | 2.2 | 1.1 | 2.4 | 2.4 | 3.2 |
| 2005 | 1.4 | 2.6 | 1.5 | 2.7 | 1.8 | 2.9 |

Source: US Department of Health and Human Services, Centers for Disease Control and Prevention, *Health United States, 2007*, table 62.

Notes: 'White' and 'Black' exclude White Hispanics and Black Hispanics, repectively.
Data is drawn from the National Youth Risk Factor Survey. Responses are for the 12 months preceding the survey.

Units: Percent of students in grades 9-12.

## Table 2.52: Health Care Coverage for Persons Under 65 Years of Age, by Type of Coverage, 1995 and 2000–2004

| | Black | White | All Races |
|---|---|---|---|
| **1995** | | | |
| Private insurance | 53.0% | 74.5% | 71.3% |
| Obtained through workplace | 49.3 | 68.4 | 65.4 |
| Medicaid or other public assistance | 28.5 | 8.9 | 11.5 |
| No health insurance coverage | 18.0 | 15.5 | 16.1 |
| **2000** | | | |
| Private insurance | 55.9% | 75.7% | 71.5% |
| Obtained through workplace | 53.1 | 70.6 | 66.7 |
| Medicaid or other public assistance | 21.2 | 7.1 | 9.5 |
| No health insurance coverage | 19.5 | 15.4 | 17.0 |
| **2001** | | | |
| Private insurance | 56.5% | 75.1% | 71.2% |
| Obtained through workplace | 54.2 | 70.2 | 66.7 |
| Medicaid or other public assistance | 22.1 | 8.0 | 10.4 |
| No health insurance coverage | 18.8 | 14.9 | 16.4 |
| **2002** | | | |
| Private insurance | 55.1% | 73.4% | 69.4% |
| Obtained through workplace | 52.4 | 68.7 | 65.0 |
| Medicaid or other public assistance | 23.2 | 9.3 | 11.8 |
| No health insurance coverage | 18.8 | 15.5 | 16.8 |

*(continued on next page)*

## Table 2.52: Health Care Coverage for Persons Under 65 Years of Age, by Type of Coverage, 1995 and 2000–2004

|  | Black | White | All Races |
|---|---|---|---|
| **2003** | | | |
| Private insurance | 54.9% | 71.5% | 68.9% |
| Obtained through workplace | 51.5 | 65.6 | 63.3 |
| Medicaid or other public assistance | 23.7 | 10.4 | 12.3 |
| No health insurance coverage | 18.4 | 16.0 | 16.5 |
| **2004** | | | |
| Private insurance | 53.9% | 71.4% | 68.8% |
| Obtained through workplace | 51.0 | 65.8 | 63.5 |
| Medicaid or other public assistance | 24.9 | 10.4 | 12.5 |
| No health insurance coverage | 17.6 | 16.1 | 16.4 |

Source : US Department of Health and Human Services, Centers for Disease Control and Prevention, National Center for Health Statistics, *Health, United States, 2006*, tables 133-135.

Notes: 'All Races' includes races not shown separately.

'Medicaid' includes persons receiving AFDC (Aid to Families with Dependent Children) or SSI (Supplemental Security Income), or those with a current Medicaid card.

Data is age-adjusted. The questionnaire changed in 1997 compared with previous years. Beginning in quarter 3 of the 2004 NHIS, persons under 65 years with no reported coverage were asked explicitly about Medicaid coverage. Estimates shown here were calculated with this additional information.

Units: Percent of the population under 65 years of age.

## Table 2.53: People Lacking Health Insurance Coverage, 2002–2006

|  | Black | White | Total |
|---|---|---|---|
| **2002** | | | |
| All people | 18.4% | 14.2% | 15.2% |
| Children under 18 | NA | 11.1 | 11.6 |
| **2003** | | | |
| All people | 18.8% | 14.6% | 15.6% |
| Children under 18 | 12.4 | 7.4 | 11.4 |
| **2004** | | | |
| All people | 16.8% | 14.9% | 15.7% |
| Children under 18 | 9.4 | 7.6 | 11.2 |
| **2005** | | | |
| All people | 19.3% | 15.0% | 15.9% |
| Children under 18 | 12.5 | 7.2 | 11.2 |
| **2006** | | | |
| All people | 20.5% | 14.9% | 15.8% |
| Children under 18 | 14.1 | 7.3 | 11.7 |

Source: US Bureau of the Census, Current Population Reports, *Income, Poverty, and Health Insurance Coverage in the United States: 2003*, table 5 and figure 7; *2004*, table 7 and figure 7; *2005*, table C-1 and figure 8; *2006*, tables C-1 and C2, and figure 8.

Notes: 'Total' includes races and ethnic groups not shown separately. 'White' and 'Black' as shown are equivalent to 'White Alone' and 'Black Alone.'
Figures may have been adjusted since their initial publication, and may not match current estimates.

Units: Percent of all people, and children under 18, not covered by government or private health insurance.

## Table 2.54: Health Care Coverage for Persons 65 Years of Age and Over, by Type of Coverage, 1992–2005

|  | Black | White | All Races |
|---|---|---|---|
| **1992** | | | |
| Employer-sponsored plan | 25.9% | 45.9% | 42.8% |
| Medicare HMO | * | 3.6 | 3.9 |
| Medicaid | 28.5 | 5.6 | 9.4 |
| Medigap | 13.6 | 37.2 | 33.9 |
| Other | 26.7 | 7.7 | 9.9 |
| **1995** | | | |
| Employer-sponsored plan | 26.7% | 41.3% | 38.6% |
| Medicare HMO | 7.9 | 8.4 | 8.9 |
| Medicaid | 30.3 | 5.4 | 9.6 |
| Medigap | 10.2 | 36.2 | 32.5 |
| Other | 25.0 | 8.7 | 10.5 |
| **2000** | | | |
| Employer-sponsored plan | 22.0% | 38.6% | 35.2% |
| Medicare HMO | 20.7 | 18.4 | 19.3 |
| Medicaid | 23.6 | 5.1 | 9.0 |
| Medigap | 7.5 | 28.3 | 25.0 |
| Other | 26.1 | 9.6 | 11.5 |
| **2005** | | | |
| Employer-sponsored plan | 27.9% | 39.5% | 36.4% |
| Medicare HMO | 17.1 | 13.2 | 14.5 |
| Medicaid | 23.6 | 6.1 | 10.1 |
| Medigap | 9.5 | 29.1 | 25.7 |
| Other | 21.9 | 12.2 | 13.3 |

Source:  US Department of Health and Human Services, Centers for Disease Control and Prevention, *Health United States, 2007*, table 140.

Notes:  'All Races' includes races not shown separately.
Medicare HMO enrollees are listed regardless of other insurance. Medicaid enrollees exclude those also enrolled in a Medicare HMO. 'Medigap' includes supplemental insurance plans purchased privately or through organizations such as AARP or professional organizations. 'Other' includes Medicare fee-for-service only or other public plans besides Medicaid.
Data is age-adjusted. The questionnaire changed in 1997 compared with previous years.
* Data drawn from a sample size of 50 or smaller, and are not shown here.

Units:  Percent of people over 65.

## Table 2.55:  Health Care Visits, 2000 and 2005

|  | Black | White | All Races |
|---|---|---|---|
| **2000** | | | |
| *All visits* | *353* | *380* | *374* |
| Physician offices | 239 | 315 | 304 |
| Hospital outpatient | 52 | 28 | 31 |
| Hospital emergency department | 62 | 37 | 40 |
| **Number of health care visits** | | | |
| None | 17.3% | 16.0% | 16.6% |
| 1-3 visits | 46.7 | 45.1 | 45.4 |
| 4-9 visits | 23.4 | 25.3 | 24.7 |
| 10 or more visits | 12.6 | 13.7 | 13.3 |
| **2005** | | | |
| *All visits* | *398* | *413* | *400* |
| Physician offices | 270 | 347 | 329 |
| Hospital outpatient | 58 | 28 | 31 |
| Hospital emergency department | 70 | 37 | 40 |
| **Number of health care visits** | | | |
| None | 16.0% | 15.2% | 15.6% |
| 1-3 visits | 47.5 | 46.0 | 46.2 |
| 4-9 visits | 23.6 | 24.9 | 24.6 |
| 10 or more visits | 12.9 | 14.0 | 13.7 |

Source:   US Department of Health and Human Services, Centers for Disease Control and Prevention, *Health, United States, 2002*, tables 72 and 83; *2007*, tables 82 and 92.

Notes:   'All visits' includes visits to physician offices and hospital outpatient and emergency departments. 'Health care visits' includes ambulatory and home health care visits during a 12-month period.
All visits per person are age-adjusted.

Units:   Number of visits per 100 persons; percent of persons with specified number of health care visits within the last 12 months.

## Table 2.56: Dental Visits in the Past Year, by Age and Poverty Status, 2000 and 2005

|  | Black | White | All Races |
|---|---|---|---|
| **2000** |  |  |  |
| **Poor** |  |  |  |
| *Age 2 and older* | *46.0%* | *52.0%* | *47.6%* |
| 2-17 years | 67.5 | 63.0 | 61.8 |
| 18-64 years | 45.3 | 52.1 | 46.7 |
| 65 years and older | 17.3 | 34.4 | 30.3 |
| **Non-Poor** |  |  |  |
| *Age 2 and older* | *66.0%* | *75.0%* | *73.1%* |
| 2-17 years | 73.9 | 82.5 | 80.1 |
| 18-64 years | 65.4 | 73.8 | 72.0 |
| 65 years and older | 55.1 | 68.3 | 66.7 |
| **2005** |  |  |  |
| **Poor** |  |  |  |
| *Age 2 and older* | *52.5%* | *51.5%* | *50.4%* |
| 2-17 years | 71.1 | 65.0 | 66.2 |
| 18-64 years | 44.1 | 49.6 | 44.6 |
| 65 years and older | 24.6 | 37.9 | 34.7 |
| **Non-Poor** |  |  |  |
| *Age 2 and older* | *67.6%* | *74.6%* | *72.6%* |
| 2-17 years | 75.9 | 84.2 | 82.0 |
| 18-64 years | 66.7 | 72.8 | 70.5 |
| 65 years and older | 50.7 | 69.7 | 67.8 |

Source: US Department of Health and Human Services, Centers for Disease Control and Prevention, *Health, United States, 2002*, table 80; *2007*, table 94.

Notes: 'All Races' includes races not shown separately. 'Black' and 'White' exclude Black Hispanics and White Hispanics, respectively. Data excludes residents of US Territories.
'Poor' persons are defined as below the poverty threshold. 'Non-poor' persons have incomes of at least 200% of the poverty threshold.

Units: Percent of persons with a dental visit in the past year.

## Table 2.57: Short Stay Hospitals: Discharges, Days of Care, and Average Length of Stay, 2000–2003

|  | Black | White | All Races |
|---|---|---|---|
| **2000** | | | |
| Discharges | 122.6 | 92.2 | 119.8 |
| Days of Care | 526.6 | 354.4 | 557.8 |
| Average length of stay | 4.3 | 3.8 | 4.7 |
| **2001** | | | |
| Discharges | 131.2 | 93.2 | 121.9 |
| Days of Care | 661.1 | 368.6 | 553.6 |
| Average length of stay | 5.0 | 4.0 | 4.5 |
| **2002** | | | |
| Discharges | 121.3 | 96.4 | 122.9 |
| Days of Care | 536.4 | 342.5 | 541.3 |
| Average length of stay | 4.4 | 3.6 | 4.4 |
| **2003** | | | |
| Discharges | 124.8 | 93.2 | 119.9 |
| Days of Care | 623.7 | 378.3 | 558.9 |
| Average length of stay | 5.0 | 4.1 | 4.7 |

Source: US Department of Health and Human Services, Centers for Disease Control and Prevention, National Center for Health Statistics, *Health, United States, 2005*, table 96.

Notes: 'All Races' includes races not shown separately.
Data is age-adjusted.

Units: Number of discharges and days of care per 1,000 population; average length of stay in days.

## Table 2.58: Sources of Payment for Health Care, 1987–2004

| | Black | | White | | All Races | |
|---|---|---|---|---|---|---|
| | Under 65 | 65 and Over | Under 65 | 65 and Over | Under 65 | 65 and Over |
| **1987** | | | | | | |
| Out of Pocket | 15.5% | 11.2% | 28.2% | 23.7% | 26.2% | 22.0% |
| Private insurance | 30.0 | *11.9 | 50.1 | 16.7 | 46.6 | 15.8 |
| Public coverage | 47.2 | 76.3 | 15.9 | 58.0 | 21.3 | 60.8 |
| Other | 7.3 | 0.6 | 5.8 | 1.6 | 6.0 | 1.5 |
| **1997** | | | | | | |
| Out of Pocket | 17.1% | 11.4% | 21.8% | 17.0% | 21.1% | 16.3% |
| Private insurance | 42.3 | 8.8 | 55.8 | 17.9 | 53.1 | 16.5 |
| Public coverage | 30.7 | 77.6 | 15.3 | 62.6 | 18.1 | 64.8 |
| Other | 9.9 | 2.2 | 7.1 | 2.5 | 7.7 | 2.5 |
| **2000** | | | | | | |
| Out of Pocket | 11.8% | 13.6% | 21.7% | 18.3% | 20.3% | 17.5% |
| Private insurance | 40.5 | 9.3 | 55.1 | 15.2 | 52.5 | 14.9 |
| Public coverage | 38.8 | 68.3 | 18.0 | 64.1 | 21.3 | 64.7 |
| Other | 8.8 | *8.9 | 5.2 | 2.4 | 6.0 | 2.9 |
| **2004** | | | | | | |
| Out of Pocket | 14.7% | 14.0% | 20.1% | 18.2% | 19.5% | 17.8% |
| Private insurance | 39.5 | 10.1 | 59.4 | 16.7 | 55.0 | 15.8 |
| Public coverage | 39.9 | 74.7 | 16.2 | 63.0 | 20.8 | 64.2 |
| Other | 5.9 | 1.2 | 4.3 | 2.2 | 4.7 | 2.2 |

**Source:** US Department of Health and Human Services, Centers for Disease Control and Prevention, *Health, United States, 2007*, table 129.

**Notes:** 'White' and 'Black' exclude Hispanics.
'Public coverage' includes Medicare, Medicaid, the Department of Veterans Affairs, and other federal sources.
* Estimates are considered unreliable and should be treated with caution.

**Units:** Percent of noninstutional population.

## Table 2.59: Health Care Expenses, by Age Group, 1987 and 2004

|  | Black | White | All Races |
|---|---|---|---|
| **1987** | | | |
| *Under 65 years of age* | | | |
| Percent with expenses | 72.2% | 86.9% | 83.2% |
| Mean annual expense | $2,446 | $2,029 | $2,022 |
| Percent with prescribed medicine expense | 44.1% | 57.7% | 54.0% |
| Mean annual out-of-pocket expense | $100 | $118 | $113 |
| *65 years old and over* | | | |
| Percent with expenses | 88.5% | 94.9% | 93.7% |
| Mean annual expense | $7,732 | $6,316 | $6,415 |
| Percent with prescribed medicine expense | 79.5% | 82.3% | 81.6% |
| Mean annual out-of-pocket expense | $276 | $359 | $353 |
| **2004** | | | |
| *Under 65 years of age* | | | |
| Percent with expenses | 75.2% | 87.7% | 82.9% |
| Mean annual expense | $2,635 | $3,406 | $3,028 |
| Percent with prescribed medicine expense | 50.6% | 64.6% | 58.5% |
| Mean annual out-of-pocket expense | $269 | $333 | $304 |
| *65 years old and over* | | | |
| Percent with expenses | 95.6% | 97.6% | 97.1% |
| Mean annual expense | $8,035 | $9,316 | $8,906 |
| Percent with prescribed medicine expense | 90.6% | 92.6% | 91.9% |
| Mean annual out-of-pocket expense | $943 | $1,062 | $1,027 |

Source: US Department of Health and Human Services, Centers for Disease Control and Prevention, *Health, United States, 2007*, table 128.

Notes: 'White' and 'Black' exclude White Hispanics and Black Hispanics, repectively.
Expenses include inpatient hospital services, physician services, prescribed medicines, home health services, dental services, and other medical equipment. Dollar figures have been updated to 2004 dollars using the Consumer Price Index.

Units: Percent of total people; mean annual expenses for people with applicable expenses.

# Chapter 3

## Education

## Chapter Three Highlights

This chapter provides statistics about education for Black persons in the United States, including both the most current data available as well as comparisons of the Black population over time. For almost all tables, corresponding data is provided for the total population of the United States as well as for White persons. This allows for easy comparison between groups.

This chapter contains enrollment statistics for students below grade 12 by age (table 3.01); control of school (public or private) and family status (tables 3.02, 3.07, and 3.10); and for nursery school and Kindergarten students (tables 3.03). We have also included tables showing percentages of persons aged 3 to 34 who are enrolled in school (table 3.06), percentage distribution of enrollment in school by state (table 3.07), and percentages of students in gifted and talented programs (table 3.08).

Along with this data on enrollment, we have included enrollment status and enrollment rates of high school graduates and college students (tables 3.23 and 3.24). Also included are statistics on high school dropouts (tables 3.16 and 3.17).

This chapter also provides data on public school teachers, such as highest degree earned and years of teaching experience (tables 3.09 and 3.10).

Also included in this chapter is a variety of data on standardized test results, both for proficiency tests (tables 3.11 and 3.12) and for the SAT and ACT tests (tables 3.14 and 3.15).

Also of note are tables on degrees conferred by field of study for Associate's Degrees (table 3.25), Bachelor's Degrees (table 3.26), Master's Degrees (table 3.27), Doctoral Degrees (table 3.28), and Professional Degrees (table 3.29).

## Table 3.01: School Enrollment by Age, 2006

| | Enrollment | | | Enrollment Rate | | |
|---|---|---|---|---|---|---|
| | **Black** | **White** | **All Races** | **Black** | **White** | **All Races** |
| *All persons 3 years and over* | *11,400* | *57,419* | *75,197* | *32.3%* | *25.3%* | *26.6%* |
| 3 and 4 years old | 732 | 3,463 | 4,534 | 59.2 | 55.6 | 55.7 |
| 5 and 6 years | 1,132 | 5,851 | 7,628 | 92.6 | 95.0 | 94.6 |
| 7 to 9 years | 1,723 | 8,717 | 11,444 | 97.1 | 98.4 | 98.2 |
| 10 to 13 years | 2,454 | 12,285 | 16,060 | 97.2 | 98.4 | 98.3 |
| 14 to 15 years | 1,325 | 6,294 | 8,252 | 97.5 | 98.4 | 98.3 |
| 16 and 17 years | 1,268 | 6,266 | 8,203 | 93.3 | 95.0 | 94.6 |
| 18 and 19 years | 796 | 4,103 | 5,306 | 64.7 | 64.9 | 65.5 |
| 20 and 21 years | 474 | 3,040 | 3,839 | 39.1 | 48.2 | 47.5 |
| 22 to 24 years | 447 | 2,436 | 3,256 | 27.2 | 25.5 | 26.7 |
| 25 to 29 years | 322 | 1,781 | 2,373 | 11.8 | 11.3 | 11.7 |
| 30 to 34 years | 209 | 1,001 | 1,376 | 8.6 | 6.7 | 7.2 |
| 35 to 44 years | 254 | 1,218 | 1,631 | 4.8 | 3.6 | 3.8 |
| 45 to 54 years | 204 | 677 | 924 | 4.0 | 1.9 | 2.1 |
| 55 years and over | 59 | 287 | 371 | 0.9 | 0.5 | 0.6 |

**Source:** US Bureau of the Census, Current Population Reports, *School Enrollment: Social and Economic Characteristics of Students, October 2006*, table 1.

**Notes:** 'All Races' includes races not shown separately. 'White' as shown is equivalent to 'White alone' and 'Black' as shown is equivalent to 'Black alone.'

**Units:** Persons enrolled in thousands; percent of the civilian noninstitutional population, by age group.

## Table 3.02: School Enrollment, by Control of School and Family Status, 2006

**Kindergarten, elementary, and high school**

|  | Black | White | All Races |
|---|---|---|---|
| *All families* | *9,377* | *63,637* | *78,099* |
| Public | 4,433 | 21,443 | 27,858 |
| Private | 287 | 2,262 | 2,733 |
| *Married couple families* | *4,168* | *50,513* | *58,507* |
| Public | 1,570 | 15,577 | 18,526 |
| Private | 113 | 1,884 | 2,137 |
| *Unmarried householder* | *5,208* | *13,124* | *19,592* |
| Public | 2,863 | 5,866 | 9,333 |
| Private | 174 | 378 | 596 |

Source: US Bureau of the Census, Current Population Reports, *School Enrollment: Social and Economic Characteristics of Students, October 2006*, table 8.

Notes: 'All Races' includes races not shown separately. 'White' as shown is equivalent to 'White alone' and 'Black' as shown is equivalent to 'Black alone.'
Includes civilian non-institutional population only.
'Public' is equivalent to 'Public only' and 'Private' is equivalent to 'Private only.'

Units: Number of families with enrolled children in thousands.

## Table 3.03: Nursery School and Kindergarten Enrollment of Children 3 to 6 Years Old

|  | Black | White | All Races |
|---|---|---|---|
| *Total Children 3–6* | *2,460* | *12,389* | *16,203* |
| **Enrolled in nursery school** |  |  |  |
| Total | 715 | 4,688 | 4,688 |
| Public | 513 | 2,519 | 2,519 |
| Private | 202 | 2,169 | 2,169 |
| **Enrolled in kindergarten** |  |  |  |
| Total | 589 | 3,062 | 3,994 |
| Public | 518 | 2,680 | 3,508 |
| Private | 71 | 382 | 487 |
| **Enrolled in elementary school** |  |  |  |
| Total | 561 | 2,628 | 3,479 |
| Public | 508 | 2,345 | 3,113 |
| Private | 53 | 284 | 366 |

Source:  US Bureau of the Census, Current Population Reports, *School Enrollment: Social and Economic Characteristics of Students, October 2006*, table 3.

Notes:  'All Races' includes races not shown separately. 'White' as shown is equivalent to 'White alone,' and 'Black' as shown is equivalent to 'Black alone.'
'Public' is equivalent to 'Public only' and 'Private' is equivalent to 'Private only.'

Units:  Number of enrolled children in thousands.

## Table 3.04: Estimates of the School-Age Population, 1980–2006

|  | Black | | White | | All Races |
|---|---|---|---|---|---|
|  | Number | Percent | Number | Percent | Number |
| 1980 | 6,840 | 14.5% | 35,220 | 74.6% | 47,232 |
| 1985 | 6,569 | 14.7 | 32,099 | 71.7 | 44,782 |
| 1990 | NA | NA | NA | NA | 45,359 |
| 1995 | NA | NA | NA | NA | 49,838 |
| 2000 | 7,989 | 15.0 | 33,016 | 62.1 | 53,177 |
| 2001 | 7,991 | 15.0 | 32,801 | 61.6 | 53,262 |
| 2002 | 7,981 | 15.0 | 32,552 | 61.0 | 53,325 |
| 2003 | 7,954 | 14.9 | 32,210 | 60.5 | 53,269 |
| 2004 | 7,913 | 14.9 | 31,877 | 59.9 | 53,198 |
| 2005 | 7,881 | 14.8 | 31,571 | 59.3 | 53,219 |
| 2006 | 7,872 | 14.8 | 31,304 | 58.7 | 53,318 |

Source: US Department of Education, Center for Education Statistics, *Digest of Education Statistics, 2007*, table 16.

Notes: 'School-age population' is defined as persons between 5 and 17 years.
'All Races' includes races not shown separately.
Some data has been revised from previously published figures.
Data for civilian non-institutionalized population, as of July 1.

Units: Population between 5 and 17 in thousands of persons; percent of total persons by age group.

## Table 3.05: Students Who are Foreign-born or Who Have Foreign-born Parents, 2005

|  | Black | White | All Races |
|---|---|---|---|
| **Elementary and high school** |  |  |  |
| Total | 1,047 | 7,636 | 10,980 |
| Foreign-born students | 310 | 1,694 | 2,465 |
| Students with at least one foreign-born parent | 737 | 5,941 | 8,485 |
| **College** |  |  |  |
| Total | 416 | 1,846 | 3,151 |
| Foreign-born students | 254 | 783 | 1,528 |
| Students with at least one foreign-born parent | 163 | 1,063 | 1,623 |
| **Graduate school** |  |  |  |
| Total | 45 | 467 | 890 |
| Foreign-born students | 32 | 236 | 525 |
| Students with at least one foreign-born parent | 13 | 231 | 364 |

Source: US Bureau of Census, *Statistical Abstract of the United States, 2008*, table 216.

Notes: 'All Races' includes races not shown separately.

Units: Number of students in thousands.

## Table 3.06: Percent of the Population
## Age 3-34 Enrolled in School, 2006

| | Black | White | All Races |
|---|---|---|---|
| **Both sexes** | | | |
| *Total, 3-34 years* | *58.1%* | *55.5%* | *56.0%* |
| 3-4 years | 59.2 | 55.6 | 55.7 |
| 5-6 years | 92.6 | 95.0 | 94.6 |
| 7-9 years | 97.1 | 98.4 | 98.2 |
| 10-13 years | 97.2 | 98.4 | 98.3 |
| 14-15 years | 97.5 | 98.4 | 98.3 |
| 16-17 years | 93.3 | 95.0 | 94.6 |
| 18-19 years | 64.7 | 64.9 | 65.5 |
| 20-21 years | 39.1 | 48.2 | 47.5 |
| 22-24 years | 27.2 | 25.5 | 26.7 |
| 25-29 years | 11.8 | 11.3 | 11.7 |
| 30-34 years | 8.6 | 6.7 | 7.2 |
| **Male** | | | |
| *Total, 3-34 years* | *58.6%* | *54.6%* | *55.5%* |
| 3-4 years | 56.6 | 55.9 | 56.0 |
| 5-6 years | 93.5 | 94.8 | 94.4 |
| 7-9 years | 97.2 | 98.3 | 98.1 |
| 10-13 years | 96.8 | 98.4 | 98.2 |
| 14-15 years | 97.7 | 98.2 | 98.2 |
| 16-17 years | 91.8 | 94.7 | 94.1 |
| 18-19 years | 63.9 | 62.7 | 63.6 |
| 20-21 years | 38.0 | 43.8 | 44.0 |
| 22-24 years | 24.2 | 24.0 | 25.0 |
| 25-29 years | 9.3 | 10.2 | 10.4 |
| 30-34 years | 6.9 | 5.5 | 5.9 |

*(continued on next page)*

## Table 3.06: Percent of the Population
## Age 3-34 Enrolled in School, 2006

|  | Black | White | All Races |
|---|---|---|---|
| **Female** | | | |
| *Total, 3-34 years* | *57.7%* | *56.3%* | *56.6%* |
| 3-4 years | 61.5 | 55.3 | 55.4 |
| 5-6 years | 91.7 | 95.2 | 94.8 |
| 7-9 years | 96.9 | 98.5 | 98.3 |
| 10-13 years | 97.6 | 98.5 | 98.4 |
| 14-15 years | 97.2 | 98.7 | 98.4 |
| 16-17 years | 94.7 | 95.3 | 95.0 |
| 18-19 years | 65.4 | 67.2 | 67.4 |
| 20-21 years | 40.2 | 52.6 | 51.1 |
| 22-24 years | 30.0 | 27.1 | 28.5 |
| 25-29 years | 14.0 | 12.4 | 13.0 |
| 30-34 years | 9.9 | 8.0 | 8.5 |

Source: US Bureau of the Census, Current Population Reports, *School Enrollment: Social and Economic Characteristics of Students, October 2006*, table 1.

Notes: 'All Races' includes races not shown separately. 'White' as shown is equivalent to 'White alone' and 'Black' as shown is equivalent to 'Black alone.'
Estimates of the civilian non-institutional population 3 years old and older as of October 1.

Units: Percent of the total population enrolled in school.

## Table 3.07: Percentage Distribution of Enrollment in Public Elementary and Secondary Schools by State, 1995 and 2005

|  | Fall 1995 | | Fall 2005 | |
|---|---|---|---|---|
|  | Black | White | Black | White |
| *United States* | *16.8%* | *64.8%* | *17.2%* | *57.1%* |
| Alabama | 36.0 | 62.1 | 36.0 | 59.4 |
| Alaska | 4.6 | 63.7 | 4.6 | 57.7 |
| Arizona | 4.3 | 56.9 | 5.2 | 47.2 |
| Arkansas | 23.6 | 73.9 | 23.0 | 68.2 |
| California | 8.8 | 40.4 | 8.0 | 31.0 |
| Colorado | 5.5 | 72.5 | 6.0 | 62.5 |
| Connecticut | 13.5 | 72.0 | 13.7 | 67.0 |
| Delaware | 29.4 | 64.7 | 32.5 | 55.1 |
| District of Columbia | 87.6 | 4.0 | 83.3 | 4.5 |
| Florida | 25.3 | 57.5 | 23.9 | 49.6 |
| Georgia | 37.8 | 58.2 | 39.2 | 49.2 |
| Hawaii | 2.6 | 22.9 | 2.4 | 19.8 |
| Idaho | 0.6 | 88.4 | 1.0 | 83.0 |
| Illinois | 21.1 | 63.6 | 20.6 | 56.4 |
| Indiana | 11.1 | 85.6 | 12.5 | 80.3 |
| Iowa | 3.3 | 92.7 | 5.1 | 86.6 |
| Kansas | 8.5 | 82.6 | 8.6 | 75.4 |
| Kentucky | 9.8 | 89.1 | 10.6 | 86.3 |
| Louisiana | 46.0 | 51.0 | 44.4 | 51.5 |
| Maine | 0.8 | 97.3 | 2.0 | 95.1 |
| Maryland | 35.0 | 57.5 | 38.1 | 48.6 |
| Massachusetts | 8.2 | 78.5 | 8.4 | 73.5 |
| Michigan | 18.4 | 76.4 | 20.3 | 71.9 |
| Minnesota | 4.8 | 87.4 | 8.5 | 78.3 |
| Mississippi | 51.0 | 47.7 | 51.2 | 46.5 |
| Missouri | 16.1 | 81.7 | 18.2 | 76.6 |
| Montana | 0.5 | 87.5 | 0.9 | 84.3 |
| Nebraska | 5.9 | 87.2 | 7.6 | 77.5 |

*(continued on next page)*

## Table 3.07: Percentage Distribution of Enrollment in Public Elementary and Secondary Schools by State, 1995 and 2005

| | Fall 1995 | | Fall 2005 | |
|---|---|---|---|---|
| | Black | White | Black | White |
| *United States* | *16.8%* | *64.8%* | *17.2%* | *57.1%* |
| Nevada | 9.8 | 66.5 | 11.1 | 46.4 |
| New Hampshire | 0.9 | 96.7 | 1.7 | 93.3 |
| New Jersey | 18.5 | 62.5 | 17.6 | 56.5 |
| New Mexico | 2.4 | 39.5 | 2.5 | 31.1 |
| New York | 20.2 | 56.9 | 19.8 | 52.7 |
| North Carolina | 30.7 | 64.6 | 31.5 | 56.6 |
| North Dakota | 0.8 | 90.8 | 1.5 | 87.2 |
| Ohio | 15.3 | 82.2 | 17.1 | 79.0 |
| Oklahoma | 10.5 | 69.4 | 10.9 | 59.6 |
| Oregon | 2.6 | 85.3 | 3.2 | 73.6 |
| Pennsylvania | 14.0 | 80.6 | 16.2 | 74.8 |
| Rhode Island | 7.0 | 78.9 | 8.6 | 70.4 |
| South Carolina | 42.1 | 56.3 | 40.3 | 54.0 |
| South Dakota | 0.9 | 83.7 | 1.6 | 85.0 |
| Tennessee | 23.1 | 75.3 | 25.1 | 69.5 |
| Texas | 14.3 | 46.4 | 14.7 | 36.5 |
| Utah | 0.7 | 90.4 | 1.3 | 81.8 |
| Vermont | 0.7 | 97.3 | 1.5 | 95.5 |
| Virginia | 26.5 | 66.6 | 27.0 | 59.8 |
| Washington | 4.7 | 78.3 | 5.7 | 69.8 |
| West Virginia | 4.0 | 95.2 | 5.0 | 93.6 |
| Wisconsin | 9.4 | 83.2 | 10.5 | 77.8 |
| Wyoming | 1.0 | 89.3 | 1.5 | 84.9 |

Source:  U.S. Department of Education, National Center for Education Statistics, *Digest of Education Statistics, 2007*, table 40.

Notes:  Both 'Black' and 'White' exclude persons of Hispanic origin. Based on students whose ethnicity was reported.

Units:  Percent of total enrollment.

## Table 3.08: Percent of Gifted and Talented Students in Public Elementary and Secondary Schools by State, 2004

|  | Black | White | All Races |
|---|---|---|---|
| *United States* | 3.5% | 7.9% | 6.7% |
| Alabama | 2.4 | 6.3 | 4.8 |
| Alaska | 2.1 | 5.8 | 4.1 |
| Arizona | 3.5 | 8.4 | 5.9 |
| Arkansas | 7.1 | 11.2 | 9.9 |
| California | 4.6 | 12.0 | 8.4 |
| Colorado | 5.2 | 7.9 | 6.7 |
| Connecticut | 1.7 | 3.5 | 3.0 |
| Delaware | 2.2 | 6.1 | 4.6 |
| Florida | 2.0 | 5.7 | 4.5 |
| Georgia | 3.7 | 13.6 | 8.9 |
| Hawaii | 2.9 | 7.7 | 5.7 |
| Idaho | 1.7 | 4.4 | 3.9 |
| Illinois | 2.5 | 6.7 | 5.4 |
| Indiana | 3.8 | 7.7 | 7.1 |
| Iowa | 4.6 | 9.0 | 8.5 |
| Kansas | 1.1 | 3.9 | 3.3 |
| Kentucky | 5.2 | 14.2 | 13.0 |
| Louisiana | 1.9 | 5.5 | 3.9 |
| Maine | 1.3 | 3.1 | 3.0 |
| Maryland | 6.7 | 17.0 | 13.8 |
| Massachusetts | 0.7 | 0.8 | 0.8 |
| Michigan | 3.0 | 4.1 | 3.9 |
| Minnesota | 5.2 | 8.3 | 8.1 |
| Mississippi | 3.3 | 9.1 | 6.0 |
| Missouri | 1.7 | 4.3 | 3.8 |
| Montana | 2.8 | 6.0 | 5.6 |
| Nebraska | 6.4 | 12.8 | 11.4 |
| Nevada | 0.8 | 2.8 | 1.9 |

*(continued on next page)*

## Table 3.08: Percent of Gifted and Talented Students in Public Elementary and Secondary Schools by State, 2004

|  | Black | White | All Races |
|---|---|---|---|
| *United States* | *3.5%* | *7.9%* | *6.7%* |
| New Hampshire | 0.6 | 2.3 | 2.3 |
| New Jersey | 3.3 | 8.4 | 6.9 |
| New Mexico | 9.6 | 12.6 | 10.7 |
| New York | 0.8 | 3.4 | 2.2 |
| North Carolina | 3.9 | 15.7 | 10.9 |
| North Dakota | 2.3 | 2.8 | 3.1 |
| Ohio | 6.5 | 7.6 | 7.4 |
| Oklahoma | 7.7 | 16.6 | 14.0 |
| Oregon | 3.6 | 8.0 | 7.1 |
| Pennsylvania | 2.7 | 5.3 | 4.8 |
| Rhode Island | 1.5 | 2.0 | 1.8 |
| South Carolina | 5.9 | 17.8 | 12.7 |
| South Dakota | 1.2 | 2.4 | 2.2 |
| Tennessee | 4.5 | 2.9 | 3.3 |
| Texas | 4.9 | 11.2 | 8.0 |
| Utah | 5.1 | 4.5 | 4.6 |
| Vermont | 0.4 | 0.8 | 0.8 |
| Virginia | 4.6 | 14.9 | 12.1 |
| Washington | 1.4 | 4.2 | 3.8 |
| West Virginia | 1.4 | 2.2 | 2.2 |
| Wisconsin | 2.0 | 7.8 | 6.8 |
| Wyoming | 1.5 | 3.5 | 3.2 |

**Source:** US Department of Education, National Center for Education Statistics, *Digest of Education Statistics, 2007*, table 51.

**Notes:** 'All Races' includes races not shown separately. 'White' as shown is equivalent to 'White alone' and 'Black' as shown is equivalent to 'Black alone.'

**Units:** Percent of all primary school and secondary school students in gifted and talented programs.

## Table 3.09: Public Elementary and Secondary School Teachers, by Selected Characteristics, 1999–2000

|  | Black | White | All Races |
|---|---|---|---|
| *Total number of teachers* | *228,000* | *2,532,000* | *3,002,000* |
| **By highest degree earned** | | | |
| Bachelor's degree | 51.5% | 51.6% | NA |
| Master's degree | 42.0 | 44.2 | NA |
| Education specialist | 4.0 | 3.0 | NA |
| Doctorate | 1.6 | 0.6 | NA |
| **By years of full-time teaching experience** | | | |
| Less than 3 years | 20.8% | 17.1% | NA |
| 3-9 years | 22.0 | 23.2 | NA |
| 10-20 years | 24.5 | 29.1 | NA |
| Over 20 years | 32.7 | 30.6 | NA |

Source:    US Bureau of Census, *Statistical Abstract of the United States, 2003*, table 249.

Notes:    'All Races' includes races not shown separately. Both 'Black' and 'White' exclude persons of Hispanic origin.

Units:    Number of public elementary and secondary teachers; percent of all public elementary and secondary school teachers.

## Table 3.10: Private Elementary and Secondary School Teachers, by Selected Characteristics, 1999–2000

|  | Black | White | All Races |
|---|---|---|---|
| *Total number of teachers* | *17,000* | *402,000* | *449,000* |
| **By highest degree earned** | | | |
| Bachelor's degree | 59.1% | 58.3% | NA |
| Master's degree | 18.7 | 31.8 | NA |
| Education specialist | 2.1 | 1.7 | NA |
| Doctorate | 0.7 | 1.8 | NA |
| **By years of full-time teaching experience** | | | |
| Less than 3 years | 37.6% | 29.1% | NA |
| 3-9 years | 24.8 | 25.0 | NA |
| 10-20 years | 22.5 | 27.4 | NA |
| Over 20 years | 15.1 | 18.5 | NA |

Source: US Bureau of Census, *Statistical Abstract of the United States, 2003*, table 263.

Notes: 'All Races' includes races not shown separately. Both 'Black' and 'White' exclude persons of Hispanic origin.

Units: Number of public elementary and secondary teachers; percent of all private elementary and secondary school teachers.

## Table 3.11: Percent of Students At or Above Selected Reading Proficiency Levels by Age, 2004

|  | Black | White | All Races |
|---|---|---|---|
| **9 year-olds** |  |  |  |
| Level 150 | 91% | 98% | 96% |
| Level 200 | 51 | 78 | 70 |
| Level 250 | 8 | 25 | 20 |
| **13 year-olds** |  |  |  |
| Level 200 | 89% | 96% | 94% |
| Level 250 | 45 | 69 | 61 |
| Level 300 | 5 | 17 | 13 |
| **17 year-olds** |  |  |  |
| Level 250 | 67% | 86% | 80% |
| Level 300 | 17 | 45 | 38 |

Source:  US Department of Education, National Center for Education Statistics, *Digest of Education Statistics, 2005*, table 111.

Notes:  'All Races' includes races not shown separately. 'White' and 'Black' exclude Hispanic. Reading level shown as score on scale:
   150: Able to follow brief written directions and carry out simple discrete reading tasks.
   200: Able to understand, combine ideas, and make inferences based on short uncompli-cated passages about specific or sequentially related information.
   250: Able to search for specific information, interrelate ideas, and make generalizations about literature, science, and social studies materials.
   300: Able to find, understand, summarize, and explain relatively complicated literary and informational material.

Units:  Percent of students scoring at or above the specified level.

## Table 3.12: Percent of Students At or Above Selected Mathematics Proficiency Levels by Age, 2004

|  | Black | White | All Races |
|---|---|---|---|
| **9 year-olds** | | | |
| Level 150 | 97.6% | 99.7% | 99.3% |
| Level 200 | 77.0 | 92.6 | 88.6 |
| Level 250 | 23.6 | 49.0 | 41.9 |
| **13 year-olds** | | | |
| Level 150 | NA | NA | NA |
| Level 200 | 97.2% | 99.1% | 98.6% |
| Level 250 | 67.2 | 90.5 | 83.5 |
| Level 300 | 9.0 | 36.0 | 29.0 |
| **17 year-olds** | | | |
| Level 250 | 91.7% | 98.4% | 96.7% |
| Level 300 | 26.0 | 69.0 | 58.6 |
| Level 350 | 0.9 | 8.5 | 6.9 |

**Source:** US Department of Education, National Center for Education Statistics, *Digest of Education Statistics, 2005*, table 111.

**Notes:** 'All Races' includes races not shown separately. 'White' and 'Black' exclude Hispanic. Mathematics level shown as score on scale:
   150: Simple arithmetic facts.
   200: Beginning skills and understanding.
   250: Numerical operations and beginning problem-solving.
   300: Moderately complex procedures and reasoning.
   350: Multi-step problem-solving and algebra.

**Units:** Percent of students scoring at or above the specified level.

## Table 3.13: Tenth-Grade Students in Schools with Specified Physical or Structural Conditions, 2002

|                              | Black  | White  | All Races |
|------------------------------|--------|--------|-----------|
| Trash on floor               | 29.2%  | 18.1%  | 21.6%     |
| Trash overflowing            | 10.2   | 5.3    | 6.4       |
| Graffiti                     | 10.1   | 2.8    | 5.6       |
| Ceiling in disrepair         | 12.0   | 6.6    | 7.8       |
| Floors/walls not clean       | 37.2   | 28.4   | 30.5      |
| Broken lights                | 5.0    | 3.2    | 3.7       |
| Chipped paint on walls       | 16.3   | 6.2    | 9.6       |
| Broken windows               | 2.1    | 0.4    | 1.0       |
| Doors not on bathroom stalls | 32.7   | 23.3   | 24.7      |

Source:  US Bureau of Census, *Statistical Abstract of the United States, 2007*, table 231.

Notes:  Conditions based on observers' physical inspection of school property. Conditions may be at any location in the school.

Units:  Percent of tenth-grade students.

## Table 3.14: Students Taking the SAT Test and the ACT (American College Testing Program), 1975–2006

| | Black | White |
|---|---|---|
| **1975** | | |
| SAT | 7.9% | 86.0% |
| ACT | 7 | 77 |
| **1980** | | |
| SAT | 9.1% | 82.1% |
| ACT | 8 | 83 |
| **1985** | | |
| SAT | 7.5% | 81.0% |
| ACT | 8 | 82 |
| **1990** | | |
| SAT | 10.0% | 73.0% |
| ACT | 9 | 79 |
| **1995** | | |
| SAT | 10.7% | 69.2% |
| ACT | 10 | 75 |
| **2000** | | |
| SAT | 11.2% | 66.4% |
| ACT | 11 | 76 |
| **2005** | | |
| SAT | 11.6% | 62.3% |
| ACT | 13 | 71 |
| **2006** | | |
| SAT | 11.3% | 62.1% |
| ACT | 13 | 70 |

**Source:** US Bureau of the Census, *Statistical Abstract of the United States, 2008*, tables 258 and 259.

**Notes:** 'All Races' includes races not shown separately.

**Units:** Percent of all students who take each test.

## Table 3.15: SAT Test Scores, 1986–2007

|  | Black | White | All Races |
|---|---|---|---|
| **1986-1987** | | | |
| Verbal score | 428 | 524 | 507 |
| Math score | 411 | 514 | 501 |
| **1990-1991** | | | |
| Verbal score | 427 | 518 | 499 |
| Math score | 419 | 513 | 500 |
| **1995-1996** | | | |
| Verbal score | 434 | 526 | 505 |
| Math score | 422 | 523 | 508 |
| **2000-2001** | | | |
| Verbal score | 433 | 529 | 506 |
| Math score | 426 | 531 | 514 |
| **2001-2002** | | | |
| Verbal score | 430 | 527 | 504 |
| Math score | 427 | 533 | 516 |
| **2002-2003** | | | |
| Verbal score | 431 | 529 | 507 |
| Math score | 426 | 534 | 519 |

*(continued on next page)*

## Chapter 3: Education

## Table 3.15: SAT Test Scores, 1986–2007

|  | Black | White | All Races |
|---|---|---|---|
| **2003-2004** | | | |
| Verbal score | 430 | 528 | 508 |
| Math score | 427 | 531 | 518 |
| **2004-2005** | | | |
| Verbal score | 433 | 532 | 508 |
| Math score | 431 | 536 | 520 |
| **2005-2006** | | | |
| Critical reading | 434 | 527 | 503 |
| Mathematics | 429 | 536 | 518 |
| Writing | 428 | 519 | 497 |
| **2006-2007** | | | |
| Critical reading | 433 | 527 | 502 |
| Mathematics | 429 | 534 | 515 |
| Writing | 425 | 518 | 494 |

Source: US Department of Education, Center for Education Statistics, *Digest of Education Statistics 2007*, table 134.

Notes: 'All Races' includes races not shown separately.
The SAT test was redesigned for the 2005-2006 school year; data from 2005-2006 and 2006-2007 may not be directly comparable with previous years.

Units: Average scores (minimum score=200, maximum score=800).

## Table 3.16: Labor Force Status of 2007 High School Graduates and 2006-2007 High School Dropouts, October 2007

|  | Black | White | All Races |
|---|---|---|---|
| **2007 high school graduates** | 420 | 2,380 | 2,955 |
| In civilian labor force | 231 | 1,224 | 1,531 |
| Employed | 151 | 1,091 | 1,307 |
| Unemployed | 80 | 132 | 224 |
| Not in labor force | 189 | 1,156 | 1,424 |
| **2006-2007 high school dropouts** | 75 | 288 | 426 |
| In civilian labor force | 45 | 156 | 239 |
| Employed | 29 | 109 | 175 |
| Unemployed | 17 | 48 | 64 |
| Not in labor force | 30 | 132 | 187 |

Source: US Department of Labor, Bureau of Labor Statistics, *College Enrollment and Work Activity of 2007 High School Graduates*, table 1.

Notes: 'All Races' includes races not shown separately. 'White' as shown is equivalent to 'White alone' and 'Black' as shown is equivalent to 'Black alone.'

Units: Number of persons 16 to 24 years old in thousands.

## Table 3.17: Percent of High School Dropouts Among Persons 16 to 24 Years Old, by Sex, 1975–2006

|  | Black | | | White | | | All Races | | |
|  | Male | Female | Total | Male | Female | Total | Male | Female | Total |
|---|---|---|---|---|---|---|---|---|---|
| 1975 | 23.0% | 22.9% | 22.9% | 11.0% | 11.8% | 11.4% | 13.3% | 14.5% | 13.9% |
| 1980 | 20.8 | 17.7 | 19.1 | 12.3 | 10.5 | 11.4 | 15.1 | 13.1 | 14.1 |
| 1985 | 16.1 | 14.3 | 15.2 | 11.1 | 9.8 | 10.4 | 13.4 | 11.8 | 12.6 |
| 1990 | 11.9 | 14.4 | 13.2 | 9.3 | 8.7 | 9.0 | 12.3 | 11.8 | 12.1 |
| 1995 | 11.1 | 12.9 | 12.1 | 9.0 | 8.2 | 8.6 | 12.2 | 11.7 | 12.0 |
| 1999 | 12.1 | 13.0 | 12.6 | 7.7 | 6.9 | 7.3 | 11.9 | 10.5 | 11.2 |
| 2000 | 15.3 | 11.1 | 13.1 | 7.0 | 6.9 | 6.9 | 12.0 | 9.9 | 10.9 |
| 2001 | 13.0 | 9.0 | 10.9 | 7.9 | 6.7 | 7.3 | 12.2 | 9.3 | 10.7 |
| 2002 | 12.8 | 9.9 | 11.3 | 6.7 | 6.3 | 6.5 | 11.8 | 9.2 | 10.5 |
| 2003 | 12.5 | 9.5 | 10.9 | 7.1 | 5.6 | 6.3 | 11.3 | 8.4 | 9.9 |
| 2004 | 13.5 | 10.2 | 11.8 | 7.1 | 6.4 | 6.8 | 11.6 | 9.0 | 10.3 |
| 2005 | 12.0 | 9.0 | 10.4 | 6.6 | 5.3 | 6.0 | 10.8 | 8.0 | 9.4 |
| 2006 | 9.7 | 11.7 | 10.7 | 6.4 | 5.3 | 5.8 | 10.3 | 8.3 | 9.3 |

**Source:**  US Department of Education, Center for Education Statistics, *Digest of Education Statistics 2007*, table 105.

**Notes:**  'All Races' includes races not shown separately. 'White' and 'Black' exclude persons of Hispanic origin.
'Dropouts' are 16 to 24 year olds who are not enrolled in school and who have not completed a high school program regardless of when they left school.
Based on October enrollment counts.

**Units:**  Percent of total population.

## Table 3.18: Attendance Status of College Students
## 15 Years Old and Over, 2004–2006

|  | Black | White | All Races |
|---|---|---|---|
| **2004** | | | |
| *Total enrolled* | *2,301* | *13,381* | *17,338* |
| Year enrolled in college | | | |
| 1st year | 690 | 3,118 | 4,150 |
| 2nd year | 497 | 2,958 | 3,807 |
| 3rd year | 424 | 2,637 | 3,291 |
| 4th year | 347 | 2,114 | 2,757 |
| 5th year | 136 | 1,006 | 1,324 |
| 6th year or higher | 207 | 1,548 | 2,054 |
| **2005** | | | |
| *Total enrolled* | *2,298* | *13,466* | *17,472* |
| Undergraduate college, year enrolled | | | |
| 1st year | 628 | 3,052 | 4,033 |
| 2nd year | 609 | 3,058 | 3,988 |
| 3rd year | 409 | 2,693 | 3,439 |
| 4th year | 325 | 2,130 | 2,708 |
| Graduate school, year enrolled | | | |
| 1st year | 114 | 806 | 1,067 |
| 2nd year or higher | 212 | 1,728 | 2,237 |
| **2006** | | | |
| *Total enrolled* | *2,333* | *13,274* | *17,232* |
| Undergraduate college, year enrolled | | | |
| 1st year | 676 | 3,085 | 4,077 |
| 2nd year | 621 | 3,038 | 4,048 |
| 3rd year | 448 | 2,577 | 3,257 |
| 4th year | 287 | 1,987 | 2,471 |
| Graduate school, year enrolled | | | |
| 1st year | 163 | 945 | 1,234 |
| 2nd year or higher | 212 | 1,642 | 2,144 |

**Source:** US Bureau of the Census, Current Population Reports, *School Enrollment, 2004*, table 10; *2005*, table 10; *2006*, table 5.

**Notes:** 'All Races' includes races not shown separately. 'White' as shown is equivalent to 'White alone' and 'Black' as shown is equivalent to 'Black alone.'
College enrollment at the undergraduate level in two year and four-year institutions including both full-time and part-time students. Based on October enrollment counts.

**Units:** College enrollment in thousands of students.

## Table 3.19: Enrollment in Institutions of Higher Education by Type of Institution, 1980–2005

| | Black | White | All Races |
|---|---|---|---|
| **1980** | | | |
| *All institutions* | *1,106.8* | *9,883.0* | *12,086.8* |
| 4-year institutions | 634.3 | 6,274.5 | 7,565.4 |
| 2-year institutions | 472.5 | 3,558.5 | 4,521.4 |
| **1990** | | | |
| *All institutions* | *1,247.0* | *10,722.5* | *13,818.6* |
| 4-year institutions | 722.8 | 6,768.1 | 8,578.6 |
| 2-year institutions | 524.3 | 3,954.3 | 5,240.1 |
| **1995** | | | |
| *All institutions* | *1,473.7* | *10,311.2* | *14,261.8* |
| 4-year institutions | 852.2 | 6,517.2 | 8,769.3 |
| 2-year institutions | 621.5 | 3,794.0 | 5,492.5 |
| **2000** | | | |
| *All institutions* | *1,730.3* | *10,462.1* | *15,312.3* |
| 4-year institutions | 995.4 | 6,658.0 | 9,363.9 |
| 2-year institutions | 734.9 | 3,804.1 | 5,948.4 |
| **2004** | | | |
| *All institutions* | *2,164.7* | *11,422.8* | *17,272.0* |
| 4-year institutions | 1,258.9 | 7,359.0 | 10,726.2 |
| 2-year institutions | 905.8 | 4,063.8 | 6,545.9 |
| **2005** | | | |
| *All institutions* | *2,214.6* | *11,495.4* | *17,487.5* |
| 4-year institutions | 1,313.4 | 7,496.9 | 10,999.4 |
| 2-year institutions | 901.1 | 3,998.6 | 6,488.1 |

Source: US Department of Education, Center for Education Statistics, *Digest of Education Statistics, 2006*, table 211.

Notes: 'All Races' includes races not shown separately. Both 'Black' and 'White' exclude persons of Hispanic origin.

Units: Number of students enrolled in college in thousands.

## Table 3.20: Enrollment in Institutions of Higher Education by State, Fall 2005

| | Black | White | All Races |
|---|---|---|---|
| *United States* | *2,214,561* | *11,495,440* | *17,487,475* |
| Alabama | 74,968 | 166,394 | 256,389 |
| Alaska | 1,016 | 21,653 | 30,231 |
| Arizona | 48,521 | 347,468 | 545,597 |
| Arkansas | 26,242 | 107,865 | 143,272 |
| California | 185,659 | 1,034,430 | 2,399,833 |
| Colorado | 15,528 | 231,165 | 302,672 |
| Connecticut | 18,528 | 126,904 | 174,675 |
| Delaware | 10,169 | 36,537 | 51,612 |
| District of Columbia | 36,007 | 50,078 | 104,897 |
| Florida | 155,357 | 493,385 | 872,662 |
| Georgia | 131,040 | 255,587 | 426,650 |
| Hawaii | 1,534 | 17,817 | 67,083 |
| Idaho | 651 | 68,692 | 77,708 |
| Illinois | 118,905 | 543,072 | 832,967 |
| Indiana | 30,315 | 298,997 | 361,253 |
| Iowa | 11,660 | 196,992 | 227,722 |
| Kansas | 11,230 | 155,703 | 191,752 |
| Kentucky | 21,322 | 212,887 | 244,969 |
| Louisiana | 59,974 | 123,371 | 197,713 |
| Maine | 1,279 | 60,093 | 65,551 |
| Maryland | 86,984 | 181,270 | 314,151 |
| Massachusetts | 34,986 | 320,791 | 443,316 |
| Michigan | 83,007 | 477,811 | 626,751 |
| Minnesota | 24,452 | 299,792 | 361,701 |
| Mississippi | 58,758 | 86,626 | 150,457 |
| Missouri | 46,582 | 296,174 | 374,445 |
| Montana | 270 | 40,775 | 47,850 |
| Nebraska | 5,094 | 104,861 | 121,236 |
| Nevada | 8,651 | 70,454 | 110,705 |

*(continued on next page)*

## Table 3.20: Enrollment in Institutions of Higher Education by State, Fall 2005

|  | Black | White | All Races |
|---|---|---|---|
| *United States* | *2,214,561* | *11,495,440* | *17,487,475* |
| New Hampshire | 1,418 | 62,925 | 69,893 |
| New Jersey | 53,971 | 226,762 | 379,758 |
| New Mexico | 3,844 | 56,581 | 131,337 |
| New York | 160,007 | 699,226 | 1,152,081 |
| North Carolina | 116,786 | 325,552 | 484,392 |
| North Dakota | 682 | 43,037 | 49,389 |
| Ohio | 74,590 | 496,461 | 616,350 |
| Oklahoma | 19,039 | 146,358 | 208,053 |
| Oregon | 4,788 | 162,662 | 200,033 |
| Pennsylvania | 71,463 | 546,328 | 692,340 |
| Rhode Island | 4,897 | 64,726 | 81,382 |
| South Carolina | 57,941 | 141,590 | 210,444 |
| South Dakota | 642 | 42,727 | 48,768 |
| Tennessee | 55,288 | 210,640 | 283,070 |
| Texas | 153,416 | 645,009 | 1,240,707 |
| Utah | 2,298 | 174,746 | 200,691 |
| Vermont | 725 | 36,445 | 39,915 |
| Virginia | 85,096 | 300,192 | 439,166 |
| Washington | 15,461 | 264,285 | 348,482 |
| West Virginia | 5,220 | 89,306 | 99,547 |
| Wisconsin | 17,185 | 288,185 | 335,258 |
| Wyoming | 336 | 31,888 | 35,334 |

Source: US Department of Education, Center for Education Statistics, *Digest of Education Statistics, 2006*, table 212.

Notes: 'All Races' includes races not shown separately. Both 'White' and 'Black' exclude those who identify as Hispanic.
Degree-granting institutions grant associate's or higher degrees and participate in Title IV federal financial aid programs.

Units: Number of students enrolled.

## Table 3.21: Enrollment Rates of 18 to 24 Year-Olds in Institutions of Higher Education, 1975–2005

| | Black | White | All Races |
|---|---|---|---|
| **Percent of 18–24 year olds enrolled** | | | |
| 1975 | 20.4% | 27.4% | 26.3% |
| 1980 | 19.4 | 27.3 | 25.7 |
| 1985 | 19.6 | 30.0 | 27.8 |
| 1990 | 25.3 | 35.2 | 32.1 |
| 1995 | 27.5 | 37.9 | 34.3 |
| 2000 | 30.5 | 38.7 | 35.5 |
| 2001 | 31.3 | 39.3 | 36.2 |
| 2002 | 31.9 | 40.9 | 36.7 |
| 2003 | 32.3 | 41.6 | 37.8 |
| 2004 | 31.8 | 41.7 | 38.0 |
| 2005 | 33.1 | 42.8 | 38.9 |
| 2006 | 32.6 | 41.0 | 37.3 |
| **Percent of high school graduates enrolled** | | | |
| 1975 | 31.5% | 32.3% | 32.5% |
| 1980 | 27.6 | 32.1 | 31.8 |
| 1985 | 26.0 | 34.9 | 33.7 |
| 1990 | 30.4 | 39.2 | 37.7 |
| 1995 | 35.4 | 44.0 | 42.3 |
| 2000 | 39.3 | 44.1 | 43.2 |
| 2001 | 40.1 | 45.3 | 44.2 |
| 2002 | 40.2 | 46.7 | 44.7 |
| 2003 | 41.4 | 47.2 | 45.7 |
| 2004 | 40.8 | 47.4 | 45.8 |
| 2005 | 41.4 | 48.6 | 46.8 |
| 2006 | 42.0 | 46.5 | 45.0 |

Source:  US Department of Education, National Center for Education Statistics, *Digest of Education Statistics, 2007*, table 195.

Notes:  'All Races' includes races not shown separately. Both 'White' and 'Black' exclude those who identify as Hispanic.

Units:  Percent of 18–24 year-olds and high school graduates.

## Table 3.22: Enrollment Status of High School Graduates by Type of School and Sex, 2006

|  | Black | White | All Races |
|---|---|---|---|
| *Total graduates* | *3,110* | *18,288* | *23,216* |
| **Both Sexes** | | | |
| Enrolled in 2-year college | 287 | 1,496 | 1,941 |
| Enrolled in 4-year college | 740 | 4,892 | 6,226 |
| Enrolled in graduate school | 95 | 624 | 831 |
| Enrolled in vocational school | 30 | 205 | 267 |
| **Male Students** | | | |
| Enrolled in 2-year college | 128 | 711 | 916 |
| Enrolled in 4-year college | 293 | 2,326 | 2,958 |
| Enrolled in graduate school | 17 | 238 | 294 |
| Enrolled in vocational school | 10 | 118 | 146 |
| **Female Students** | | | |
| Enrolled in 2-year college | 160 | 785 | 1,025 |
| Enrolled in 4-year college | 447 | 2,566 | 3,269 |
| Enrolled in graduate school | 78 | 386 | 537 |
| Enrolled in vocational school | 20 | 87 | 121 |

Source: US Bureau of the Census, Current Population Reports, *School Enrollment, 2006*, table 7.

Notes: 'All Races' includes races not shown separately. 'White' as shown is equivalent to 'White alone' and 'Black' as shown is equivalent to 'Black alone.' Numbers are for full-time students only.

Units: Enrollment in thousands of students aged 15–24.

## Table 3.23: Enrollment of Persons 14 to 34 Years Old in Institutions of Higher Education by Sex, 1975–1999

| | Enrollment | | | Percent distribution | | |
|---|---|---|---|---|---|---|
| | Black | White | All Races | Black | White | All Races |
| **1975** | | | | | | |
| *Total* | 927 | 8,141 | 9,697 | 9.6% | 84.0% | 100% |
| Men | 433 | 4,566 | 5,342 | 4.5 | 47.1 | 55.1 |
| Women | 494 | 3,576 | 4,355 | 5.1 | 36.9 | 44.9 |
| **1980** | | | | | | |
| *Total* | 996 | 8,453 | 10,181 | 9.8% | 83.0% | 100% |
| Men | 431 | 4,225 | 5,193 | 4.2 | 41.5 | 51.0 |
| Women | 565 | 4,228 | 5,244 | 5.5 | 41.5 | 49.0 |
| **1985** | | | | | | |
| *Total* | 1,036 | 8,781 | 10,863 | 9.5% | 80.0% | 100% |
| Men | 458 | 4,361 | 5,345 | 4.2 | 40.1 | 49.2 |
| Women | 578 | 4,420 | 5,518 | 5.3 | 40.7 | 50.8 |
| **1990** | | | | | | |
| *Total* | 1,167 | 8,892 | 11,303 | 10.3% | 78.7% | 100% |
| Men | 508 | 4,289 | NA | 4.5 | 38.0 | NA |
| Women | 659 | 4,594 | NA | 5.8 | 40.6 | NA |
| **1993** | | | | | | |
| *Total* | 1,227 | 8,592 | 11,409 | 10.8% | 75.3% | 100% |
| Men | 515 | 4,168 | NA | 4.5 | 36.5 | NA |
| Women | 713 | 4,424 | NA | 6.2 | 38.8 | NA |
| **1999** | | | | | | |
| *Total* | 1,609 | 8,853 | 12,506 | 12.9% | 70.8% | 100% |
| Men | 686 | 4,310 | NA | 5.5 | 34.5 | NA |
| Women | 924 | 4,543 | NA | 7.4 | 36.3 | NA |

Source: US Department of Education, Center for Education Statistics, *Digest of Education Statistics, 2000*, table 213.

Notes: 'All Races' includes races not shown separately. Both 'White' and 'Black' exclude those identifying as Hispanic.
Totals may not add to 100% due to other groups not shown.

Units: Enrollment in thousands of students; percent of 14–34 year-olds.

## Table 3.24: Enrollment Status of Persons 18 to 21 Years Old, 2003–2005

| | Black | White | All Races |
|---|---|---|---|
| **2003** | | | |
| *Total Persons 18–21 yrs* | *2,159* | *11,917* | *15,167* |
| Enrolled in high school | 14.8% | 8.8% | 9.7% |
| High school graduates | | | |
| Total | 72.5 | 79.5 | 78.6 |
| In college | 35.0 | 46.0 | 45.2 |
| Not high school graduates | 12.7 | 11.7 | 11.7 |
| **2004** | | | |
| *Total Persons 18–21 yrs* | *2,213* | *12,325* | *15,677* |
| Enrolled in high school | 11.7% | 8.4% | 8.9% |
| High school graduates | | | |
| Total | 72.3 | 80.4 | 79.4 |
| In college | 37.9 | 48.4 | 47.6 |
| Not high school graduates | 16.0 | 11.2 | 11.7 |
| **2005** | | | |
| *Total Persons 18–21 yrs* | *2,271* | *12,510* | *15,916* |
| Enrolled in high school | 12.7% | 8.8% | 9.4% |
| High school graduates | | | |
| Total | 74.9 | 80.7 | 80.1 |
| In college | 37.4 | 49.1 | 48.2 |
| Not high school graduates | 12.4 | 10.5 | 10.6 |

Source: US Bureau of Census, *Statistical Abstract of the United States, 2006*, table 260; *2007*, table 262; *2008*, table 266.

Notes: 'All Races' includes races not shown separately.

Units: 'Total Persons' in thousands; percent of total by category.

## Table 3.25: Associate's Degrees Conferred by Major Field of Study, 2005–2006

|  | Black | White | All Races |
|---|---|---|---|
| *All fields, total* | *89,784* | *485,297* | *713,066* |
| Agriculture and natural resources | 59 | 5,733 | 6,168 |
| Architecture and related services | 49 | 416 | 656 |
| Area, ethnic, cultural, and gender studies | 21 | 22 | 124 |
| Biological and biomedical sciences | 162 | 1,031 | 1,827 |
| Business | 17,764 | 73,280 | 114,095 |
| Communications, journalism, and related programs | 253 | 1,905 | 2,629 |
| Communications technologies | 395 | 2,449 | 3,380 |
| Computer and information sciences | 5,011 | 20,474 | 31,246 |
| Construction trades | 239 | 3,262 | 3,850 |
| Education | 2,532 | 8,994 | 14,475 |
| Engineering | 224 | 1,378 | 2,162 |
| Engineering technologies | 3,336 | 22,101 | 30,461 |
| English language and literature/letters | 94 | 694 | 1,105 |
| Family and consumer sciences | 2,032 | 5,172 | 9,488 |
| Foreign languages, literatures, and linguistics | 64 | 771 | 1,161 |
| Health professions and related clinical sciences | 17,615 | 98,252 | 134,931 |
| Legal professions and studies | 1,768 | 6,960 | 10,509 |
| Liberal arts and sciences, general studies, and humanities | 26,878 | 164,099 | 244,689 |
| Library science | 3 | 114 | 136 |
| Mathematics and statistics | 36 | 400 | 753 |
| Mechanics and repair technologies | 1,028 | 11,152 | 14,454 |

*(continued on next page)*

## Table 3.25: Associate's Degrees Conferred by Major Field of Study, 2005–2006

| | Black | White | All Races |
|---|---|---|---|
| Military technologies | 113 | 399 | 610 |
| Multi/interdisciplinary studies | 1,646 | 8,889 | 14,473 |
| Parks, recreation, leisure and fitness studies | 141 | 816 | 1,128 |
| Philosophy and religious studies | 4 | 332 | 367 |
| Physical sciences and science technologies | 259 | 1,907 | 2,902 |
| Precision production | 73 | 1,710 | 1,977 |
| Psychology | 207 | 1,205 | 1,944 |
| Public administration and social service professions | 1,235 | 2,312 | 4,415 |
| Security and protective services | 3,673 | 18,379 | 26,425 |
| Social sciences and history | 735 | 3,893 | 6,730 |
| Social sciences | 716 | 3,592 | 6,308 |
| History | 19 | 301 | 422 |
| Theology and religious vocations | 148 | 376 | 570 |
| Transportation and materials moving | 87 | 1,149 | 1,472 |
| Visual and performing arts | 1,900 | 15,271 | 21,754 |

Source: US Department of Education, Center for Education Statistics, *Digest of Education Statistics 2007*, table 272.

Notes: 'All Races' includes races not shown separately. Both 'White' and 'Black' exclude those identifying as Hispanic.

Units: Number of earned Associate's degrees conferred.

## Table 3.26: Bachelor's Degrees Conferred
## by Major Field of Study, 2005–2006

|  | Black | White | All Races |
|---|---|---|---|
| *All fields, total* | *142,420* | *1,075,561* | *1,485,242* |
| Agriculture and natural resources | 685 | 20,190 | 23,053 |
| Architecture and related services | 455 | 6,991 | 9,515 |
| Area, ethnic, cultural, and gender studies | 1,167 | 4,307 | 7,879 |
| Biological and biomedical sciences | 5,409 | 46,877 | 69,178 |
| Business | 36,195 | 216,567 | 318,042 |
| Communications, journalism, and related programs | 7,325 | 56,648 | 73,955 |
| Communications technologies | 295 | 2,191 | 2,981 |
| Computer and information sciences | 5,875 | 29,864 | 47,480 |
| Construction trades | 9 | 123 | 141 |
| Education | 6,864 | 91,279 | 107,238 |
| Engineering | 3,355 | 45,465 | 67,045 |
| Engineering technologies | 1,536 | 10,600 | 14,178 |
| English language and literature/letters | 4,242 | 43,872 | 55,096 |
| Family and consumer sciences | 2,227 | 16,083 | 20,775 |
| Foreign languages, literatures, and linguistics | 799 | 13,819 | 19,410 |
| Health professions and related clinical sciences | 10,268 | 69,092 | 91,973 |
| Legal professions and studies | 578 | 2,081 | 3,302 |
| Liberal arts and sciences, general studies, and humanities | 5,701 | 30,162 | 44,898 |
| Library science | 2 | 73 | 76 |
| Mathematics and statistics | 871 | 10,700 | 14,770 |
| Mechanics and repair technologies | 19 | 173 | 246 |

*(continued on next page)*

## Table 3.26: Bachelor's Degrees Conferred by Major Field of Study, 2005–2006

| | Black | White | All Races |
|---|---|---|---|
| Military technologies | 0 | 32 | 33 |
| Multi/interdisciplinary studies | 2,746 | 22,495 | 32,012 |
| Parks, recreation, leisure and fitness studies | 2,271 | 20,189 | 25,490 |
| Philosophy and religious studies | 689 | 9,801 | 11,985 |
| Physical sciences and science technologies | 1,178 | 15,421 | 20,318 |
| Precision production | 1 | 46 | 55 |
| Psychology | 9,663 | 62,645 | 88,134 |
| Public administration and social service professions | 5,187 | 13,168 | 21,986 |
| Security and protective services | 6,412 | 23,208 | 35,319 |
| Social sciences and history | 14,683 | 115,808 | 161,485 |
| Social sciences | 12,995 | 88,131 | 128,332 |
| History | 1,688 | 27,677 | 33,153 |
| Theology and religious vocations | 553 | 7,275 | 8,548 |
| Transportation and materials moving | 305 | 4,382 | 5,349 |
| Visual and performing arts | 4,855 | 63,934 | 83,297 |

Source:   US Department of Education, Center for Education Statistics, *Digest of Education Statistics 2007*, table 275.

Notes:   'All Races' includes races not shown separately. Both 'White' and 'Black' exclude those identifying as Hispanic.

Units:   Number of earned Bachelor's degrees conferred.

## Table 3.27: Master's Degrees Conferred
## by Major Field of Study, 2005–2006

|  | Black | White | All Races |
|---|---|---|---|
| *All fields, total* | *58,976* | *393,357* | *594,065* |
| Agriculture and natural resources | 128 | 3,480 | 4,640 |
| Architecture and related services | 237 | 3,791 | 5,743 |
| Area, ethnic, cultural, and gender studies | 184 | 1,223 | 2,080 |
| Biological and biomedical sciences | 468 | 5,602 | 8,681 |
| Business | 17,933 | 86,404 | 146,406 |
| Communications, journalism, and related programs | 702 | 4,730 | 7,244 |
| Communications technologies | 62 | 227 | 501 |
| Computer and information sciences | 996 | 6,680 | 17,055 |
| Construction trades | 0 | 0 | 0 |
| Education | 18,237 | 134,221 | 174,620 |
| Engineering | 880 | 12,570 | 30,989 |
| Engineering technologies | 235 | 1,363 | 2,541 |
| English language and literature/letters | 465 | 7,247 | 8,845 |
| Family and consumer sciences | 225 | 1,417 | 1,983 |
| Foreign languages, literatures, and linguistics | 77 | 2,076 | 3,539 |
| Health professions and related clinical sciences | 5,054 | 36,452 | 51,380 |
| Legal professions and studies | 259 | 1,549 | 4,453 |
| Liberal arts and sciences, general studies, and humanities | 298 | 2,946 | 3,702 |
| Library science | 306 | 5,485 | 6,448 |
| Mathematics and statistics | 163 | 2,268 | 4,730 |
| Mechanics and repair technologies | 0 | 0 | 0 |

*(continued on next page)*

## Table 3.27: Master's Degrees Conferred
## by Major Field of Study, 2005–2006

|  | Black | White | All Races |
|---|---|---|---|
| Military technologies | 0 | 0 | 0 |
| Multi/interdisciplinary studies | 325 | 3,134 | 4,491 |
| Parks, recreation, leisure and fitness studies | 327 | 3,197 | 3,992 |
| Philosophy and religious studies | 89 | 1,358 | 1,739 |
| Physical sciences and science technologies | 195 | 3,583 | 5,922 |
| Precision production | 0 | 6 | 9 |
| Psychology | 2,403 | 14,340 | 19,770 |
| Public administration and social service professions | 5,474 | 19,529 | 30,510 |
| Security and protective services | 754 | 2,965 | 4,277 |
| Social sciences and history | 1,333 | 10,932 | 17,369 |
| Social sciences | 1,198 | 8,439 | 14,377 |
| History | 135 | 2,493 | 2,992 |
| Theology and religious vocations | 501 | 4,490 | 6,092 |
| Transportation and materials moving | 68 | 601 | 784 |
| Visual and performing arts | 598 | 9,491 | 13,530 . |

**Source:** US Department of Education, Center for Education Statistics, *Digest of Education Statistics 2007*, table 278.

**Notes:** 'All Races' includes races not shown separately. Both 'White' and 'Black' exclude those identifying as Hispanic.

**Units:** Number of earned Master's degrees conferred.

## Table 3.28: Doctoral Degrees Conferred
by Major Field of Study, 2005–2006

|  | Black | White | All Races |
|---|---|---|---|
| *All fields, total* | *3,122* | *31,601* | *56,067* |
| Agriculture and natural resources | 33 | 592 | 1,194 |
| Architecture and related services | 3 | 59 | 201 |
| Area, ethnic, cultural, and gender studies | 44 | 110 | 226 |
| Biological and biomedical sciences | 175 | 3,243 | 5,775 |
| Business | 137 | 787 | 1,711 |
| Communications, journalism, and related programs | 24 | 275 | 461 |
| Communications technologies | 0 | 1 | 3 |
| Computer and information sciences | 24 | 410 | 1,416 |
| Construction trades | 0 | 0 | 0 |
| Education | 1,093 | 5,107 | 7,584 |
| Engineering | 116 | 1,960 | 7,396 |
| Engineering technologies | 5 | 30 | 75 |
| English language and literature/letters | 67 | 965 | 1,254 |
| Family and consumer sciences | 33 | 193 | 340 |
| Foreign languages, literatures, and linguistics | 18 | 536 | 1,074 |
| Health professions and related clinical sciences | 356 | 5,340 | 7,128 |
| Legal professions and studies | 5 | 46 | 129 |
| Liberal arts and sciences, general studies, and humanities | 2 | 72 | 84 |
| Library science | 2 | 23 | 44 |
| Mathematics and statistics | 21 | 465 | 1,293 |
| Mechanics and repair technologies | 0 | 0 | 0 |

*(continued on next page)*

## Table 3.28: Doctoral Degrees Conferred
## by Major Field of Study, 2005–2006

|  | Black | White | All Races |
|---|---|---|---|
| Military technologies | 0 | 0 | 0 |
| Multi/interdisciplinary studies | 43 | 615 | 987 |
| Parks, recreation, leisure and fitness studies | 10 | 130 | 194 |
| Philosophy and religious studies | 41 | 410 | 578 |
| Physical sciences and science technologies | 63 | 2,092 | 4,489 |
| Precision production | 0 | 0 | 0 |
| Psychology | 315 | 3,687 | 4,921 |
| Public administration and social service professions | 106 | 412 | 704 |
| Security and protective services | 7 | 57 | 80 |
| Social sciences and history | 182 | 2,244 | 3,914 |
| Social sciences | 146 | 1,591 | 3,062 |
| History | 36 | 653 | 852 |
| Theology and religious vocations | 171 | 840 | 1,429 |
| Transportation and materials moving | 0 | 0 | 0 |
| Visual and performing arts | 26 | 900 | 1,383 |

**Source:** US Department of Education, Center for Education Statistics, *Digest of Education Statistics 2007*, table 281.

**Notes:** 'All Races' includes races not shown separately. Both 'White' and 'Black' exclude those identifying as Hispanic.

**Units:** Number of earned Doctoral degrees conferred.

## Table 3.29: First-professional Degrees Conferred by Field of Study, 2005–2006

|  | Black | White | All Races |
|---|---|---|---|
| *All fields, total* | *6,223* | *63,590* | *87,655* |
| Dentistry | 214 | 2,810 | 4,389 |
| Medicine | 1,159 | 10,172 | 15,455 |
| Optometry | 34 | 790 | 1,198 |
| Osteopathic medicine | 95 | 2,113 | 2,718 |
| Pharmacy | 744 | 5,966 | 9,292 |
| Podiatry or podiatric medicine | 41 | 209 | 347 |
| Veterinary medicine | 51 | 2,148 | 2,370 |
| Chiropractic medicine | 114 | 1,968 | 2,564 |
| Naturopathic medicine | 5 | 177 | 216 |
| Law | 2,939 | 33,154 | 43,440 |
| Theology | 827 | 4,083 | 5,666 |

Source: US Department of Education, National Center for Education Statistics, *Digest of Education Statistics, 2007*, table 284.

Notes: 'All Races' includes races not shown separately. Both 'White' and 'Black' exclude those identifying as Hispanic.

Units: Number of earned first-professional degrees conferred.

## Table 3.30: Historically Black Institutions of Higher Education, Enrollment, Fall 2005, and Earned Degrees Conferred, 2005–2006

| | Public | | Private | | |
|---|---|---|---|---|---|
| | 4-year | 2-year | 4-year | 2-year | Total |
| **Enrollment, fall 2005** | | | | | |
| *Total* | *197,200* | *38,675* | *75,466* | *427* | *311,768* |
| Men | 74,824 | 15,253 | 29,775 | 171 | 120,023 |
| Women | 122,376 | 23,422 | 45,691 | 256 | 191,745 |
| *Full-time enrollment* | *153,655* | *21,356* | *69,171* | *368* | *244,550* |
| Men | 61,013 | 8,427 | 27,310 | 150 | 96,900 |
| Women | 92,642 | 12,929 | 41,861 | 218 | 147,650 |
| *Part-time enrollment* | *43,545* | *17,319* | *6,295* | *59* | *67,218* |
| Men | 13,811 | 6,826 | 2,465 | 21 | 23,123 |
| Women | 29,734 | 10,493 | 3,830 | 38 | 44,095 |
| **Earned degrees conferred, 2005–2006** | | | | | |
| Associate's degrees | 832 | 2,848 | 106 | 33 | 3,819 |
| Men | 189 | 926 | 29 | 9 | 1,153 |
| Women | 643 | 1,922 | 77 | 24 | 2,666 |
| Bachelor's degrees | 20,090 | NA | 10,458 | NA | 30,548 |
| Men | 6,958 | NA | 3,406 | NA | 10,364 |
| Women | 13,132 | NA | 7,052 | NA | 20,184 |
| Master's degrees | 5,962 | NA | 816 | NA | 6,778 |
| Men | 1,616 | NA | 242 | NA | 1,858 |
| Women | 4,346 | NA | 574 | NA | 4,920 |
| Doctoral degrees | 255 | NA | 189 | NA | 444 |
| Men | 106 | NA | 82 | NA | 188 |
| Women | 149 | NA | 107 | NA | 256 |
| First-professional degrees | 681 | NA | 1,042 | NA | 1,723 |
| Men | 235 | NA | 383 | NA | 618 |
| Women | 446 | NA | 659 | NA | 1,105 |

Source: US Department of Education, National Center for Education Statistics, *Digest of Education Statistics, 2007*, table 231.

Notes: Historically black colleges and universities are accredited institutions of higher education established prior to 1964 (with some exceptions) with the principal mission of educating Black Americans. Most institutions are in the southern and border States.
'First-professional degrees' include degrees awarded in chiropractic, dentistry, law, medicine, optometry, osteopathy, pharmacy, podiatry, theology, and veterinary medicine.

Units: Number of students enrolled and earned degrees conferred.

**Black Americans: A Statistical Sourcebook 2008** **153**

## Table 3.31: Enrollment in Schools of Medicine, Dentistry, and Related Fields, 1990–1991, 2003–2004, and 2004–2005

|  | Black | White |
|---|---|---|
| **1990–1991** | | |
| Dentistry | 5.9% | 70.1% |
| Allopathic medicine | 6.5 | 73.5 |
| Osteopathic medicine | 3.2 | 83.6 |
| Podiatry | 10.6 | 75.2 |
| Optometry | 2.8 | 77.9 |
| Pharmacy | 5.7 | 80.5 |
| Registered nursing | 10.4 | 82.8 |
| **2003–2004** | | |
| Dentistry | 5.4% | 65.6% |
| Allopathic medicine | 7.4 | 63.0 |
| Osteopathic medicine | 3.6 | 73.8 |
| Podiatry | 14.0 | 58.7 |
| Optometry | 3.2 | 60.3 |
| Pharmacy | 9.7 | 58.4 |
| Registered nursing | NA | NA |
| **2004–2005** | | |
| Dentistry | 5.4% | 66.1% |
| Allopathic medicine | 7.4 | 63.3 |
| Osteopathic medicine | 3.7 | 73.5 |
| Podiatry | 14.4 | 60.4 |
| Optometry | 3.5 | 63.2 |
| Pharmacy | 8.6 | 59.7 |
| Registered nursing | NA | NA |

Source: US Department of Health and Human Services, Centers for Disease Control and Prevention, National Center for Health Statistics, *Health in the United States, 2006*, table 111.

Notes: 'All Races' includes races not shown separately. Both 'White' and 'Black' exclude those identifying as Hispanic.

Units: Percent of all students 25 years old and older enrolled in schools for each occupation.

## Table 3.32: Educational Attainment by Sex, 1960–2006

| | Black | | White | | All Races | |
|---|---|---|---|---|---|---|
| | **Male** | **Female** | **Male** | **Female** | **Male** | **Female** |
| **High school graduate or higher** | | | | | | |
| 1960 | 18.2% | 21.8% | 41.6% | 44.7% | 39.5% | 42.5% |
| 1970 | 30.1 | 32.5 | 54.0 | 55.0 | 51.9 | 52.8 |
| 1980 | 50.8 | 51.5 | 69.6 | 68.1 | 67.3 | 65.8 |
| 1990 | 65.8 | 66.5 | 79.1 | 79.0 | 77.7 | 77.5 |
| 1995 | 73.4 | 74.1 | 83.0 | 83.0 | 81.7 | 81.6 |
| 2000 | 78.7 | 78.3 | 84.8 | 85.0 | 84.2 | 84.0 |
| 2003 | 79.6 | 80.3 | 84.5 | 85.7 | 84.1 | 85.0 |
| 2004 | 80.4 | 80.8 | 85.3 | 86.3 | 84.8 | 85.4 |
| 2005 | 81.0 | 81.2 | 85.2 | 86.2 | 84.9 | 85.5 |
| 2006 | 80.1 | 81.2 | 85.5 | 86.7 | 85.0 | 85.9 |
| **College graduate or higher** | | | | | | |
| 1960 | 2.8% | 3.3% | 10.3% | 6.0% | 9.7% | 5.8% |
| 1970 | 4.2 | 4.6 | 14.4 | 8.4 | 13.5 | 8.1 |
| 1980 | 8.4 | 8.3 | 21.3 | 13.3 | 20.1 | 12.8 |
| 1990 | 11.9 | 10.8 | 25.3 | 19.0 | 24.4 | 18.4 |
| 1995 | 13.6 | 12.9 | 27.2 | 21.0 | 26.0 | 20.2 |
| 2000 | 16.3 | 16.7 | 28.5 | 23.9 | 27.8 | 23.6 |
| 2003 | 16.7 | 17.8 | 29.4 | 25.9 | 28.9 | 25.7 |
| 2004 | 16.6 | 18.5 | 30.0 | 26.4 | 29.4 | 26.1 |
| 2005 | 16.0 | 18.8 | 29.4 | 26.8 | 28.9 | 26.5 |
| 2006 | 17.2 | 19.4 | 29.7 | 27.1 | 29.2 | 26.9 |

**Source:** US Bureau of Census, *Statistical Abstract of the United States, 2008*, table 218.

**Notes:** Beginning in 2003, 'White' as shown is equivalent to 'White alone' and 'Black' as shown is equivalent to 'Black alone.'
'High school graduate' indicates those who have completed 4 years of high school or more.
'College graduate' indicates having completed 4 years of college or more.
Figures are as of April 1 of the respective years.

**Units:** Percent of total population 25 years old and over.

## Table 3.33: College Completion, Persons 25 Years Old and Older, 1970–2006

|  | Black | White | All Races |
|---|---|---|---|
| **1970** | | | |
| Total | 4.5% | 11.6% | 11.0% |
| Men | 4.6 | 15.0 | 14.1 |
| Women | 4.4 | 8.6 | 8.2 |
| **1980** | | | |
| Total | 7.9% | 17.8% | 17.0% |
| Men | 7.7 | 22.1 | 20.9 |
| Women | 8.1 | 14.0 | 13.6 |
| **1990** | | | |
| Total | 11.3% | 22.0% | 21.3% |
| Men | 11.9 | 25.3 | 24.4 |
| Women | 10.8 | 19.0 | 18.4 |
| **2000** | | | |
| Total | 16.6% | 28.1% | 25.6% |
| Men | 16.4 | 30.8 | 27.8 |
| Women | 16.8 | 25.5 | 23.6 |
| **2003** | | | |
| Total | 17.6% | 28.2% | 27.7% |
| Men | 16.6 | 30.0 | 29.4 |
| Women | 18.5 | 26.4 | 26.1 |
| **2006** | | | |
| Total | 18.5% | 28.4% | 28.0% |
| Men | 17.2 | 29.7 | 29.2 |
| Women | 19.4 | 27.1 | 26.9 |

Source:   US Bureau of the Census, Current Population Reports, *Educational Attainment in the United States: March 1998 (update)*, table 1; *2000*, table 1a; *2002*, table 1a; *2003*, table 1a; *2004*; table 1a; *2006*, table 1a.

Notes:   'All Races' includes other races not shown separately.
For For 2003 and later, 'White' and 'Black' are equivalent to 'White Alone' and 'Black Alone,' and refer to people who reported 'White' and 'Black,' respectively, and did not report any other race category.

Units:   Percent as a percent of all persons 25 years old and older completing four or more years of college (1970-1991) or Bachelor's degree or more (1992 and later).

## Table 3.34: Educational Attainment, Persons 25 Years Old and Older, 2000 and 2006

|  | Black | White | All Races |
|---|---|---|---|
| **2000** | | | |
| *All persons 25 years old and over* | *20,036* | *147,067* | *175,230* |
| Percent of the population: | | | |
| Not a high school graduate | 21.5% | 15.1% | 15.8% |
| High school graduate | 35.2 | 33.4 | 33.1 |
| With some college, no degree | 20.0 | 17.4 | 17.6 |
| With associate's degree | 6.8 | 8.0 | 7.8 |
| With bachelor's degree | 11.4 | 17.3 | 17.0 |
| With advanced degree | 5.1 | 8.8 | 8.6 |
| **2006** | | | |
| *All persons 25 years old and over* | *21,600* | *157,566* | *191,884* |
| Percent of the population: | | | |
| Not a high school graduate | 19.3% | 13.9% | 14.5% |
| High school graduate | 35.6 | 31.8 | 31.7 |
| With some college, no degree | 19.0 | 16.9 | 17.0 |
| With associate's degree | 7.7 | 9.0 | 8.7 |
| With bachelor's degree | 12.6 | 18.6 | 18.3 |
| With advanced degree | 5.8 | 9.8 | 9.7 |

**Source:** US Bureau of the Census, *Statistical Abstract of the United States, 2001*, table 217.
US Bureau of the Census, Current Population Reports: *Educational Attainment in the United States, 2006*, table 1.

**Notes:** 'Advanced degree' indicates Master's, Doctoral, or first-professional degree.
'All Races' includes races not shown separately.
Data as of March.
Percentages calculated by Information Publications.

**Units:** Number of persons 25 years old and older in thousands; percent of the population 25 years old and older.

## Table 3.35: Undergraduates Receiving Financial Aid: Average Amount Awarded per Student by Type and Source of Aid, 2003–2004

|  | Black | White | All Races |
|---|---|---|---|
| **Undergraduates receiving aid** |  |  |  |
| *All full-time, full-year enrolled undergraduates* | *2,666* | *12,025* | *19,054* |
| Receiving aid | 75.8% | 61.5% | 63.2% |
| From grants | 64.3 | 47.8 | 50.7 |
| From loans | 43.2 | 35.5 | 35.2 |
| From work-study | 8.5 | 7.3 | 7.5 |
| **Average aid from:** |  |  |  |
| Any source | $10,520 | $9,919 | $9,899 |
| Federal source | 7,901 | 7,318 | 7,304 |
| Non-federal sources | 5,256 | 5,733 | 5,586 |
| **Grants** | **$5,694** | **$5,479** | **$5,565** |
| From federal source | 3,442 | 3,075 | 3,247 |
| Fom non-federal sources | 4,754 | 4,887 | 4,828 |
| **Loans** | **$7,111** | **$7,443** | **$7,336** |
| From federal source | 6,510 | 6,450 | 6,426 |
| From non-federal sources | 5,401 | 6,222 | 6,089 |
| **Work-study funds, total** | **$1,959** | **$1,917** | **$1,942** |

Source:   US Department of Education, Center for Education Statistics, *Digest of Education Statistics, 2005*, tables 316 and 317.

Notes:   'All Races' includes races not shown separately.

Units:   Number of undergraduates in thousands; percent of total undergraduates receiving financial aid; average financial aid in dollars.

## Table 3.36: Average Total Price of Attendance of Undergraduate Education, 2003-2004

|  | Black | White | All Races |
|---|---|---|---|
| *Overall* | *$10,511* | *$11,625* | *$11,256* |
| Public 2-year | 6,321 | 6,161 | 6,149 |
| Public 4-year: |  |  |  |
| Doctorate | 11,445 | 10,698 | 10,812 |
| Non-doctorate | 13,516 | 13,922 | 13,809 |
| Public not-for-profit 4-year: |  |  |  |
| Doctorate | 16,163 | 19,778 | 18,700 |
| Non-doctorate | 25,451 | 30,659 | 30,340 |
| Private for-profit | 14,551 | 15,736 | 15,657 |

Source: US Bureau of the Census, *Statistical Abstract of the United States, 2007*, table 276.

Notes: Excludes students attending more than one institution.
Price includes tuition, fees, books, suplies, room and board, transportation, and other expenses. Based on the 2003-2004 National Postsecondary Student-Aid Study (NPSAS:04).

Units: Cost of attendance in dollars.

# Chapter 4

# Government & Elections

## Chapter Four Highlights

This chapter provides information about government and elections as they pertain to Black persons in the United States, including both the most current data available as well as comparisons of the Black population over time. For almost all tables, corresponding data is provided for the total population of the United States as well as for White persons. This allows for easy comparison between groups.

The chapter contains data on Black public officials, organizing information by year (table 4.01), by state (table 4.02), and by type of office held (tables 4.01 and 4.02). Also included is information on members of Congress (table 4.19).

This chapter also includes a variety of information on the voting-age population (tables 4.03, 4.04, 4.07, 4.10, and 4.13), persons registered to vote (tables 4.03, 4.05, 4.08, 4.11, and 4.14), and persons voting (tables 4.03, 4.06, 4.09, 4.12, and 4.15). We have also provided data on the reasons given for not registering to vote (table 4.16) and for not voting (table 4.17), as well as party breakdown of voting in the last two presidential elections (table 4.18).

## Table 4.01: Black Elected Public Officials,
## by Type of Office Held, 1970–2002

|  | Education | Law enforcement | City & county officials | US & State legislatures | Total |
|---|---|---|---|---|---|
| 1970 | 368 | 213 | 719 | 179 | 1,479 |
| 1980 | 1,232 | 491 | 2,871 | 326 | 4,963 |
| 1985 | 1,531 | 685 | 3,689 | 407 | 6,312 |
| 1990 | 1,645 | 769 | 4,481 | 440 | 7,335 |
| 1995 | 1,840 | 987 | 4,954 | 604 | 8,385 |
| 1996 | 1,922 | 994 | 5,023 | 606 | 8,545 |
| 1997 | 1,952 | 996 | 5,056 | 613 | 8,617 |
| 1998 | 2,008 | 998 | 5,210 | 614 | 8,830 |
| 1999 | 1,927 | 997 | 5,354 | 618 | 8,896 |
| 2000 | 1,923 | 1,037 | 5,420 | 621 | 9,001 |
| 2001 | 1,928 | 1,044 | 5,456 | 633 | 9,061 |
| 2002 | 1,960 | 1,081 | 5,753 | 636 | 9,430 |

Source: US Bureau of the Census, *Statistical Abstract of the United States, 1994*, table 443; 2001, table 399; *2002*, table 391; *2003*, table 417; *2008*, table 402.

Notes: 'US and State legislatures' includes elected state administrators. 'City & county officials' includes county commissioners and mayors, councilmen, vice-mayors, aldermen, regional officials and others. 'Law enforcement' includes judges, magistrates, sheriffs, justices of the peace, and others. 'Education' includes members of state education agencies, college boards, school boards, and others.
Data are as of February for 1970, July for 1980, and January for 1970–2002.

Units: Number of Black elected public officials.

## Table 4.02: Black Elected Public Officials, by State and Type of Office Held, 2002

| | US & state legislatures | City & county offices | Law enforcement | Education | Total |
|---|---|---|---|---|---|
| *United States* | 636 | 5,753 | 1,081 | 1,960 | 9,430 |
| Alabama | 36 | 569 | 56 | 96 | 757 |
| Alaska | 1 | 1 | 0 | 0 | 2 |
| Arizona | 1 | 1 | 6 | 5 | 13 |
| Arkansas | 15 | 374 | 17 | 129 | 535 |
| California | 10 | 78 | 76 | 70 | 234 |
| Colorado | 4 | 5 | 8 | 0 | 17 |
| Connecticut | 14 | 46 | 3 | 6 | 69 |
| Delaware | 4 | 18 | 0 | 7 | 29 |
| District of Columbia | 2 | 169 | 0 | 3 | 174 |
| Florida | 25 | 180 | 43 | 27 | 275 |
| Georgia | 53 | 413 | 48 | 126 | 640 |
| Hawaii | 1 | 0 | 0 | 0 | 1 |
| Idaho | 0 | 1 | 0 | 0 | 1 |
| Illinois | 28 | 327 | 59 | 205 | 619 |
| Indiana | 13 | 54 | 13 | 14 | 94 |
| Iowa | 1 | 8 | 1 | 2 | 12 |
| Kansas | 7 | 4 | 3 | 2 | 16 |
| Kentucky | 5 | 45 | 6 | 6 | 62 |
| Louisiana | 32 | 408 | 132 | 167 | 739 |
| Maine | 0 | 1 | 0 | 1 | 2 |
| Maryland | 40 | 101 | 41 | 10 | 192 |
| Massachusetts | 6 | 60 | 2 | 11 | 79 |
| Michigan | 24 | 153 | 62 | 114 | 353 |
| Minnesota | 2 | 4 | 10 | 4 | 20 |
| Mississippi | 46 | 646 | 121 | 137 | 950 |
| Missouri | 19 | 145 | 17 | 25 | 206 |
| Montana | 0 | 0 | 0 | 0 | 0 |
| Nebraska | 1 | 5 | 0 | 3 | 9 |
| Nevada | 5 | 4 | 2 | 2 | 13 |

*(continued on next page)*

## Table 4.02: Black Elected Public Officials, by State and Type of Office Held, 2002

| | US & state legislatures | City & county offices | Law enforcement | Education | Total |
|---|---|---|---|---|---|
| *United States* | *636* | *5,753* | *1,081* | *1,960* | *9,430* |
| New Hampshire | 5 | 0 | 0 | 0 | 5 |
| New Jersey | 18 | 162 | 0 | 89 | 269 |
| New Mexico | 1 | 0 | 2 | 1 | 4 |
| New York | 34 | 90 | 84 | 120 | 328 |
| North Carolina | 28 | 369 | 31 | 95 | 523 |
| North Dakota | 0 | 1 | 0 | 0 | 1 |
| Ohio | 21 | 197 | 35 | 52 | 305 |
| Oklahoma | 6 | 85 | 4 | 20 | 115 |
| Oregon | 3 | 1 | 1 | 0 | 5 |
| Pennsylvania | 19 | 85 | 75 | 36 | 215 |
| Rhode Island | 7 | 1 | 0 | 0 | 8 |
| South Carolina | 32 | 345 | 12 | 158 | 547 |
| South Dakota | 0 | 0 | 0 | 0 | 0 |
| Tennessee | 18 | 118 | 28 | 31 | 195 |
| Texas | 19 | 306 | 47 | 94 | 466 |
| Utah | 1 | 3 | 1 | 0 | 5 |
| Vermont | 1 | 0 | 0 | 0 | 1 |
| Virginia | 16 | 132 | 16 | 84 | 248 |
| Washington | 2 | 9 | 11 | 2 | 24 |
| West Virginia | 2 | 13 | 3 | 1 | 19 |
| Wisconsin | 8 | 15 | 5 | 5 | 33 |
| Wyoming | 0 | 1 | 0 | 0 | 1 |

**Source:** US Bureau of the Census, *Statistical Abstract of the United States*, 2008, table 402.

**Notes:** 'US and state legislatures' includes elected state administrators; 'City & county officials' includes county commissioners and mayors, councilmen, vice-mayors, aldermen, regional officials and others; 'Law enforcement' includes judges, magistrates, sheriffs, justices of the peace, and others; 'Education' includes members of state education agencies, college boards, school boards, and others.

**Units:** Number of Black elected public officials.

## Table 4.03: Voting-Age Population, Registration, and Voting, 1984–2006

|  | Black | White | All Races |
|---|---|---|---|
| **Voting-age population** | | | |
| 1984 | 18.4 | 146.8 | 170.0 |
| 1986 | 19.0 | 149.9 | 173.9 |
| 1988 | 19.7 | 152.8 | 178.1 |
| 1990 | 20.4 | 155.6 | 182.1 |
| 1992 | 21.0 | 157.8 | 185.7 |
| 1994 | 21.8 | 160.3 | 190.3 |
| 1996 | 22.5 | 162.8 | 193.7 |
| 1998 | 23.3 | 165.8 | 198.2 |
| 2000 | 24.1 | 168.7 | 202.6 |
| 2002 | 24.4 | 174.1 | 210.4 |
| 2004* | 24.9 | 176.6 | 215.7 |
| 2006* | 25.7 | 179.9 | 220.6 |
| **Presidential election years** | | | |
| *Percent reporting registration* | | | |
| 1984 | 66.3% | 69.6% | 68.3% |
| 1988 | 64.5 | 67.9 | 66.6 |
| 1992 | 63.9 | 70.1 | 68.2 |
| 1996 | 63.5 | 67.7 | 65.9 |
| 2000 | 67.5 | 70.4 | 63.9 |
| 2004* | 64.4 | 67.9 | 65.9 |
| *Percent reporting voting* | | | |
| 1984 | 55.8% | 61.4% | 59.9% |
| 1988 | 51.5 | 59.1 | 57.4 |
| 1992 | 54.0 | 63.6 | 61.3 |
| 1996 | 50.6 | 56.0 | 54.2 |
| 2000 | 56.8 | 60.5 | 54.7 |
| 2004* | 56.3 | 60.3 | 58.3 |

*(continued on next page)*

## Table 4.03: Voting-Age Population,
### Registration, and Voting, 1984–2006

| | Black | White | All Races |
|---|---|---|---|
| **Congressional election years (non-presidential election years)** | | | |
| *Percent reporting registration* | | | |
| 1982 | 59.1% | 65.6% | 64.1% |
| 1986 | 64.0 | 65.3 | 64.3 |
| 1990 | 58.8 | 63.8 | 62.2 |
| 1994 | 58.5 | 64.6 | 62.5 |
| 1998 | 60.2 | 63.9 | 62.1 |
| 2002 | 58.8 | 63.1 | 60.9 |
| 2006* | 57.4 | 64.0 | 61.6 |
| *Percent reporting voting* | | | |
| 1982 | 43.0% | 49.9% | 48.5% |
| 1986 | 43.2 | 47.0 | 46.0 |
| 1990 | 39.2 | 46.7 | 45.0 |
| 1994 | 37.1 | 47.3 | 45.0 |
| 1998 | 39.6 | 43.3 | 41.9 |
| 2002 | 39.7 | 44.1 | 42.3 |
| 2006* | 38.6 | 45.8 | 43.6 |

Source:   US Bureau of the Census, *Statistical Abstract of the United States, 1989*, table 432;
          *1999*, table 487; *2008*, table 404.
          US Bureau of the Census, Current Population Reports: *Voting and Registration in the
          Election of November, 1988*, table 8; *1990*, table 2; *1992*, table 2; *1994*, tables 1 and
          VI; *1996*, table 23; *2000*, table A; *2002*, table 2; *2004*, table 2.

Notes:    'All Races' includes races not shown separately.
          * For 2004 and 2006, 'Black' and 'White' are equivalent to 'Black Alone' and 'White
          Alone' respectively.

Units:    Voting-age population in millions of persons; percent reporting registration and
          percent reporting voting out of the voting-age population.

## Table 4.04: Selected Characteristics of the Voting-Age Population, 1990

|  | Black | White | All Races |
|---|---|---|---|
| *Total 18 years and over* | *20,371* | *155,587* | *182,118* |
| **by Age** | | | |
| 18-20 years old | 1,671 | 8,722 | 10,800 |
| 21-24 years old | 1,854 | 11,635 | 14,031 |
| 25-34 years old | 5,352 | 35,682 | 45,652 |
| 35-44 years old | 4,153 | 32,281 | 37,889 |
| 45-54 years old | 2,669 | 21,983 | 25,648 |
| 55-64 years old | 2,144 | 18,477 | 21,223 |
| 65-74 years old | 1,609 | 16,180 | 18,126 |
| 75 years and over | 919 | 10,627 | 11,748 |
| **by Sex** | | | |
| Male | 9,093 | 74,625 | 86,621 |
| Female | 11,277 | 80,962 | 95,496 |
| **by Years of school completed** | | | |
| *Elementary* | | | |
| 0-4 years of school | 712 | 2,617 | 3,669 |
| 5-7 years of school | 1,038 | 5,096 | 6,445 |
| 8 years of school | 832 | 6,564 | 7,617 |
| *High school* | | | |
| 1-3 years high school | 3,729 | 16,733 | 20,956 |
| 4 years high school | 8,241 | 61,342 | 71,492 |
| *College* | | | |
| 1-3 years college | 3,714 | 31,481 | 36,300 |
| 4 years college | 1,331 | 18,900 | 21,350 |
| 5 or more years college | 774 | 12,855 | 14,288 |

*(continued on next page)*

## Table 4.04: Selected Characteristics of the Voting-Age Population, 1990

|  | **Black** | **White** | **All Races** |
|---|---|---|---|
| **by Family income** |  |  |  |
| Under $5,000 | 1,981 | 4,503 | 6,799 |
| $5,000-$9,999 | 2,395 | 6,978 | 9,808 |
| $10,000-$14,999 | 2,173 | 11,049 | 13,759 |
| $15,000-$19,999 | 1,439 | 8,677 | 10,496 |
| $20,000-$24,999 | 1,284 | 10,619 | 12,304 |
| $25,000-$34,999 | 2,120 | 20,827 | 23,627 |
| $35,000-$49,999 | 1,852 | 22,698 | 25,367 |
| $50,000 and over | 1,348 | 30,330 | 32,818 |
| Income not reported | 1,547 | 9,555 | 11,576 |

**Source:** US Bureau of the Census, Current Population Reports: *Voting and Registration in the Election of November, 1990*, tables 2, 8, and 13.

**Notes:** 'All Races' includes races not shown separately.

**Units:** Voting-age population (18 years and over) in thousands.

## Table 4.05: Selected Characteristics of Persons Registered to Vote, 1990

|  | Black | White | All Races |
|---|---|---|---|
| *Total 18 years and over* | *58.8%* | *63.8%* | *62.2%* |
| **by Age** |  |  |  |
| 18-20 years old | 30.4 | 37.0 | 35.4 |
| 21-24 years old | 49.1 | 43.1 | 43.3 |
| 25-34 years old | 52.1 | 53.2 | 52.0 |
| 35-44 years old | 63.6 | 67.2 | 65.5 |
| 45-54 years old | 67.0 | 71.3 | 69.8 |
| 55-64 years old | 71.4 | 74.9 | 73.5 |
| 65-74 years old | 72.5 | 79.7 | 78.3 |
| 75 years and over | 68.9 | 74.8 | 73.7 |
| **by Sex** |  |  |  |
| Male | 56.0% | 63.0% | 61.2% |
| Female | 60.9 | 64.6 | 63.1 |
| **by Years of school completed** |  |  |  |
| *Elementary* |  |  |  |
| 0-4 years of school | 50.7% | 26.4% | 29.5% |
| 5-7 years of school | 58.2 | 38.7 | 41.1 |
| 8 years of school | 53.2 | 54.3 | 53.3 |
| *High school* |  |  |  |
| 1-3 years high school | 49.5% | 48.2% | 47.9% |
| 4 years high school | 57.1 | 61.2 | 60.0 |
| *College* |  |  |  |
| 1-3 years college | 65.4% | 70.2% | 68.7% |
| 4 years college | 72.2 | 77.1 | 74.5 |
| 5 or more years college | 80.4 | 83.5 | 81.5 |

*(continued on next page)*

## Table 4.05: Selected Characteristics of Persons Registered to Vote, 1990

|  | Black | White | All Races |
|---|---|---|---|
| **by Family income** | | | |
| Under $5,000 | 47.5% | 53.1% | 50.7% |
| $5,000-$9,999 | 53.5 | 47.6 | 48.3 |
| $10,000-$14,999 | 58.6 | 55.4 | 54.8 |
| $15,000-$19,999 | 61.4 | 57.5 | 56.8 |
| $20,000-$24,999 | 58.8 | 59.0 | 58.0 |
| $25,000-$34,999 | 62.3 | 65.0 | 63.9 |
| $35,000-$49,999 | 67.9 | 69.4 | 68.3 |
| $50,000 and over | 74.4 | 77.8 | 76.4 |
| Income not reported | 55.0 | 59.7 | 57.6 |

Source: US Bureau of the Census, Current Population Reports: *Voting and Registration in the Election of November, 1990*, tables 2, 8 and 13.

Notes: 'All Races' includes races not shown separately.

Units: Percent of voting-age population reporting being registered to vote in election.

## Table 4.06: Selected Characteristics of Persons Voting, 1990

|  | Black | White | All Races |
|---|---|---|---|
| *Total 18 years and over* | *39.2%* | *46.7%* | *45.0%* |
| **by Age** |  |  |  |
| 18-20 years old | 15.0 | 19.4 | 18.4 |
| 21-24 years old | 24.9 | 21.8 | 22.0 |
| 25-34 years old | 32.4 | 34.9 | 33.8 |
| 35-44 years old | 44.7 | 50.0 | 48.4 |
| 45-54 years old | 45.7 | 54.9 | 53.2 |
| 55-64 years old | 54.0 | 60.4 | 58.9 |
| 65-74 years old | 54.6 | 65.7 | 64.1 |
| 75 years and over | 45.4 | 55.8 | 54.5 |
| **by Sex** |  |  |  |
| Male | 37.3% | 46.4% | 44.6% |
| Female | 40.6 | 46.9 | 45.4 |
| **by Years of school completed** |  |  |  |
| *Elementary* |  |  |  |
| 0-4 years of school | 27.4% | 14.8% | 16.5% |
| 5-7 years of school | 37.9 | 23.7 | 25.7 |
| 8 years of school | 33.3 | 35.7 | 34.8 |
| *High school* |  |  |  |
| 1-3 years high school | 30.7% | 31.3% | 30.9% |
| 4 years high school | 36.2 | 43.6 | 42.2 |
| *College* |  |  |  |
| 1-3 years college | 45.8% | 51.4% | 50.0% |
| 4 years college | 58.1 | 61.6 | 59.0 |
| 5 or more years college | 65.9 | 69.6 | 67.8 |

*(continued on next page)*

## Table 4.06: Selected Characteristics of Persons Voting, 1990

|  | Black | White | All Races |
|---|---|---|---|
| **by Family income** |  |  |  |
| Under $5,000 | 26.8% | 35.1% | 32.2% |
| $5,000-$9,999 | 31.9 | 31.3 | 30.9 |
| $10,000-$14,999 | 38.2 | 38.5 | 37.7 |
| $15,000-$19,999 | 39.2 | 39.9 | 38.8 |
| $20,000-$24,999 | 38.2 | 42.5 | 41.3 |
| $25,000-$34,999 | 42.6 | 47.5 | 46.4 |
| $35,000-$49,999 | 51.2 | 51.8 | 51.0 |
| $50,000 and over | 54.3 | 60.5 | 59.2 |
| Income not reported | 39.1 | 45.1 | 43.3 |

**Source:** US Bureau of the Census, Current Population Reports: *Voting and Registration in the Election of November, 1990*, tables 2, 8 and 13.

**Notes:** 'All Races' includes races not shown separately.

**Units:** Pecent of voting-age population reporting voting in election.

## Table 4.07: Selected Characteristics of the Voting-Age Population, 2000

| | Black | White | All Races |
|---|---|---|---|
| *Total, 18 years and over* | *24,132* | *168,733* | *202,609* |
| **by Sex** | | | |
| Male | 10,771 | 81,720 | 97,087 |
| Female | 13,361 | 87,014 | 105,523 |
| **by Age** | | | |
| 18-24 years old | 3,944 | 21,295 | 26,712 |
| 25-44 years old | 10,816 | 66,378 | 81,780 |
| 45-64 years old | 6,585 | 52,038 | 61,352 |
| 65-74 years old | 1,754 | 15,493 | 17,819 |
| 75 years and over | 1,033 | 13,529 | 14,945 |
| **by Educational attainment** | | | |
| Less than 9th grade | 1,497 | 10,626 | 12,894 |
| 9th to 12th grade, no diploma | 3,569 | 15,822 | 20,108 |
| High school graduate or GED | 8,382 | 55,530 | 66,339 |
| Some college or associate degree | 7,041 | 45,923 | 55,308 |
| Bachelor's degree | 2,545 | 27,382 | 32,254 |
| Advanced degree | 1,096 | 13,450 | 15,706 |
| **by Employment status** | | | |
| In civilian labor force | 16,561 | 115,103 | 138,378 |
| Unemployed | 1,137 | 3,544 | 4,944 |
| **by Family income** | | | |
| Less than $5,000 | 660 | 1,405 | 2,230 |
| $5,000-$9,999 | 1,299 | 2,732 | 4,242 |
| $10,000-$14,999 | 1,534 | 5,390 | 7,286 |
| $15,000-$24,999 | 2,341 | 11,568 | 14,600 |
| $25,000-$34,999 | 2,292 | 14,578 | 17,692 |
| $35,000-$49,999 | 2,419 | 18,907 | 22,349 |
| $50,000-$74,999 | 2,661 | 24,250 | 28,144 |
| $75,000 and over | 1,907 | 31,021 | 35,030 |
| Income not reported | 2,311 | 17,518 | 20,721 |

**Source:** US Bureau of the Census, Current Population Reports: *Voting and Registration in the Election of November, 2000*, tables 2, 6, 7, and 9.

**Notes:** 'All Races' includes races not shown separately.

**Units:** Voting-age population (18 years and over) in thousands.

## Table 4.08:  Selected Characteristics of Persons Registered to Vote, 2000

|  | Black | White | All Races |
|---|---|---|---|
| *Total, 18 years and over* | 63.6% | 65.6% | 63.9% |
| **by Sex** |  |  |  |
| Male | 59.6% | 64.0% | 62.2% |
| Female | 66.8 | 67.2 | 65.6 |
| **by Age** |  |  |  |
| 18-24 years old | 48.0% | 46.3% | 45.4% |
| 25-44 years old | 62.0 | 61.2 | 59.6 |
| 45-64 years old | 70.9 | 72.7 | 71.2 |
| 65-74 years old | 75.2 | 77.3 | 76.2 |
| 75 years and over | 73.0 | 77.2 | 76.1 |
| **by Educational attainment** |  |  |  |
| Less than 9th grade | 54.5% | 34.8% | 36.1% |
| 9th to 12th grade, no diploma | 54.3 | 44.8 | 45.9 |
| High school graduate or GED | 59.4 | 61.3 | 60.1 |
| Some college or associate degree | 68.8 | 71.8 | 70.0 |
| Bachelor's degree | 75.5 | 79.6 | 76.3 |
| Advanced degree | 77.7 | 83.1 | 79.4 |
| **by Employment status** |  |  |  |
| In civilian labor force | 64.8% | 65.5% | 64.0% |
| Unemployed | 54.7 | 44.9 | 46.1 |
| **by Family income** |  |  |  |
| Less than $5,000 | 58.9% | 40.7% | 44.0% |
| $5,000-$9,999 | 59.6 | 45.3 | 48.8 |
| $10,000-$14,999 | 62.1 | 47.5 | 49.8 |
| $15,000-$24,999 | 61.9 | 55.1 | 54.9 |
| $25,000-$34,999 | 65.3 | 61.9 | 61.0 |
| $35,000-$49,999 | 66.5 | 68.8 | 67.1 |
| $50,000-$74,999 | 71.4 | 75.9 | 73.8 |
| $75,000 and over | 79.4 | 80.7 | 78.4 |
| Income not reported | 53.3 | 55.5 | 54.2 |

Source:  US Bureau of the Census, Current Population Reports: *Voting and Registration in the Election of November, 2000*, tables 2, 6, 7, and 9.

Notes:  'All Races' includes races not shown separately.

Units:  Percent of voting-age population reporting being registered to vote in election.

## Table 4.09: Selected Characteristics of Persons Voting, 2000

| | Black | White | All Races |
|---|---|---|---|
| *Total, 18 years and over* | *53.5%* | *56.4%* | *54.7%* |
| **by Sex** | | | |
| Male | 49.5% | 54.9% | 53.1% |
| Female | 56.8 | 57.7 | 56.2 |
| **by Age** | | | |
| 18-24 years old | 33.9% | 33.0% | 32.3% |
| 25-44 years old | 52.1 | 51.2 | 49.8 |
| 45-64 years old | 62.9 | 65.6 | 64.1 |
| 65-74 years old | 68.1 | 71.1 | 69.9 |
| 75 years and over | 58.8 | 66.2 | 64.9 |
| **by Educational attainment** | | | |
| Less than 9th grade | 41.1% | 25.8% | 26.8% |
| 9th to 12th grade, no diploma | 40.5 | 32.7 | 33.6 |
| High school graduate or GED | 49.1 | 50.4 | 49.4 |
| Some college or associate degree | 59.0 | 62.0 | 60.3 |
| Bachelor's degree | 69.9 | 73.4 | 70.3 |
| Advanced degree | 73.2 | 79.3 | 75.5 |
| **by Employment status** | | | |
| In civilian labor force | 55.2% | 56.2% | 54.8% |
| Unemployed | 41.2 | 34.6 | 35.1 |
| **by Family income** | | | |
| Less than $5,000 | 35.0% | 27.3% | 28.2% |
| $5,000-$9,999 | 41.3 | 32.5 | 34.7 |
| $10,000-$14,999 | 48.3 | 35.6 | 37.7 |
| $15,000-$24,999 | 50.5 | 43.3 | 43.4 |
| $25,000-$34,999 | 54.7 | 51.8 | 51.0 |
| $35,000-$49,999 | 58.9 | 58.8 | 57.5 |
| $50,000-$74,999 | 63.7 | 67.1 | 65.2 |
| $75,000 and over | 73.0 | 73.8 | 71.5 |
| Income not reported | 45.7 | 49.6 | 48.2 |

**Source:** US Bureau of the Census, Current Population Reports: *Voting and Registration in the Election of November, 2000*, tables 2, 6, 7, and 9.

**Notes:** 'All Races' includes races not shown separately.

**Units:** Pecent of voting-age population reporting voting in election.

## Table 4.10: Selected Characteristics of the Voting-Age Population, 2002

|  | Black | White | All Races |
|---|---|---|---|
| *Total, 18 years and over* | *24,445* | *174,099* | *210,421* |
| **by Sex** | | | |
| Male | 10,811 | 84,466 | 100,939 |
| Female | 13,634 | 89,633 | 109,481 |
| **by Age** | | | |
| 18-24 years old | 3,930 | 21,728 | 27,377 |
| 25-44 years old | 10,478 | 66,238 | 82,228 |
| 45-64 years old | 7,207 | 56,204 | 66,924 |
| 65-74 years old | 1,618 | 15,653 | 17,967 |
| 75 years and over | 1,212 | 14,276 | 15,925 |
| **by Educational attainment** | | | |
| Less than 9th grade | 1,310 | 10,195 | 12,333 |
| 9th to 12th grade, no diploma | 3,748 | 16,161 | 20,908 |
| High school graduate or GED | 8,869 | 57,210 | 68,866 |
| Some college or associate degree | 6,969 | 47,538 | 57,343 |
| Bachelor's degree | 2,538 | 28,693 | 34,095 |
| Advanced degree | 1,012 | 14,302 | 16,877 |
| **by Employment status** | | | |
| In civilian labor force | 16,338 | 118,094 | 142,635 |
| Unemployed | 1,680 | 5,488 | 7,735 |
| **by Family income** | | | |
| Less than $5,000 | 716 | 1,280 | 2,159 |
| $5,000-$9,999 | 1,128 | 2,707 | 4,051 |
| $10,000-$14,999 | 1,288 | 4,960 | 6,696 |
| $15,000-$24,999 | 2,290 | 11,696 | 14,665 |
| $25,000-$34,999 | 2,378 | 13,412 | 16,868 |
| $35,000-$49,999 | 2,500 | 18,200 | 21,945 |
| $50,000-$74,999 | 2,535 | 24,932 | 28,921 |
| $75,000 and over | 1,977 | 35,540 | 40,309 |
| Income not reported | 2,760 | 18,188 | 22,278 |

**Source:** US Bureau of the Census, Current Population Reports: *Voting and Registration in the Election of November, 2002*, tables 2, 6, 7, and 9.

**Notes:** 'All Races' includes races not shown separately.

**Units:** Voting-age population (18 years and over) in thousands.

## Table 4.11: Selected Characteristics of Persons Registered to Vote, 2002

|  | Black | White | All Races |
|---|---|---|---|
| *Total, 18 years and over* | *58.5%* | *63.1%* | *60.9%* |
| **by Sex** | | | |
| Male | 53.3% | 61.3% | 58.9% |
| Female | 62.7 | 64.8 | 62.8 |
| **by Age** | | | |
| 18-24 years old | 39.6% | 39.2% | 38.2% |
| 25-44 years old | 55.8 | 57.4 | 55.4 |
| 45-64 years old | 66.9 | 71.3 | 69.4 |
| 65-74 years old | 74.0 | 77.9 | 76.1 |
| 75 years and over | 72.8 | 76.7 | 75.5 |
| **by Educational attainment** | | | |
| Less than 9th grade | 48.4% | 31.6% | 32.4% |
| 9th to 12th grade, no diploma | 49.6 | 41.1 | 41.6 |
| High school graduate or GED | 54.5 | 58.7 | 57.1 |
| Some college or associate degree | 63.6 | 68.8 | 66.7 |
| Bachelor's degree | 72.4 | 76.7 | 73.3 |
| Advanced degree | 69.9 | 81.3 | 76.6 |
| **by Employment status** | | | |
| In civilian labor force | 59.5% | 62.8% | 60.9% |
| Unemployed | 52.6 | 48.6 | 48.1 |
| **by Family income** | | | |
| Less than $5,000 | 59.5% | 39.5% | 45.2% |
| $5,000-$9,999 | 47.5 | 40.1 | 41.5 |
| $10,000-$14,999 | 56.8 | 50.3 | 49.7 |
| $15,000-$24,999 | 60.0 | 51.0 | 51.3 |
| $25,000-$34,999 | 56.0 | 58.5 | 56.2 |
| $35,000-$49,999 | 61.4 | 64.1 | 62.0 |
| $50,000-$74,999 | 67.8 | 72.0 | 69.8 |
| $75,000 and over | 73.8 | 77.8 | 75.5 |
| Income not reported | 49.4 | 54.4 | 52.0 |

**Source:** US Bureau of the Census, Current Population Reports: *Voting and Registration in the Election of November, 2002*, tables 2, 6, 7, and 9.

**Notes:** 'All Races' includes races not shown separately.

**Units:** Percent of voting-age population reporting being registered to vote in election.

## Table 4.12: Selected Characteristics of Persons Voting, 2002

| | Black | White | All Races |
|---|---|---|---|
| *Total, 18 years and over* | *39.7%* | *44.1%* | *42.3%* |
| **by Sex** | | | |
| Male | 35.3% | 43.5% | 41.4% |
| Female | 43.1 | 44.6 | 43.0 |
| **by Age** | | | |
| 18-24 years old | 19.3% | 17.4% | 17.2% |
| 25-44 years old | 36.1 | 35.3 | 34.1 |
| 45-64 years old | 50.0 | 54.8 | 53.1 |
| 65-74 years old | 57.0 | 65.1 | 63.1 |
| 75 years and over | 51.9 | 60.1 | 58.6 |
| **by Educational attainment** | | | |
| Less than 9$^{th}$ grade | 28.7% | 19.0% | 19.4% |
| 9$^{th}$ to 12$^{th}$ grade, no diploma | 27.6 | 23.1 | 23.3 |
| High school graduate or GED | 34.8 | 38.3 | 37.1 |
| Some college or associate degree | 44.7 | 47.3 | 45.8 |
| Bachelor's degree | 58.9 | 59.1 | 56.2 |
| Advanced degree | 58.1 | 67.7 | 63.2 |
| **by Employment status** | | | |
| In civilian labor force | 40.7% | 42.7% | 41.3% |
| Unemployed | 27.1 | 28.2 | 27.2 |
| **by Family income** | | | |
| Less than $5,000 | 30.0% | 19.6% | 22.0% |
| $5,000-$9,999 | 23.9 | 19.8 | 20.7 |
| $10,000-$14,999 | 34.5 | 31.1 | 30.5 |
| $15,000-$24,999 | 37.5 | 31.9 | 32.0 |
| $25,000-$34,999 | 37.2 | 40.2 | 38.3 |
| $35,000-$49,999 | 42.9 | 44.2 | 42.7 |
| $50,000-$74,999 | 50.6 | 51.7 | 50.1 |
| $75,000 and over | 58.3 | 58.3 | 56.6 |
| Income not reported | 37.2 | 40.5 | 38.6 |

Source: US Bureau of the Census, Current Population Reports: *Voting and Registration in the Election of November, 2002*, tables 2, 6, 7, and 9.

Notes: 'All Races' includes races not shown separately.

Units: Pecent of voting-age population reporting voting in election.

## Table 4.13: Selected Characteristics of the Voting-Age Population, 2004

| | Black | White | All Races |
|---|---|---|---|
| *Total, 18 years and over* | *24,910* | *176,618* | *215,694* |
| **by Sex** | | | |
| Male | 11,072 | 85,984 | 103,812 |
| Female | 13,838 | 90,634 | 111,882 |
| **by Age** | | | |
| 18-24 years old | 3,942 | 21,764 | 27,808 |
| 25-44 years old | 10,368 | 65,317 | 82,133 |
| 45-64 years old | 7,690 | 59,196 | 71,014 |
| 65-74 years old | 1,725 | 15,783 | 18,363 |
| 75 years and over | 1,185 | 14,557 | 16,375 |
| **by Educational attainment** | | | |
| Less than 9th grade | 1,218 | 10,431 | 12,574 |
| 9th to 12th grade, no diploma | 3,742 | 15,793 | 20,719 |
| High school graduate or GED | 8,853 | 56,254 | 68,545 |
| Some college or associate degree | 7,280 | 48,154 | 58,913 |
| Bachelor's degree | 2,670 | 30,678 | 36,591 |
| Advanced degree | 1,147 | 15,308 | 18,352 |
| **by Employment status** | | | |
| In civilian labor force | 16,600 | 119,726 | 146,082 |
| Unemployed | 1,693 | 5,030 | 7,251 |
| **by Family income** | | | |
| Less than $10,000 | 1,817 | 4,088 | 6,404 |
| $10,000-$14,999 | 1,230 | 4,874 | 6,565 |
| $15,000-$19,999 | 999 | 4,386 | 5,859 |
| $20,000-$29,999 | 2,290 | 12,339 | 15,574 |
| $30,000-$39,999 | 1,989 | 14,042 | 17,194 |
| $40,000-$49,999 | 1,342 | 11,170 | 13,281 |
| $50,000-$74,999 | 2,684 | 25,568 | 30,179 |
| $75,000-$99,999 | 1,208 | 15,707 | 18,123 |
| $100,000-$149,999 | 842 | 12,894 | 14,905 |
| $150,000 and over | 343 | 8,003 | 9,120 |
| Income not reported | 3,163 | 19,886 | 24,723 |

**Source:**  US Bureau of the Census, Current Population Reports: *Voting and Registration in the Election of November, 2004*, tables 2, 6, 7, and 9.

**Notes:**  'All Races' includes races not shown separately. 'White' and 'Black' are equivalent to 'White Alone' and 'Black Alone' respectively.

**Units:**  Voting-age population (18 years and over) in thousands.

## Table 4.14: Selected Characteristics of Persons Registered to Vote, 2004

|  | Black | White | All Races |
|---|---|---|---|
| *Total, 18 years and over* | *64.4%* | *67.9%* | *65.9%* |
| **by Sex** |  |  |  |
| Male | 60.0% | 66.2% | 64.0% |
| Female | 67.9 | 69.5 | 67.6 |
| **by Age** |  |  |  |
| 18-24 years old | 53.1% | 52.5% | 51.5% |
| 25-44 years old | 62.2 | 62.0 | 60.1 |
| 45-64 years old | 69.6 | 74.6 | 72.7 |
| 65-74 years old | 73.2 | 78.4 | 76.9 |
| 75 years and over | 74.5 | 78.4 | 76.8 |
| **by Educational attainment** |  |  |  |
| Less than 9th grade | 51.7% | 31.5% | 32.5% |
| 9th to 12th grade, no diploma | 55.1 | 44.6 | 45.7 |
| High school graduate or GED | 61.1 | 62.7 | 61.5 |
| Some college or associate degree | 70.9 | 75.6 | 73.7 |
| Bachelor's degree | 72.2 | 80.9 | 77.0 |
| Advanced degree | 73.9 | 85.5 | 80.3 |
| **by Employment status** |  |  |  |
| In civilian labor force | 65.6% | 68.5% | 66.5% |
| Unemployed | 64.8 | 55.2 | 56.3 |
| **by Family income** |  |  |  |
| Less than $10,000 | 64.6% | 43.8% | 49.5% |
| $10,000-$14,999 | 64.1 | 46.2 | 49.0 |
| $15,000-$19,999 | 64.5 | 52.6 | 53.9 |
| $20,000-$29,999 | 66.1 | 58.2 | 58.1 |
| $30,000-$39,999 | 70.3 | 63.9 | 62.9 |
| $40,000-$49,999 | 68.5 | 71.9 | 69.8 |
| $50,000-$74,999 | 75.4 | 77.8 | 75.6 |
| $75,000-$99,999 | 76.3 | 82.3 | 79.4 |
| $100,000-$149,999 | 77.4 | 84.9 | 82.2 |
| $150,000 and over | 74.2 | 85.2 | 82.6 |
| Income not reported | 43.7 | 56.1 | 53.0 |

Source:   US Bureau of the Census, Current Population Reports: *Voting and Registration in the Election of November, 2004*, tables 2, 6, 7, and 9.

Notes:    'All Races' includes races not shown separately. 'White' and 'Black' are equivalent to 'White Alone' and 'Black Alone' respectively.

Units:    Percent of voting-age population reporting being registered to vote in election.

## Table 4.15: Selected Characteristics of Persons Voting, 2004

|  | Black | White | All Races |
|---|---|---|---|
| *Total, 18 years and over* | *56.3%* | *60.3%* | *58.3%* |
| **by Sex** |  |  |  |
| Male | 51.8% | 58.6% | 56.3% |
| Female | 59.8 | 62.0 | 60.1 |
| **by Age** |  |  |  |
| 18-24 years old | 44.1% | 42.6% | 41.9% |
| 25-44 years old | 54.0 | 54.0 | 52.2 |
| 45-64 years old | 62.6 | 68.6 | 66.6 |
| 65-74 years old | 66.3 | 72.4 | 70.8 |
| 75 years and over | 60.9 | 68.4 | 66.7 |
| **by Educational attainment** |  |  |  |
| Less than 9th grade | 38.5% | 22.7% | 23.6% |
| 9th to 12th grade, no diploma | 43.1 | 33.3 | 34.6 |
| High school graduate or GED | 52.4 | 53.4 | 52.4 |
| Some college or associate degree | 63.6 | 68.0 | 66.1 |
| Bachelor's degree | 68.7 | 76.7 | 72.6 |
| Advanced degree | 72.6 | 82.7 | 77.4 |
| **by Employment status** |  |  |  |
| In civilian labor force | 58.6% | 61.1% | 59.3% |
| Unemployed | 55.5 | 45.1 | 46.4 |
| **by Family income** |  |  |  |
| Less than $10,000 | 49.4% | 31.7% | 36.5% |
| $10,000-$14,999 | 52.0 | 36.7 | 39.1 |
| $15,000-$19,999 | 56.1 | 44.0 | 45.2 |
| $20,000-$29,999 | 55.2 | 49.7 | 49.4 |
| $30,000-$39,999 | 62.7 | 55.0 | 54.3 |
| $40,000-$49,999 | 61.0 | 64.4 | 62.3 |
| $50,000-$74,999 | 69.4 | 70.2 | 68.1 |
| $75,000-$99,999 | 73.7 | 76.8 | 74.1 |
| $100,000-$149,999 | 74.4 | 80.4 | 77.8 |
| $150,000 and over | 72.8 | 81.0 | 78.3 |
| Income not reported | 39.6 | 50.4 | 47.6 |

**Source:** US Bureau of the Census, Current Population Reports: *Voting and Registration in the Election of November, 2004*, tables 2, 6, 7, and 9.

**Notes:** 'All Races' includes races not shown separately. 'White' and 'Black' are equivalent to 'White Alone' and 'Black Alone' respectively.

**Units:** Pecent of voting-age population reporting voting in election.

## Table 4.16: Reasons for Not Registering to Vote, 2004

|  | Black | White | All Races |
|---|---|---|---|
| Total not registered | 3,376 | 26,185 | 32,432 |
| *Percent distribution* |  |  |  |
| Not interested in the election or not involved in politics | 38.3% | 48.2% | 46.6% |
| Did not meet registration deadlines | 18.3 | 17.5 | 17.4 |
| Not eligible to vote | 9.6 | 6.0 | 6.7 |
| Don't know or refused | 9.0 | 5.6 | 6.2 |
| Permanent illness or disability | 7.1 | 5.5 | 5.6 |
| Did not know where or how to register | 5.3 | 4.2 | 4.5 |
| Did not meet residency requirements | 3.3 | 3.7 | 3.7 |
| My vote would not make a difference | 4.4 | 3.8 | 3.7 |
| Difficulty with English | 0.1 | 0.8 | 1.0 |

**Source:** US Bureau of the Census, Current Population Reports: *Voting and Registration in the Election of November, 2004*, table E.

**Notes:** 'All Races' includes races not shown separately. 'White' and 'Black' are equivalent to 'White Alone' and 'Black Alone' respectively.

**Units:** Number of non-registered persons in thousands; percent distribution of reasons for not registering to vote among voting-age population.

## Table 4.17: Reasons for Not Voting, 2004

|  | Black | White | All Races |
|---|---|---|---|
| Total not voting | 2,019 | 13,341 | 16,334 |
| *Percent distribution* |  |  |  |
| Too busy, conflicting schedule | 20.7% | 19.4% | 19.9% |
| Illness or disability | 16.5 | 15.6 | 15.4 |
| Other reason | 9.8 | 10.9 | 10.9 |
| Not interested | 10.0 | 10.8 | 10.7 |
| Did not like candidates or issues | 6.4 | 10.6 | 9.9 |
| Out of town | 5.5 | 9.4 | 9.0 |
| Don't know or refused | 13.0 | 7.9 | 8.5 |
| Registration problems | 7.2 | 6.8 | 6.8 |
| Forgot to vote | 3.9 | 3.4 | 3.4 |
| Inconvenient polling place | 2.6 | 3.0 | 3.0 |
| Transportation problems | 4.2 | 1.9 | 2.1 |
| Bad weather conditions | 0.3 | 0.4 | 0.5 |

**Source:** US Bureau of the Census, Current Population Reports: *Voting and Registration in the Election of November, 2004*, table F.

**Notes:** 'All Races' includes races not shown separately. 'White' and 'Black' are equivalent to 'White Alone' and 'Black Alone' respectively.

**Units:** Number of non-voters in thousands; percent distribution of reasons for not voting.

## Table 4.18: Percent Voting Democratic or Republican in Presidential Elections, 2000 and 2004

|  | Black | White | Total |
|---|---|---|---|
| **2000** |  |  |  |
| Democratic | 92% | 46% | 52% |
| Republican | 8 | 54 | 48 |
| **2004** |  |  |  |
| Democratic | 90% | 42% | 50% |
| Republican | 10 | 58 | 50 |

Source: US Bureau of the Census, *Statistical Abstract of the United States, 2006*, table 386.

Notes: Third-party or independent votes are not included. Percentages for Democratic presidential vote are computed by subtracting the percentage Republican vote from 100 percent. Includes voting-age citizens living in private housing units in the contiguous United States.

Units: Percent of total voting Democratic or Republican.

## Table 4.19: Members of Congress, 1981–2007

|  | Black | White | All Races |
|---|---|---|---|
| **House of Representatives** | | | |
| 97th Congress, 1981 | 17 | 415 | 434 |
| 98th Congress, 1983 | 21 | 411 | " |
| 99th Congress, 1985 | 20 | 412 | 435 |
| 100th Congress, 1987 | 23 | 408 | 433 |
| 101st Congress, 1989 | 24 | 406 | 435 |
| 102nd Congress, 1991 | 25 | 407 | " |
| 103rd Congress, 1993 | 38 | 393 | " |
| 104th Congress, 1995 | 40 | 391 | " |
| 106th Congress, 1999 | 39 | NA | " |
| 107th Congress, 2001 | 39 | NA | 443 |
| 108th Congress, 2003 | 39 | NA | 435 |
| 109th Congress, 2005 | 42 | NA | " |
| 110th Congress, 2007 | 39 | NA | " |
| **Senate** | | | |
| 97th Congress, 1981 | 0 | 97 | 100 |
| 98th Congress, 1983 | 0 | 98 | " |
| 99th Congress, 1985 | 0 | 98 | " |
| 100th Congress, 1987 | 0 | 98 | " |
| 101st Congress, 1989 | 0 | 98 | " |
| 102nd Congress, 1991 | 0 | 98 | " |
| 103rd Congress, 1993 | 1 | 97 | " |
| 104th Congress, 1995 | 1 | 97 | " |
| 106th Congress, 1999 | 0 | NA | " |
| 107th Congress, 2001 | 0 | NA | " |
| 108th Congress, 2003 | 0 | NA | " |
| 109th Congress, 2005 | 1 | 96 | " |
| 110th Congress, 2007 | 1 | 95 | " |

Source: US Bureau of the Census, *Statistical Abstract of the United States, 2006*, table 395; *2007*, table 395.

US House of Representatives, 'House Press Gallery' (accessed online at http://www.house.gov/daily/hpg.htm).

US Senate, 'Ethnic Diversity in the Senate' (accessed online at http://www.senate.gov/artandhistory/history/common/briefing/minority_senators.htm).

Notes: 'All Races' includes races not shown separately.

Units: Number of members of the House and Senate respectively, as shown.

# Chapter 5

## Crime, Law
## Enforcement & Corrections

## Chapter Five Highlights

This chapter provides statistics about crime, law enforcement, and corrections on Black persons in the United States, including both the most current data available as well as comparisons of the Black population over time. For almost all tables, corresponding data is provided for the total population of the United States as well as for White persons. This allows for easy comparison between groups.

This chapter includes data on crime victimization for both households (tables 5.05–5.07) and persons (tables 5.01–5.04).

This chapter also provides data on arrests by offense charged (tables 5.13–5.22), on arrests of minors (tables 5.16–5.18), and arrests in cities and suburban areas (tables 5.19–5.22).

We have also included statistics on incarceration, including incarceration rates (tables 5.23, 5.26, and 5.27), type of commitment offense (table 5.29), prisoners under sentence of death (tables 5.31–5.33), and HIV and AIDS rates in prisons and jails (tables 5.26 and 5.37). We have also provided data on the incarceration of minors (tables 5.40 and 5.41).

More detailed data on hate crimes has begun to be collected by the Census, and we have included a table detailing the bias motivation of hate crimes as well as a table showing the type of offense committed (tables 5.42 and 5.43).

Also of note are tables on the attitudes of Black Americans on a variety of current social issues, including the death penalty (table 5.45), crime victimization (table 5.46), the legality of homosexual relations (table 5.47), and the fairness and prevalence of racial profiling (table 5.48).

## Table 5.01: Victimization Rates for Personal Crimes by Type of Crime, 2005

| | Black Victims | White Victims | Victims of All Races |
|---|---|---|---|
| *All personal crimes* | *28.7* | *20.9* | *22.1* |
| **Crimes of violence** | 27.0 | 20.1 | 21.2 |
| Completed | 12.4 | 5.9 | 6.8 |
| Attempted/threatened | 14.7 | 14.2 | 14.4 |
| **Rape/sexual assault** | 1.8 | 0.6 | 0.8 |
| Rape/attempted rape | 1.1* | 0.4 | 0.5 |
| - Rape | 1.0* | 0.2 | 0.3 |
| - Attempted rape | 0.1* | 0.2 | 0.2 |
| Sexual assault | 0.7* | 0.2 | 0.3 |
| **Robbery** | 4.6 | 2.2 | 2.6 |
| Completed/property taken | 4.3 | 1.3 | 1.7 |
| - With injury | 1.0* | 0.5 | 0.6 |
| - Without injury | 3.4 | 0.7 | 1.1 |
| Attempted to take property | 0.3* | 1.0 | 0.9 |
| - With injury | 0.1* | 0.3 | 0.3 |
| - Without injury | 0.2* | 0.7 | 0.6 |
| **Assault** | 20.6 | 17.2 | 17.8 |
| Aggravated | 7.6 | 3.8 | 4.3 |
| - With injury | 2.9 | 1.1 | 1.4 |
| - Threatened with weapon | 4.8 | 2.7 | 3.0 |
| Simple | 13.0 | 13.4 | 13.5 |
| - With minor injury | 3.6 | 3.2 | 3.3 |
| - Without injury | 9.4 | 10.2 | 10.3 |
| **Purse-snatching/pocket-picking** | 1.7 | 0.9 | 0.9 |

**Source:** US Department of Justice, Office of Justice Programs, *Criminal Victimization 2005*, tables 5 and 7.

**Notes:** 'Victims of All Races' includes victims of races not shown separately.
'Personal crimes' include completed and attempted rape, robbery, assault, and larceny, but exclude homicide.
The National Crime Victimization Survey has been redesigned: comparisons of estimates of crime based on previous survey procedures (before 1993) are not recommended.
Data for persons 12 years old and over.
* Based on fewer than 10 sample cases.

**Units:** Rate per 1,000 persons 12 years old and over.

## Table 5.02: Victimization Rates for Personal Crimes, 2001–2005

| | Black Victims | White Victims | Victims of All Races |
|---|---|---|---|
| **2001** | | | |
| Crimes of violence | 31.2 | 24.5 | 25.1 |
| Rape/sexual assault | 1.1 | 1.0 | 1.1 |
| Robbery | 3.6 | 2.6 | 2.8 |
| Assault | 26.4 | 20.8 | 21.2 |
| Personal theft | 0.8* | 0.8 | 0.8 |
| **2002** | | | |
| Crimes of violence | 27.9 | 22.8 | 23.1 |
| Rape/sexual assault | 2.5 | 0.8 | 1.1 |
| Robbery | 4.1 | 1.9 | 2.2 |
| Assault | 21.3 | 20.0 | 19.8 |
| Personal theft | 0.7* | 0.7 | 0.7 |
| **2003** | | | |
| Crimes of violence | 29.1 | 21.5 | 22.6 |
| Rape/sexual assault | 0.8* | 0.8 | 0.8 |
| Robbery | 5.9 | 1.9 | 2.5 |
| Assault | 22.3 | 18.8 | 19.3 |
| Personal theft | 1.7 | 0.6 | 0.8 |
| **2004** | | | |
| Crimes of violence | 26.0 | 21.0 | 21.4 |
| Rape/sexual assault | 1.7 | 0.8 | 0.9 |
| Robbery | 3.7 | 1.8 | 2.1 |
| Assault | 20.7 | 18.4 | 18.5 |
| Personal theft | 1.5 | 0.8 | 0.9 |

*(continued on next page)*

## Table 5.02: Victimization Rates for Personal Crimes, 2001–2005

|  | Black Victims | White Victims | Victims of All Races |
|---|---|---|---|
| **2005** | | | |
| *All Personal Crimes* | *28.7* | *20.9* | *22.1* |
| Crimes of violence | 27.0 | 20.1 | 21.2 |
| Rape/sexual assault | 1.8 | 0.6 | 0.8 |
| Robbery | 4.6 | 2.2 | 2.6 |
| Assault | 20.6 | 17.2 | 17.8 |
| Personal theft | 1.7 | 0.9 | 0.9 |

Source:   US Department of Justice, Office of Justice Programs, *Criminal Victimization, 2001*, tables 1 and 2; *2002*, tables 3 and 6; *2003*, tables 3 and 6; *2004*; tables 3 and 6; *2005*, tables 5 and 7.

Notes:   'Victims of All Races' includes victims of races not shown separately.
'Personal crimes' include completed and attempted rape, robbery, assault, and larceny, but exclude homicide. 'Personal Theft' includes purse-snatching and pocket-picking.
The National Crime Victimization Survey has been redesigned: comparisons of estimates of crime based on previous survey procedures (before 1993) are not recommended.
Data for persons 12 years old and over.
* Based on 10 or fewer sample cases.

Units:   Rates per 1,000 persons, 12 years old and over.

## Table 5.03: Victimization Rates for Personal Crimes by Age of the Victim, 2005

| | Black Victims | White Victims | Victims of All Races |
|---|---|---|---|
| **Persons 12-15 years old** | | | |
| Crimes of violence | 59.5 | 39.9 | 44.0 |
| Completed | 25.4 | 11.7 | 14.7 |
| Attempted | 34.4 | 28.2 | 29.3 |
| Purse-snatching/Pocket-picking | 2.6* | 1.1* | 1.3* |
| **Persons 16-19 years old** | | | |
| Crimes of violence | 62.6 | 42.3 | 44.2 |
| Completed | 41.1 | 13.9 | 17.8 |
| Attempted | 21.5 | 28.4 | 26.4 |
| Purse-snatching/Pocket-picking | 4.2* | 1.2* | 1.6* |
| **Persons 20-24 years old** | | | |
| Crimes of violence | 45.8 | 49.0 | 46.9 |
| Completed | 19.9 | 14.4 | 14.7 |
| Attempted | 26.0 | 34.6 | 32.2 |
| Purse-snatching/Pocket-picking | 0.0* | 1.9* | 1.5* |
| **Persons 25-34 years old** | | | |
| Crimes of violence | 21.9 | 22.4 | 23.6 |
| Completed | 10.0 | 6.7 | 7.5 |
| Attempted | 11.8 | 15.8 | 16.1 |
| Purse-snatching/Pocket-picking | 0.6* | 1.2* | 1.0 |

*(continued on next page)*

## Table 5.03: Victimization Rates for Personal Crimes by Age of the Victim, 2005

|  | Black Victims | White Victims | Victims of All Races |
|---|---|---|---|
| **Persons 35-49 years old** |  |  |  |
| Crimes of violence | 17.9 | 17.4 | 17.5 |
| Completed | 6.4 | 5.2 | 5.3 |
| Attempted | 11.6 | 12.1 | 12.1 |
| Purse-snatching/Pocket-picking | 2.7* | 0.8 | 1.0 |
| **Persons 50-64 years old** |  |  |  |
| Crimes of violence | 16.2 | 10.6 | 11.4 |
| Completed | 6.2* | 2.4 | 3.0 |
| Attempted | 10.0 | 8.2 | 8.4 |
| Purse-snatching/Pocket-picking | 0.7* | 0.6* | 0.6* |
| **Persons 65 years old and over** |  |  |  |
| Crimes of violence | 2.2* | 2.4 | 2.4 |
| Completed | 0.0* | 0.6* | 0.6* |
| Attempted | 2.2* | 1.7 | 1.9 |
| Purse-snatching/Pocket-picking | 1.2* | 0.3* | 0.4* |

Source: US Department of Justice, Office of Justice Programs, *Criminal Victimization, 2005*, tables 3 and 9.

Notes: 'Victims of All Races' includes races not shown separately.
The National Crime Victimization Survey has been redesigned. Comparisons of estimates of crime based on previous survey procedures (before 1993) are not recommended.
*Based on 10 or fewer sample cases.

Units: Rates per 1,000 persons.

## Table 5.04: Victimization Rates for Personal Crimes by Sex of the Victim, 2005

|  | Black Victims | | White Victims | | Victims of All Races | |
|---|---|---|---|---|---|---|
|  | Male | Female | Male | Female | Male | Female |
| *All personal crimes* | *32.6* | *25.5* | *25.5* | *16.5* | *26.3* | *18.1* |
| Crimes of violence | 31.6 | 23.2 | 24.6 | 15.6 | 25.5 | 17.1 |
| Completed | 15.8 | 9.5 | 7.1 | 4.7 | 8.2 | 5.5 |
| Attempted/threatened | 15.7 | 13.8 | 17.5 | 10.9 | 17.3 | 11.6 |
| Rape/sexual assault | 0.2* | 3.1 | 0.1* | 1.1 | 0.1* | 1.4 |
| Robbery | 7.3 | 2.4 | 3.3 | 1.2 | 3.8 | 1.4 |
| Completed/property taken | 6.9 | 2.2* | 1.6 | 0.9 | 2.3 | 1.1 |
| - With injury | 1.0* | 0.9* | 0.8 | 0.3* | 0.8 | 0.4 |
| - Without injury | 5.9 | 1.3* | 0.8 | 0.6 | 1.5 | 0.7 |
| Attempted to take property | 0.4* | 0.2* | 1.7 | 0.3* | 1.5 | 0.3* |
| - With injury | 0.0* | 0.2* | 0.6 | 0.0* | 0.5 | 0.0* |
| - Without injury | 0.4* | 0.0* | 1.1 | 0.3* | 1.0 | 0.2* |
| Assault | 24.0 | 17.8 | 21.2 | 13.3 | 21.5 | 14.3 |
| Aggravated | 9.1 | 6.4 | 5.3 | 2.3 | 5.6 | 3.1 |
| - With injury | 3.5 | 2.4 | 1.5 | 0.7 | 1.8 | 1.0 |
| - Threatened with weapon | 5.6 | 4.0 | 3.8 | 1.7 | 3.8 | 2.1 |
| Simple | 14.9 | 11.4 | 15.9 | 11.0 | 15.9 | 11.2 |
| - With minor injury | 5.3 | 2.2* | 4.0 | 2.4 | 4.0 | 2.5 |
| - Without injury | 9.6 | 9.2 | 12.0 | 8.6 | 11.9 | 8.7 |
| Purse-snatching/pocket-picking | 1.1* | 2.2* | 0.9 | 0.9 | 0.8 | 1.0 |

Source: US Department of Justice, Office of Justice Programs, *Criminal Victimization, 2005*, tables 2 and 6.

Notes: 'Victims of All Races' includes races not shown separately.
The National Crime Victimization Survey has been redesigned: comparisons of estimates of crime based on previous survey procedures (before 1993) are not recommended.
Data for persons 12 years old and over.
*Based on 10 or fewer sample cases.

Units: Rates per 1,000 persons, 12 years old and over.

## Table 5.05: Household Victimization Rates for Property Crimes by Type of Crime, 2005

| | Black Households | White Households | All Households |
|---|---|---|---|
| *All property crimes* | *144.6* | *155.7* | *154.0* |
| Household burglary | 35.0 | 28.6 | 29.5 |
| Completed | 30.3 | 24.0 | 24.8 |
| - Forcible entry | 16.1 | 8.2 | 9.1 |
| - Unlawful entry without force | 14.2 | 15.8 | 15.6 |
| Attempted forcible entry | 4.7 | 4.6 | 4.7 |
| Theft | 12.7 | 7.6 | 8.4 |
| Completed | 11.7 | 5.8 | 6.6 |
| - Less than $50 | 1.0* | 1.8 | 1.7 |
| - $50-$249 | 96.9 | 119.6 | 116.2 |
| - $250 or more | 93.3 | 115.6 | 112.0 |
| - Amount not available | 24.6 | 36.7 | 34.8 |
| Attempted | 36.5 | 40.6 | 39.8 |
| Motor vehicle theft | 23.3 | 28.0 | 27.6 |
| Completed | 8.8 | 10.3 | 9.8 |
| Attempted | 3.6 | 4.0 | 4.2 |

Source:   US Department of Justice, Office of Justice Programs, *Criminal Victimization, 2005*, table 16.

Notes:   Data based on race of the head of household. 'All Households' includes households of races not shown separately.
The National Crime Victimization Survey has been redesigned: comparisons of estimates of crime based on previous survey procedures (before 1993) are not recommended.

Units:   Rates per 1,000 households.

## Table 5.06: Victimization Rates for Property Crimes by Locality of Residence, 1999–2005

| | Black Households | White Households | All Households |
|---|---|---|---|
| **1999** | | | |
| *All areas* | *249.9* | *190.0* | *198.0* |
| Urban | 299.0 | 247.5 | 256.3 |
| Suburban | 207.1 | 177.9 | 181.4 |
| Rural | 175.0 | 157.2 | 159.8 |
| **2002** | | | |
| *All areas* | *173.7* | *157.6* | *159.0* |
| Urban | 211.7 | 220.0 | 215.3 |
| Suburban | 150.4 | 145.9 | 145.3 |
| Rural | 95.7 | 120.6 | 118.3 |
| **2003** | | | |
| *All areas* | *190.2* | *159.1* | *163.2* |
| Urban | 224.0 | 218.1 | 216.3 |
| Suburban | 168.9 | 142.1 | 144.8 |
| Rural | 125.1 | 136.4 | 136.6 |
| **2005** | | | |
| *All areas* | *144.6* | *155.7* | *154.0* |
| Urban | 170.4 | 213.1 | 200.0 |
| Suburban | 131.7 | 142.4 | 141.4 |
| Rural | 90.6 | 127.7 | 125.1 |

Source:   US Department of Justice, Office of Justice Programs, *Criminal Victimization, 1999*, tables 53 and 55; *2002*, tables 53 and 55; *2003*, tables 53 and 55; *2005*, tables 53 and 55.

Notes:   Data based on race of the head of household. 'All Households' includes households of races not shown separately.
The National Crime Victimization Survey has been redesigned: comparisons of estimates of crime based on previous survey procedures (before 1993) are not recommended.

Units:   Rate per 1,000 households.

## Table 5.07: Victimization Rates for Property Crimes, Type of Crime by Housing Tenure, 2005

| | Black Households | White Households | All Households |
|---|---|---|---|
| **Owner-occupied** | | | |
| *All property crimes* | *118.5* | *138.3* | *136.5* |
| Household burglary | 27.8 | 24.9 | 25.3 |
| Completed | 24.0 | 21.0 | 21.3 |
| - Forcible entry | 13.5 | 6.7 | 7.3 |
| - Unlawful entry without force | 10.5 | 14.3 | 14.0 |
| Attempted forcible entry | 3.7* | 3.9 | 4.0 |
| Motor vehicle theft | 11.0 | 5.5 | 6.1 |
| Completed | 10.3 | 4.0 | 4.7 |
| Attempted | 0.7* | 1.6 | 1.4 |
| Theft | 79.7 | 107.9 | 105.1 |
| Completed | 76.7 | 104.0 | 101.1 |
| - Less than $50 | 20.5 | 33.8 | 32.3 |
| - $50-$249 | 29.5 | 35.3 | 34.4 |
| - $250 or more | 17.1 | 24.0 | 23.8 |
| - Amount not available | 9.6 | 10.9 | 10.6 |
| Attempted | 3.0* | 3.9 | 4.0 |
| **Renter-occupied** | | | |
| *All property crimes* | *170.3* | *201.2* | *192.3* |
| Household burglary | 42.2 | 38.1 | 38.6 |
| Completed | 36.5 | 31.8 | 32.4 |
| - Forcible entry | 18.7 | 12.3 | 13.1 |
| - Unlawful entry without force | 17.8 | 19.6 | 19.2 |
| Attempted forcible entry | 5.6 | 6.3 | 6.3 |
| Motor vehicle theft | 14.3 | 12.9 | 13.3 |
| Completed | 13.0 | 10.5 | 10.9 |
| Attempted | 1.3* | 2.4 | 2.4 |
| Theft | 113.8 | 150.1 | 140.3 |
| Completed | 109.6 | 145.7 | 135.7 |
| - Less than $50 | 28.6 | 44.2 | 40.3 |
| - $50-$249 | 43.5 | 54.3 | 51.5 |
| - $250 or more | 29.5 | 38.6 | 35.8 |
| - Amount not available | 8.2 | 8.6 | 8.2 |
| Attempted | 4.2* | 4.3 | 4.6 |

Source: US Department of Justice, Office of Justice Programs, *Criminal Victimization, 2005*, table 56.

Notes: 'All Households' includes households of races not shown separately.
Data based on race of the head of household.
*Based on 10 or fewer sample cases.

Units: Rates per 1,000 households.

## Table 5.08: Characteristics of Murders, 1976–2005

| | By Race of Victim | | | By Race of Offender | | |
|---|---|---|---|---|---|---|
| | **Black** | **White** | **Other Races** | **Black** | **White** | **Other Races** |
| *All Murders* | *50.9%* | *46.9%* | *2.1%* | *45.8%* | *52.2%* | *2.0%* |
| **Victim/offender relationship** | | | | | | |
| Intimate | 56.6% | 41.2% | 2.2% | 54.4% | 43.4% | 2.2% |
| Family | 60.7 | 36.9 | 2.2 | 59.2 | 38.5 | 2.3 |
| Infanticide | 55.9 | 41.6 | 2.5 | 55.4 | 42.1 | 2.5 |
| Eldercide | 69.2 | 29.1 | 1.6 | 54.5 | 43.8 | 1.6 |
| **Circumstances** | | | | | | |
| Felony muder | 54.7% | 42.7% | 2.6% | 39.1% | 59.3% | 1.6% |
| Sex related | 66.9 | 30.5 | 2.5 | 54.7 | 43.4 | 1.9 |
| Drug related | 37.4 | 61.6 | 0.9 | 33.9 | 65.0 | 1.1 |
| Gang related | 57.5 | 39.0 | 3.5 | 54.3 | 41.2 | 4.4 |
| Argument | 48.6 | 49.3 | 2.1 | 46.8 | 51.1 | 2.2 |
| Workplace | 84.6 | 12.2 | 3.2 | 70.5 | 26.7 | 2.8 |
| **Weapon** | | | | | | |
| Gun | 47.2% | 50.9% | 1.9% | 41.9% | 56.4% | 1.7% |
| Arson | 58.9 | 38.1 | 2.9 | 55.7 | 42.0 | 2.3 |
| Poison | 80.6 | 16.9 | 2.5 | 79.8 | 18.4 | 1.8 |
| **Multiple victims or offenders** | | | | | | |
| Multiple victims | 63.4% | 33.2% | 3.3% | 55.7% | 40.8% | 3.5% |
| Multiple offenders | 54.8 | 42.5 | 2.7 | 44.6 | 53.0 | 2.4 |

Source: US Department of Justice, Bureau of Justice Statistics, *Homicide Trends in the US,* accessed online at http://www.ojp.usdoj.gov/bjs/homicide/race.htm on May 7, 2008.

Notes: 'Other Races' refers to anyone identifying as neither Black nor White.

Units: Percent of all murders from 1976 to 2005.

## Table 5.09: Number of Murder Victims by Age and Sex, Selected Years, 1980–2005

| | Black Victims | | White Victims | |
|---|---|---|---|---|
| | **Male** | **Female** | **Male** | **Female** |
| **1980** | | | | |
| 14-17 years | 295 | 76 | 352 | 170 |
| 18-24 years | 1780 | 463 | 2,038 | 652 |
| 25 years and older | 5,478 | 1,217 | 6,306 | 2,037 |
| **1985** | | | | |
| 14-17 years | 259 | 79 | 238 | 113 |
| 18-24 years | 1,421 | 334 | 1,465 | 489 |
| 25 years and older | 4,243 | 1,106 | 5,384 | 2,167 |
| **1990** | | | | |
| 14-17 years | 614 | 104 | 412 | 131 |
| 18-24 years | 2,827 | 395 | 1,874 | 428 |
| 25 years and older | 5,652 | 1,327 | 5,672 | 2,051 |
| **1995** | | | | |
| 14-17 years | 734 | 134 | 512 | 151 |
| 18-24 years | 2,765 | 324 | 1,792 | 417 |
| 25 years and older | 4,696 | 1,242 | 4,754 | 2,036 |
| **2000** | | | | |
| 14-17 years | 326 | 54 | 269 | 88 |
| 18-24 years | 1,979 | 271 | 1,296 | 299 |
| 25 years and older | 3,505 | 851 | 3,436 | 1,583 |
| **2005** | | | | |
| 14-17 years | 378 | 55 | 301 | 70 |
| 18-24 years | 2,205 | 248 | 1,432 | 278 |
| 25 years and older | 3,944 | 755 | 3,776 | 1,593 |

**Source:** US Department of Justice, Bureau of Justice Statistics, *Homicide Trends in the US*, accessed online at http://www.ojp.usdoj.gov/bjs/homicide/tables/varstab.htm#numbers on May 7, 2008.

**Notes:** Some data has been revised and may differ from previous publications.

**Units:** Number of murder victims.

## Table 5.10: Murder Victims by Age, 2006

|  | Black | White | All Races |
|---|---|---|---|
| *All murders* | *7,421* | *6,956* | *14,990* |
| **By Age of the victim** | | | |
| Under 1 year old | 51 | 141 | 203 |
| 1-4 years old | 145 | 141 | 299 |
| 5-8 years old | 29 | 61 | 95 |
| 9-12 years old | 31 | 46 | 83 |
| 13-16 years old | 259 | 217 | 485 |
| 17-19 years old | 860 | 563 | 1,485 |
| 20-24 years old | 1,653 | 1,077 | 2,831 |
| 25-29 years old | 1,304 | 913 | 2,273 |
| 30-34 years old | 863 | 628 | 1,549 |
| 35-39 years old | 587 | 615 | 1,250 |
| 40-44 years old | 493 | 595 | 1,123 |
| 45-49 years old | 393 | 540 | 985 |
| 50-54 years old | 270 | 420 | 727 |
| 55-59 years old | 157 | 276 | 455 |
| 60-64 years old | 87 | 214 | 316 |
| 65-69 years old | 48 | 94 | 147 |
| 70-74 years old | 39 | 101 | 144 |
| 75 years old and older | 52 | 203 | 263 |
| Age unknown | 100 | 111 | 277 |

**Source:** US Federal Bureau of Investigation, *Crime in the United States 2006, Expanded Homicide Data*, table 2.

**Notes:** 'All Races' includes races not shown separately.
Data covers only those murders and non-negligent homicides in which there was a single offender and single victim.

**Units:** Number of murders and non-negligent homicides known to police.

## Table 5.11: Self-Protective Measures Used by Victims of Violent Crime, 2004 and 2005

|  | Black | White | All Races |
|---|---|---|---|
| **2004** | | | |
| Attacked offender with weapon | 1.4%* | 0.9% | 0.9% |
| Attacked offender without weapon | 13.3 | 8.9 | 9.6 |
| Threatened offender with weapon | 0.9* | 1.1 | 1.0 |
| Threatened offender without weapon | 1.4* | 1.4 | 1.5 |
| Resisted or captured offender | 26.3 | 25.1 | 24.7 |
| Scared or warned offender | 12.0 | 12.9 | 12.8 |
| Persuaded or appeased offender | 13.4 | 9.2 | 10.0 |
| Ran away or hid | 10.6 | 13.4 | 12.8 |
| Got help or gave alarm | 12.5 | 13.2 | 13.3 |
| Screamed from pain or fear | 2.2* | 2.5 | 2.4 |
| Took other measures | 6.1 | 11.5 | 10.7 |
| **2005** | | | |
| Attacked offender with weapon | 0.6%* | 0.9%* | 0.8% |
| Attacked offender without weapon | 9.7 | 8.2 | 8.6 |
| Threatened offender with weapon | 2.2* | 0.7* | 0.9 |
| Threatened offender without weapon | 0.8* | 1.6 | 1.4 |
| Resisted or captured offender | 22.4 | 26.4 | 25.6 |
| Scared or warned offender | 11.2 | 10.1 | 10.4 |
| Persuaded or appeased offender | 13.9 | 10.1 | 11.1 |
| Ran away or hid | 11.9 | 15.0 | 14.4 |
| Got help or gave alarm | 14.6 | 14.3 | 14.2 |
| Screamed from pain or fear | 2.5* | 1.7 | 1.7 |
| Took other measures | 10.3 | 11.0 | 10.8 |

Source: US Department of Justice, Office of Justice Programs, *Criminal Victimization, 2004*, table 71; *2005*, table 71.

Notes: 'All Races' includes races not shown separately.
Some respondents may have reported using more than one method.
The National Crime Victimization Survey has been redesigned: comparisons of estimates of crime based on previous survey procedures (before 1993) are not recommended.
Data for persons 12 years old and over.
* Based on 10 or fewer sample cases.

Units: Percent of violent crime victims using self-protective measures.

## Table 5.12: Lifetime Likelihood of Victimization by Crime by Type of Crime and Number of Likely Victimizations, 1997

| | Black | White | All Races |
|---|---|---|---|
| **All violent crimes** | | | |
| *Both sexes* | | | |
| One or more victimizations | 87% | 82% | 83% |
| One victimization | 26 | 31 | 30 |
| Two victimization | 27 | 26 | 27 |
| Three or more victimizations | 34 | 24 | 25 |
| *Male* | | | |
| One or more victimizations | 92% | 88% | 89% |
| One victimization | 21 | 25 | 24 |
| Two victimization | 26 | 27 | 27 |
| Three or more victimizations | 45 | 37 | 38 |
| *Female* | | | |
| One or more victimizations | 81% | 71% | 73% |
| One victimization | 31 | 36 | 35 |
| Two victimization | 26 | 22 | 23 |
| Three or more victimizations | 24 | 13 | 14 |
| **All completed violent crimes** | | | |
| *Both sexes* | | | |
| One or more victimizations | 53% | 41% | 42% |
| One victimization | 35 | 31 | 32 |
| Two victimization | 13 | 8 | 9 |
| Three or more victimizations | 4 | 2 | 2 |

*(continued on next page)*

## Table 5.12: Lifetime Likelihood of Victimization by Crime by Type of Crime and Number of Likely Victimizations, 1997

|  | Black | White | All Races |
|---|---|---|---|
| **Rape (female victimization)** |  |  |  |
| One or more victimizations | 11% | 8% | 8% |
| One victimization | 10 | 7 | 8 |
| Two victimization | 1 | * | * |
| Three or more victimizations | * | * | * |
| **Robbery** |  |  |  |
| One or more victimizations | 51% | 27% | 30% |
| One victimization | 35 | 23 | 25 |
| Two victimization | 12 | 4 | 5 |
| Three or more victimizations | 4 | * | 1 |
| **Assault** |  |  |  |
| One or more victimizations | 73% | 74% | 74% |
| One victimization | 35 | 35 | 35 |
| Two victimization | 25 | 24 | 24 |
| Three or more victimizations | 12 | 16 | 15 |

Source: US Department of Justice, Bureau of Justice Statistics, *Technical Report: Lifetime Likelihood of Victimization, March 1997*, table 1.

Notes: 'All Races' includes races not shown separately.
Estimates are lifetime likelihoods, starting from age 12.
* Less than 0.5%.

Units: Estimated percent of persons who will be victimized by crime, starting at 12 years of age.

## Table 5.13: Arrests by Offense Charged, 2002

| | Number of Arrests | | | Percent Distribution | |
|---|---|---|---|---|---|
| | **Black** | **White** | **All Races** | **Black** | **White** |
| *All arrests* | *2,633,632* | *6,923,390* | *9,797,385* | *26.9%* | *70.7%* |
| For Index crimes | 514,769 | 1,057,846 | 1,614,134 | 31.9 | 65.5 |
| **For Violent crimes** | 169,525 | 266,681 | 446,356 | 38.0 | 59.7 |
| Murder and non-negligent manslaughter | 5,047 | 4,814 | 10,099 | 50.0 | 47.7 |
| Forcible rape | 6,852 | 12,766 | 20,127 | 34.0 | 63.4 |
| Robbery | 41,837 | 34,109 | 77,280 | 54.1 | 44.1 |
| Aggravated assault | 115,789 | 214,992 | 338,850 | 34.2 | 63.4 |
| **For Property crimes** | 345,244 | 791,165 | 1,167,778 | 29.6 | 67.7 |
| Burglary | 56,647 | 144,958 | 205,873 | 27.5 | 70.4 |
| Lacreny-theft | 246,946 | 572,515 | 843,066 | 29.3 | 67.9 |
| Motor vehicle theft | 39,114 | 64,625 | 107,031 | 36.5 | 60.4 |
| Arson | 2,537 | 9,067 | 11,808 | 21.5 | 76.8 |

Source:    US Department of Justice, Bureau of Justice Statistics, *Sourcebook of Criminal Justice Statistics, 2003*, table 4.10.

Notes:    'All Races' includes races not shown separately.
The Crime Index is comprised of the four violent crimes (murder and non-negligent homicide, rape, robbery, and aggravated assault), and four property crimes (burglary, larceny-theft, motor vehicle theft, and arson) which are tracked by the FBI.

Units:    Number of arrests; percent of total arrests by offense.

## Table 5.14: Arrests by Offense Charged, 2005

|  | Number of Arrests | | | Percent Distribution | |
|---|---|---|---|---|---|
|  | Black | White | All Races | Black | White |
| *All arrests* | *2,830,778* | *7,117,040* | *10,189,691* | *27.8%* | *69.8%* |
| **For Violent crimes** | 171,675 | 260,984 | 442,520 | 38.8 | 59.0 |
| Murder and non-negligent manslaughter | 4,898 | 4,955 | 10,083 | 48.6 | 49.1 |
| Forcible rape | 6,015 | 11,980 | 18,405 | 32.7 | 65.1 |
| Robbery | 47,700 | 35,796 | 84,785 | 56.3 | 42.2 |
| Aggravated assault | 113,062 | 208,253 | 329,247 | 34.3 | 63.3 |
| **For Property crimes** | 338,635 | 814,754 | 1,183,491 | 28.6 | 68.8 |
| Burglary | 62,045 | 151,757 | 217,894 | 28.5 | 69.6 |
| Lacreny-theft | 236,608 | 586,393 | 846,213 | 28.0 | 69.3 |
| Motor vehicle theft | 37,489 | 67,578 | 107,604 | 34.8 | 62.8 |
| Arson | 2,493 | 9,026 | 11,780 | 21.2 | 76.6 |

**Source:** US Department of Justice, Bureau of Justice Statistics, *Sourcebook of Criminal Justice Statistics Online*, table 4.10.2005.

**Notes:** 'All Races' includes races not shown separately.
The Crime Index, used to measure the four violent crimes and four property crimes tracked by the FBI, was discontinued in June 2004. Violent crime and property crime totals are used instead.

**Units:** Number of arrests; percent of total arrests by offense.

## Table 5.15: Arrests by Offense Charged, 2006

| | Number of Arrests | | | Percent Distribution | |
|---|---|---|---|---|---|
| | Black | White | All Races | Black | White |
| *All offenses* | *2,924,724* | *7,270,214* | *10,437,620* | *28.0%* | *69.7%* |
| Murder and non-negligent manslaughter | 4,990 | 4,595 | 9,801 | 50.9 | 46.9 |
| Forcible rape | 5,536 | 11,122 | 17,042 | 32.5 | 65.3 |
| Robbery | 52,541 | 39,419 | 93,393 | 56.3 | 42.2 |
| Aggravated assault | 112,645 | 206,417 | 326,721 | 34.5 | 63.2 |
| Burglary | 64,655 | 152,965 | 221,732 | 29.2 | 69.0 |
| Larceny-theft | 230,980 | 548,057 | 798,983 | 28.9 | 68.6 |
| Motor vehicle theft | 35,116 | 63,090 | 100,612 | 34.9 | 62.7 |
| Arson | 2,591 | 9,101 | 11,972 | 21.6 | 76.0 |
| Violent crimes | 175,712 | 261,553 | 446,957 | 39.3 | 58.5 |
| Property crimes | 333,342 | 773,213 | 1,133,299 | 29.4 | 68.2 |
| Other assaults | 306,078 | 619,825 | 949,940 | 32.2 | 65.2 |
| Forgery and counterfeiting | 22,337 | 55,562 | 79,258 | 28.2 | 70.1 |
| Fraud | 59,087 | 135,329 | 196,930 | 30.0 | 68.7 |
| Embezzlement | 4,741 | 9,668 | 14,705 | 32.2 | 65.7 |
| Stolen property | 30,267 | 58,066 | 89,850 | 33.7 | 64.6 |
| Vandalism | 48,781 | 165,518 | 219,652 | 22.2 | 75.4 |
| Weapons: carrying, possessing, etc. | 59,863 | 84,929 | 147,312 | 40.6 | 57.7 |
| Prostitution and commercialized vice | 23,612 | 33,827 | 59,616 | 39.6 | 56.7 |

*(continued on next page)*

## Table 5.15: Arrests by Offense Charged, 2006

|  | Number of Arrests | | | Percent Distribution | |
|---|---|---|---|---|---|
|  | **Black** | **White** | **All Races** | **Black** | **White** |
| Sex offenses | 15,465 | 46,194 | 63,048 | 24.5% | 73.3% |
| Drug abuse violations | 483,886 | 875,101 | 1,376,792 | 35.1 | 63.6 |
| Gambling | 6,467 | 2,358 | 9,001 | 71.8 | 26.2 |
| Offenses against the family and children | 28,086 | 61,278 | 91,618 | 30.7 | 66.9 |
| Driving under the influence | 95,260 | 914,226 | 1,034,651 | 9.2 | 88.4 |
| Liquor laws | 50,035 | 398,068 | 466,323 | 10.7 | 85.4 |
| Drunkenness | 54,113 | 344,155 | 408,439 | 13.2 | 84.3 |
| Disorderly conduct | 179,733 | 325,991 | 517,264 | 34.7 | 63.0 |
| Vagrancy | 11,238 | 15,308 | 27,016 | 41.6 | 56.7 |
| Suspicion | 658 | 1,011 | 1,723 | 38.2 | 58.7 |
| Curfew and loitering law violations | 42,496 | 69,624 | 114,166 | 37.2 | 61.0 |
| Runaways | 20,896 | 57,393 | 83,749 | 25.0 | 68.5 |
| All other offenses (except traffic) | 872,571 | 1,962,017 | 2,906,311 | 30.0 | 67.5 |

Source: US Federal Bureau of Investigation, *Crime in the United States 2006*, table 43A.

Notes: 'All Races' includes races not shown separately. Violent crimes are offenses of murder and non-negligent manslaughter, forcible rape, robbery, and aggravated assault. Property crimes are offenses of burglary, larceny-theft, motor vehicle theft, and arson. 'Sex offenses' exclude forcible rape and prostitution.

Units: Number of arrests; percent of total arrests by offense.

# Chapter 5: Crime, Law Enforcement & Corrections

## Table 5.16: Arrests for Persons Under 18 Years of Age, By Offense, 2002

| | Number of arrests | | | Percent distribution | |
| --- | --- | --- | --- | --- | --- |
| | Black | White | All Races | Black | White |
| *All arrests* | *415,854* | *1,158,776* | *1,620,594* | *25.7%* | *71.5%* |
| For Index crimes | 123,127 | 278,547 | 414,670 | 29.7 | 67.2 |
| **For Violent crimes** | 28,448 | 36,297 | 66,390 | 42.8 | 54.7 |
| Murder and non-negligent manslaughter | 487 | 446 | 972 | 50.1 | 45.9 |
| Forcible rape | 1,207 | 2,079 | 3,355 | 36.0 | 62.0 |
| Robbery | 10,537 | 6,895 | 17,878 | 58.9 | 38.6 |
| Aggravated assault | 16,217 | 26,877 | 44,185 | 36.7 | 60.8 |
| **For Property crimes** | 94,679 | 242,250 | 348,280 | 27.2 | 69.6 |
| Burglary | 15,558 | 44,680 | 61,754 | 25.2 | 72.4 |
| Lacreny-theft | 65,667 | 173,910 | 248,202 | 26.5 | 70.1 |
| Motor vehicle theft | 12,428 | 18,949 | 32,487 | 38.3 | 58.3 |
| Arson | 1,026 | 4,711 | 5,837 | 17.6 | 80.7 |

**Source:** US Department of Justice, Bureau of Justice Statistics, *Sourcebook of Criminal Justice Statistics, 2003*, table 4.10.

**Notes:** 'All Races' includes races not shown separately.
The Crime Index is comprised of the four violent crimes (murder and non-negligent homicide, rape, robbery, and aggravated assault), and four property crimes (burglary, larceny-theft, motor vehicle theft, and arson) which are tracked by the FBI.

**Units:** Number of arrests for persons under 18; percent of total arrests by offense.

## Table 5.17: Arrests for Persons Under 18 Years of Age, By Offense, 2005

| | Number of arrests | | | Percent distribution | |
|---|---|---|---|---|---|
| | **Black** | **White** | **All Races** | **Black** | **White** |
| *All arrests* | *469,382* | *1,059,742* | *1,570,282* | *29.9%* | *67.5%* |
| **For Violent crimes** | 34,897 | 33,780 | 70,080 | 49.8 | 48.2 |
| Murder and non-negligent manslaughter | 499 | 397 | 924 | 54.0 | 43.0 |
| Forcible rape | 969 | 1,834 | 2,851 | 34.0 | 64.3 |
| Robbery | 14,487 | 6,598 | 21,460 | 67.5 | 30.7 |
| Aggravated assault | 18,942 | 24,951 | 44,845 | 42.2 | 55.6 |
| **For Property crimes** | 92,089 | 207,414 | 308,723 | 29.8 | 67.2 |
| Burglary | 17,663 | 38,287 | 57,054 | 31.0 | 67.2 |
| Lacreny-theft | 61,407 | 149,754 | 218,383 | 28.1 | 68.6 |
| Motor vehicle theft | 11,943 | 14,798 | 27,499 | 43.4 | 53.8 |
| Arson | 1,076 | 4,575 | 5,787 | 18.6 | 79.1 |

**Source:** US Department of Justice, Bureau of Justice Statistics, *Sourcebook of Criminal Justice Statistics Online*, table 4.10.2005.

**Notes:** 'All Races' includes races not shown separately.
The Crime Index, used to measure the four violent crimes and four property crimes tracked by the FBI, was discontinued in June 2004. Violent crime and property crime totals are used instead.

**Units:** Number of arrests for persons under 18; percent of total arrests by offense.

## Table 5.18: Arrests for Persons Under 18 Years of Age, By Offense, 2006

| | Number of Arrests | | | Percent Distribution | |
|---|---|---|---|---|---|
| | **Black** | **White** | **All Races** | **Black** | **White** |
| *All offenses* | *490,838* | *1,088,376* | *1,621,167* | *30.3%* | *67.1%* |
| Murder and non-negligent manslaughter | 566 | 374 | 956 | 59.2 | 39.1 |
| Forcible rape | 863 | 1,592 | 2,507 | 34.4 | 63.5 |
| Robbery | 17,569 | 8,074 | 26,060 | 67.4 | 31.0 |
| Aggravated assault | 18,652 | 24,697 | 44,314 | 42.1 | 55.7 |
| Burglary | 19,221 | 40,426 | 60,987 | 31.5 | 66.3 |
| Larceny-theft | 60,545 | 138,577 | 205,201 | 29.5 | 67.5 |
| Motor vehicle theft | 10,965 | 13,576 | 25,285 | 43.4 | 53.7 |
| Arson | 1,075 | 4,646 | 5,868 | 18.3 | 79.2 |
| Violent crimes | 37,650 | 34,737 | 73,837 | 51.0 | 47.0 |
| Property crimes | 91,806 | 197,225 | 297,341 | 30.9 | 66.3 |
| Other assaults | 70,639 | 106,785 | 181,288 | 39.0 | 58.9 |
| Forgery and counterfeiting | 617 | 1,892 | 2,568 | 24.0 | 73.7 |
| Fraud | 1,938 | 3,623 | 5,656 | 34.3 | 64.1 |
| Embezzlement | 391 | 624 | 1,036 | 37.7 | 60.2 |
| Stolen property | 6,522 | 8,750 | 15,574 | 41.9 | 56.2 |
| Vandalism | 16,417 | 67,487 | 85,850 | 19.1 | 78.6 |
| Weapons: carrying, possessing, etc. | 12,745 | 21,142 | 34,611 | 36.8 | 61.1 |
| Prostitution and commercialized vice | 651 | 533 | 1,207 | 53.9 | 44.2 |

*(continued on next page)*

## Table 5.18: Arrests for Persons Under 18 Years of Age, By Offense, 2006

|  | Number of Arrests | | | Percent Distribution | |
|---|---|---|---|---|---|
|  | Black | White | All Races | Black | White |
| Sex offenses | 3,086 | 8,185 | 11,465 | 26.9% | 71.4% |
| Drug abuse violations | 43,080 | 97,800 | 143,267 | 30.1 | 68.3 |
| Gambling | 1,471 | 140 | 1,620 | 90.8 | 8.6 |
| Offenses against the family and children | 823 | 2,737 | 3,621 | 22.7 | 75.6 |
| Driving under the influence | 506 | 13,328 | 14,225 | 3.6 | 93.7 |
| Liquor laws | 4,987 | 93,368 | 102,230 | 4.9 | 91.3 |
| Drunkenness | 977 | 10,764 | 12,035 | 8.1 | 89.4 |
| Disorderly conduct | 61,438 | 88,420 | 152,869 | 40.2 | 57.8 |
| Vagrancy | 823 | 2,872 | 3,734 | 22.0 | 76.9 |
| Suspicion | 108 | 205 | 316 | 34.2 | 64.9 |
| Curfew and loitering law violations | 42,496 | 69,624 | 114,166 | 37.2 | 61.0 |
| Runaways | 20,896 | 57,393 | 83,749 | 25.0 | 68.5 |
| All other offenses (except traffic) | 70,771 | 200,742 | 278,902 | 25.4 | 72.0 |

Source: US Federal Bureau of Investigation, *Crime in the United States 2006*, table 43B.

Notes: 'All Races' includes races not shown separately. Violent crimes are offenses of murder and non-negligent manslaughter, forcible rape, robbery, and aggravated assault. Property crimes are offenses of burglary, larceny-theft, motor vehicle theft, and arson. 'Sex offenses' exlude forcible rape and prostitution.

Units: Number of arrests for persons under 18; percent of total arrests by offense.

## Table 5.19: Arrests in Cities by Offense Charged, 2002

| | Number of arrests | | | Percent distribution | |
|---|---|---|---|---|---|
| | **Black** | **White** | **All Races** | **Black** | **White** |
| *All arrests* | *2,155,660* | *5,006,302* | *7,351,904* | *29.3%* | *68.1%* |
| For Index crimes | 442,470 | 830,427 | 1,308,137 | 33.8 | 63.5 |
| **For Violent crimes** | 144,839 | 196,061 | 348,642 | 41.5 | 56.2 |
| Murder and non-negligent manslaughter | 4,225 | 3,073 | 7,463 | 56.6 | 41.2 |
| Forcible rape | 5,719 | 8,394 | 14,491 | 39.5 | 57.9 |
| Robbery | 37,104 | 28,509 | 66,784 | 55.6 | 42.7 |
| Aggravated assault | 97,791 | 156,085 | 259,904 | 37.6 | 60.1 |
| **For Property crimes** | 297,631 | 634,366 | 959,495 | 31.0 | 66.1 |
| Burglary | 46,761 | 101,169 | 151,127 | 30.9 | 66.9 |
| Lacreny-theft | 213,858 | 479,268 | 714,476 | 29.9 | 67.1 |
| Motor vehicle theft | 34,947 | 47,798 | 85,542 | 40.9 | 55.9 |
| Arson | 2,065 | 6,131 | 8,350 | 24.7 | 73.4 |

Source:   US Department of Justice, Bureau of Justice Statistics, *Sourcebook of Criminal Justice Statistics, 2003*, table 4.12.

Notes:   'All Races' includes races not shown separately.
The Crime Index is comprised of the four violent crimes (murder and non-negligent homicide, rape, robbery, and aggravated assault), and four property crimes (burglary, larceny-theft, motor vehicle theft, and arson) which are tracked by the FBI.

Units:   Number of arrests in cities; percent of total arrests by offense.

## Table 5.20:  Arrests in Cities by Offense Charged, 2005

| | Number of arrests | | | Percent distribution | |
|---|---|---|---|---|---|
| | Black | White | All Races | Black | White |
| *All arrests* | *2,310,786* | *5,153,928* | *7,652,725* | *30.2%* | *67.3%* |
| **For Violent crimes** | 142,729 | 190,582 | 340,729 | 41.9 | 55.9 |
| Murder and non-negligent manslaughter | 3,958 | 3,244 | 7,340 | 53.9 | 44.2 |
| Forcible rape | 4,947 | 7,870 | 13,091 | 37.8 | 60.1 |
| Robbery | 41,177 | 29,548 | 71,815 | 57.3 | 41.1 |
| Aggravated assault | 92,647 | 149,920 | 248,483 | 37.3 | 60.3 |
| **For Property crimes** | 286,523 | 645,677 | 957,742 | 29.9 | 67.4 |
| Burglary | 50,672 | 105,001 | 158,662 | 31.9 | 66.2 |
| Lacreny-theft | 201,425 | 485,287 | 707,109 | 28.5 | 68.6 |
| Motor vehicle theft | 32,507 | 49,209 | 83,684 | 38.8 | 58.8 |
| Arson | 1,919 | 6,180 | 8,287 | 23.2 | 74.6 |

**Source:**   US Department of Justice, Bureau of Justice Statistics, *Sourcebook of Criminal Justice Statistics Online*, table 4.12.2005.

**Notes:**   'All Races' includes races not shown separately.
The Crime Index, used to measure the four violent crimes and four property crimes tracked by the FBI, was discontinued in June 2004. Violent crime and property crime totals are used instead.

**Units:**   Number of arrests in cities; percent of total arrests by offense.

## Table 5.21: Arrests in Cities by Offense Charged, 2006

|  | Number of Arrests | | | Percent Distribution | |
| --- | --- | --- | --- | --- | --- |
|  | Black | White | All Races | Black | White |
| *All offenses* | *2,411,609* | *5,289,134* | *7,894,606* | *30.5%* | *67.0%* |
| Murder and non-negligent manslaughter | 4,054 | 2,999 | 7,210 | 56.2 | 41.6 |
| Forcible rape | 4,524 | 7,346 | 12,162 | 37.2 | 60.4 |
| Robbery | 46,051 | 32,818 | 80,094 | 57.5 | 41.0 |
| Aggravated assault | 93,092 | 148,322 | 247,200 | 37.7 | 60.0 |
| Burglary | 53,360 | 107,527 | 163,865 | 32.6 | 65.6 |
| Larceny-theft | 197,904 | 453,091 | 668,651 | 29.6 | 67.8 |
| Motor vehicle theft | 30,588 | 45,711 | 78,263 | 39.1 | 58.4 |
| Arson | 2,074 | 6,385 | 8,677 | 23.9 | 73.6 |
| Violent crimes | 147,721 | 191,485 | 346,666 | 42.6 | 55.2 |
| Property crimes | 283,926 | 612,714 | 919,456 | 30.9 | 66.6 |
| Other assaults | 253,587 | 450,556 | 723,628 | 35.0 | 62.3 |
| Forgery and counterfeiting | 17,948 | 41,431 | 60,502 | 29.7 | 68.5 |
| Fraud | 36,007 | 72,475 | 110,207 | 32.7 | 65.8 |
| Embezzlement | 3,662 | 7,414 | 11,321 | 32.3 | 65.5 |
| Stolen property | 25,416 | 41,854 | 68,481 | 37.1 | 61.1 |
| Vandalism | 41,837 | 128,541 | 174,816 | 23.9 | 73.5 |
| Weapons: carrying, possessing, etc. | 51,263 | 65,368 | 118,595 | 43.2 | 55.1 |
| Prostitution and commercialized vice | 22,759 | 31,990 | 56,689 | 40.1 | 56.4 |

*(continued on next page)*

## Table 5.21: Arrests in Cities by Offense Charged, 2006

| | Number of Arrests | | | Percent Distribution | |
|---|---|---|---|---|---|
| | **Black** | **White** | **All Races** | **Black** | **White** |
| Sex offenses | 12,709 | 31,771 | 45,587 | 27.9% | 69.7% |
| Drug abuse violations | 410,240 | 635,190 | 1,059,063 | 38.7 | 60.0 |
| Gambling | 6,084 | 1,587 | 7,796 | 78.0 | 20.4 |
| Offenses against the family and children | 11,912 | 29,951 | 43,084 | 27.6 | 69.5 |
| Driving under the influence | 62,806 | 567,649 | 647,719 | 9.7 | 87.6 |
| Liquor laws | 44,621 | 314,553 | 375,270 | 11.9 | 83.8 |
| Drunkenness | 49,436 | 291,715 | 350,099 | 14.1 | 83.3 |
| Disorderly conduct | 162,956 | 276,664 | 449,678 | 36.2 | 61.5 |
| Vagrancy | 10,302 | 13,317 | 24,059 | 42.8 | 55.4 |
| Suspicion | 378 | 607 | 1,000 | 37.8 | 60.7 |
| Curfew and loitering law violations | 41,677 | 65,596 | 109,221 | 38.2 | 60.1 |
| Runaways | 17,261 | 41,344 | 63,192 | 27.3 | 65.4 |
| All other offenses (except traffic) | 697,101 | 1,375,362 | 2,128,477 | 32.8 | 64.6 |

**Source:** US Federal Bureau of Investigation, *Crime in the United States, 2006*, table 49A.

**Notes:** 'All Races' includes races not shown separately. Violent crimes are offenses of murder and non-negligent manslaughter, forcible rape, robbery, and aggravated assault. Property crimes are offenses of burglary, larceny-theft, motor vehicle theft, and arson. 'Sex offenses' exlude forcible rape and prostitution.

**Units:** Number of arrests in cities; percent of total arrests by offense.

## Table 5.22: Arrests in Suburban Areas by Offense Charged, 2006

| | Number of Arrests | | | Percent Distribution | |
|---|---|---|---|---|---|
| | Black | White | All Races | Black | White |
| *All offenses* | *925,822* | *3,119,705* | *4,105,074* | *22.6%* | *76.0%* |
| Murder and non-negligent manslaughter | 1,254 | 1,775 | 3,073 | 40.8 | 57.8 |
| Forcible rape | 1,656 | 4,782 | 6,534 | 25.3 | 73.2 |
| Robbery | 13,238 | 13,057 | 26,578 | 49.8 | 49.1 |
| Aggravated assault | 32,189 | 83,484 | 117,565 | 27.4 | 71.0 |
| Burglary | 18,944 | 62,896 | 82,916 | 22.8 | 75.9 |
| Larceny-theft | 81,391 | 215,585 | 302,288 | 26.9 | 71.3 |
| Motor vehicle theft | 7,574 | 23,258 | 31,243 | 24.2 | 74.4 |
| Arson | 886 | 4,297 | 5,261 | 16.8 | 81.7 |
| Violent crimes | 48,337 | 103,098 | 153,750 | 31.4 | 67.1 |
| Property crimes | 108,795 | 306,036 | 421,708 | 25.8 | 72.6 |
| Other assaults | 92,780 | 263,017 | 361,321 | 25.7 | 72.8 |
| Forgery and counterfeiting | 8,341 | 23,591 | 32,325 | 25.8 | 73.0 |
| Fraud | 28,017 | 68,071 | 96,872 | 28.9 | 70.3 |
| Embezzlement | 1,945 | 3,885 | 5,907 | 32.9 | 65.8 |
| Stolen property | 10,621 | 26,500 | 37,602 | 28.2 | 70.5 |
| Vandalism | 14,413 | 70,887 | 86,493 | 16.7 | 82.0 |
| Weapons: carrying, possessing, etc. | 15,589 | 32,765 | 49,077 | 31.8 | 66.8 |
| Prostitution and commercialized vice | 1,784 | 4,056 | 6,263 | 28.5 | 64.8 |

*(continued on next page)*

## Table 5.22:  Arrests in Suburban Areas by Offense Charged, 2006

| | Number of Arrests | | | Percent Distribution | |
|---|---|---|---|---|---|
| | **Black** | **White** | **All Races** | **Black** | **White** |
| Sex offenses | 4,434 | 18,931 | 23,732 | 18.7% | 79.8% |
| Drug abuse violations | 121,184 | 365,791 | 491,999 | 24.6 | 74.3 |
| Gambling | 545 | 942 | 1,554 | 35.1 | 60.6 |
| Offenses against the family and children | 16,214 | 33,185 | 50,024 | 32.4 | 66.3 |
| Driving under the influence | 41,600 | 434,381 | 483,197 | 8.6 | 89.9 |
| Liquor laws | 14,930 | 176,212 | 196,333 | 7.6 | 89.8 |
| Drunkenness | 13,537 | 127,333 | 142,756 | 9.5 | 89.2 |
| Disorderly conduct | 51,400 | 140,866 | 195,112 | 26.3 | 72.2 |
| Vagrancy | 2,166 | 3,860 | 6,060 | 35.7 | 63.7 |
| Suspicion | 396 | 581 | 987 | 40.1 | 58.9 |
| Curfew and loitering law violations | 4,655 | 18,407 | 23,337 | 19.9 | 78.9 |
| Runaways | 6,381 | 23,118 | 30,094 | 21.2 | 76.8 |
| All other offenses (except traffic) | 317,758 | 874,192 | 1,208,571 | 26.3 | 72.3 |

**Source:**  US Federal Bureau of Investigation, *Crime in the United States, 2006*, table 67A.

**Notes:**  'All Races' includes races not shown separately.

Violent crimes are offenses of murder and non-negligent manslaughter, forcible rape, robbery, and aggravated assault. Property crimes are offenses of burglary, larceny-theft, motor vehicle theft, and arson. 'Sex offenses' exlude forcible rape and prostitution.

Suburban area data is taken from law enforcement agencies in cities with less than 50,000 inhabitants and county law enforcement agencies that are within a Metropolitan Statistical Area. It excludes all metropolitan agencies associated with a principal city.

**Units:**  Number of arrests in suburban areas; percent of total arrests by offense.

## Table 5.23: Number of Jail Inmates per 100,000 US Residents, 1990–2006

|  | Black | White |
|---|---|---|
| 1990 | 560 | 89 |
| 1991 | 594 | 92 |
| 1992 | 618 | 93 |
| 1993 | 633 | 94 |
| 1994 | 656 | 98 |
| 1995 | 670 | 104 |
| 1996 | 640 | 111 |
| 1997 | 706 | 117 |
| 1998 | 716 | 125 |
| 1999 | 730 | 127 |
| 2000 | 736 | 132 |
| 2001 | 703 | 138 |
| 2002 | 740 | 147 |
| 2003 | 748 | 151 |
| 2004 | 765 | 160 |
| 2005 | 800 | 166 |
| 2006 | 815 | 170 |

Source:   US Department of Justice, Bureau of Justice Statistics, *The Annual Survey of Jails and Census of Jail Inmates, 1997, 1998-2006.*

Notes:   'White' and 'Black' are equivalent to 'White alone' and 'Black alone.' Both groups exclude Hispanics.

Units:   Jail inmates per 100,000 US Residents.

## Table 5.24: Jail Population, 1990–2006

|      | Black   | White   |
|------|---------|---------|
| 1990 | 172,300 | 169,400 |
| 1991 | 185,100 | 175,300 |
| 1992 | 196,300 | 178,300 |
| 1993 | 203,200 | 180,700 |
| 1994 | 215,300 | 191,800 |
| 1995 | 224,100 | 206,600 |
| 1996 | 213,100 | 215,700 |
| 1997 | 237,900 | 230,300 |
| 1998 | 244,000 | 244,900 |
| 1999 | 251,800 | 249,900 |
| 2000 | 256,300 | 260,500 |
| 2001 | 256,200 | 271,700 |
| 2002 | 264,900 | 291,800 |
| 2003 | 271,000 | 301,200 |
| 2004 | 275,400 | 317,400 |
| 2005 | 290,500 | 331,000 |
| 2006 | 296,000 | 336,600 |

Source: US Department of Justice, Bureau of Justice Statistics, *The Annual Survey of Jails and Census of Jail Inmates, 1997, 1998-2006.*

Notes: 'White' and 'Black' are equivalent to 'White alone' and 'Black alone.' Both groups exclude Hispanics.

Units: Number of persons incarcerated as determined by a one-day count.

## Table 5.25: Distribution of Jail Inmates, 1990–2006

|      | Black  | White  |
|------|--------|--------|
| 1990 | 42.5%  | 41.8%  |
| 1991 | 43.4   | 41.1   |
| 1992 | 44.1   | 40.1   |
| 1993 | 44.2   | 39.3   |
| 1994 | 43.9   | 39.1   |
| 1995 | 43.5   | 40.1   |
| 1996 | 41.1   | 41.6   |
| 1997 | 42.0   | 40.6   |
| 1998 | 41.2   | 41.3   |
| 1999 | 41.5   | 41.3   |
| 2000 | 41.3   | 41.9   |
| 2001 | 40.6   | 43.0   |
| 2002 | 39.8   | 43.8   |
| 2003 | 39.2   | 43.6   |
| 2004 | 38.6   | 44.4   |
| 2005 | 38.9   | 44.3   |
| 2006 | 38.6   | 43.9   |

Source: US Department of Justice, Bureau of Justice Statistics, *Sourcebook of Criminal Justice Statistics Online*, table 6.17.2006.

Notes: Race totals may not add to total due to other groups not included here. 'White' and 'Black' are equivalent to 'White alone' and 'Black alone.' Both groups exclude Hispanics.

Units: Percent of local jail inmates.

## Table 5.26: Incarceration Rate in State or Federal Prisons and Local Jails by Age, January 2006

|  | Black | | White | | All Races | |
|---|---|---|---|---|---|---|
|  | **Male** | **Female** | **Male** | **Female** | **Male** | **Female** |
| *Total* | *3,145* | *156* | *471* | *45* | *929* | *65* |
| 18-19 years | 1,920 | 61 | 274 | 20 | 619 | 29 |
| 20-24 years | 6,345 | 248 | 948 | 85 | 2,016 | 118 |
| 25-29 years | 8,082 | 339 | 1,098 | 113 | 2,342 | 153 |
| 30-34 years | 7,726 | 391 | 1,172 | 138 | 2,234 | 177 |
| 35-39 years | 6,630 | 435 | 1,067 | 134 | 1,953 | 185 |
| 40-44 years | 5,472 | 345 | 923 | 102 | 1,641 | 145 |
| 45-54 years | 3,136 | 163 | 493 | 41 | 899 | 63 |
| 55 or older | 697 | 19 | 135 | 6 | 208 | 8 |

**Source:** US Department of Justice, Bureau of Justice Statistics, *Prisoners in 2005*, table 11.

**Notes:** 'All Races' includes races not shown separately. 'Black' and 'White' exclude Hispanics and persons who reported two or more races.
Counts are as of January 1, 2006.

**Units:** Number of inmates per 100,000 residents.

## Table 5.27: Incarceration Rate in State Prisons and Local Jails by State, June 2005

|  | Black | White | All Races |
|---|---|---|---|
| *United States* | *2,290* | *412* | *738* |
| Alabama | 1,916 | 542 | 890 |
| Alaska | 2,163 | 500 | 705 |
| Arizona | 3,294 | 590 | 808 |
| Arkansas | 1,846 | 478 | 673 |
| California | 2,992 | 460 | 682 |
| Colorado | 3,491 | 525 | 728 |
| Connecticut | 2,532 | 211 | 544 |
| Delaware | 2,517 | 396 | 820 |
| District of Columbia | 1,065 | 56 | NA |
| Florida | 2,615 | 588 | 835 |
| Georgia | 2,068 | 623 | 1,021 |
| Hawaii | 851 | 453 | 447 |
| Idaho | 2,869 | 675 | 784 |
| Illinois | 2,020 | 223 | 507 |
| Indiana | 2,526 | 463 | 637 |
| Iowa | 4,200 | 309 | 412 |
| Kansas | 3,096 | 443 | 582 |
| Kentucky | 2,793 | 561 | 720 |
| Louisiana | 2,452 | 523 | 1,138 |
| Maine | 1,992 | 262 | 273 |
| Maryland | 1,579 | 288 | 636 |
| Massachusetts | 1,635 | 201 | 356 |
| Michigan | 2,262 | 412 | 663 |
| Minnesota | 1,937 | 212 | 300 |
| Mississippi | 1,742 | 503 | 955 |
| Missouri | 2,556 | 487 | 715 |
| Montana | 3,569 | 433 | 526 |
| Nebraska | 2,418 | 290 | 421 |
| Nevada | 2,916 | 627 | 756 |

*(continued on next page)*

## Table 5.27: Incarceration Rate in State Prisons and Local Jails by State, June 2005

|  | Black | White | All Races |
|---|---|---|---|
| *United States* | *2,290* | *412* | *738* |
| New Hampshire | 2,666 | 289 | 319 |
| New Jersey | 2,352 | 190 | 532 |
| New Mexico | NA | NA | 782 |
| New York | 1,627 | 174 | 482 |
| North Carolina | 1,727 | 320 | 620 |
| North Dakota | 2,683 | 267 | 359 |
| Ohio | 2,196 | 344 | 559 |
| Oklahoma | 3,252 | 740 | 919 |
| Oregon | 2,930 | 502 | 531 |
| Pennsylvania | 2,792 | 305 | 607 |
| Rhode Island | 1,838 | 191 | 313 |
| South Carolina | 1,856 | 415 | 830 |
| South Dakota | 4,710 | 470 | 622 |
| Tennessee | 2,006 | 487 | 732 |
| Texas | 3,162 | 667 | 976 |
| Utah | 3,588 | 392 | 466 |
| Vermont | 3,797 | 304 | 317 |
| Virginia | 2,331 | 396 | 759 |
| Washington | 2,522 | 393 | 465 |
| West Virginia | 2,188 | 392 | 443 |
| Wisconsin | 4,416 | 415 | 653 |
| Wyoming | NA | NA | 690 |

**Source:** US Department of Justice, Bureau of Justice Statistics, *Prison and Jail Inmates at Midyear 2005*, tables 12 and 14.

**Notes:** 'All Races' includes races not shown separately. 'Black' and 'White' exclude Hispanics and persons who reported two or more races. Figures are as of June 30, 2005.

**Units:** Number of inmates per 100,000 residents.

## Table 5.28: Prisoners Under Jurisdiction of Federal and State Correctional Authorities, 1995 and 2000

|  | Black | White | All Races |
|---|---|---|---|
| **December 31, 1995** |  |  |  |
| *Total* | *544,005* | *455,021* | *1,126,287* |
| Federal Institutions | 37,055 | 60,261 | 100,250 |
| State Institutions | 506,950 | 394,760 | 1,026,037 |
| **June 30, 2000** |  |  |  |
| *Total* | *587,300* | *453,300* | *1,305,253* |
| Federal Institutions | 44,800 | 29,800 | 110,974 |
| State Institutions | 506,408 | 395,637 | 1,101,202 |
| Private institutions | 36,066 | 27,905 | 93,077 |

Source:  US Department of Justice, Bureau of Justice Statistics, *Sourcebook of Criminal Justice Statistics, 1999*, table 6.34; *2002*, table 6.24 and 6.28.

Notes:  'All Races' includes races not shown separately. 'Black' and 'White' exclude Hispanic persons.

Units:  Number of prisoners under jurisdictional authority.

## Table 5.29:  Type of Commitment Offense by Gender, 2003

| | Black | | White | |
|---|---|---|---|---|
| | **Male** | **Female** | **Male** | **Female** |
| *Total offenses* | *60,986* | *3,716* | *80,811* | *6,539* |
| Drug | 36,662 | 2,353 | 41,139 | 4,282 |
| Robbery | 5,349 | 194 | 4,298 | 167 |
| Property | 2,369 | 198 | 3,646 | 408 |
| Extortion, fraud, bribery | 1,679 | 515 | 3,768 | 702 |
| Violent | 2,448 | 111 | 1,190 | 49 |
| Weapons, explosives, arson | 9,545 | 174 | 7,689 | 178 |
| White collar | 272 | 66 | 499 | 162 |
| Immigration | 673 | 14 | 15,423 | 388 |
| Court, corrections | 187 | 44 | 367 | 92 |
| Sex offenses | 475 | 4 | 397 | 9 |
| National security | 11 | 5 | 59 | 7 |
| Continuing criminal enterprise | 278 | 3 | 320 | 12 |
| Other | 638 | 35 | 2,016 | 83 |

**Source:**  US Department of Justice, Bureau of Justice Statistics, *Sourcebook of Criminal Justice Statistics Online*, table 6.56.

**Notes:**  'White' and 'Black' are equivalent to 'White alone' and 'Black alone.'
'Violent' refers to crimes such as homicide, aggravated assault, and kidnapping. 'White collar' refers to crimes such as banking and insurance offenses, counterfeiting, and embezzlement. 'Court, corrections' refers to crimes such as harboring a fugitive, possesing or bringing contraband into a prison, and perjury.

**Units:**  Number of persons incarcerated, by offense.

## Table 5.30: Chances of Going to State or Federal Prison, 1997 and 2001

|  | Black | White | All Races |
|---|---|---|---|
| **1997** | | | |
| *Incarcerated for the first time, by age* | | | |
| 20 | 4.1% | 0.4% | 1.1% |
| 25 | 8.4 | 0.9 | 2.4 |
| 30 | 11.6 | 1.4 | 3.3 |
| 35 | 13.6 | 1.7 | 4.0 |
| 40 | 14.9 | 2.0 | 4.4 |
| 45 | 15.4 | 2.1 | 4.7 |
| 50 | 15.7 | 2.3 | 4.9 |
| 55 | 15.8 | 2.4 | 5.0 |
| 65 | 16.0 | 2.5 | 5.1 |
| Lifetime | 16.2 | 2.5 | 5.1 |
| | | | |
| *At some time during the rest of life, by age* | | | |
| Birth | 16.2% | 2.5% | 5.1% |
| 20 | 14.1 | 2.3 | 4.5 |
| 25 | 9.6 | 1.7 | 3.1 |
| 30 | 6.0 | 1.2 | 2.1 |
| 35 | 3.6 | 0.9 | 1.4 |
| 40 | 2.0 | 0.6 | 0.9 |
| 45 | 1.2 | 0.4 | 0.6 |

*(continued on next page)*

## Table 5.30: Chances of Going to State or Federal Prison, 1997 and 2001

| | Black | | | White | | |
|---|---|---|---|---|---|---|
| | **Male** | **Female** | **Total** | **Male** | **Female** | **Total** |
| **2001** | | | | | | |
| *Percent of adult population ever incarcerated, by age* | | | | | | |
| 18-24 | 8.5% | 0.4% | 4.4% | 1.1% | 0.1% | 0.6% |
| 25-34 | 20.4 | 2.1 | 10.9 | 2.8 | 0.3 | 1.6 |
| 35-44 | 22.0 | 2.8 | 12.1 | 3.5 | 0.5 | 2.0 |
| 45-54 | 17.7 | 1.9 | 9.5 | 3.1 | 0.3 | 1.7 |
| 55-64 | 13.0 | 1.1 | 6.7 | 2.5 | 0.2 | 1.4 |
| 65 and older | 11.6 | 0.9 | 5.9 | 2.0 | 0.2 | 1.1 |

Source:   US Department of Justice, Bureau of Justice Statistics, *Lifetime Likelihood of Going to State or Federal Prison, March 1997*, tables 1 and 2.
US Department of Justice, Bureau of Justice Statistics, *Prevalence of Imprisonment in the US Population, 1974-2001*, table 7.

Notes:   Chances of going to State or Federal Prison for the first time are cumulative percents. These estimates were obtained by sequentially applying age-specific first-incarceration rates and mortality rates for each group to a hypothetical population of 100,000 births. Chances of going to State or Federal Prison at some time are for persons not previously incarcerated. These estimates were obtained by subtracting the cumulative percent first incarcerated for each age from the lifetime likelihood of incarceration.
'White' and 'Black' exclude persons of Hispanic origin.

Units:   Percent of total resident population.

## Table 5.31: Prisoners Under Sentence of Death by State, January 1, 2007

|  | Black | White | All Races |
|---|---|---|---|
| *United States*\* | *1,397* | *1,517* | *3,350* |
| Alabama | 93 | 100 | 195 |
| Arizona | 13 | 88 | 124 |
| Arkansas | 23 | 14 | 37 |
| California | 235 | 254 | 660 |
| Colorado | 1 | 0 | 2 |
| Connecticut | 3 | 3 | 8 |
| Delaware | 7 | 8 | 18 |
| Florida | 139 | 221 | 397 |
| Georgia | 50 | 53 | 107 |
| Idaho | 0 | 20 | 20 |
| Illinois | 3 | 5 | 11 |
| Indiana | 7 | 16 | 23 |
| Kansas | 4 | 5 | 9 |
| Kentucky | 9 | 31 | 41 |
| Louisiana | 55 | 30 | 88 |
| Maryland | 5 | 3 | 8 |
| Mississippi | 35 | 30 | 66 |
| Missouri | 21 | 30 | 51 |
| Montana | 0 | 2 | 2 |
| Nebraska | 1 | 5 | 9 |
| Nevada | 29 | 42 | 80 |

*(continued on next page)*

## Table 5.31: Prisoners Under Sentence of Death by State, January 1, 2007

|  | Black | White | All Races |
|---|---|---|---|
| *United States\** | *1,397* | *1,517* | *3,350* |
| New Hampshire | 0 | 0 | 0 |
| New Jersey | 6 | 5 | 11 |
| New Mexico | 0 | 2 | 2 |
| New York | 1 | 0 | 1 |
| North Carolina | 98 | 72 | 185 |
| Ohio | 96 | 88 | 191 |
| Oklahoma | 33 | 48 | 88 |
| Oregon | 3 | 26 | 33 |
| Pennsylvania | 137 | 68 | 226 |
| South Carolina | 38 | 29 | 67 |
| South Dakota | 0 | 4 | 4 |
| Tennessee | 43 | 59 | 107 |
| Texas | 161 | 121 | 393 |
| Utah | 1 | 6 | 9 |
| Virginia | 12 | 8 | 20 |
| Washington | 4 | 5 | 9 |
| Wyoming | 0 | 2 | 2 |

**Source:** US Department of Justice, Bureau of Justice Statistics, *Sourcebook of Criminal Justice Statistics, Online (2003 and later)*, table 6.80.2007.

**Notes:** 'All Races' includes races and ethnic groups not shown separately.
Only states that use the death penalty are shown.
\* Includes prisoners under Federal and US Military jurisdiction.

**Units:** Number of prisoners under sentence of death.

## Table 5.32: Prisoners Under Sentence of Death and Elapsed Time from Sentence to Execution, 1980–2005

| | Black | White | All Races |
|---|---|---|---|
| **Prisoners under sentence of death** | | | |
| 1980 | 268 | 425 | 697 |
| 1990 | 940 | 1,368 | 2,346 |
| April, 1995 | 1,217 | 1,455 | 3,009 |
| April, 1996 | 1,272 | 1,493 | 3,122 |
| April, 1998 | 1,420 | 1,611 | 3,387 |
| April, 1999 | 1,516 | 1,657 | 3,565 |
| April, 2000 | 1,574 | 1,698 | 3,670 |
| April, 2001 | 1,593 | 1,700 | 3,711 |
| April, 2002 | 1,593 | 1,678 | 3,701 |
| April, 2004 | 1,462 | 1,591 | 3,487 |
| January, 2006 | 1,411 | 1,531 | 3,373 |
| January, 2007 | 1,397 | 1,517 | 3,350 |
| **Average elapsed time (in months) from sentence to execution** | | | |
| 1990 | 91 | 97 | 95 |
| 1995 | 144 | 128 | 134 |
| 1996 | 153 | 112 | 125 |
| 1997 | 147 | 126 | 133 |
| 1998 | 132 | 128 | 130 |
| 1999 | 141 | 143 | 143 |
| 2000 | 142 | 134 | 137 |
| 2001 | 166 | 134 | 142 |
| 2002 | 120 | 130 | 127 |
| 2003 | 120 | 135 | 131 |
| 2004 | 132 | 132 | 132 |
| 2005 | 155 | 144 | 147 |

**Source:** US Bureau of the Census, *Statistical Abstract of the United States, 1989*, table 325.
US Department of Justice, Bureau of Justice Statistics, *Sourcebook of Criminal Justice Statistics, 1993*, tables 6.108 and 6.110; *1994*, table 6.70; *1995*, table 6.74; *1997*, table 6.76; *1998*, table 6.81; *1999*, table 6.83; *2000*, table 6.83; *2001*, table 6.76; *2002*, table 6.77; *Online (2003 and later)*, tables 6.80.2006 and 6.80.2007.
US Department of Justice, Bureau of Justice Statistics, *Bureau of Justice Statistics Bulletin: Capital Punishment 2005*, table 11.

**Notes:** 'All Races' includes races not shown separately.

**Units:** Number of prisoners under sentence of death; average elapsed time from sentence to execution in months.

## Table 5.33:  Criminal History Profile of Prisoners Under Sentence of Death, 2006

|  | Black | White | All Races |
|---|---|---|---|
| *United States total* | *1,352* | *1,802* | *3,228* |
| **Prior felony convictions** | | | |
| Yes | 70.9% | 62.1% | 65.5% |
| No | 29.1 | 37.9 | 34.5 |
| **Prior homicide convictions** | | | |
| Yes | 8.8% | 8.4% | 8.4% |
| No | 91.2 | 91.6 | 91.6 |
| **Legal status at time of capital offense** | | | |
| Charges pending | 7.4% | 9.0% | 7.8% |
| Probation | 12.1 | 8.9 | 10.6 |
| Parole | 16.8 | 14.0 | 16.0 |
| Prison escapee | 0.9 | 1.7 | 1.4 |
| Prison inmate | 3.3 | 4.0 | 3.5 |
| Other status | 0.6 | 0.4 | 0.5 |
| None | 58.9 | 62.0 | 60.2 |

Source:  US Department of Justice, Bureau of Justice Statistics, *Capital Punishment 2006*, tables 4 and 8.

Notes:  'All Races' includes races not shown separately. 'Black' and 'White' exclude persons of Hispanic origin.
Prisoner counts are as of December 31, 2008.

Units:  Number of prisoners; percent of total.

## Table 5.34: Prisoners Executed Under Civil Authority, 1930-2006

|  | Black | White | All Races |
|---|---|---|---|
| *All years, 1930–2006* | *2,428* | *2,431* | *4,916* |
| 1930-1939 | 816 | 827 | 1,667 |
| 1940-1949 | 781 | 490 | 1,284 |
| 1950-1959 | 376 | 336 | 717 |
| 1960-1967 | 93 | 98 | 191 |
| 1968-1976 | 0 | 0 | 0 |
| 1977-2006 | 362 | 680 | 1,057 |
| 1985 | 7 | 11 | 18 |
| 1990 | 7 | 16 | 23 |
| 1991 | 7 | 7 | 14 |
| 1992 | 11 | 19 | 31 |
| 1993 | 14 | 23 | 38 |
| 1994 | 11 | 20 | 31 |
| 1995 | 22 | 33 | 56 |
| 1996 | 14 | 31 | 45 |
| 1997 | 27 | 45 | 74 |
| 1998 | 18 | 48 | 68 |
| 1999 | 33 | 61 | 98 |
| 2000 | 35 | 49 | 85 |
| 2001 | 17 | 48 | 66 |
| 2002 | 18 | 53 | 71 |
| 2003 | 20 | 44 | 65 |
| 2004 | 19 | 39 | 59 |
| 2005 | 19 | 41 | 60 |
| 2006 | 21 | 32 | 53 |

**Source:** US Bureau of the Census, *Statistical Abstract of the United States, 2008*, table 343.

**Notes:** 'All Races' includes races not shown separately. 'White' as shown is equivalent to 'White alone' and 'Black' as shown is equivalent to 'Black alone.'

**Units:** Number of prisoners executed under civil authority.

## Table 5.35: Prisoners Executed for Murder Under Civil Authority, 1930–2006

|  | Black | White | All Races |
|---|---|---|---|
| *All years, 1930–2006* | *1,992* | *2,344* | *4,391* |
| 1930-1939 | 687 | 803 | 1,514 |
| 1940-1949 | 595 | 458 | 1,064 |
| 1950-1959 | 280 | 316 | 601 |
| 1960-1967 | 68 | 87 | 155 |
| 1968-1976 | 0 | 0 | 0 |
| 1977-2006 | 362 | 680 | 1,057 |
| 1985 | 7 | 11 | 18 |
| 1990 | 7 | 16 | 23 |
| 1991 | 7 | 7 | 14 |
| 1992 | 11 | 19 | 31 |
| 1993 | 14 | 23 | 38 |
| 1994 | 11 | 20 | 31 |
| 1995 | 22 | 33 | 56 |
| 1996 | 14 | 31 | 45 |
| 1997 | 27 | 45 | 74 |
| 1998 | 18 | 48 | 68 |
| 1999 | 33 | 61 | 98 |
| 2000 | 35 | 49 | 85 |
| 2001 | 17 | 48 | 66 |
| 2002 | 18 | 53 | 71 |
| 2003 | 20 | 44 | 65 |
| 2004 | 19 | 39 | 59 |
| 2005 | 19 | 41 | 60 |
| 2006 | 21 | 32 | 53 |

**Source:** US Bureau of the Census, *Statistical Abstract of the United States, 2008*, table 343.

**Notes:** 'All Races' includes races not shown separately. 'White' as shown is equivalent to 'White alone' and 'Black' as shown is equivalent to 'Black alone.'

**Units:** Number of prisoners executed under civil authority.

## Table 5.36: Inmates Ever Tested for HIV and Results, 1996–1997, 2002, and 2004

| | Black | White | All Races |
|---|---|---|---|
| **1996** | | | |
| Local jails | | | |
| Number | 125,259 | 110,023 | 289,991 |
| Percent HIV positive | 2.6% | 1.4% | 2.2% |
| **1997** | | | |
| State prisons | | | |
| Number | 384,870 | 257,919 | 790,128 |
| Percent HIV positive | 2.8% | 1.4% | 2.2% |
| Federal prisons | | | |
| Number | 28,178 | 21,128 | 70,902 |
| Percent HIV positive | 0.8% | 0.3% | 0.6% |
| **2002** | | | |
| State prisons | | | |
| Number | 163,219 | 136,069 | 374,711 |
| Percent HIV positive | 1.2% | 0.8% | 1.3% |
| **2004** | | | |
| State prisons | | | |
| Number | 409,000 | 336,100 | 967,200 |
| Percent HIV positive | 2.0% | 1.0% | 1.6% |
| Federal prisons | | | |
| Number | 46,600 | 26,800 | 102,600 |
| Percent HIV positive | 1.7% | 0.5% | 1.0% |

Source: US Department of Justice, Bureau of Justice Statistics, *HIV in Prisons and Jails, 1996*, table 8; *2002*, table 9; *2004*, table 10.

Notes: 'All Races' includes races not shown separately. 'White' and 'Black' exclude Hispanics.

Units: Number of inmates tested who reported results, rounded to nearest hundred; percent of inmates testing positive for HIV (Human Immunodeficiency Virus).

## Table 5.37: AIDS-related Deaths in State Prisons, 2004–2006

|  | Black | White | All Races |
|---|---|---|---|
| **2004** | | | |
| Number | 122 | 46 | 185 |
| Rate | 24 | 11 | 14 |
| **2005** | | | |
| Number | 120 | 33 | 176 |
| Rate | 24 | 8 | 13 |
| **2006** | | | |
| Number | 114 | 29 | 155 |
| Rate | 21 | 6 | 11 |

**Source:** U.S. Department of Justice, Bureau of Justice Statistics, *HIV in Prisons*, 2006, table 7.

**Notes:** 'All Races' includes races not shown separately. 'White' and 'Black' exclude Hispanics.

**Units:** Number of AIDS-related deaths; rate per 100,000 inmates.

## Table 5.38: High School Students Who Reported Carrying a Weapon, 2001, 2003, and 2005

|  | Black | White | All Races |
|---|---|---|---|
| **2001** | | | |
| Anywhere | 15.2% | 17.9% | 17.4% |
| On school property | 6.3 | 6.1 | 6.4 |
| **2003** | | | |
| Anywhere | 17.3% | 16.7% | 17.1% |
| On school property | 6.9 | 5.5 | 6.1 |
| **2005** | | | |
| Anywhere | 16.4% | 18.7% | 18.5% |
| On school property | 5.1 | 6.1 | 6.5 |

**Source:** US Census Bureau, *Statistical Abstract of the United States, 2008*, table 237.

**Notes:** 'All Races' includes races not shown separately. 'White' and 'Black' are equivalent to 'White alone' and 'Black alone,' respectively.
Weapons are such things as guns, knives, and clubs. Responses indicate students who reported carrying a weapon in the previous 30 days.

**Units:** Percent of students in grades 9 to 12.

## Table 5.39: Type of Offense by Juvenile Offenders, 1999 and 2000

|  | Black | White |
|---|---|---|
| **1999** | | |
| *All offenses* | *28.4%* | *68.2%* |
| Person | 34.3 | 62.7 |
| Property | 25.8 | 70.1 |
| Drug | 26.6 | 71.1 |
| Public order | 28.0 | 69.0 |
| **2000** | | |
| *All offenses* | *28.1%* | *68.6%* |
| Person | 35.1 | 61.9 |
| Property | 26.3 | 69.7 |
| Drug | 22.2 | 75.4 |
| Public order | 27.3 | 69.6 |

Source: U.S. Department of Justice, Bureau of Justice Statistics, *Sourcebook of Criminal Justice Statistics, 2001*, table 5.59; *2002*, table 5.61.

Notes: Cases disposed by juvenile courts.

Units: Percent of all offenses committed by juvenile offenders, as disposed by juvenile courts.

## Table 5.40: Juveniles in Public and Private Residential Custody Facilities, 2003

|  | Black | White | All Races |
|---|---|---|---|
| *All offenses* | *36,740* | *37,347* | *96,655* |
| Delinquency offenses | 35,091 | 35,036 | 91,831 |
| Violent offenses | 13,510 | 12,043 | 33,197 |
| Index offenses | 9,086 | 7,535 | 22,055 |
| Other | 4,424 | 4,508 | 11,142 |
| Property offenses | 9,630 | 11,086 | 26,843 |
| Index offenses | 8,086 | 9,218 | 22,356 |
| Other | 1,544 | 1,868 | 4,487 |
| Drug offenses | 3,322 | 2,770 | 8,002 |
| Public order offenses | 3,520 | 3,621 | 9,654 |
| Technical violation | 5,109 | 5,516 | 14,135 |
| Status offenses | 1,649 | 2,311 | 4,824 |

**Source:** US Department of Justice, Bureau of Justice Statistics, *Sourcebook of Criminal Justice Statistics, 2003*, table 6.10.2003.

**Notes:** 'All Races' includes races not shown separately. 'Black' and 'White' exclude Hispanics. 'Status offenses' include running away, underage drinking, truancy, curfew violations, and other offenses that are illegal for juveniles but not for adults. States vary as to what behaviors are considered status offenses.
'Index offenses' include murder and non-negligent homicide, rape, robbery, and aggravated assault for violent crimes; and burglary, larceny-theft, motor vehicle theft, and arson for property crimes.

**Units:** Number of juveniles by offense type.

## Table 5.41: Deaths of Juveniles in State Juvenile Correctional Facilities, 2002–2005

|         | Black | White | All Races |
|---------|-------|-------|-----------|
| *Total* | *18*  | *16*  | *43*      |
| 2002    | 4     | 6     | 13        |
| 2003    | 6     | 1     | 10        |
| 2004    | 4     | 4     | 11        |
| 2005    | 4     | 5     | 9         |

**Source:** U.S. Department of Justice, Bureau of Justice Statistics, *Sourcebook of Criminal Justice Statistics Online (2003 and later)*, table 6.0014.2005.

**Notes:** 'All Races' includes races not shown separately. 'White' and 'Black' are equivalent to 'White alone' and 'Black alone.' Both groups exclude Hispanics.
Breakdowns may not add to totals due to missing data.

**Units:** Number of juvenile deaths in state juvenile correctional facilities.

## Table 5.42: Offenders in Hate Crimes by Bias Motivation, 2006

| | Black | White | All Races |
|---|---|---|---|
| *Total* | *1,026* | *3,710* | *9,080* |
| Single-Bias Incidents | 1,026 | 3,708 | 9,076 |
| **Race** | 551 | 2,110 | 4,737 |
| Anti-White | 403 | 210 | 1,008 |
| Anti-Black | 93 | 1,680 | 3,136 |
| Anti-American Indian/Alaskan Native | 12 | 26 | 72 |
| Anti-Asian/Pacific Islander | 30 | 101 | 230 |
| Anti-Multiple Races, Group | 13 | 93 | 291 |
| **Religion** | 51 | 333 | 1,597 |
| Anti-Jewish | 15 | 178 | 1,027 |
| Anti-Catholic | 7 | 16 | 81 |
| Anti-Protestant | 2 | 13 | 62 |
| Anti-Islamic | 15 | 80 | 191 |
| Anti-Other Religion | 1 | 28 | 140 |
| Anti-Multiple Religions, Group | 7 | 17 | 88 |
| Anti-Atheism/Agnosticism/etc. | 4 | 1 | 8 |
| **Sexual Orientation** | 241 | 620 | 1,415 |
| Anti-Male Homosexual | 153 | 418 | 881 |
| Anti-Female Homosexual | 31 | 64 | 192 |
| Anti-Homosexual | 48 | 119 | 293 |
| Anti-Heterosexual | 3 | 12 | 28 |
| Anti-Bisexual | 6 | 7 | 21 |
| **Ethnicity/National Origin** | 163 | 607 | 1,233 |
| Anti-Hispanic | 118 | 404 | 770 |
| Anti-Other Ethnicity/National Origin | 45 | 203 | 463 |
| **Disability** | 20 | 38 | 94 |
| Anti-Physical | 6 | 4 | 20 |
| Anti-Mental | 14 | 34 | 74 |
| **Multiple-Bias Incidents** | 0 | 2 | 4 |

Source: US Federal Bureau of Investigation, *Crime in the United States 2006*, table 5.

Notes: 'All Races' includes races not shown separately. 'White' as shown is equivalent to 'White alone' and 'Black' as shown is equivalent to 'Black alone.'
In a multiple-bias incident, more than one offense type must occur in the incident and at least two offense types must be motivated by different biases.

Units: Number of hate crime offenders.

## Table 5.43: Offenders in Hate Crimes by Type of Offense, 2006

|  | Black | White | All Races |
|---|---|---|---|
| *Total* | *1,026* | *3,710* | *9,080* |
| **Crimes against persons** | 839 | 3,122 | 5,449 |
| Murder and non-negligent manslaughter | 0 | 2 | 3 |
| Forcible rape | 0 | 4 | 6 |
| Aggravated assault | 248 | 715 | 1,178 |
| Simple assault | 368 | 1,041 | 1,737 |
| Intimidation | 215 | 1,356 | 2,508 |
| Other | 8 | 4 | 17 |
| **Crimes against property** | 173 | 573 | 3,593 |
| Robbery | 61 | 47 | 142 |
| Burglary | 15 | 27 | 155 |
| Larceny-theft | 23 | 58 | 261 |
| Motor vehicle theft | 3 | 4 | 25 |
| Arson | 2 | 7 | 41 |
| Destruction/damage/vandalism | 59 | 409 | 2,911 |
| Other | 10 | 21 | 58 |
| **Crimes against society** | 14 | 15 | 38 |

**Source:** U.S. Federal Bureau of Investigation, *Crime in the United States, 2006*, table 3.

**Notes:** 'All Races' includes races not shown separately. 'White' as shown is equivalent to 'White alone' and 'Black' as shown is equivalent to 'Black alone.'
In a multiple-bias incident, more than one offense type must occur in the incident and at least two offense types must be motivated by different biases.

**Units:** Number of hate crime offenders.

## Table 5.44:  Law Enforcement Officers Killed, 1978–2006

|      | Black Percent | White Percent | Total Number |
|------|:---:|:---:|:---:|
| 1978 | 9% | 91% | 93 |
| 1979 | 9 | 88 | 106 |
| 1980 | 13 | 86 | 104 |
| 1981 | 14 | 85 | 91 |
| 1982 | 15 | 84 | 92 |
| 1983 | 13 | 84 | 80 |
| 1984 | 14 | 85 | 72 |
| 1985 | 10 | 88 | 78 |
| 1986 | 11 | 89 | 66 |
| 1987 | 10 | 90 | 73 |
| 1988 | 9 | 91 | 78 |
| 1989 | 11 | 89 | 66 |
| 1990 | 18 | 80 | 65 |
| 1991 | 13 | 87 | 71 |
| 1992 | 16 | 82 | 62 |
| 1993 | 14 | 86 | 70 |
| 1994 | 14 | 84 | 76 |
| 1995 | 12 | 84 | 74 |
| 1996 | 15 | 80 | 55 |
| 1997 | 17 | 80 | 65 |
| 1998 | 11 | 87 | 61 |
| 1999 | 7 | 88 | 42 |
| 2000 | 22 | 76 | 51 |
| 2001 | 11 | 87 | 70* |
| 2002 | 7 | 91 | 56 |
| 2003 | 15 | 79 | 52 |
| 2004 | 18 | 81 | 57 |
| 2005 | 15 | 85 | 55 |
| 2006 | 10 | 79 | 48 |

Source:   US Department of Justice, Bureau of Justice Statistics, *Sourcebook of Criminal Justice Statistics Online (2003 and later)*, table 3.158.2006.

Notes:   'All Races' includes races not shown separately.
   * Does not include the deaths of 72 law enforcement officers (12 Black and 59 White) resulting from the events of Sept. 11, 2001.

Units:   Percent distribution of law enforcement officers killed; total number of law enforcement officers killed.

## Table 5.45: Attitudes Toward the Death Penalty, 2007

*Question: "Generally speaking, do you believe the death penalty is applied fairly or unfairly in this country today?"*

|  | Black | White | All Races |
|---|---|---|---|
| Applied fairly | 20% | 62% | 57% |
| Applied unfairly | 72 | 33 | 38 |
| Don't know/refused | 8 | 5 | 5 |

*Question: "Are you in favor of the death penalty for a person convicted of murder?"*

|  | Black | White | All Races |
|---|---|---|---|
| Yes, in favor | 33% | 73% | 69% |
| No, not in favor | 58 | 23 | 27 |
| Don't know/refused | 9 | 4 | 4 |

**Source:** US Department of Justice, Bureau of Justice Statistics, *Sourcebook of Criminal Justice Statistics Online*, tables 2.54.2007 and 2.52.2007.

**Notes:** Table constructed by *Sourcebook of Criminal Justice Statistics* staff from data provided by The Gallup Organization, Inc.

**Units:** Percent of persons taking survey who answered with given response.

## Table 5.46: Reported Concern About Crime Victimization, 2007

*Question: "How often do you, yourself, worry about the following things–frequently, occasionally, rarely, or never?"*

| | Black | White | All Races |
|---|---|---|---|
| Your home being burglarized when you are not there | 49% | 46% | 47% |
| Having your car stolen or broken into | 50 | 42 | 44 |
| Being a victim of terrorism | 43 | 34 | 36 |
| Having a school-aged child of yours physically harmed at school | 62 | 28 | 34 |
| Getting mugged | 44 | 27 | 29 |
| Your home being burglarized when you are there | 27 | 27 | 29 |
| Being attacked while driving your car | 31 | 22 | 24 |
| Being sexually assaulted | 31 | 16 | 19 |
| Being the victim of a hate crime | 57 | 12 | 18 |
| Getting murdered | 40 | 15 | 19 |
| Being assaulted or killed by another employee where you work | 8 | 5 | 6 |

**Source:** US Department of Justice, Bureau of Justice Statistics, *Sourcebook of Criminal Justice Statistics Online*, table 2.39.2007.

**Notes:** Table constructed by *Sourcebook of Criminal Justice Statistics* staff from data provided by The Gallup Organization, Inc.

**Units:** Percent of persons taking the survey who answered 'frequently' or 'occasionally.'

## Table 5.47: Attitudes Toward the Legality of Homosexual Relations, 2004–2007

*Question: "Do you think homosexual relations between consenting adults should or should not be legal?"*

|  | Black | White | All Races |
|---|---|---|---|
| **2004** | | | |
| Should be legal | 36% | 55% | 52% |
| Should be illegal | 59 | 41 | 43 |
| Don't know/refused | 5 | 4 | 5 |
| **2005** | | | |
| Should be legal | 49% | 53% | 52% |
| Should be illegal | 48 | 42 | 43 |
| Don't know/refused | 3 | 5 | 5 |
| **2006** | | | |
| Should be legal | 33% | 58% | 56% |
| Should be illegal | 64 | 38 | 40 |
| Don't know/refused | 4 | 4 | 4 |
| **2007** | | | |
| Should be legal | 53% | 60% | 59% |
| Should be illegal | 40 | 37 | 37 |
| Don't know/refused | 7 | 3 | 4 |

**Source:**   US Department of Justice, Bureau of Justice Statistics, *Sourcebook of Criminal Justice Statistics Online*, tables 2.99, 2.99.2005, 2.99.2006, and 2.99.2007.

**Notes:**   Table constructed by *Sourcebook of Criminal Justice Statistics* staff from data provided by The Gallup Organization, Inc.

**Units:**   Percent of persons taking survey who answered with given response.

## Table 5.48: Attitudes Toward Racial Profiling, 2004

*Question: "It has been reported that some police officers or security guards stop people of certain racial or ethnic groups because these officials believe that these groups are more likely than others to commit certain types of crimes. For each of the following situations, please say if you think this practice, known as 'racial profiling,' is widespread, or not, and whether it is justified, or not?"*

|  | Black | White | All Races |
|---|---|---|---|
| When motorists are stopped on roads and highways |  |  |  |
| Racial profiling is widespread | 67% | 50% | 53% |
| Racial profiling is justified | 23 | 31 | 31 |
| When passengers are stopped at security checkpoints in airports |  |  |  |
| Racial profiling is widespread | 48% | 40% | 42% |
| Racial profiling is justified | 32 | 46 | 45 |
| When shoppers are questioned/attempting to prevent theft in stores |  |  |  |
| Racial profiling is widespread | 65% | 45% | 49% |
| Racial profiling is justified | 19 | 24 | 25 |

**Source:** US Department of Justice, Bureau of Justice Statistics, *Sourcebook of Criminal Justice Statistics Online (2003 and later)*, table 2.26.

**Notes:** Table constructed by *Sourcebook of Criminal Justice Statistics* staff from data provided by The Gallup Organization, Inc.

**Units:** Percent of people surveyed answering 'yes' to questions.

# Chapter 6

## Labor, Employment & Unemployment

## Chapter Six Highlights

This chapter provides statistics about labor and employment for Black persons in the United States, including both the most current data available as well as comparisons of the Black population over time. For almost all tables, corresponding data is provided for the total population of the United States as well as for White persons. This allows for easy comparison between groups.

The chapter contains a variety of information on the United States' labor force, including labor force participation (tables 6.01–6.04), full-time and part-time status (tables 6.06 and 6.07), occupation and industry (tables 6.19 and 6.20), sex (tables 6.03–6.05), age (tables 6.02 and 6.03), and region of employment (table 6.13).

The chapter also provides data on unemployment, and includes data organized by age (tables 6.11 and 6.12), sex (table 6.12), region (tables 6.12 and 6.16), and reason for unemployment (table 6.14).

We have also included data on tenure of employment (table 6.21), educational attainment of workers (tables 6.19, 6.23, and 6.24), and workers paid at or below minimum wage (table 6.27).

## Table 6.01: Civilian Population, Employment, and Unemployment Rate, 1980–2006

|  | Black | White | All Races |
|---|---|---|---|
| **1980** | | | |
| Civilian noninstitutional population | 17,824 | 146,122 | 167,745 |
| Percent in labor force | 61.0% | 64.1% | 63.8% |
| Percent of labor force unemployed | 14.3 | 6.3 | 7.1 |
| **1990** | | | |
| Civilian noninstitutional population | 21,477 | 160,425 | 189,164 |
| Percent in labor force | 64.0% | 66.9% | 66.5% |
| Percent of labor force unemployed | 11.4 | 4.8 | 5.6 |
| **2000** | | | |
| Civilian noninstitutional population | 24,902 | 176,220 | 212,577 |
| Percent in labor force | 65.8% | 67.3% | 67.1% |
| Percent of labor force unemployed | 7.6 | 3.5 | 4.0 |
| **2005** | | | |
| Civilian noninstitutional population | 26,517 | 184,446 | 226,082 |
| Percent in labor force | 64.2% | 66.3% | 66.0% |
| Percent of labor force unemployed | 10.0 | 4.4 | 5.1 |
| **2006** | | | |
| Civilian noninstitutional population | 27,007 | 186,264 | 228,815 |
| Percent in labor force | 64.1% | 66.5% | 66.2% |
| Percent of labor force unemployed | 8.9 | 4.0 | 4.6 |

**Source:** US Bureau of the Census, *Statistical Abstract of the United States, 2008*, tables 569 and 571.

**Notes:** 'All Races' includes races not shown separately. For data after 2003, 'White' and 'Black' are equivalent to 'White alone' and 'Black alone,' respectively.

**Units:** Civilian noninstitutional population in thousands; percent of civilian population in labor force; percent of labor force unemployed.

## Table 6.02: Labor Force Participation of the Civilian Noninstitutional Population 16 Years Old and Over, by Age, 1980–2007

| | Black | White | All Races |
|---|---|---|---|
| **1980** | | | |
| *Civilian noninstitutional population* | | | |
| All persons 16 years old and over | 17,824 | 146,122 | 167,745 |
| 16-19 years old | 2,289 | 13,854 | 16,543 |
| 20 years old and over | 15,535 | 132,268 | 151,202 |
| 65 years old and over | 2,030 | 22,050 | 24,350 |
| *Civilian labor force* | | | |
| All persons 16 years old and over | 10,865 | 93,600 | 106,940 |
| 16-19 years old | 891 | 8,312 | 9,378 |
| 20 years old and over | 9,975 | 85,286 | 97,561 |
| 65 years old and over | 257 | 2,759 | 3,054 |
| *Labor force participation rate* | | | |
| All persons 16 years old and over | 61.0% | 64.1% | 63.8% |
| 16-19 years old | 38.9 | 60.0 | 56.7 |
| 20 years old and over | 64.1 | 64.5 | 64.5 |
| 65 years old and over | 13.0 | 12.5 | 12.5 |
| **1990** | | | |
| *Civilian noninstitutional population* | | | |
| All persons 16 years old and over | 21,300 | 160,415 | 188,049 |
| 16-19 years old | 2,150 | 11,095 | 13,794 |
| 20 years old and over | 19,150 | 149,320 | 174,255 |
| 65 years old and over | 2,506 | 26,643 | 29,730 |
| *Civilian labor force* | | | |
| All persons 16 years old and over | 13,493 | 107,177 | 124,787 |
| 16-19 years old | 831 | 6,374 | 7,410 |
| 20 years old and over | 12,662 | 100,803 | 117,377 |
| 65 years old and over | 279 | 3,189 | 3,535 |
| *Labor force participation rate* | | | |
| All persons 16 years old and over | 63.3% | 66.8% | 66.4% |
| 16-19 years old | 38.6 | 57.5 | 53.7 |
| 20 years old and over | 59.4 | 62.8 | 62.4 |
| 65 years old and over | 11.1 | 12.0 | 11.9 |

*(continued on next page)*

## Table 6.02: Labor Force Participation of the Civilian Noninstitutional Population 16 Years Old and Over, by Age, 1980–2007

| | Black | White | All Races |
|---|---|---|---|
| **2000** | | | |
| *Civilian noninstitutional population* | | | |
| All persons 16 years old and over | 25,218 | 174,428 | 209,699 |
| 16-19 years old | 2,468 | 12,707 | 16,042 |
| 65 years old and over | 2,778 | 28,947 | 32,705 |
| *Civilian labor force* | | | |
| All persons 16 years old and over | 16,603 | 117,574 | 140,863 |
| 16-19 years old | 967 | 7,075 | 8,369 |
| 65 years old and over | 322 | 3,749 | 4,200 |
| *Labor force participation rate* | | | |
| All persons 16 years old and over | 65.8% | 67.4% | 67.2% |
| 16-19 years old | 39.2 | 55.7 | 52.2 |
| 65 years old and over | 11.6 | 13.0 | 12.8 |
| **2007** | | | |
| *Civilian noninstitutional population* | | | |
| All persons 16 years old and over | 27,485 | 188,253 | 231,867 |
| 16-19 years old | 2,640 | 13,043 | 16,982 |
| 65 years old and over | 3,080 | 31,426 | 36,228 |
| *Civilian labor force* | | | |
| All persons 16 years old and over | 17,496 | 124,935 | 153,124 |
| 16-19 years old | 801 | 5,795 | 7,012 |
| 65 years old and over | 432 | 5,085 | 5,804 |
| *Labor force participation rate* | | | |
| All persons 16 years old and over | 63.7% | 66.4% | 66.0% |
| 16-19 years old | 30.3 | 44.4 | 41.3 |
| 65 years old and over | 14.0 | 16.2 | 16.0 |

Source: US Department of Labor, Bureau of Labor Statistics, *Handbook of Labor Statistics, 1989*, tables 3-5.
US Department of Labor, Bureau of Labor Statistics, *Employment and Earnings, 1991*, table 3; *2001*, table 3; *2007*, table 3.

Notes: 'All Races' includes races not shown separately.

Units: Civilian noninstitutional population and civilian labor force in thousands of persons; participation rate as a percent (the civilian labor force divided by the civilian noninstitutional population).

## Table 6.03: Labor Force Participation of the Civilian Noninstitutional Population Age 16 and Older, by Sex and Age, 1980–2007

| | Black | | White | | All Races | |
|---|---|---|---|---|---|---|
| | **Male** | **Female** | **Male** | **Female** | **Male** | **Female** |
| **1980** | | | | | | |
| *Civilian noninstitutional population* | | | | | | |
| All persons 16 years old and over | 7,944 | 9,880 | 69,634 | 76,489 | 79,398 | 88,348 |
| 16-19 years old | 1,110 | 1,180 | 6,941 | 6,914 | 8,260 | 8,283 |
| 20 years old and over | 6,834 | 8,700 | 62,694 | 69,575 | 71,138 | 80,065 |
| 65 years old and over | 822 | 1,208 | 9,027 | 13,022 | 9,979 | 14,372 |
| *Civilian labor force* | | | | | | |
| All persons 16 years old and over | 5,612 | 5,253 | 54,473 | 39,127 | 61,453 | 45,487 |
| 16-19 years old | 479 | 412 | 4,424 | 3,888 | 4,999 | 4,381 |
| 20 years old and over | 5,134 | 4,841 | 50,049 | 35,239 | 56,455 | 41,106 |
| 65 years old and over | 138 | 119 | 1,727 | 1,032 | 1,893 | 1,161 |
| *Labor force participation rate* | | | | | | |
| All persons 16 years old and over | 70.3% | 53.1% | 78.2% | 51.2% | 77.4% | 51.5% |
| 16-19 years old | 43.2 | 34.9 | 63.7 | 56.2 | 60.5 | 52.9 |
| 20 years old and over | 75.1 | 55.6 | 79.8 | 50.6 | 79.4 | 51.3 |
| 65 years old and over | 16.9 | 10.2 | 19.1 | 7.9 | 19.0 | 8.1 |
| **1990** | | | | | | |
| *Civilian noninstitutional population* | | | | | | |
| All persons 16 years old and over | 9,567 | 11,773 | 77,082 | 83,332 | 89,650 | 98,399 |
| 16-19 years old | 1,065 | 1,085 | 5,600 | 5,495 | 6,947 | 6,847 |
| 20 years old and over | 8,502 | 10,648 | 71,482 | 77,837 | 82,703 | 91,552 |
| 65 years old and over | 1,012 | 1,493 | 11,129 | 15,514 | 12,392 | 17,337 |
| *Civilian labor force* | | | | | | |
| All persons 16 years old and over | 6,708 | 6,785 | 58,298 | 47,879 | 68,234 | 56,554 |
| 16-19 years old | 433 | 398 | 3,329 | 3,046 | 3,866 | 3,544 |
| 20 years old and over | 6,275 | 6,387 | 54,969 | 44,833 | 64,368 | 53,010 |
| 65 years old and over | 131 | 148 | 1,865 | 1,325 | 2,033 | 1,502 |
| *Labor force participation rate* | | | | | | |
| All persons 16 years old and over | 70.1% | 57.8% | 76.9% | 57.5% | 76.1% | 57.5% |
| 16-19 years old | 40.6 | 36.7 | 59.4 | 55.4 | 55.7 | 51.8 |
| 20 years old and over | 73.8 | 60.0 | 78.3 | 57.6 | 77.8 | 57.9 |
| 65 years old and over | 13.0 | 9.9 | 16.8 | 8.5 | 16.4 | 8.7 |

*(continued on next page)*

## Table 6.03: Labor Force Participation of the Civilian Noninstitutional Population Age 16 and Older, by Sex and Age, 1980–2007

| | Black | | White | | All Races | |
|---|---|---|---|---|---|---|
| | **Male** | **Female** | **Male** | **Female** | **Male** | **Female** |
| **2000** | | | | | | |
| *Civilian noninstitutional population* | | | | | | |
| All persons 16 years old and over | 11,320 | 13,898 | 84,647 | 89,781 | 100,731 | 108,968 |
| 16-19 years old | 1,213 | 1,255 | 6,496 | 6,211 | 8,151 | 7,890 |
| 65 years old and over | 1,105 | 1,673 | 12,390 | 16,557 | 13,925 | 18,780 |
| *Civilian labor force* | | | | | | |
| All persons 16 years old and over | 7,816 | 8,787 | 63,861 | 53,714 | 75,247 | 65,616 |
| 16-19 years old | 473 | 494 | 3,679 | 3,396 | 4,317 | 4,051 |
| 65 years old and over | 157 | 165 | 2,198 | 1,550 | 2,439 | 1,762 |
| *Labor force participation rate* | | | | | | |
| All persons 16 years old and over | 69.0% | 63.2% | 75.4% | 59.8% | 74.7% | 60.2% |
| 16-19 years old | 39.0 | 39.4 | 56.6 | 54.7 | 53.0 | 51.3 |
| 65 years old and over | 14.2 | 9.9 | 17.7 | 9.4 | 17.5 | 9.4 |
| **2007** | | | | | | |
| *Civilian noninstitutional population* | | | | | | |
| All persons 16 years old and over | 12,361 | 15,124 | 92,073 | 96,180 | 112,173 | 119,694 |
| 16-19 years old | 1,305 | 1,336 | 6,653 | 6,390 | 8,618 | 8,364 |
| 65 years old and over | 1,186 | 1,893 | 13,591 | 17,835 | 15,525 | 20,703 |
| *Civilian labor force* | | | | | | |
| All persons 16 years old and over | 8,252 | 9,244 | 68,158 | 56,777 | 82,136 | 70,988 |
| 16-19 years old | 384 | 417 | 2,944 | 2,851 | 3,541 | 3,471 |
| 65 years old and over | 206 | 227 | 2,821 | 2,264 | 3,188 | 2,615 |
| *Labor force participation rate* | | | | | | |
| All persons 16 years old and over | 66.8% | 61.1% | 74.0% | 59.0% | 73.2% | 59.3% |
| 16-19 years old | 29.4 | 31.2 | 44.3 | 44.6 | 41.1 | 41.5 |
| 65 years old and over | 17.3 | 12.0 | 20.8 | 12.7 | 20.5 | 12.6 |

**Source:**   US Department of Labor, Bureau of Labor Statistics, *Handbook of Labor Statistics, 1989,* tables 3-5.
US Department of Labor, Bureau of Labor Statistics, *Employment and Earnings, 1991,* table 3; *2001,* table 3; *2007,* table 3.

**Notes:**   'All Races' includes races not shown separately.

**Units:**   Civilian noninstitutional population and civilian labor force in thousands of persons; participation rate as a percent (the civilian labor force divided by the civilian noninstitutional population).

## Table 6.04: Civilian Labor Force and Civilian Labor Force Participation Rates, Projections for 2014

|  | Black | White | All Races |
|---|---|---|---|
| *Civilian labor force* |  |  |  |
| Total | 19.4 | 129.9 | 162.1 |
| Men | 9.1 | 70.3 | 86.2 |
| Women | 10.4 | 59.6 | 75.9 |
| *Labor force participation rate* |  |  |  |
| Total | 63.4% | 65.9% | 65.6% |
| Men | 64.7 | 72.7 | 71.8 |
| Women | 62.3 | 59.3 | 59.7 |

**Source:** US Bureau of the Census, *Statistical Abstract of the United States, 2008*, table 570.

**Notes:** 'All Races' includes races not shown separately.

**Units:** Civilian labor force population 16 years old and over in millions of persons; labor force participation rate as a percent (the civilian labor force divided by the civilian noninstitutional population).

## Table 6.05: Employed Members of the Civilian Labor Force, by Sex and Age, 1980–2007

| | Black | | White | | All Races | |
|---|---|---|---|---|---|---|
| | **Male** | **Female** | **Male** | **Female** | **Male** | **Female** |
| **1980** | | | | | | |
| *All employed persons,* | | | | | | |
| *16 years old and over* | *4,798* | *4,515* | *51,127* | *36,587* | *57,186* | *42,177* |
| 16-19 years old | 299 | 248 | 3,708 | 3,314 | 4,085 | 3,625 |
| 20 years old and over | 4,498 | 4,267 | 47,419 | 33,275 | 53,101 | 38,492 |
| 65 years old and over | 126 | 113 | 1,684 | 1,001 | 1,835 | 1,125 |
| **1990** | | | | | | |
| *All employed persons,* | | | | | | |
| *16 years old and over* | *5,915* | *6,051* | *56,432* | *45,654* | *64,435* | *53,479* |
| 16-19 years old | 294 | 279 | 2,856 | 2,662 | 3,237 | 3,024 |
| 20 years old and over | 5,621 | 5,780 | 53,576 | 42,992 | 61,198 | 50,455 |
| 65 years old and over | 125 | 139 | 1,812 | 1,288 | 1,972 | 1,455 |
| **2000** | | | | | | |
| *All employed persons,* | | | | | | |
| *16 years old and over* | *7,180* | *8,154* | *61,696* | *51,780* | *72,293* | *62,915* |
| 16-19 years old | 348 | 380 | 3,227 | 3,043 | 3,713 | 3,563 |
| 65 years old and over | 147 | 155 | 2,130 | 1,512 | 2,357 | 1,713 |
| **2007** | | | | | | |
| *All employed persons,* | | | | | | |
| *16 years old and over* | *7,500* | *8,551* | *65,289* | *54,503* | *78,254* | *67,792* |
| 16-19 years old | 254 | 311 | 2,483 | 2,507 | 2,917 | 2,994 |
| 65 years old and over | 195 | 218 | 2,727 | 2,193 | 3,080 | 2,534 |

**Source:** US Department of Labor, Bureau of Labor Statistics, *Handbook of Labor Statistics, 1989*, tables 3-5.
US Department of Labor, Bureau of Labor Statistics, *Employment and Earnings, 1991*, table 3; *2001*, table 3; *2007*, table 3.

**Notes:** 'All Races' includes races not shown separately.
Data covers members of the civilian labor force.

**Units:** Employed members of the civilian labor force in thousands of persons, by age group as shown.

## Table 6.06:  Full-Time and Part-Time Status of the Labor Force, by Region, 2003

|  | Black | White | Total |
|---|---|---|---|
| **Northeast** | | | |
| *Employed persons* | | | |
| Full-time workers, total | 2,225 | 17,600 | 21,024 |
| 35 hours of more | 1,957 | 15,428 | 18,451 |
| At work 1 to 34 hours for economic reasons | 182 | 1,507 | 1,779 |
| Not at work | 86 | 666 | 793 |
| Part-time workers, total | 375 | 4,218 | 4,792 |
| At work for economic reasons | 91 | 424 | 539 |
| Not at work | 15 | 249 | 276 |
| *Unemployed persons* | | | |
| Looking for full-time work | 291 | 971 | 1,332 |
| Looking for part-time work | 38 | 215 | 267 |
| **Midwest** | | | |
| *Employed persons* | | | |
| Full-time workers, total | 2,124 | 22,907 | 25,950 |
| 35 hours of more | 1,854 | 19,977 | 22,640 |
| At work 1 to 34 hours for economic reasons | 193 | 2,096 | 2,367 |
| Not at work | 77 | 834 | 943 |
| Part-time workers, total | 392 | 5,706 | 6,316 |
| At work for economic reasons | 91 | 587 | 710 |
| Not at work | 22 | 362 | 398 |
| *Unemployed persons* | | | |
| Looking for full-time work | 323 | 1,262 | 1,671 |
| Looking for part-time work | 48 | 289 | 353 |

*(continued on next page)*

## Table 6.06: Full-Time and Part-Time Status of the Labor Force, by Region, 2003

| | Black | White | Total |
|---|---|---|---|
| **South** | | | |
| *Employed persons* | | | |
| Full-time workers, total | 7,124 | 31,882 | 40,798 |
| 35 hours of more | 6,313 | 28,176 | 36,077 |
| At work 1 to 34 hours for economic reasons | 580 | 2,646 | 3,375 |
| Not at work | 231 | 1,061 | 1,345 |
| Part-time workers, total | 1,147 | 5,986 | 7,479 |
| At work for economic reasons | 270 | 728 | 1,051 |
| Not at work | 60 | 381 | 464 |
| *Unemployed persons* | | | |
| Looking for full-time work | 809 | 1,589 | 2,523 |
| Looking for part-time work | 100 | 308 | 429 |
| **West** | | | |
| *Employed persons* | | | |
| Full-time workers, total | 1,107 | 20,867 | 25,306 |
| 35 hours of more | 976 | 18,223 | 22,158 |
| At work 1 to 34 hours for economic reasons | 90 | 1,934 | 2,295 |
| Not at work | 41 | 710 | 853 |
| Part-time workers, total | 213 | 4,806 | 5,764 |
| At work for economic reasons | 42 | 705 | 878 |
| Not at work | 17 | 318 | 384 |
| *Unemployed persons* | | | |
| Looking for full-time work | 151 | 1,366 | 1,814 |
| Looking for part-time work | 22 | 295 | 361 |

Source: US Department of Labor, Bureau of Labor Statistics, *Geographic Profile of Employment and Unemployment, 2003*, table 3.

Notes: 'Total' includes races and ethnic groups not shown separately.
The full-time labor force includes persons working part time for economic reasons (slack work, material shortages, repairs to plant or equipment, start or termination of a job during the week, and inability to find full-time work).

Units: Members of the civilian labor force in thousands.

## Table 6.07:  Full-Time and Part-Time Status of Employed Persons in Nonagricultural Industries, 1980–2007

|  | Black | White | All Races |
|---|---|---|---|
| **1980** | | | |
| *All employed persons in nonagricultural industries* | *8,502* | *79,614* | *90,209* |
| Full-time | 6,998 | 64,835 | 73,590 |
| Part-time | 1,504 | 14,780 | 16,619 |
| Part time for economic reasons | 601 | 3,375 | 4,064 |
| **1990** | | | |
| *All employed persons in nonagricultural industries* | *11,184* | *93,886* | *108,697* |
| Full-time | 9,358 | 76,697 | 89,081 |
| Part-time | 1,826 | 17,188 | 19,616 |
| Part time for economic reasons | 721 | 3,989 | 4,860 |
| **2000** | | | |
| *All employed persons in nonagricultural industries* | *14,590* | *105,736* | *126,433* |
| Full-time | 11,692 | 81,132 | 97,701 |
| Part-time | 2,897 | 24,604 | 28,732 |
| Part time for economic reasons | 488 | 2,404 | 3,045 |
| **2007** | | | |
| *All employed persons in nonagricultural industries* | *15,442* | *113,128* | *138,321* |
| Full-time | 12,389 | 86,328 | 106,419 |
| Part-time | 3,053 | 26,800 | 31,902 |
| Part time for economic reasons | 616 | 3,407 | 4,317 |

Source: US Department of Labor, Bureau of Labor Statistics, *Handbook of Labor Statistics, 1989*, table 23.
US Department of Labor, Bureau of Labor Statistics, *Employment and Earnings, 1991*, tables 32 and 33; *2001*, table 22; *2007*, table 22.

Notes: 'All Races' includes races not shown separately.
Economic reasons for persons who are employed part-time are: slack work, material shortages, repairs to plant or equipment, start or termination of a job during the week, and inability to find full-time work. Employed workers are 16 years old and over. Full-time employment is defined as 35 hours or more a week.

Units: Employed members of the civilian labor force in thousands of persons, by status, as shown.

## Table 6.08: Employment Status of Families, 2005 and 2007

|  | Black | White | All Races |
|---|---|---|---|
| **2005** | | | |
| *Total families* | *8,952* | *62,567* | *76,443* |
| With employed member(s) | 6,986 | 51,645 | 62,933 |
| Some usually work full time | 6,353 | 47,883 | 58,276 |
| With no employed member(s) | 1,966 | 10,922 | 13,509 |
| With unemployed member(s) | 1,140 | 3,801 | 5,318 |
| Some member(s) employed | 657 | 2,782 | 3,717 |
| Some usually work full time | 583 | 2,477 | 3,310 |
| **2007** | | | |
| *Total families* | *9,184* | *63,667* | *77,894* |
| With employed member(s) | 7,249 | 52,669 | 64,330 |
| Some usually work full time | 6,608 | 48,879 | 59,616 |
| With no employed member(s) | 1,935 | 10,997 | 13,564 |
| With unemployed member(s) | 990 | 3,587 | 4,914 |
| Some member(s) employed | 591 | 2,653 | 3,497 |
| Some usually work full time | 519 | 2,350 | 3,096 |

Source: US Department of Labor, Bureau Labor Statistics, *Employment and unemployment in families by race and Hispanic or Latino ethnicity, 2005-2006 annual averages*, table 1; *2006-07 annual averages*, table 1.

Notes: 'All Races' includes races not shown separately.

Units: Number of families in thousands.

### Table 6.09: Employment Status for Native-born and Foreign-born Workers, 2006

|  | Black | White | All Races |
|---|---|---|---|
| **Native-born** | | | |
| Civilian noninstititutional population | 23,668 | 150,979 | 195,082 |
| Civilian labor force | 14,905 | 100,126 | 128,280 |
| Participation rate | 63.0% | 66.3% | 65.8% |
| Employed | 13,500 | 96,262 | 122,202 |
| Unemployed | 1,405 | 3,864 | 6,078 |
| Unemployment rate | 9.4% | 3.9% | 4.7% |
| **Foreign-born** | | | |
| Civilian noninstititutional population | 2,450 | 7,329 | 33,733 |
| Civilian labor force | 1,807 | 4,503 | 23,148 |
| Participation rate | 73.7% | 61.4% | 68.6% |
| Employed | 1,708 | 4,344 | 22,225 |
| Unemployed | 99 | 159 | 923 |
| Unemployment rate | 5.5% | 3.5% | 4.0% |

Source: US Bureau of the Census, *Statistical Abstract of the United States, 2008*, table 572.

Notes: 'All Races' includes races not shown separately. 'White' and 'Black' exclude people of Hispanic origin, who may be of any race.

Units: Civilian labor force population, employed persons, and unemployed persons in thousands; labor force participation and unemployment rate as percents.

## Table 6.10: Work at Home, 2001 and 2004

|  | Black | White | All Races |
|---|---|---|---|
| **2001** | | | |
| Worked at home | 173 | 3,138 | 3,436 |
| Less than 8 hours per week | 24.4% | 24.4% | 24.5% |
| 8 hours or more | 48.1 | 48.0 | 47.6 |
| 35 hours or more | 28.9 | 15.0 | 15.7 |
| Mean hours worked per week | 23.2 | 17.7 | 18.0 |
| **2004** | | | |
| Worked at home | 176 | 2,999 | 3,349 |
| Less than 8 hours per week | 33.6% | 20.9% | 21.1% |
| 8 hours or more | 29.6 | 50.8 | 49.5 |
| 35 hours or more | 5.4 | 15.3 | 14.8 |
| Mean hours worked per week | 11.7 | 19.0 | 18.6 |

**Source:** US Department of Labor, Bureau of Labor Statistics, *Work at Home in 2001*, table 3; *2004*, table 3.

**Notes:** Data refers to employed persons (excluding self-employed) in nonagricultural industries who reported that they usually work at home at least once per week as part of their primary job.
'All Races' includes races not shown separately.

**Units:** Numbers of workers in thousands; percent of persons working at home.

## Table 6.11: Unemployment Rates for the Civilian Labor Force, by Age, 1980–2007

|  | Black | White | All Races |
|---|---|---|---|
| **1980** | | | |
| *All workers 16 years and older* | *14.3%* | *6.3%* | *7.1%* |
| 16-19 years old | 38.5 | 15.5 | 17.8 |
| 20 years old and over | 12.1 | 5.4 | 6.1 |
| 65 years old and over | 6.9 | 2.7 | 3.1 |
| **1985** | | | |
| *All workers 16 years and older* | *15.1%* | *6.2%* | *7.2%* |
| 16-19 years old | 40.2 | 15.7 | 18.6 |
| 20 years old and over | 13.1 | 5.5 | 6.4 |
| 65 years old and over | 7.0 | 2.9 | 3.2 |
| **1990** | | | |
| *All workers 16 years and older* | *11.3%* | *4.7%* | *5.5%* |
| 16-19 years old | 31.3 | 13.4 | 15.5 |
| 20-24 years old | 19.9 | 7.2 | 8.8 |
| 25-54 years old | 9.0 | 3.9 | 4.5 |
| 55-64 years old | 4.6 | 3.2 | 3.3 |
| 65 years old and over | 5.3 | 2.8 | 3.0 |

*(continued on next page)*

## Table 6.11: Unemployment Rates for the Civilian Labor Force, by Age, 1980–2007

|  | Black | White | All Races |
|---|---|---|---|
| **2000** | | | |
| *All workers 16 years and older* | *7.6%* | *3.5%* | *4.0%* |
| 16-19 years old | 24.7 | 11.4 | 13.1 |
| 20-24 years old | 15.0 | 5.8 | 7.1 |
| 25-54 years old | 5.6 | 2.7 | 3.1 |
| 55-64 years old | 3.0 | 2.4 | 2.5 |
| 65 years old and over | 6.1 | 2.8 | 3.1 |
| **2006** | | | |
| *All workers 16 years and older* | *8.9%* | *4.0%* | *4.6%* |
| 16-19 years old | 29.1 | 13.2 | 15.4 |
| 20-24 years old | 16.2 | 6.9 | 8.2 |
| 25-54 years old | 7.1 | 3.3 | 4.7 |
| 55-64 years old | 4.6 | 2.8 | 3.0 |
| 65 years old and over | 4.7 | 2.8 | 2.9 |
| **2007** | | | |
| *All workers 16 years and older* | *8.3%* | *4.1%* | *4.6%* |
| 16-19 years old | 29.4 | 13.9 | 15.7 |
| 20-24 years old | 15.2 | 7.0 | 8.2 |
| 25-54 years old | 6.5 | 3.3 | 3.7 |
| 55-64 years old | 4.3 | 2.9 | 3.1 |
| 65 years old and over | 4.5 | 3.2 | 3.3 |

**Source:** US Department of Labor, Bureau of Labor Statistics, *Handbook of Labor Statistics, 1989*, table 28.

US Department of Labor, Bureau of Labor Statistics, *Employment and Earnings, 1991*, table 3; *2001*, table 3; *2006*, table 3; *2007*, table 3.

**Notes:** 'All Races' includes races not shown separately.
Data covers members of the civilian labor force.

**Units:** Unemployment rate as percent of labor force.

## Table 6.12: Unemployment Rates for the Civilian Labor Force, by Sex and Age, 1980–2007

| | Black | | White | | All Races | |
|---|---|---|---|---|---|---|
| | Male | Female | Male | Female | Male | Female |
| **1980** | | | | | | |
| *All workers 16 and older* | *14.5%* | *14.0%* | *6.1%* | *6.5%* | *6.9%* | *7.4%* |
| 16-19 years old | 37.5 | 39.8 | 16.2 | 14.8 | 18.3 | 17.2 |
| 20 years old and over | 12.4 | 11.9 | 5.3 | 5.6 | 5.9 | 6.4 |
| 65 years old and over | 8.7 | 4.9 | 2.5 | 3.0 | 3.1 | 3.1 |
| **1985** | | | | | | |
| *All workers 16 and older* | *15.3%* | *14.9%* | *6.1%* | *6.4%* | *7.0%* | *7.4%* |
| 16-19 years old | 41.0 | 39.2 | 16.5 | 14.8 | 19.5 | 17.6 |
| 20 years old and over | 13.2 | 13.1 | 5.4 | 5.7 | 6.2 | 6.6 |
| 65 years old and over | 8.9 | 5.2 | 2.7 | 3.1 | 3.1 | 3.3 |
| **1990** | | | | | | |
| *All workers 16 and older* | *11.3%* | *10.8%* | *4.8%* | *4.6%* | *5.6%* | *5.4%* |
| 16-19 years old | 31.1 | 30.0 | 14.2 | 12.6 | 16.3 | 14.7 |
| 20-24 years old | 19.9 | 19.7 | 7.6 | 6.8 | 9.1 | 8.5 |
| 25-54 years old | 9.0 | 8.7 | 3.9 | 3.9 | 4.5 | 4.5 |
| 55-64 years old | 4.6 | 3.7 | 3.6 | 2.7 | 3.8 | 2.8 |
| 65 years old and over | 5.3 | 5.8 | 2.8 | 2.8 | 3.0 | 3.1 |
| **2000** | | | | | | |
| *All workers 16 and older* | *8.1%* | *7.2%* | *3.4%* | *3.6%* | *3.9%* | *4.1%* |
| 16-19 years old | 26.4 | 23.0 | 12.3 | 10.4 | 14.0 | 12.1 |
| 20-24 years old | 16.7 | 13.5 | 5.9 | 5.8 | 7.3 | 7.0 |
| 25-54 years old | 5.9 | 5.4 | 2.5 | 2.9 | 2.9 | 3.3 |
| 55-64 years old | 2.7 | 3.3 | 2.4 | 2.4 | 2.4 | 2.5 |
| 65 years old and over | 6.3 | 6.0 | 3.1 | 2.4 | 3.4 | 2.8 |

*(continued on next page)*

## Table 6.12: Unemployment Rates for the Civilian Labor Force, by Sex and Age, 1980–2007

| | Black | | White | | All Races | |
|---|---|---|---|---|---|---|
| | **Male** | **Female** | **Male** | **Female** | **Male** | **Female** |
| **2003** | | | | | | |
| *All workers 16 and older* | *11.6%* | *10.2%* | *5.6%* | *4.8%* | *6.3%* | *5.7%* |
| 16-19 years old | 36.0 | 30.3 | 17.1 | 13.3 | 19.3 | 15.6 |
| 20-24 years old | 20.9 | 18.8 | 9.1 | 7.6 | 10.6 | 9.3 |
| 25-54 years old | 9.2 | 8.2 | 4.6 | 4.1 | 5.2 | 4.8 |
| 55-64 years old | 6.8 | 5.9 | 4.2 | 3.4 | 4.5 | 3.7 |
| 65 years old and over | 5.6 | 5.3 | 3.8 | 3.5 | 4.0 | 3.6 |
| **2006** | | | | | | |
| *All workers 16 and older* | *9.5%* | *8.4%* | *4.0%* | *4.0%* | *4.6%* | *4.6%* |
| 16-19 years old | 32.7 | 25.9 | 14.6 | 11.7 | 16.9 | 13.8 |
| 20-24 years old | 17.2 | 15.2 | 7.3 | 6.3 | 8.7 | 7.6 |
| 25-54 years old | 7.3 | 7.0 | 3.2 | 3.4 | 3.6 | 3.9 |
| 55-64 years old | 5.5 | 3.9 | 2.8 | 2.8 | 3.0 | 2.9 |
| 65 years old and over | 5.8 | 3.7 | 2.7 | 3.0 | 2.8 | 3.0 |
| **2007** | | | | | | |
| *All workers 16 and older* | *9.1%* | *7.5%* | *4.2%* | *4.0%* | *4.7%* | *4.5%* |
| 16-19 years old | 33.8 | 25.3 | 15.7 | 12.1 | 17.6 | 13.8 |
| 20-24 years old | 16.9 | 13.6 | 7.6 | 6.2 | 8.9 | 7.3 |
| 25-54 years old | 6.9 | 6.2 | 3.3 | 3.4 | 3.7 | 3.8 |
| 55-64 years old | 5.2 | 3.7 | 3.0 | 2.8 | 3.2 | 3.0 |
| 65 years old and over | 5.0 | 4.0 | 3.3 | 3.1 | 3.4 | 3.1 |

**Source:**  US Department of Labor, Bureau of Labor Statistics, *Handbook of Labor Statistics, 1989*, table 28.
US Department of Labor, Bureau of Labor Statistics, *Employment and Earnings, 1991*, table 3; *2001*, table 3; *2006*, table 3; *2007*, table 3.

**Notes:**  'All Races' includes races not shown separately.
Data covers members of the civilian labor force.

**Units:**  Unemployment rate as percent of labor force.

## Table 6.13: Civilian Labor Force and Unemployment Rate, by State, 2006

| | Civilian Labor Force | | | Unemployment Rate | | |
|---|---|---|---|---|---|---|
| | Black | White | All Races | Black | White | All Races |
| *United States* | *17,314* | *123,834* | *151,428* | *8.9%* | *4.0%* | *4.6%* |
| Alabama | 516 | 1,640 | 2,210 | 7.5 | 3.0 | 4.1 |
| Alaska | 11 | 273 | 349 | 10.7 | 5.3 | 6.9 |
| Arizona | 113 | 2,670 | 2,969 | 6.1 | 4.0 | 4.2 |
| Arkansas | 194 | 1,137 | 1,374 | 10.3 | 4.4 | 5.3 |
| California | 1,058 | 13,833 | 17,751 | 9.4 | 4.7 | 4.8 |
| Colorado | 85 | 2,389 | 2,610 | 6.6 | 4.0 | 4.2 |
| Connecticut | 182 | 1,592 | 1,858 | 8.1 | 3.8 | 4.3 |
| Delaware | 91 | 337 | 448 | 5.5 | 3.0 | 3.5 |
| District of Columbia | 131 | 144 | 291 | 10.0 | 2.3 | 5.8 |
| Florida | 1,310 | 7,413 | 9,054 | 5.9 | 2.8 | 3.2 |
| Georgia | 1,342 | 3,177 | 4,694 | 7.9 | 3.3 | 4.6 |
| Hawaii | NA | 147 | 657 | NA | 2.6 | 2.7 |
| Idaho | NA | 724 | 759 | NA | 3.3 | 3.5 |
| Illinois | 846 | 5,358 | 6,584 | 10.0 | 3.7 | 4.5 |
| Indiana | 258 | 2,947 | 3,253 | 10.9 | 4.5 | 5.0 |
| Iowa | 34 | 1,619 | 1,701 | 16.5 | 3.2 | 3.6 |
| Kansas | 67 | 1,338 | 1,480 | 12.4 | 3.7 | 4.4 |
| Kentucky | 132 | 1,870 | 2,042 | 10.8 | 5.3 | 5.6 |
| Louisiana | 539 | 1,370 | 1,960 | 9.1 | 2.7 | 4.6 |
| Maine | NA | 695 | 715 | NA | 4.5 | 4.6 |
| Maryland | 825 | 1,990 | 3,001 | 6.3 | 2.9 | 3.9 |
| Massachusetts | 192 | 2,976 | 3,368 | 9.0 | 4.7 | 5.1 |
| Michigan | 610 | 4,232 | 5,086 | 12.8 | 6.2 | 7.0 |
| Minnesota | 107 | 2,667 | 2,933 | 10.7 | 3.6 | 4.0 |
| Mississippi | 424 | 841 | 1,296 | 11.3 | 4.0 | 6.4 |
| Missouri | 339 | 2,634 | 3,069 | 12.2 | 3.9 | 4.8 |
| Montana | NA | 475 | 505 | NA | 3.2 | 3.6 |
| Nebraska | 34 | 906 | 982 | 9.2 | 2.7 | 3.1 |

*(continued on next page)*

## Table 6.13: Civilian Labor Force and Unemployment Rate, by State, 2006

| | Civilian Labor Force | | | Unemployment Rate | | |
|---|---|---|---|---|---|---|
| | Black | White | All Races | Black | White | All Races |
| *United States* | *17,314* | *123,834* | *151,428* | *8.9%* | *4.0%* | *4.6%* |
| Nevada | 92 | 1,052 | 1,296 | 6.8 | 3.8 | 4.1 |
| New Hampshire | NA | 710 | 741 | NA | 3.3 | 3.4 |
| New Jersey | 599 | 3,473 | 4,490 | 9.7 | 4.2 | 4.8 |
| New Mexico | 24 | 814 | 944 | 5.5 | 4.3 | 4.4 |
| New York | 1,451 | 7,187 | 9,464 | 7.8 | 3.9 | 4.4 |
| North Carolina | 902 | 3,344 | 4,426 | 9.0 | 3.5 | 4.7 |
| North Dakota | NA | 338 | 368 | NA | 2.6 | 3.3 |
| Ohio | 649 | 5,163 | 5,975 | 12.3 | 4.5 | 5.4 |
| Oklahoma | 113 | 1,380 | 1,733 | 8.2 | 3.3 | 3.9 |
| Oregon | 28 | 1,719 | 1,897 | 16.1 | 5.1 | 5.4 |
| Pennsylvania | 558 | 5,606 | 6,308 | 8.2 | 4.3 | 4.7 |
| Rhode Island | 33 | 519 | 577 | 7.2 | 4.9 | 5.2 |
| South Carolina | 592 | 1,492 | 2,124 | 10.2 | 5.0 | 6.5 |
| South Dakota | NA | 408 | 434 | NA | 2.4 | 3.1 |
| Tennessee | 460 | 2,483 | 3,028 | 10.0 | 4.3 | 5.2 |
| Texas | 1,286 | 9,509 | 11,465 | 10.7 | 4.1 | 4.8 |
| Utah | NA | 1,231 | 1,309 | NA | 2.8 | 2.9 |
| Vermont | NA | 352 | 365 | NA | 3.6 | 3.6 |
| Virginia | 761 | 2,973 | 3,971 | 5.7 | 2.5 | 3.1 |
| Washington | 110 | 2,802 | 3,335 | 7.8 | 4.9 | 5.0 |
| West Virginia | 23 | 782 | 815 | 6.7 | 5.1 | 5.1 |
| Wisconsin | 145 | 2,830 | 3,079 | 11.9 | 4.3 | 4.8 |
| Wyoming | NA | 275 | 287 | NA | 3.1 | 3.4 |

Source: US Department of Labor, Bureau of Labor Statistics, *Geographic Profile of Employment and Unemployment*, 2006 Annual Averages.

Notes: 'All Races' includes races not shown separately.
Data covers members of the civilian labor force.

Units: Civilian labor force in thousands; percent unemployed in civilian labor force.

## Table 6.14: Unemployment, by Reason for Unemployment, 1990–2007

|  | Black | White | All Races |
|---|---|---|---|
| **1990** | | | |
| *Total unemployed* | *1,527* | *5,091* | *6,874* |
| Job losers | 678 | 2,534 | 3,322 |
| Job leavers | 187 | 787 | 1,014 |
| Re-entrants to the labor force | 461 | 1,346 | 1,883 |
| New entrants to the labor force | 201 | 423 | 654 |
| **2000** | | | |
| *Total unemployed* | *1,269* | *4,099* | *5,655* |
| Job losers | 514 | 1,866 | 2,492 |
| Job leavers | 145 | 593 | 775 |
| Re-entrants to the labor force | 494 | 1,356 | 1,957 |
| New entrants to the labor force | 115 | 284 | 431 |
| **2006** | | | |
| *Total unemployed* | *1,549* | *5,002* | *7,001* |
| Job losers | 660 | 2,479 | 3,321 |
| Job leavers | 161 | 608 | 827 |
| Re-entrants to the labor force | 564 | 1,514 | 2,237 |
| New entrants to the labor force | 164 | 401 | 616 |
| **2007** | | | |
| *Total unemployed* | *1,445* | *5,143* | *7,078* |
| Job losers | 637 | 2,667 | 3,515 |
| Job leavers | 139 | 595 | 793 |
| Re-entrants to the labor force | 500 | 1,474 | 2,142 |
| New entrants to the labor force | 169 | 407 | 627 |

**Source:** US Department of Labor, Bureau of Labor Statistics, *Employment and Earnings, 1991*, table 12; *2001*, table 28, *2007*, tables 27 and 28.

**Notes:** 'All Races' includes races not shown separately.
Data covers members of the civilian labor force.

**Units:** Unemployed members of the civilian labor force in thousands of persons, by reason for unemployment as shown.

## Table 6.15: Unemployment Rate by Marital Status, 2005–2007

| | Black | | White | | All Races | |
|---|---|---|---|---|---|---|
| | **Male** | **Female** | **Male** | **Female** | **Male** | **Female** |
| **2005** | | | | | | |
| *Total unemployed* | *10.5%* | *9.5%* | *4.4%* | *4.4%* | *5.1%* | *5.1%* |
| Married, spouse present | 5.1 | 5.2 | 2.5 | 3.0 | 2.8 | 3.3 |
| Widowed, divorced, or separated | 9.5 | 7.3 | 5.0 | 4.9 | 5.6 | 5.4 |
| Single (never married) | 16.9 | 13.9 | 8.2 | 6.8 | 9.5 | 8.3 |
| **2006** | | | | | | |
| *Total unemployed* | *9.5%* | *8.4%* | *4.0%* | *4.0%* | *4.6%* | *4.6%* |
| Married, spouse present | 4.7 | 4.4 | 2.2 | 2.7 | 2.4 | 2.9 |
| Widowed, divorced, or separated | 8.3 | 6.4 | 4.7 | 4.7 | 5.2 | 4.9 |
| Single (never married) | 15.2 | 12.5 | 7.5 | 6.4 | 8.6 | 7.7 |
| **2007** | | | | | | |
| *Total unemployed* | *9.1%* | *7.5%* | *4.2%* | *4.0%* | *4.7%* | *4.5%* |
| Married, spouse present | 4.3 | 4.3 | 2.4 | 2.6 | 2.5 | 2.8 |
| Widowed, divorced, or separated | 7.5 | 5.7 | 4.9 | 4.9 | 5.3 | 5.0 |
| Single (never married) | 15.0 | 10.8 | 7.8 | 6.3 | 8.8 | 7.2 |

**Source:** US Department of Labor, Bureau of Labor Statistics, *Employment and Earnings, 2006*, table 24; *2007*, table 24.

**Notes:** 'All Races' includes races not shown separately.
All persons 16 years old and over.

**Units:** Percent unemployed by marital status.

## Table 6.16: Duration of Unemployment by Region of Residence, 2000 and 2003

| | Black | White | All Races |
|---|---|---|---|
| **2000** | | | |
| *Northeast* | | | |
| Less than 5 weeks | 35.0% | 42.0% | 40.1% |
| 5-14 weeks | 32.1 | 31.9 | 32.1 |
| 15 weeks and over | 32.9 | 26.1 | 27.9 |
| 27 weeks and over | 18.4 | 13.0 | 14.3 |
| 52 weeks and over | 11.5 | 7.4 | 8.5 |
| *Midwest* | | | |
| Less than 5 weeks | 37.9% | 50.1% | 47.4% |
| 5-14 weeks | 34.9 | 31.1 | 32.0 |
| 15 weeks and over | 26.8 | 18.8 | 20.6 |
| 27 weeks and over | 14.5 | 8.4 | 9.8 |
| 52 weeks and over | NA | NA | 4.5 |
| *South* | | | |
| Less than 5 weeks | 37.5% | 49.1% | 45.2% |
| 5-14 weeks | 34.2 | 31.6 | 32.4 |
| 15 weeks and over | 28.3 | 19.4 | 22.5 |
| 27 weeks and over | 14.3 | 8.8 | 10.8 |
| 52 weeks and over | 7.6 | 4.8 | 5.9 |
| *West* | | | |
| Less than 5 weeks | 43.0% | 47.1% | 46.0% |
| 5-14 weeks | 27.1 | 31.3 | 31.2 |
| 15 weeks and over | 30.8 | 21.6 | 22.9 |
| 27 weeks and over | 17.8 | 10.5 | 11.5 |
| 52 weeks and over | 10.3 | 5.1 | 5.7 |

*(continued on next page)*

## Table 6.16: Duration of Unemployment by Region of Residence, 2000 and 2003

|  | Black | White | All Races |
|---|---|---|---|
| **2003** | | | |
| *Northeast* | | | |
| Less than 5 weeks | 23.1% | 29.1% | 27.5% |
| 5-14 weeks | 28.6 | 29.3 | 29.2 |
| 15-26 weeks | 18.5 | 17.9 | 17.9 |
| 27-51 weeks | 12.8 | 11.8 | 11.9 |
| 52 weeks and over | 17.3 | 11.9 | 13.4 |
| Median duration | 13.9 | 11.1 | 11.8 |
| *Midwest* | | | |
| Less than 5 weeks | 26.4% | 33.2% | 31.9% |
| 5-14 weeks | 30.5 | 30.6 | 30.5 |
| 15-26 weeks | 16.4 | 15.4 | 15.7 |
| 27-51 weeks | 10.2 | 10.5 | 10.5 |
| 52 weeks and over | 16.4 | 10.3 | 11.4 |
| Median duration | 12.2 | 9.4 | 9.9 |
| *South* | | | |
| Less than 5 weeks | 25.4% | 36.2% | 32.8% |
| 5-14 weeks | 28.7 | 29.8 | 29.6 |
| 15-26 weeks | 19.1 | 15.6 | 16.7 |
| 27-51 weeks | 11.4 | 8.6 | 9.5 |
| 52 weeks and over | 15.3 | 9.7 | 11.4 |
| Median duration | 12.9 | 8.8 | 9.8 |
| *West* | | | |
| Less than 5 weeks | 24.9% | 35.4% | 33.4% |
| 5-14 weeks | 29.5 | 29.8 | 29.7 |
| 15 weeks and over | 19.1 | 15.6 | 15.6 |
| 27 weeks and over | 12.7 | 9.2 | 9.7 |
| 52 weeks and over | 14.5 | 10.2 | 11.6 |
| Median duration | 13.1 | 9.0 | 9.6 |

Source: US Department of Labor, Bureau of Labor Statistics, *Geographic Profile of Employment and Unemployment, 2000*, table 11; *2003*, table 13.

Notes: 'All Races' includes races not shown separately.

Units: Percent of total unemployed in each region; median duration in weeks.

## Table 6.17: Duration of Unemployment by Sex, 2006 and 2007

| | Black | | White | | All Races | |
|---|---|---|---|---|---|---|
| | Male | Female | Male | Female | Male | Female |
| **2006** | | | | | | |
| Total unemployed | 774 | 775 | 2,730 | 2,271 | 3,753 | 3,247 |
| *by Duration* | | | | | | |
| Less than 5 weeks | 231 | 225 | 1,073 | 919 | 1,391 | 1,222 |
| 5-14 weeks | 218 | 240 | 825 | 710 | 1,112 | 1,009 |
| 15-26 weeks | 140 | 149 | 372 | 308 | 549 | 482 |
| 27 weeks and over | 186 | 161 | 461 | 335 | 700 | 534 |
| Average duration | 21.0 | 19.8 | 16.3 | 14.7 | 17.5 | 16.1 |
| Median duration | 11.3 | 10.8 | 7.7 | 7.2 | 8.5 | 8.1 |
| **2007** | | | | | | |
| Total unemployed | 752 | 693 | 2,869 | 2,274 | 3,882 | 3,196 |
| *by Duration* | | | | | | |
| Less than 5 weeks | 205 | 208 | 1,070 | 877 | 1,370 | 1,172 |
| 5-14 weeks | 228 | 214 | 913 | 721 | 1,228 | 1,004 |
| 15-26 weeks | 133 | 120 | 413 | 335 | 578 | 483 |
| 27 weeks and over | 185 | 152 | 474 | 341 | 706 | 537 |
| Average duration | 21.6 | 19.8 | 16.3 | 15.1 | 17.3 | 16.2 |
| Median duration | 11.7 | 10.4 | 8.0 | 7.8 | 8.7 | 8.4 |

Source:  US Department of Labor, Bureau of Labor Statistics, *Employment and Earnings, 2006*, table 31; *2007*, table 31.

Notes:  'All Races' includes races not shown separately.

Units:  Thousands of unemployed persons; average (mean) and median duration of unemployment in weeks.

## Table 6.18: Unemployed Jobseekers by Active Job Search Methods Used, 2005 and 2007

|  | Black | White | All Races |
|---|---|---|---|
| **2005** |  |  |  |
| Total unemployed | 1,700 | 5,350 | 7,591 |
| Total jobseekers | 1,563 | 4,595 | 6,657 |
| *Methods used as a percent of total jobseekers* |  |  |  |
| Employer directly | 60.3% | 61.1% | 60.6% |
| Sent out resumes or filled out applications | 55.6 | 55.6 | 55.4 |
| Placed or answered ads | 14.3 | 15.2 | 14.8 |
| Friends or relatives | 17.1 | 17.7 | 17.7 |
| Public employment agency | 22.0 | 17.2 | 18.3 |
| Private employment agency | 6.5 | 6.6 | 6.7 |
| Other | 9.2 | 11.6 | 11.1 |
| **2007** |  |  |  |
| Total unemployed | 1,445 | 5,143 | 7,078 |
| Total jobseekers | 1,323 | 4,337 | 6,102 |
| *Methods used as a percent of total jobseekers* |  |  |  |
| Employer directly | 58.1% | 57.5% | 57.4% |
| Sent out resumes or filled out applications | 49.7 | 51.1 | 50.7 |
| Placed or answered ads | 15.0 | 16.5 | 16.0 |
| Friends or relatives | 20.7 | 21.8 | 21.7 |
| Public employment agency | 22.3 | 16.5 | 17.7 |
| Private employment agency | 8.2 | 7.3 | 7.6 |
| Other | 10.7 | 13.3 | 12.9 |
| Average number of methods used | 1.85 | 1.85 | 1.84 |

**Source:** US Department of Labor, Bureau of Labor Statistics, *Employment and Earnings, 2005*, table 33; *2007*, table 33.

**Notes:** 'All Races' includes races not shown separately.
'Jobseekers' does not include persons on temporary layoff.
Percents will add to more than 100% because people used multiple job search methods.

**Units:** Unemployed persons in thousands; percent of jobseekers using specified search methods.

## Table 6.19: Employed Black Persons as Percent of the Civilian Labor Force, by Selected Occupation, 2007

| | Black | All Races |
|---|---|---|
| *All occupations* | 11.0% | 146,047 |
| *Management occupations* | 6.3 | 15,486 |
| Chief executive | 3.5 | 1,649 |
| General and operations managers | 4.6 | 971 |
| Computer and information systems managers | 7.7 | 467 |
| Financial managers | 7.1 | 1,181 |
| Education administrators | 12.6 | 810 |
| Medical and health services managers | 11.3 | 536 |
| *Business and financial operations occupations* | 10.5 | 6,091 |
| Accountants and auditors | 10.5 | 1,806 |
| Insurance underwriters | 14.3 | 94 |
| Wholesale and retail buyers, except farm products | 7.2 | 200 |
| *Computer and mathematical occupations* | 7.2 | 3,441 |
| Computer scientists and systems analysts | 8.8 | 825 |
| Computer programmers | 5.2 | 526 |
| Computer software engineers | 4.9 | 907 |
| Database administrators | 5.8 | 104 |
| Operations research analysts | 13.1 | 87 |
| *Architecture and engineering occupations* | 5.3 | 2,932 |
| Architects, except naval | 4.4 | 240 |
| Aerospace engineers | 6.6 | 123 |
| Chemical engineers | 10.3 | 75 |
| Civil engineers | 2.9 | 382 |
| Engineering technicians, except drafters | 8.3 | 420 |
| *Life, physical, and social science occupations* | 5.8 | 1,382 |
| Medical scientists | 7.4 | 152 |
| Environmental scientists and geoscientists | 5.4 | 98 |
| Psychologists | 7.0 | 185 |
| *Legal occupations* | 6.7 | 1,668 |
| Lawyers | 4.9 | 1,001 |
| Judges, magistrate, and other judicial workers | 9.1 | 68 |
| *Education, training and library occupations* | 9.6 | 8,485 |
| Librarians | 6.0 | 215 |
| *Arts, design, entertainment, sports and media occupations* | 5.7 | 2,789 |
| Writers and authors | 2.6 | 179 |

*(continued on next page)*

## Table 6.19: Employed Black Persons as Percent of the Civilian Labor Force, by Selected Occupation, 2007

|  | Black | All Races |
|---|---|---|
| *Healthcare practitioner and technical occupations* | 10.2% | 7,248 |
| Dentists | 5.4 | 184 |
| Physicians and surgeons | 5.6 | 888 |
| Registered nurses | 9.9 | 2,629 |
| *Healthcare support occupations* | 24.0 | 3,138 |
| *Protective service occupations* | 18.9 | 3,071 |
| Fire fighters | 10.0 | 288 |
| Police and sheriff's patrol officers | 12.7 | 669 |
| *Food preparation and serving related occupations* | 11.5 | 7,699 |
| *Building and grounds cleaning and maintenance* | 15.2 | 5,469 |
| *Personal care and service occupations* | 14.3 | 4,760 |
| *Sales and related occupations* | 9.9 | 16,698 |
| Cashiers | 17.4 | 3,022 |
| Retail salespersons | 10.9 | 3,492 |
| Real estate brokers and sales agents | 5.3 | 1,050 |
| *Office and administrative occupations* | 13.0 | 19,513 |
| *Farming, fishing, and forestry occupations* | 4.9 | 960 |
| *Construction and extraction occupations* | 6.7 | 9,535 |
| Carpenters | 5.6 | 1,824 |
| Construction laborers | 8.6 | 1,771 |
| Electricians | 5.9 | 912 |
| *Installation, maintenance, and repair* | 8.3 | 5,245 |
| *Production occupations* | 12.6 | 9,395 |
| Electrical and electronic assemblers | 13.1 | 205 |
| Machinist | 5.0 | 422 |
| Printing machine operators | 11.7 | 222 |
| Medical, dental, ophthalmic laboratory technicians | 7.7 | 107 |
| *Transportation and material moving* | 16.8 | 8,776 |
| Aircraft pilots and flight engineers | 0.5 | 123 |
| Bus drivers | 26.8 | 578 |
| Industrial truck and tractor operators | 23.0 | 571 |
| Refuse and recyclable material collectors | 23.8 | 79 |

**Source:** US Department of Labor, Bureau of Labor Statistics, *Employment and Earnings, 2007*, table 11.

**Notes:** Only selected subcategories of occupational groups displayed.

**Units:** Employed Black persons as a percent of all employed persons, by occupation; total employed persons in thousands.

## Table 6.20: Employed Black Persons as Percent of the Civilian Labor Force, by Industry Group, 2007

|  | Black | All Races |
|---|---|---|
| *All industries* | 11.0% | 146,047 |
| Agriculture, forestry, fishing, and hunting | 2.5 | 2,095 |
| Mining | 4.3 | 736 |
| Construction | 5.7 | 11,856 |
| Manufacturing | 9.7 | 16,302 |
| Durable goods | 8.4 | 10,363 |
| Nondurable goods | 11.9 | 5,938 |
| Wholesale and retail trade | 10.0 | 20,937 |
| Wholesale trade | 8.1 | 4,367 |
| Retail trade | 10.4 | 16,570 |
| Transportation and warehousing | 18.4 | 6,457 |
| Utilities | 11.7 | 1,193 |
| Information | 11.9 | 3,566 |
| Finance and insurance | 10.6 | 7,306 |
| Real estate, rental, and leasing | 9.0 | 3,182 |
| Legal services | 6.6 | 1,642 |
| Architectural, engineering, and related services | 5.1 | 1,658 |
| Scientific research and development services | 6.0 | 533 |
| Management, administrative, and waste services | 14.3 | 6,412 |
| Educational services | 10.6 | 12,828 |
| Hospitals | 15.5 | 5,955 |
| Health services, except hospitals | 15.6 | 8,733 |
| Social assistance | 19.1 | 3,147 |
| Arts, entertainment, and recreation | 8.8 | 2,833 |
| Accommodation and food services | 11.2 | 9,582 |
| Services | 10.4 | 6,972 |
| Public administration | 15.8 | 6,746 |

**Source:** US Department of Labor, Bureau of Labor Statistics, *Employment and Earnings, 2007*, table 18.

**Notes:** Only selected subcategories of industry groups are displayed.
Data includes workers 16 years and older.

**Units:** Employed Black persons as a percent of all employed persons, by industry group; total employed persons in thousands.

## Table 6.21: Tenure of Workers with Current Employer, by Sex, 2006

| | Black | | White | | All Races | |
|---|---|---|---|---|---|---|
| | **Male** | **Female** | **Male** | **Female** | **Male** | **Female** |
| Number of workers | 6,501 | 7,764 | 54,241 | 48,659 | 65,212 | 60,456 |
| *Tenure:* | | | | | | |
| Under 1 year | 26.4% | 26.1% | 23.4% | 24.6% | 23.9% | 24.9% |
| 1-2 years | 6.7 | 6.6 | 6.7 | 7.2 | 6.8 | 7.2 |
| 2 years | 6.4 | 5.1 | 5.1 | 5.0 | 5.3 | 5.0 |
| 3-4 years | 17.8 | 16.7 | 16.6 | 17.0 | 16.7 | 17.2 |
| 5-9 years | 19.8 | 22.2 | 20.7 | 21.1 | 20.7 | 21.2 |
| 10-14 years | 8.6 | 8.2 | 9.9 | 9.4 | 9.6 | 9.3 |
| 15-19 years | 5.5 | 7.5 | 6.9 | 6.9 | 6.6 | 6.8 |
| 20+ years | 8.9 | 7.7 | 10.8 | 8.7 | 10.3 | 8.4 |

**Source:**   US Bureau of the Census, *Statistical Abstract of the United States, 2008*, table 593.

**Notes:**   'All Races' includes races not shown separately.
Data is for employed wage and salary workers 16 years old and over, and excludes self-employed workers.

**Units:**   Number of workers in thousands; percent of total.

## Table 6.22: Labor Force Status of the Civilian Noninstitutional Population 16–24 Years of Age, by School Enrollment, 2001 and 2007

| | Black | White | All Races |
|---|---|---|---|
| **2001** | | | |
| *All persons enrolled in school* | *2,759* | *14,906* | *18,949* |
| Civilian labor force | 1,009 | 7,531 | 9,047 |
| Employed | 817 | 6,911 | 8,174 |
| Unemployed | 193 | 619 | 873 |
| Below college level | 1,480 | 7,027 | NA |
| Civilian labor force | 349 | 2,862 | NA |
| Employed | 247 | 2,530 | NA |
| Unemployed | 102 | 332 | NA |
| At college level | 1,279 | 7,879 | 9,958 |
| Civilian labor force | 660 | 4,669 | 5,721 |
| Employed | 570 | 4,381 | 5,311 |
| Unemployed | 91 | 288 | 470 |
| *All persons not enrolled in school* | *2,497* | *13,107* | *16,246* |
| Civilian labor force | 1,898 | 10,995 | 13,411 |
| Employed | 1,482 | 9,901 | 11,822 |
| Unemployed | 416 | 1,094 | 1,588 |
| **2007** | | | |
| *All persons enrolled in school* | *3,013* | *16,282* | *21,061* |
| Civilian labor force | 968 | 7,379 | 8,979 |
| Employed | 829 | 6,812 | 8,181 |
| Unemployed | 139 | 567 | 798 |
| Below college level | 1,590 | 7,370 | 9,724 |
| Civilian labor force | 294 | 2,371 | 2,855 |
| Employed | 222 | 2,053 | 2,421 |
| Unemployed | 72 | 318 | 434 |
| At college level | 1,423 | 8,912 | 11,337 |
| Civilian labor force | 674 | 5,008 | 6,124 |
| Employed | 607 | 4,759 | 5,760 |
| Unemployed | 67 | 249 | 364 |
| *All persons not enrolled in school* | *2,542* | *12,740* | *16,419* |
| Civilian labor force | 1,938 | 10,441 | 13,264 |
| Employed | 1,521 | 9,441 | 11,740 |
| Unemployed | 417 | 1,000 | 1,524 |

Source: US Bureau of the Census, *Statistical Abstract of the United States, 2002*, table 567.
US Department of Labor, Bureau of Labor Statistics, *College Enrollment and Work Activity of 2007 High School Graduates*, table 2.

Notes: 'All Races' includes races not shown separately. Data as of October of the year indicated.

Units: Civilian noninstitutional population, civilian labor force, employed, and unemployed in thousands of persons.

## Table 6.23: Educational Attainment of Persons 16 Years and Over, by Labor Force Status and Sex, 2000 and 2006

| | Black | | White | | All Races | |
|---|---|---|---|---|---|---|
| | **Male** | **Female** | **Male** | **Female** | **Male** | **Female** |
| **2000** | | | | | | |
| *High school graduate* | | | | | | |
| Employed | 2,605 | 2,747 | 19,043 | 16,232 | 22,377 | 19,681 |
| Unemployed | 259 | 272 | 828 | 641 | 1,136 | 951 |
| Not in labor force | 981 | 1,511 | 5,968 | 12,740 | 7,173 | 14,757 |
| *Bachelor's degree* | | | | | | |
| Employed | 916 | 1,116 | 11,312 | 9,846 | 13,028 | 11,786 |
| Unemployed | 27 | 22 | 186 | 188 | 250 | 225 |
| Not in labor force | 122 | 223 | 1,961 | 3,444 | 2,248 | 4,032 |
| **2006** | | | | | | |
| *High school graduate* | | | | | | |
| Employed | 2,657 | 2,717 | 19,377 | 14,875 | 23,898 | 18,565 |
| Unemployed | 363 | 321 | 1,046 | 645 | 1,497 | 1,009 |
| Not in labor force | 1,297 | 1,728 | 7,175 | 13,459 | 8,938 | 15,983 |
| *Bachelor's degree* | | | | | | |
| Employed | 947 | 1,320 | 12,135 | 11,128 | 14,322 | 13,684 |
| Unemployed | 55 | 51 | 330 | 267 | 430 | 350 |
| Not in labor force | 192 | 317 | 2,601 | 4,482 | 3,037 | 5,344 |

**Source:**  US Bureau of the Census, Current Population Reports: *Educational Attainment in the United States: 2000*, table 5a; *2006*, table 5a.

**Notes:**  'All Races' includes other races not shown separately.
For 2006 data, 'White' and 'Black' are equivalent to 'White Alone' and 'Black Alone' and refer to people who reported 'White' and 'Black,' respectively, and did not report any other race category.

**Units:**  Number of persons 16 years old and over in thousands.

## Table 6.24: Unemployment Rates of the Civilian Labor Force, by Educational Attainment, 1992–2006

|  | Black | White | All Races |
|---|---|---|---|
| **1992** | | | |
| Number of unemployed | 1,269 | 4,978 | 65 |
| *All levels of education* | *11.0%* | *5.5%* | *6.1%* |
| Less than 4 years of high school | 15.3 | 10.7 | 11.5 |
| 4 years of high school only | 12.3 | 6.0 | 6.8 |
| 1-3 years of college | 9.8 | 5.0 | 5.6 |
| 4 or more years of college | 4.4 | 3.0 | 3.2 |
| **2000** | | | |
| Number of unemployed | 731 | 2,644 | 3,589 |
| *All levels of education* | *5.4%* | *2.6%* | *3.0%* |
| Less than 4 years of high school | 10.7 | 5.6 | 6.3 |
| 4 years of high school only | 6.4 | 2.9 | 3.4 |
| 1-3 years of college | 4.0 | 2.4 | 2.7 |
| 4 or more years of college | 2.5 | 1.6 | 1.7 |
| **2005** | | | |
| Number of unemployed | 1,075 | 3,627 | 5,070 |
| *All levels of education* | *7.5%* | *3.5%* | *4.0%* |
| Less than 4 years of high school | 14.4 | 6.5 | 7.6 |
| 4 years of high school only | 8.5 | 4.0 | 4.7 |
| 1-3 years of college | 6.9 | 3.4 | 3.9 |
| 4 or more years of college | 3.5 | 2.1 | 2.3 |
| **2006** | | | |
| Number of unemployed | 979 | 3,376 | 4,648 |
| *All levels of education* | *6.8%* | *3.2%* | *3.6%* |
| Less than 4 years of high school | 12.8 | 5.9 | 6.8 |
| 4 years of high school only | 8.0 | 3.7 | 4.3 |
| 1-3 years of college | 6.2 | 3.2 | 3.6 |
| 4 or more years of college | 2.8 | 2.0 | 2.0 |

**Source:** US Bureau of the Census, Statistical Abstract of the United States, *2007*, table 614; *2008*, table 609.

**Notes:** 'All Races' includes races not shown separately.
Data is for persons 25 years old and over.

**Units:** Unemployment rates as a percent of the total civilian labor force; number of unemployed in thousands.

## Table 6.25: Self-Employed Workers, 1980–2007

| Year | Black | White | All Races |
|------|-------|-------|-----------|
| 1980 | 342 | 8,116 | 8,642 |
| 1985 | 379 | 8,659 | 9,269 |
| 1990 | 461 | 9,377 | 10,160 |
| 1991 | 475 | 9,512 | 10,341 |
| 1992 | 452 | 9,215 | 10,017 |
| 1993 | 468 | 9,486 | 10,335 |
| 1994 | 458 | 8,179 | 9,003 |
| 1995 | 488 | 8,105 | 8,902 |
| 1996 | 481 | 8,106 | 8,971 |
| 1997 | 471 | 8,153 | 9,056 |
| 1998 | 497 | 8,030 | 8,962 |
| 1999 | 520 | 7,846 | 8,790 |
| 2000 | 583 | 7,692 | 8,674 |
| 2001 | 544 | 7,639 | 8,594 |
| 2002 | 582 | 7,914 | 8,923 |
| 2003 | 593 | 8,160 | 9,344 |
| 2004 | 600 | 8,252 | 9,467 |
| 2005 | 648 | 8,247 | 9,509 |
| 2006 | 635 | 8,342 | 9,685 |
| 2007 | 614 | 8,268 | 9,557 |

**Source:** US Bureau of the Census, *Statistical Abstract of the United States, 1989*, table 627.
US Department of Labor, Bureau of Labor Statistics, *Employment and Earnings, 1991*, table 41; *1992*, table 41; *1993*, table 41; *1994*, table 41; *1999*, table 12; *2000*, table 12; *2001*, table 12; *2002*, table 12; *2004*, table 12; *2005*, table 12; *2006*, table 12; *2007*, table 12.

**Notes:** 'All Races' includes races not shown separately.
Data shown for non-agricultural workers only.

**Units:** Self-employed workers in thousands.

## Table 6.26: Union Membership, by Sex, 2006 and 2007

| | Black | White | All Races |
|---|---|---|---|
| **2006** | | | |
| *Men* | | | |
| Total employed | 6,788 | 55,459 | 66,811 |
| Members of unions | 1,056 | 7,115 | 8,657 |
| Percent of total | 15.6% | 12.8% | 13.0% |
| Represented by unions | 1,158 | 7,668 | 9,360 |
| Percent of total | 17.1% | 13.8% | 14.0% |
| *Women* | | | |
| Total employed | 8,090 | 49,209 | 61,426 |
| Members of unions | 1,107 | 5,144 | 6,702 |
| Percent of total | 13.7% | 10.5% | 10.9% |
| Represented by unions | 1,233 | 5,756 | 7,501 |
| Percent of total | 15.2% | 11.7% | 12.2% |
| **2007** | | | |
| *Men* | | | |
| Total employed | 6,945 | 55,771 | 67,468 |
| Members of unions | 1,097 | 7,134 | 8,767 |
| Percent of total | 15.8% | 12.8% | 13.0% |
| Represented by unions | 1,205 | 7,708 | 9,494 |
| Percent of total | 17.3% | 13.8% | 14.1% |
| *Women* | | | |
| Total employed | 8,232 | 49,743 | 62,299 |
| Members of unions | 1,067 | 5,352 | 6,903 |
| Percent of total | 13.0% | 10.8% | 11.1% |
| Represented by unions | 1,198 | 6,007 | 7,749 |
| Percent of total | 14.6% | 12.1% | 12.4% |

**Source:** US Department of Labor, Bureau of Labor Statistics, *Employment and Earnings, 2007*, table 40.

**Notes:** 'All Races' includes races not shown separately.
'Members of unions' includes members of a labor union or an employee association similar to a union. 'Represented by unions' includes members of a labor union or an employee association similar to a union as well as workers who report no union affiliation but whose jobs are covered by a union or an employee association contract.

**Units:** Total employed, members of unions, and workers represented by unions in thousands; percent of total.

## Table 6.27:  Workers Paid Hourly Rates With Earnings at or Below the Minimum Wage, 2001 and 2007

|  | Black | White | All Races |
|---|---|---|---|
| **2001** | | | |
| *Number of workers* | | | |
| All workers paid hourly rates | 10,014 | 59,152 | 72,486 |
| At or below $5.15 per hour | 297 | 1,861 | 2,238 |
| At $5.15 per hour | 114 | 502 | 636 |
| Below $5.15 per hour | 183 | 1,359 | 1,602 |
| *Percent of workers paid hourly rates* | | | |
| All at or below $5.15 per hour | 3.0% | 3.1% | 3.1% |
| At $5.15 per hour | 1.1 | 0.8 | 0.9 |
| Below $5.15 per hour | 1.8 | 2.3 | 2.2 |
| Median hourly earnings | $9.66 | $10.25 | $10.17 |
| **2007** | | | |
| *Number of workers* | | | |
| All workers paid hourly rates | 9,965 | 61,061 | 75,873 |
| At or below $5.15 per hour | 205 | 1,420 | 1,729 |
| At $5.15 per hour | 55 | 204 | 267 |
| Below $5.15 per hour | 150 | 1,216 | 1,462 |
| *Percent of workers paid hourly rates* | | | |
| All at or below $5.15 per hour | 2.1% | 2.3% | 2.3% |
| At $5.15 per hour | 0.6 | 0.3 | 0.4 |
| Below $5.15 per hour | 1.5 | 2.0 | 1.9 |

Source:   US Bureau of the Census, *Statistical Abstract of the United States, 2003,* table 617.
US Department of Labor, Bureau of Labor Statistics, *Employment and Earnings, 2007,* table 44.

Notes:   'All Races' includes races not shown separately.
Data is for workers 16 years and over.
Figures may not add to total due to rounding.

Units:   Number of workers in thousands; percent of total workers paid hourly; median hourly earnings in dollars per hour.

# Chapter 7

## Earnings, Income, Poverty & Wealth

### Chapter Seven Highlights

This chapter provides information about earnings, income, poverty, and wealth of Black persons in the United States, including both the most current data available as well as comparisons of the Black population over time. For almost all tables, corresponding data is provided for the total population of the United States as well as for White persons. This allows for easy comparison between groups.

The chapter includes data on the income of households (tables 7.01–7.03) and families (tables 7.04–7.09) organized in a variety of ways, including by age and by state (table 7.03 for households and table 7.07 for families)..

We have also included data on individual persons by selected characteristics for the years 1985, 1990, and 2006. The chapter also contains data on per capita income by state (table 7.15) and per capita income by work experience (tables 7.10 and 7.11).

The chapter features data on poverty levels of families (tables 7.18 and 7.19), individual persons (table 7.20), children (table 7.21), and persons over 65 (table 7.22).

Also of note are statistics on social assistance and welfare (table 7.23) and child support payments (table 7.24).

## Table 7.01: Money Income of Households, 1980–2006

| | Black | White | All Races |
|---|---|---|---|
| **Median income** | | | |
| 1980 | $25,076 | $43,527 | $41,258 |
| 1985 | 26,481 | 44,510 | 42,205 |
| 1990 | 27,929 | 46,705 | 44,778 |
| 1995 | 29,417 | 46,985 | 44,764 |
| 2000 | 34,735 | 51,418 | 49,163 |
| 2001 | 33,562 | 50,698 | 48,091 |
| 2002 | 32,531 | 50,530 | 47,530 |
| 2003 | 32,499 | 50,023 | 47,488 |
| 2004 | 32,124 | 49,803 | 47,323 |
| 2005 | 31,870 | 50,146 | 47,845 |
| 2006 | 31,969 | 50,673 | 48,201 |
| **Mean Income** | | | |
| 1980 | $32,545 | $51,050 | $49,070 |
| 1985 | 34,551 | 54,072 | 51,940 |
| 1990 | 37,108 | 58,191 | 55,934 |
| 1995 | 39,935 | 61,386 | 59,033 |
| 2000 | 45,870 | 69,376 | 66,895 |
| 2001 | 44,697 | 68,914 | 66,290 |
| 2002 | 44,842 | 67,431 | 64,837 |
| 2003 | 43,994 | 67,515 | 64,753 |
| 2004 | 43,372 | 67,150 | 64,542 |
| 2005 | 43,846 | 68,125 | 65,421 |
| 2006 | 45,127 | 69,107 | 66,570 |

**Source:** US Bureau of the Census, Current Population Reports, *Income, Poverty, and Health Insurance in the United States: 2006*, table A1.

**Notes:** 'All Races' includes races not shown separately. Data after 2002 uses a changed race classification: 'White' is equivalent to 'White alone' (people who reported White and not any other race category) and 'Black' is equivalent to 'Black alone' (people who reported Black and not any other race category.)

**Units:** Median and mean money income in 2006 CPI-U-RS adjusted dollars.

## Table 7.02:  Money Income of Households, by Selected Household Characteristics, 2001 and 2006

| | Black | White | All Races |
|---|---|---|---|
| **2001** | | | |
| *Number of households* | *13,315* | *90,682* | *109,297* |
| **Percent of households with current dollar incomes:** | | | |
| Under $5,000 | 6.8% | 2.4% | 3.1% |
| $5,000-$9,999 | 10.9 | 5.2 | 5.9 |
| $10,000-$14,999 | 8.7 | 6.7 | 6.9 |
| $15,000-$24,999 | 16.5 | 13.0 | 13.3 |
| $25,000-$34,999 | 14.3 | 12.2 | 12.4 |
| $35,000-$49,999 | 14.9 | 15.5 | 15.4 |
| $50,000-$74,999 | 15.4 | 18.8 | 18.4 |
| $75,000-$99,999 | 6.8 | 11.4 | 10.8 |
| $100,000 and over | 5.6 | 14.8 | 13.8 |
| Median income | $29,470 | $44,517 | $42,228 |
| Mean income | $39,248 | $60,512 | $58,208 |
| **Median income:** | | | |
| By type of residence | | | |
| Inside metropolitan area | $30,726 | $47,759 | $45,219 |
| Outside metropolitan area | 21,328 | 34,971 | 33,601 |
| By type of household | | | |
| Family households | $35,080 | $55,051 | $52,275 |
| Married couple families | 51,557 | 61,137 | 60,471 |
| Non-family households | 20,610 | 26,114 | 25,631 |
| Male householder living alone | 22,544 | 29,049 | 28,283 |
| Female householder living alone | 15,508 | 18,199 | 17,868 |

*(continued on next page)*

## Table 7.02: Money Income of Households, by Selected Household Characteristics, 2001 and 2006

| | Black | White | All Races |
|---|---|---|---|
| **2001 (continued)** | | | |
| **Median income:** | | | |
| By age of householder | | | |
| 15-24 years old | $18,386 | $30,860 | $28,196 |
| 25-34 years old | 30,206 | 47,412 | 45,080 |
| 35-44 years old | 36,794 | 56,642 | 53,320 |
| 45-54 years old | 36,824 | 61,643 | 58,045 |
| 55-64 years old | 30,281 | 47,907 | 45,864 |
| 65 years old and over | 16,761 | 23,769 | 23,118 |
| By size of household | | | |
| One person | $18,176 | $22,079 | $21,761 |
| Two persons | 29,936 | 47,109 | 45,245 |
| Three persons | 33,752 | 58,007 | 54,481 |
| Four persons | 42,425 | 65,815 | 62,595 |
| Five persons | 42,655 | 62,931 | 59,898 |
| Six persons | 50,465 | 59,573 | 57,548 |
| Seven or more persons | 40,695 | 57,488 | 54,560 |
| By number of earners | | | |
| No earners | $9,142 | $16,765 | $15,452 |
| One earner | 26,115 | 35,830 | 34,104 |
| Two earners or more | 56,453 | 69,522 | 68,106 |
| By work experience of the householder | | | |
| All civilian householders | $29,470 | $44,517 | $42,228 |
| Worked | 37,436 | 55,618 | 53,002 |
| Worked year-round full-time | 42,343 | 60,783 | 58,608 |
| Did not work | 12,505 | 22,192 | 20,887 |

*(continued on next page)*

## Table 7.02: Money Income of Households, by Selected Household Characteristics, 2001 and 2006

|  | Black | White | All Races |
|---|---|---|---|
| **2006** |  |  |  |
| *Number of households* | *14,354* | *94,705* | *116,011* |
| **Percent of households with current dollar incomes:** |  |  |  |
| Under $5,000 | 6.6% | 2.5% | 3.1% |
| $5,000-$9,999 | 9.2 | 3.7 | 4.4 |
| 10,000-$14,999 | 8.6 | 5.6 | 5.9 |
| $15,000-$24,999 | 15.2 | 11.5 | 11.8 |
| $25,000-$34,999 | 13.5 | 11.3 | 11.5 |
| $35,000-$49,999 | 14.8 | 14.6 | 14.6 |
| $50,000-$74,999 | 15.2 | 18.8 | 18.2 |
| $75,000-$99,999 | 7.7 | 11.8 | 11.3 |
| $100,000 and over | 9.1 | 20.2 | 19.1 |
| Median income | $31,969 | $50,673 | $48,201 |
| Mean income | $45,127 | $69,107 | $66,570 |
| **Median income:** |  |  |  |
| **By type of residence** |  |  |  |
| Inside metropolitan area | $32,890 | $52,694 | $50,616 |
| Outside metropolitan area | 25,400 | 40,311 | 38,293 |
| **By type of household** |  |  |  |
| Family households | $40,015 | $62,277 | $59,894 |
| Married couple families | 59,337 | 70,353 | 69,716 |
| Non-family households | 21,783 | 30,260 | 29,083 |
| Male householder living alone | 22,112 | 32,431 | 31,268 |
| Female householder living alone | 18,476 | 21,723 | 21,346 |
| **By age of householder** |  |  |  |
| 15-24 years old | $20,513 | $32,504 | $30,937 |
| 25-34 years old | 30,897 | 51,579 | 49,164 |
| 35-44 years old | 40,452 | 63,663 | 60,405 |
| 45-54 years old | 41,162 | 68,869 | 64,874 |
| 55-64 years old | 33,714 | 57,126 | 54,592 |
| 65 years old and over | 19,742 | 28,580 | 27,798 |

*(continued on next page)*

## Table 7.02: Money Income of Households, by Selected Household Characteristics, 2001 and 2006

|  | Black | White | All Races |
|---|---|---|---|
| **2006 (continued)** | | | |
| **Median income:** | | | |
| By size of household | | | |
| One person | $20,354 | $26,365 | $25,504 |
| Two persons | 34,354 | 53,796 | 51,536 |
| Three persons | 40,358 | 65,196 | 61,436 |
| Four persons | 49,502 | 75,915 | 72,870 |
| Five persons | 49,178 | 69,810 | 66,823 |
| Six persons | 42,757 | 65,680 | 61,859 |
| Seven or more persons | 45,363 | 62,182 | 60,864 |
| **By number of earners** | | | |
| No earners | $10,028 | $19,705 | $17,865 |
| One earner | 30,033 | 41,110 | 39,309 |
| Two earners or more | 65,082 | 80,310 | 78,994 |
| **By work experience of the householder** | | | |
| All civilian householders | $31,969 | $50,673 | $48,201 |
| Worked | 41,632 | 62,863 | 60,613 |
| Worked year-round full-time | 47,550 | 68,997 | 66,210 |
| Did not work | 13,943 | 26,581 | 24,840 |

Source:   US Bureau of the Census, Current Population Reports, *Historical Income Tables*, tables 1 and H-17.
US Bureau of the Census, Current Population Reports, *Annual Social and Economic Supplement, 2007*, household income table HINC-01.

Notes:   'All Races' includes races not shown separately. 'White' and 'Black' as shown here are equivalent to 'White Alone' and 'Black Alone'.
Number of households as of March of the following year.
'Occupation of the householder' represents the longest job held by the householder.

Units:   Number of households in thousands; mean and median income in current dollars.

## Table 7.03: Median Household Income by State, 2006

| | Black | White | All Races |
|---|---|---|---|
| *United States* | *$32,372* | *$51,429* | *$48,451* |
| Alabama | 25,203 | 44,788 | 38,783 |
| Alaska | 40,499 | 65,641 | 59,393 |
| Arizona | 41,198 | 49,566 | 47,265 |
| Arkansas | 23,265 | 40,009 | 36,599 |
| California | 40,709 | 60,415 | 56,645 |
| Colorado | 34,563 | 54,690 | 52,015 |
| Connecticut | 41,648 | 67,852 | 63,422 |
| Delaware | 41,640 | 55,907 | 52,833 |
| District of Columbia | 34,484 | 88,969 | 51,847 |
| Florida | 32,554 | 47,749 | 45,495 |
| Georgia | 33,563 | 53,936 | 46,832 |
| Hawaii | 49,486 | 61,616 | 61,160 |
| Idaho | 32,074 | 43,347 | 42,865 |
| Illinois | 33,151 | 56,379 | 52,006 |
| Indiana | 29,309 | 47,291 | 45,394 |
| Iowa | 27,017 | 45,222 | 44,491 |
| Kansas | 29,076 | 46,946 | 45,478 |
| Kentucky | 26,595 | 40,521 | 39,372 |
| Louisiana | 23,986 | 46,691 | 39,337 |
| Maine | 35,941 | 43,915 | 43,439 |
| Maryland | 51,726 | 71,195 | 65,144 |
| Massachusetts | 38,496 | 62,443 | 59,963 |
| Michigan | 31,276 | 50,309 | 47,182 |
| Minnesota | 30,120 | 55,724 | 54,023 |
| Mississippi | 21,969 | 43,139 | 34,473 |
| Missouri | 27,808 | 45,331 | 42,841 |
| Montana | 24,365 | 41,604 | 40,627 |
| Nebraska | 28,423 | 46,525 | 45,474 |

*(continued on next page)*

## Table 7.03: Median Household Income by State, 2006

|  | Black | White | All Races |
|---|---|---|---|
| *United States* | *$32,372* | *$51,429* | *$48,451* |
| Nevada | 43,027 | 55,225 | 52,998 |
| New Hampshire | 43,993 | 59,560 | 59,683 |
| New Jersey | 44,866 | 69,836 | 64,470 |
| New Mexico | 38,006 | 43,731 | 40,629 |
| New York | 37,107 | 57,021 | 51,384 |
| North Carolina | 29,243 | 48,179 | 42,625 |
| North Dakota | 22,931 | 43,317 | 41,919 |
| Ohio | 27,140 | 47,412 | 44,532 |
| Oklahoma | 24,119 | 41,741 | 38,770 |
| Oregon | 29,293 | 47,036 | 46,230 |
| Pennsylvania | 29,111 | 48,768 | 46,259 |
| Rhode Island | 35,183 | 55,133 | 51,814 |
| South Carolina | 26,473 | 47,902 | 41,100 |
| South Dakota | 48,623 | 44,494 | 42,791 |
| Tennessee | 28,067 | 42,919 | 40,315 |
| Texas | 32,159 | 49,207 | 44,922 |
| Utah | 39,744 | 52,179 | 51,309 |
| Vermont | NA | 47,970 | 47,665 |
| Virginia | 40,267 | 61,067 | 56,277 |
| Washington | 40,659 | 54,118 | 52,583 |
| West Virginia | 21,554 | 35,454 | 35,059 |
| Wisconsin | 26,161 | 50,794 | 48,772 |
| Wyoming | 41,170 | 48,528 | 47,423 |

**Source:** US Bureau of the Census, *American Community Survey, 2006*, table B19013.

**Notes:** Use caution when comparing this data to other Census data.

**Units:** Income in current (2006) dollars.

## Table 7.04: Money Income of Families by Selected Family Characteristics, 1985

| | Black | White | All Races |
|---|---|---|---|
| *Number of families* | *6,921* | *54,991* | *63,558* |
| **Percent of families with incomes:** | | | |
| Under $2,500 | 4.2% | 1.6% | 1.9% |
| $2,500-$4,499 | 9.3 | 2.1 | 2.9 |
| $5,000-$7,499 | 9.4 | 3.6 | 4.2 |
| $7,500-$9,999 | 7.7 | 3.9 | 4.3 |
| $10,000-$12,499 | 7.9 | 4.8 | 5.2 |
| $12,500-$14,999 | 6.4 | 4.9 | 5.0 |
| $15,000-$19,999 | 13.0 | 10.3 | 10.5 |
| $20,000-$24,999 | 9.0 | 10.4 | 10.3 |
| $25,000-$34,999 | 14.3 | 19.2 | 18.6 |
| $35,000-$49,999 | 11.8 | 19.7 | 18.8 |
| $50,000 and over | 7.0 | 19.6 | 18.3 |
| Median income | $16,786 | $29,152 | $27,735 |
| Mean income | $21,359 | $34,375 | $32,944 |
| **Mean family income:** | | | |
| By occupation of the householder | | | |
| Managerial, professional specialty | $38,870 | $52,649 | $51,820 |
| Technical, sales, administrative support | 24,732 | 38,798 | 37,436 |
| Service occupations | 19,485 | 26,604 | 24,846 |
| Farming, forestry, fishing | 16,185 | 21,305 | 21,285 |
| Precision production, craft, repair | 30,315 | 33,691 | 33,507 |
| Operators, fabricators, laborers | 24,223 | 29,449 | 28,725 |
| By work experience of the householder | | | |
| Worked at full-time jobs | $28,022 | $39,510 | $38,437 |
| Worked 50-52 weeks | 30,281 | 41,992 | 40,968 |

*(continued on next page)*

## Table 7.04: Money Income of Families
### by Selected Family Characteristics, 1985

|  | Black | White | All Races |
|---|---|---|---|
| **Median income (continued)** | | | |
| By type of family | | | |
| Married-couple families | $28,163 | $36,911 | $36,267 |
| Wife in paid labor force | 33,120 | 41,818 | 41,058 |
| Wife not in paid labor force | 19,306 | 31,934 | 30,650 |
| Male householder, no wife present | 18,205 | 29,041 | 27,525 |
| Female householder, no husband present | 13,050 | 19,468 | 17,647 |
| | | | |
| By type of income | | | |
| Wages and salaries | $21,651 | $31,277 | $30,258 |
| Non-farm self-employment | 10,165 | 14,565 | 14,420 |
| Farm self-employment | NA | 4,593 | 4,557 |
| Property income | 1,042 | 3,486 | 3,327 |
| Interest income | 722 | 2,440 | 2,328 |
| Transfer payments and all other income | 5,491 | 7,776 | 7,469 |
| Social Security or railroad retirement | 5,801 | 7,684 | 7,488 |
| Public assistance and suplemental income | 3,475 | 3,416 | 3,498 |

Source: US Bureau of the Census, Current Population Reports: *Money Income of Households: Families and Persons in the United States, March 1985* (Series P-60, #156), tables 9, 10, 13, 14, 17, and 25.

Notes: 'All Races' includes races not shown separately.
Number of families as of March of the following year.
'Occupation of the householder' represents the longest job held by the householder.
'Property income' includes interest, dividends, net rental income, income from trusts and estates, and net royalty income.

Units: Number of families and families with income in thousands; percent of total families; mean and median income in current dollars.

## Table 7.05: Money Income of Families
## by Selected Family Characteristics, 1990

| | Black | White | All Races |
|---|---|---|---|
| *Number of families* | *7,471* | *58,803* | *66,322* |
| **Percent of families with current dollar incomes:** | | | |
| Under $5,000 | 11.5% | 2.5% | 3.6% |
| $5,000-$9,999 | 14.1 | 4.7 | 5.8 |
| $10,000-$14,999 | 11.3 | 7.0 | 7.5 |
| $15,000-$24,999 | 19.5 | 16.0 | 16.4 |
| $25,000-$34,999 | 14.0 | 16.5 | 16.2 |
| $35,000-$49,999 | 15.0 | 20.8 | 20.0 |
| $50,000-$74,999 | 9.8 | 19.3 | 18.2 |
| $75,000-$99,999 | 3.4 | 7.3 | 6.9 |
| $100,000 and over | 1.3 | 5.9 | 5.4 |
| Mean income | $27,554 | $44,532 | $42,652 |
| Median income | $21,423 | $36,915 | $35,353 |
| **Median income:** | | | |
| By type of residence | | | |
| Nonfarm | $21,467 | $36,974 | $35,376 |
| Farm | NA | 34,476 | 34,171 |
| Inside metropolitan area | 22,924 | 40,086 | 37,893 |
| Outside metropolitan area | 15,677 | 29,693 | 28,272 |
| By type of family | | | |
| Married-couple families | $33,784 | $40,331 | $39,895 |
| Wife in paid labor force | 40,038 | 47,247 | 46,777 |
| Wife not in paid labor force | 20,333 | 30,781 | 30,265 |
| Male householder, no wife present | 21,848 | 30,570 | 29,046 |
| Female householder, no husband present | 12,125 | 19,528 | 16,932 |

*(continued on next page)*

## Table 7.05: Money Income of Families
### by Selected Family Characteristics, 1990

|  | Black | White | All Races |
|---|---|---|---|
| **Median income (continued)** | | | |
| By age of householder | | | |
| 15-24 years old | $7,218 | $18,234 | $16,219 |
| 25-34 years old | 17,130 | 33,457 | 31,497 |
| 35-44 years old | 27,025 | 42,632 | 41,061 |
| 45-54 years old | 30,847 | 49,249 | 47,165 |
| 55-64 years old | 25,442 | 40,416 | 39,035 |
| 65 years old and over | 16,585 | 25,864 | 25,049 |
| **By size of family** | | | |
| Two persons | $19,020 | $31,734 | $30,428 |
| Three persons | 20,602 | 38,858 | 36,644 |
| Four persons | 25,758 | 43,352 | 41,451 |
| Five persons | 22,455 | 41,037 | 39,452 |
| Six persons | 26,926 | 40,387 | 38,379 |
| Seven or more persons | 22,501 | 39,845 | 35,363 |
| **By number of earners** | | | |
| No earners | $6,305 | $17,369 | $15,047 |
| One earner | 16,308 | 27,670 | 25,878 |
| Two earners or more | 36,741 | 46,261 | 45,462 |

Source:  US Bureau of the Census, Current Population Reports: *Money Income of Households, Families, and Persons in the United States: March 1990* (Series P-60, #174), tables 13 and 14.

Notes:  'All Races' includes races not shown separately.
Number of families as of March of the following year.

Units:  Number of families and families with income in thousands; percent of total families; mean and median income in current dollars.

## Table 7.06: Money Income of Families by Selected Family Characteristics, 2006

| | Black | White | All Races |
|---|---|---|---|
| *Number of families* | *9,274* | *64,120* | *78,454* |
| **With current dollar incomes of:** | | | |
| Under $5,000 | 570 | 1,252 | 1,948 |
| $5,000-$9,999 | 534 | 1,215 | 1,884 |
| $10,000-$14,999 | 635 | 1,891 | 2,714 |
| $15,000-$24,999 | 1,272 | 5,526 | 7,216 |
| $25,000-$34,999 | 1,244 | 6,486 | 8,208 |
| $35,000-$49,999 | 1,428 | 9,277 | 11,351 |
| $50,000-$74,999 | 1,455 | 11,832 | 14,126 |
| $75,000-$99,999 | 863 | 9,083 | 10,601 |
| $100,000 and over | 1,115 | 16,389 | 19,000 |
| Median income | $38,269 | $61,280 | $58,407 |
| Mean income | $52,463 | $80,271 | $77,315 |
| **Median income by:** | | | |
| By type of family | | | |
| Married couple families | $59,115 | $70,182 | $69,404 |
| Wife in paid labor force | 70,632 | 83,807 | 82,788 |
| Wife not in paid labor force | 35,594 | 46,134 | 45,757 |
| Male householder, no wife present | 32,057 | 44,308 | 41,844 |
| Female householder, no husband present | 23,952 | 30,973 | 28,829 |
| By age of householder | | | |
| 15-24 years old | $18,724 | $34,025 | $31,471 |
| 25-34 years old | 29,179 | 52,733 | 50,122 |
| 35-44 years old | 42,528 | 68,949 | 65,282 |
| 45-54 years old | 50,506 | 79,588 | 75,692 |
| 55-64 years old | 47,013 | 70,903 | 68,747 |
| 65 years old and over | 30,775 | 40,252 | 39,649 |

*(continued on next page)*

## Table 7.06: Money Income of Families by Selected Family Characteristics, 2006

|  | Black | White | All Races |
|---|---|---|---|
| **Median income (continued)** | | | |
| By size of family | | | |
| Two persons | $32,905 | $52,032 | $50,107 |
| Three persons | 38,663 | 64,094 | 60,415 |
| Four persons | 46,547 | 76,342 | 73,415 |
| Five persons | 49,700 | 70,333 | 67,158 |
| Six persons | 43,126 | 65,723 | 62,032 |
| Seven or more persons | 41,338 | 60,622 | 58,428 |
| By number of earners | | | |
| No earners | $11,334 | $27,099 | $24,564 |
| One earner | 29,006 | 42,635 | 40,717 |
| Two earners or more | 66,898 | 82,552 | 81,413 |

Source:  US Bureau of the Census, Current Population Reports, *Annual Social and Economic Supplement 2007*, Income table FINC-01.

Notes:  'All Races' includes races not shown separately. 'White' and 'Black' as shown are equivalent to 'White Alone' and 'Black Alone.'
Number of families as of March of the following year.

Units:  Number of families and families with income in thousands; mean and median income in current dollars.

## Table 7.07:  Median Family Income by State, 2006

|  | Black | White | All Races |
|---|---|---|---|
| *United States* | *$38,385* | *$62,712* | *$58,526* |
| Alabama | 31,116 | 55,868 | 49,207 |
| Alaska | 39,690 | 77,172 | 69,872 |
| Arizona | 46,314 | 59,548 | 55,709 |
| Arkansas | 29,956 | 48,486 | 45,093 |
| California | 50,041 | 71,241 | 64,563 |
| Colorado | 42,346 | 68,472 | 64,614 |
| Connecticut | 49,273 | 83,797 | 78,154 |
| Delaware | 47,784 | 67,961 | 62,623 |
| District of Columbia | 40,997 | 157,685 | 61,105 |
| Florida | 37,907 | 58,079 | 54,445 |
| Georgia | 39,145 | 65,078 | 56,112 |
| Hawaii | 49,610 | 73,527 | 70,277 |
| Idaho | 33,350 | 52,237 | 51,640 |
| Illinois | 38,917 | 69,865 | 63,121 |
| Indiana | 33,612 | 58,028 | 55,781 |
| Iowa | 29,801 | 56,640 | 55,735 |
| Kansas | 38,351 | 59,426 | 56,857 |
| Kentucky | 32,937 | 50,342 | 48,726 |
| Louisiana | 29,681 | 56,762 | 48,261 |
| Maine | 32,540 | 53,772 | 52,793 |
| Maryland | 59,372 | 85,465 | 77,839 |
| Massachusetts | 43,647 | 79,213 | 74,463 |
| Michigan | 36,530 | 61,471 | 57,996 |
| Minnesota | 32,181 | 69,223 | 66,809 |
| Mississippi | 26,218 | 53,539 | 42,805 |
| Missouri | 33,957 | 55,827 | 53,026 |
| Montana | 33,125 | 52,149 | 51,006 |
| Nebraska | 34,678 | 58,642 | 56,940 |
| Nevada | 50,063 | 64,520 | 61,466 |

*(continued on next page)*

## Table 7.07: Median Family Income by State, 2006

|  | Black | White | All Races |
|---|---|---|---|
| *United States* | *$38,385* | *$62,712* | *$58,526* |
| New Hampshire | NA | 71,153 | 71,176 |
| New Jersey | 52,949 | 85,199 | 77,875 |
| New Mexico | 41,412 | 53,655 | 48,199 |
| New York | 45,090 | 70,582 | 62,138 |
| North Carolina | 34,660 | 59,051 | 52,336 |
| North Dakota | 22,002 | 57,203 | 55,385 |
| Ohio | 32,799 | 59,279 | 56,148 |
| Oklahoma | 29,668 | 51,592 | 47,955 |
| Oregon | 31,700 | 57,339 | 55,923 |
| Pennsylvania | 35,651 | 61,013 | 58,148 |
| Rhode Island | 43,517 | 70,468 | 64,733 |
| South Carolina | 30,731 | 59,024 | 50,334 |
| South Dakota | 47,762 | 55,943 | 53,806 |
| Tennessee | 31,923 | 53,024 | 49,804 |
| Texas | 37,941 | 58,558 | 52,355 |
| Utah | 38,523 | 59,793 | 58,141 |
| Vermont | NA | 58,288 | 58,163 |
| Virginia | 45,759 | 73,505 | 66,886 |
| Washington | 47,936 | 66,409 | 63,705 |
| West Virginia | 29,844 | 44,527 | 44,012 |
| Wisconsin | 29,844 | 63,170 | 60,634 |
| Wyoming | NA | 58,476 | 57,505 |

Source: US Bureau of the Census, *American Community Survey, 2006*, table B19013.

Notes: Use caution when comparing this data to other Census data.

Units: Income in current (2006) dollars.

## Table 7.08:  Money Income of Families, 1980–2006

|  | Black | White | All Races |
|---|---|---|---|
| **Median income** | | | |
| 1980 | $25,788 | $44,569 | $42,776 |
| 1985 | 26,339 | 45,742 | 43,518 |
| 1990 | 28,135 | 48,480 | 46,429 |
| 1995 | 29,956 | 49,191 | 46,843 |
| 2000 | 34,616 | 54,509 | 52,148 |
| 2001 | 33,598 | 54,067 | 51,407 |
| 2002 | 33,525 | 54,633 | 51,680 |
| 2003 | 34,369 | 55,768 | 52,680 |
| 2004 | 35,158 | 56,700 | 54,061 |
| 2005 | 35,464 | 59,317 | 56,194 |
| 2006 | 38,269 | 61,280 | 58,407 |
| **Mean income** | | | |
| 1980 | $32,161 | $50,744 | $48,781 |
| 1985 | 33,514 | 53,937 | 51,692 |
| 1990 | 36,187 | 58,484 | 56,015 |
| 1995 | 39,231 | 61,821 | 59,234 |
| 2000 | 45,078 | 70,386 | 67,609 |
| 2001 | 43,938 | 69,856 | 66,863 |
| 2002 | 45,485 | 69,803 | 66,970 |
| 2003 | 45,278 | 71,770 | 68,563 |
| 2004 | 46,075 | 73,395 | 70,402 |
| 2005 | 48,448 | 76,546 | 73,304 |
| 2006 | 52,463 | 80,271 | 77,315 |

Source:   US Bureau of the Census, Current Population Reports, *Historical Income Tables for Families, 1967-2003*, table F-23.
US Bureau of the Census, Current Population Reports, *Annual Social and Economic Supplement, 2003*; family income table FINC-01; *2004*, table FINC-01; *2005*, table FINC-01; *2006*, table FINC-01.

Notes:   'All Races' includes races not shown separately.
Data from 2002 forward use a changed race classification: 'White' or 'White alone' refers to people who reported White and no other race category. 'Black' or 'Black alone' refers to people who reported Black and no other race category.

Units:   Median and mean money income in 2001 CPI-U-RS adjusted dollars, except for 2002-2006, which are in current dollars for that year.

## Table 7.09: Median Weekly Earnings of Families by Type of Family and Number of Earners, 1985, 1990, and 1993

|  | Black | White | All Races |
|---|---|---|---|
| **1985** |  |  |  |
| *All families with earners* | $378 | $543 | $522 |
| Married couple families | 487 | 589 | 582 |
| With one earner | 257 | 395 | 385 |
| With two or more earners | 622 | 723 | 715 |
| Families maintained by women | 259 | 311 | 297 |
| Families maintained by men | 360 | 475 | 450 |
| **1990** |  |  |  |
| All families with earners | $459 | $681 | $653 |
| Married couple families | 601 | 745 | 732 |
| With one earner | 304 | 473 | 455 |
| With two or more earners | 748 | 892 | 880 |
| Families maintained by women | 314 | 382 | 363 |
| Families maintained by men | 397 | 539 | 514 |
| **1993** |  |  |  |
| *All families with earners* | $490 | $739 | $707 |
| Married couple families | 674 | 816 | 804 |
| With one earner | 344 | 492 | 481 |
| With two or more earners | 846 | 984 | 973 |
| Families maintained by women | 334 | 415 | 393 |
| Families maintained by men | 413 | 547 | 523 |

**Source:** US Department of Labor, Bureau of Labor Statistics, *Handbook of Labor Statistics, 1989*, table 44.
US Department of Labor, Bureau of Labor Statistics, *Employment and Earnings, January, 1991*, table 52; *1994*, table 52.

**Notes:** 'All Races' includes races not shown separately.
Data excludes families in which there is no wage or salary earner, or in which the husband, wife, or other person maintaining the family is either self-employed or in the armed forces.

**Units:** Median weekly earnings in dollars.

## Table 7.10: Money Income of Persons 15 Years Old and Older by Selected Characteristics, 1985

| | Black | | White | | All Races | |
|---|---|---|---|---|---|---|
| | Male | Female | Male | Female | Male | Female |
| *Number of persons* | *9,309* | *11,263* | *76,617* | *82,345* | *88,474* | *96,354* |
| **Percent with current dollar incomes:** | | | | | | |
| Under $2,000 | 909 | 1,301 | 5,180 | 14,024 | 6,304 | 15,848 |
| $2,000-$2,999 | 400 | 871 | 1,808 | 4,420 | 2,297 | 5,425 |
| $3,000-$3,999 | 407 | 993 | 2,190 | 4,856 | 2,671 | 5,958 |
| $4,000-$4,999 | 479 | 946 | 2,095 | 4,635 | 2,642 | 5,693 |
| $5,000-$5,999 | 351 | 540 | 2,169 | 4,201 | 2,595 | 4,848 |
| $6,000-$6,999 | 353 | 556 | 2,278 | 3,992 | 2,708 | 4,648 |
| $7,000-$8,499 | 584 | 707 | 3,402 | 5,006 | 4,132 | 5,855 |
| $8,500-$9,999 | 365 | 416 | 2,896 | 3,779 | 3,353 | 4,288 |
| $10,000-$12,499 | 737 | 788 | 5,895 | 6,579 | 6,859 | 7,576 |
| $12,500-$14,999 | 598 | 530 | 4,527 | 4,672 | 5,245 | 5,339 |
| $15,000-$17,499 | 673 | 531 | 4,940 | 4,359 | 5,739 | 5,012 |
| $17,500-$19,999 | 453 | 363 | 3,869 | 2,980 | 4,423 | 3,432 |
| $20,000-$24,999 | 672 | 483 | 7,521 | 4,839 | 8,410 | 5,513 |
| $25,000-$29,999 | 454 | 336 | 6,374 | 2,759 | 7,018 | 3,194 |
| $30,000-$34,999 | 301 | 135 | 5,324 | 1,437 | 5,767 | 1,633 |
| $35,000-$49,999 | 289 | 99 | 7,730 | 1,450 | 8,211 | 1,585 |
| $50,000-$74,999 | 80 | 14 | 3,421 | 484 | 3,588 | 509 |
| $75,000 and over | 32 | 4 | 1,603 | 169 | 1,669 | 177 |
| Median income | $10,768 | $6,277 | $17,111 | $7,357 | $16,311 | $7,217 |
| Mean income | $13,376 | $9,001 | $21,523 | $10,317 | $20,652 | $10,173 |
| **Mean income:** | | | | | | |
| By occupation | | | | | | |
| Managerial, professional specialty | $25,575 | $18,273 | $34,711 | $17,763 | $34,201 | $17,857 |
| Technical, sales, administrative | 16,026 | 11,645 | 24,050 | 10,988 | 23,293 | 11,076 |
| Service occupations | 10,270 | 6,800 | 13,161 | 5,935 | 12,549 | 6,104 |
| Farming, forestry, fishing | 4,800 | NA | 8,241 | 3,865 | 8,024 | 3,762 |
| Precision production, craft, repair | 16,314 | 11,217 | 20,593 | 12,998 | 20,277 | 12,595 |
| Operators, fabricators, laborers | 13,808 | 9,649 | 16,378 | 9,528 | 15,971 | 9,548 |

*(continued on next page)*

## Table 7.10: Money Income of Persons 15 Years Old and Older by Selected Characteristics, 1985

| | Black | | White | | All Races | |
| | Male | Female | Male | Female | Male | Female |
|---|---|---|---|---|---|---|
| **Median income (continued)** | | | | | | |
| **By work experience** | | | | | | |
| Worked at full-time jobs | $16,618 | $12,988 | $24,531 | $14,556 | $23,767 | $14,364 |
| Worked 50-52 weeks | 19,940 | 15,448 | 28,140 | 17,249 | 27,414 | 17,028 |
| **By educational attainment** | | | | | | |
| Less than 8 years of school | $7,962 | $4,684 | $10,593 | $5,809 | $10,016 | $5,582 |
| High school graduates | 15,392 | 10,155 | 21,584 | 10,121 | 20,916 | 10,120 |
| 1-3 years of college | 18,658 | 12,687 | 25,768 | 12,763 | 24,987 | 12,754 |
| 4 or more years of college | 27,210 | 19,587 | 38,460 | 18,367 | 37,570 | 18,410 |
| **By type of income** | | | | | | |
| Wages and salaries | $14,446 | $10,668 | $21,848 | $11,295 | $21,056 | $11,239 |
| Non-farm self-employment | 10,222 | 5,565 | 16,083 | 5,885 | 15,834 | 5,867 |
| Farm self-employment | NA | NA | 4,234 | 1,654 | 4,184 | 1,695 |
| Property income | 709 | 708 | 1,866 | 2,021 | 1,794 | 1,937 |
| Interest income | 505 | 483 | 1,305 | 1,454 | 1,254 | 1,395 |
| Transfer payments and all other income | 4,777 | 3,641 | 6,812 | 4,428 | 6,572 | 4,318 |
| Social security or railroad retirement | 4,757 | 3,620 | 5,803 | 4,330 | 5,701 | 4,261 |
| Public assistance and supplemental income | 2,383 | 2,922 | 2,526 | 2,881 | 2,560 | 2,919 |

Source: US Bureau of the Census, Current Population Reports: *Money Income of Households in the United States: March 1985* (Series P-60, #156), tables 31, 35, 37, 40, and 41.

Notes: 'All Races' includes races not shown separately.
Number of persons as of March of the following year. Data is based on persons living in households. Persons with incomes under $2,000 includes those with a loss. Occupation represents the longest job held by the person during the year. Educational attainment covers persons 25 years old and older; income covers persons 15 years old and older. 'Property income' includes interest, dividends, net rental income, income from trusts and estates, and net royalty income.

Units: Number of persons in thousands; median and mean income in current dollars.

## Table 7.11: Money Income of Persons 15 Years Old and Older by Selected Characteristics, 1990

| | Black | | White | | All Races | |
|---|---|---|---|---|---|---|
| | Male | Female | Male | Female | Male | Female |
| *Number of persons* | *10,074* | *12,124* | *79,555* | *85,012* | *92,240* | *100,680* |
| **With current dollar incomes:** | | | | | | |
| Under $5,000 | 1,866 | 3,455 | 8,539 | 22,062 | 10,820 | 26,337 |
| $5,000-$9,999 | 1,643 | 2,561 | 9,249 | 16,358 | 11,312 | 19,563 |
| $10,000-$14,999 | 1,323 | 1,487 | 9,529 | 11,652 | 11,253 | 13,566 |
| $15,000-$24,999 | 1,859 | 1,793 | 16,679 | 15,162 | 19,166 | 17,516 |
| $25,000-$34,999 | 1,112 | 883 | 12,707 | 7,547 | 14,185 | 8,707 |
| $35,000-$49,999 | 716 | 392 | 10,531 | 3,895 | 11,604 | 4,457 |
| $50,000-$74,999 | 237 | 83 | 5,973 | 1,382 | 6,433 | 1,535 |
| $75,000 and over | 64 | 32 | 3,274 | 509 | 3,446 | 565 |
| Median income | $12,868 | $8,328 | $21,170 | $10,317 | $20,293 | $10,070 |
| Mean income | $16,985 | $12,049 | $27,142 | $14,138 | $26,041 | $13,913 |
| **Mean income:** | | | | | | |
| By work experience | | | | | | |
| Worked at full-time jobs | $20,729 | $16,992 | $30,498 | $19,269 | $29,524 | $19,010 |
| Worked 50-52 weeks | 24,021 | 19,976 | 34,300 | 22,198 | 33,334 | 21,977 |
| By educational attainment | | | | | | |
| Less than 8 years of school | $13,719 | $7,565 | $15,057 | $8,598 | $14,914 | $8,602 |
| High school graduates | 18,879 | 14,146 | 25,520 | 13,955 | 24,727 | 13,999 |
| 1-3 years of college | 23,877 | 17,499 | 31,235 | 17,148 | 30,340 | 17,188 |
| 4 or more years of college | 33,404 | 26,195 | 45,709 | 25,230 | 44,864 | 25,388 |
| By age | | | | | | |
| 15-24 years old | $7,254 | $6,105 | $8,915 | $7,161 | $8,693 | $6,998 |
| 25-34 years old | 16,948 | 12,436 | 25,442 | 15,317 | 24,365 | 14,955 |
| 35-44 years old | 23,266 | 17,271 | 35,723 | 17,724 | 34,468 | 17,667 |
| 45-54 years old | 24,268 | 16,963 | 38,632 | 17,845 | 37,182 | 17,831 |
| 55-64 years old | 18,585 | 11,234 | 33,396 | 14,159 | 31,899 | 13,834 |
| 65 years old and over | 10,954 | 7,136 | 20,918 | 11,864 | 20,011 | 11,441 |

*(continued on next page)*

## Table 7.11: Money Income of Persons 15 Years Old and Older by Selected Characteristics, 1990

| | Black | | White | | All Races | |
|---|---|---|---|---|---|---|
| | **Male** | **Female** | **Male** | **Female** | **Male** | **Female** |
| **Mean income (continued)** | | | | | | |
| **By marital status** | | | | | | |
| Single | $11,997 | $10,306 | $16,902 | $14,504 | $16,112 | $13,656 |
| Married | 21,648 | 13,711 | 32,362 | 13,828 | 31,488 | 13,858 |
| Spouse present | 22,457 | 14,261 | 32,627 | 13,805 | 31,888 | 13,883 |
| Spouse absent | 16,790 | 11,910 | 25,396 | 14,255 | 23,158 | 13,508 |
| Widowed | 10,873 | 8,985 | 18,528 | 13,822 | 17,440 | 13,190 |
| Divorced | 19,120 | 16,781 | 26,830 | 19,448 | 25,787 | 19,058 |

**Source:** US Bureau of the Census, Current Population Reports: *Money Income of Households, Families, and Persons in the United States: March 1990* (Series P-60, #174), tables 24-26, 28-29, and 31.

**Notes:** 'All Races' includes races not shown separately.
Number of persons as of March of the following year. Data is based on persons living in households. Persons with incomes under $2,000 includes those with a loss. Occupation represents the longest job held by the person during the year. Educational attainment covers persons 25 years old and older; income covers persons 15 years old and older. 'Property income' includes interest, dividends, net rental income, income from trusts and estates, and net royalty income.

**Units:** Number of persons in thousands; median and mean income in current dollars.

## Table 7.12: Money Income of Persons 15 Years Old and Older by Selected Characteristics, 2006

| | Black | | White | | All Races | |
|---|---|---|---|---|---|---|
| | Male | Female | Male | Female | Male | Female |
| *Total persons* | *12,716* | *15,413* | *94,029* | *97,550* | *114,576* | *121,443* |
| Total with income | 10,434 | 12,840 | 86,674 | 84,955 | 103,909 | 104,502 |
| **Persons with incomes:** | | | | | | |
| $1-$2,499 or loss | 498 | 810 | 3,344 | 7,140 | 4,214 | 8,610 |
| $2,500-$4,999 | 371 | 655 | 1,948 | 3,952 | 2,529 | 4,939 |
| $5,000-$7,499 | 647 | 1,024 | 2,628 | 5,952 | 3,584 | 7,444 |
| $7,500-$9,999 | 548 | 1,047 | 2,647 | 5,561 | 3,432 | 7,071 |
| $10,000-$12,499 | 713 | 1,029 | 4,047 | 6,421 | 5,096 | 7,903 |
| $12,500-$14,999 | 468 | 691 | 2,894 | 4,561 | 3,594 | 5,554 |
| $15,000-$17,499 | 573 | 805 | 4,098 | 5,218 | 5,033 | 6,399 |
| $17,500-$19,999 | 401 | 560 | 3,070 | 3,521 | 3,671 | 4,338 |
| $20,000-$22,499 | 643 | 733 | 4,412 | 4,636 | 5,413 | 5,781 |
| $22,500-$24,999 | 341 | 439 | 2,635 | 2,801 | 3,166 | 3,445 |
| $25,000-$27,499 | 605 | 638 | 3,837 | 3,905 | 4,696 | 4,827 |
| $27,500-$29,999 | 231 | 396 | 2,229 | 2,227 | 2,596 | 2,767 |
| $30,000-$32,499 | 669 | 713 | 4,463 | 3,597 | 5,440 | 4,596 |
| $32,500-$34,999 | 185 | 199 | 2,022 | 1,735 | 2,341 | 2,035 |
| $35,000-$37,499 | 482 | 483 | 3,388 | 2,815 | 4,096 | 3,516 |
| $37,500-$39,999 | 188 | 212 | 1,686 | 1,458 | 1,974 | 1,764 |
| $40,000-$42,499 | 429 | 415 | 3,723 | 2,529 | 4,399 | 3,186 |
| $42,500-$44,999 | 134 | 134 | 1,316 | 1,159 | 1,531 | 1,372 |
| $45,000-$47,499 | 256 | 229 | 2,566 | 1,603 | 3,012 | 1,950 |
| $47,500-$49,999 | 127 | 134 | 1,345 | 1,015 | 1,559 | 1,212 |
| $50,000-$52,499 | 348 | 234 | 3,459 | 1,832 | 4,047 | 2,221 |
| $52,500-$54,999 | 77 | 105 | 1,044 | 766 | 1,195 | 924 |
| $55,000-$57,499 | 148 | 125 | 1,608 | 1,029 | 1,855 | 1,233 |
| $57,500-$59,999 | 73 | 59 | 858 | 616 | 981 | 703 |

*(continued on next page)*

## Table 7.12: Money Income of Persons 15 Years Old and Older by Selected Characteristics, 2006

| | Black | | White | | All Races | |
|---|---|---|---|---|---|---|
| | Male | Female | Male | Female | Male | Female |
| $60,000-$62,499 | 188 | 154 | 2,222 | 1,250 | 2,630 | 1,513 |
| $62,500-$64,999 | 61 | 36 | 782 | 450 | 880 | 510 |
| $65,000-$67,499 | 120 | 134 | 1,380 | 701 | 1,595 | 915 |
| $67,500-$69,999 | 29 | 39 | 739 | 325 | 807 | 397 |
| $70,000-$72,499 | 105 | 89 | 1,437 | 721 | 1,667 | 899 |
| $72,500-$74,999 | 37 | 29 | 528 | 363 | 600 | 425 |
| $75,000-$77,499 | 104 | 66 | 1,192 | 470 | 1,407 | 602 |
| $77,500-$79,999 | 24 | 41 | 506 | 276 | 579 | 336 |
| $80,000-$82,499 | 69 | 54 | 1,069 | 474 | 1,230 | 579 |
| $82,500-$84,999 | 14 | 6 | 461 | 170 | 521 | 188 |
| $85,000-$87,499 | 59 | 38 | 645 | 288 | 768 | 353 |
| $87,500-$89,999 | 16 | 25 | 310 | 127 | 345 | 166 |
| $90,000-$92,499 | 68 | 17 | 760 | 230 | 894 | 284 |
| $92,500-$94,999 | 33 | 9 | 329 | 126 | 393 | 155 |
| $95,000-$97,499 | 40 | 14 | 445 | 203 | 511 | 229 |
| $97,500-$99,999 | 15 | 9 | 299 | 127 | 330 | 146 |
| $100,000 and over | 299 | 213 | 8,304 | 2,605 | 9,295 | 3,091 |
| Median income | $25,064 | $19,103 | $33,843 | $20,082 | $32,265 | $20,014 |
| Mean income | $32,230 | $25,910 | $48,315 | $28,612 | $46,677 | $28,416 |

Source:   US Bureau of the Census, Current Population Reports, *Annual Social and Economic Supplement 2007*, person income table PINC-01.

Notes:   'All Races' includes races and ethnic groups not shown separately. 'White' and 'Black' as shown here are equivalent to 'White Alone' and 'Black Alone.'
Number of persons as of March of the following year.

Units:   Number of persons with income in thousands of persons; mean and median income in current dollars.

## Table 7.13: Median Weekly Earnings of Full-Time and Part-Time Wage and Salary Workers, by Sex and Age, 2006 and 2007

| | Black | | White | | All Races | |
|---|---|---|---|---|---|---|
| | Male | Female | Male | Female | Male | Female |
| **2006** | | | | | | |
| **Full-Time Wage and Salary Workers** | | | | | | |
| *All full-time wage and salary workers* | $591 | $519 | $761 | $609 | $743 | $600 |
| 16-24 years old | NA | NA | NA | NA | 418 | 395 |
| 25 years old and over | NA | NA | NA | NA | 797 | 627 |
| **Part-Time Wage and Salary Workers** | | | | | | |
| *All part-time wage and salary workers* | $190 | $191 | $193 | $216 | $192 | $213 |
| 16-24 years old | NA | NA | NA | NA | 153 | 148 |
| 25 years old and over | NA | NA | NA | NA | 255 | 253 |
| **2007** | | | | | | |
| **Full-Time Wage and Salary Workers** | | | | | | |
| *All full-time wage and salary workers* | $630 | $533 | $788 | $626 | $766 | $614 |
| 16-24 years old | NA | NA | NA | NA | 443 | 409 |
| 25 years old and over | NA | NA | NA | NA | 823 | 646 |
| **Part-Time Wage and Salary Workers** | | | | | | |
| *All part-time wage and salary workers* | $205 | $200 | $203 | $220 | $203 | $218 |
| 16-24 years old | NA | NA | NA | NA | 162 | 155 |
| 25 years old and over | NA | NA | NA | NA | 264 | 259 |

**Source:** U.S. Department of Labor, Bureau of Labor Statistics, *Employment and Earnings, 2007*, tables 37 and 38.

**Notes:** 'All Races' includes other races not shown separately.

**Units:** Median weekly earning in dollars.

## Table 7.14: Median Income of Year-Round, Full-Time Workers by Sex, 1980–2006

|      | Black | | White | | All Races | |
|------|-------|--------|-------|--------|-------|--------|
|      | **Male** | **Female** | **Male** | **Female** | **Male** | **Female** |
| 1980 | $23,094 | $18,193 | $32,658 | $19,224 | $31,729 | $19,088 |
| 1985 | 22,791 | 18,656 | 32,678 | 20,596 | 31,548 | 20,372 |
| 1990 | 22,665 | 19,365 | 31,002 | 21,521 | 29,711 | 21,278 |
| 1995 | 24,798 | 21,079 | 33,515 | 24,264 | 32,199 | 23,777 |
| 2000 | 30,893 | 25,745 | 40,350 | 29,659 | 39,020 | 28,823 |
| 2001 | 31,921 | 27,297 | 40,790 | 30,849 | 40,136 | 30,420 |
| 2002 | 31,932 | 27,625 | 41,375 | 31,400 | 40,507 | 30,970 |
| 2003 | 33,429 | 27,622 | 42,142 | 32,192 | 41,503 | 31,653 |
| 2004 | 31,732 | 29,145 | 42,601 | 32,683 | 41,667 | 32,101 |
| 2005 | 34,233 | 30,363 | 43,696 | 34,100 | 42,188 | 33,256 |
| 2006 | 35,477 | 30,936 | 45,933 | 35,525 | 44,958 | 34,989 |

**Source:** US Bureau of the Census, Current Population Reports, *Money Income of Households, Families, and Persons in the United States: March 1992* (Series P-60, #184), table B-17; *1996* (Series P-60, #197), table 7.
US Bureau of the Census, *Current Population Reports: Income 2001*, table 7.
US Bureau of the Census, Current Population Reports, *Annual Social and Economic Supplement, 2002,* Person income table PINC-01; *2003*, table PINC-01; *2004*, table PINC-01, *2005*, table PINC-01; *2006*, table PINC-01; 2007, PINC-01.

**Notes:** 'All Races' includes races not shown separately. For 2002 and later, 'White' and 'Black' as shown here are equivalent to 'White alone' and 'Black alone.'
Data covers the earnings of wage and salary workers who usually worked 35 or more hours per week for 50 to 52 weeks during the year. Data prior to 1989 is for civilian workers only.

**Units:** Median annual money earnings in dollars.

## Table 7.15: Per Capita Income by State, 2006

| | Black | White | All Races |
|---|---|---|---|
| *United States* | *$16,559* | *$27,951* | *$25,267* |
| Alabama | 13,494 | 24,463 | 21,270 |
| Alaska | 20,025 | 31,771 | 26,919 |
| Arizona | 18,808 | 26,715 | 24,110 |
| Arkansas | 12,447 | 21,752 | 19,758 |
| California | 20,264 | 31,634 | 26,974 |
| Colorado | 19,323 | 29,762 | 27,750 |
| Connecticut | 19,638 | 37,272 | 34,048 |
| Delaware | 19,192 | 29,456 | 26,812 |
| District of Columbia | 20,904 | 64,812 | 37,043 |
| Florida | 15,116 | 28,112 | 25,297 |
| Georgia | 16,408 | 28,001 | 23,716 |
| Hawaii | 27,832 | 36,963 | 27,251 |
| Idaho | 13,572 | 21,534 | 21,000 |
| Illinois | 16,239 | 30,362 | 26,514 |
| Indiana | 15,162 | 23,954 | 22,781 |
| Iowa | 13,154 | 23,800 | 23,115 |
| Kansas | 16,565 | 25,174 | 23,818 |
| Kentucky | 14,949 | 21,823 | 21,112 |
| Louisiana | 12,025 | 24,671 | 20,367 |
| Maine | 12,769 | 23,680 | 23,226 |
| Maryland | 23,692 | 36,772 | 31,888 |
| Massachusetts | 17,900 | 32,969 | 30,686 |
| Michigan | 15,622 | 25,968 | 24,097 |
| Minnesota | 14,376 | 29,216 | 27,591 |
| Mississippi | 11,162 | 22,612 | 18,165 |
| Missouri | 15,318 | 24,320 | 22,916 |
| Montana | 11,464 | 22,086 | 21,067 |
| Nebraska | 15,077 | 24,389 | 23,248 |

*(continued on next page)*

## Table 7.15: Per Capita Income by State, 2006

|  | Black | White | All Races |
|---|---|---|---|
| *United States* | *$16,559* | *$27,951* | *$25,267* |
| Nevada | 20,648 | 28,741 | 26,340 |
| New Hampshire | 20,112 | 29,172 | 28,828 |
| New Jersey | 21,242 | 35,644 | 31,877 |
| New Mexico | 15,915 | 24,044 | 20,913 |
| New York | 18,282 | 32,758 | 28,024 |
| North Carolina | 14,954 | 26,399 | 22,945 |
| North Dakota | 13,084 | 23,679 | 22,619 |
| Ohio | 15,448 | 24,914 | 23,543 |
| Oklahoma | 13,788 | 23,217 | 20,935 |
| Oregon | 15,118 | 25,725 | 24,418 |
| Pennsylvania | 15,583 | 26,296 | 24,694 |
| Rhode Island | 15,526 | 28,306 | 25,937 |
| South Carolina | 13,236 | 25,902 | 21,875 |
| South Dakota | 19,173 | 23,936 | 22,066 |
| Tennessee | 14,582 | 24,009 | 22,074 |
| Texas | 16,333 | 25,453 | 22,501 |
| Utah | 14,499 | 21,884 | 21,016 |
| Vermont | 15,002 | 25,293 | 25,016 |
| Virginia | 19,907 | 33,383 | 29,899 |
| Washington | 19,340 | 29,262 | 27,346 |
| West Virginia | 14,444 | 19,540 | 19,417 |
| Wisconsin | 12,596 | 26,331 | 24,875 |
| Wyoming | 15,331 | 25,337 | 24,544 |

Source: US Bureau of the Census, *American Community Survey, 2006,* table B19013.

Notes: Use caution when comparing this data to other Census data.

Units: Income in current (2006) dollars.

## Table 7.16: Income of Persons from Specified Sources, 2006

|  | Black | White | All Races |
|---|---|---|---|
| *All persons, 15 years and over* | *23,274* | *171,629* | *208,491* |
| **Number with income from:** | | | |
| Earnings | 17,538 | 129,265 | 157,611 |
| Unemployment compensation | 732 | 4,211 | 5,230 |
| Workers' compensation | 190 | 1,423 | 1,710 |
| Social Security | 3,981 | 35,559 | 41,191 |
| SSI (Supplemental Security Income) | 1,236 | 3,340 | 4,992 |
| Public assistance (total) | 638 | 1,074 | 1,857 |
| Veterans' benefits | 282 | 2,039 | 2,416 |
| Survivors benefits | 183 | 2,535 | 2,812 |
| Disability benefits | 274 | 1,415 | 1,793 |
| Rents, royalties, estates or trusts | 594 | 9,340 | 10,517 |
| Educational assistance | 1,051 | 5,334 | 7,007 |
| Child support | 908 | 3,988 | 3,470 |
| Alimony | 28 | 352 | 395 |
| *Mean income, all persons 15 years and older* | *$28,743* | *$38,562* | *$37,517* |
| **Mean income from:** | | | |
| Earnings | $31,939 | $41,586 | $40,649 |
| Unemployment compensation | 4,415 | 3,817 | 3,952 |
| Workers' compensation | 5,196 | 6,998 | 6,769 |
| Social Security | 10,211 | 11,594 | 11,418 |
| SSI (Supplemental Security Income) | 6,422 | 6,417 | 6,406 |
| Public assistance (total) | 3,256 | 3,317 | 3,365 |
| Veterans' benefits | 11,903 | 11,357 | 11,424 |
| Survivors benefits | 13,587 | 14,151 | 14,040 |
| Disability benefits | 9,379 | 13,467 | 12,615 |
| Rents, royalties, estates or trusts | 4,821 | 7,661 | 7,368 |
| Educational assistance | 4,628 | 5,767 | 5,698 |
| Child support | 4,286 | 5,168 | 5,034 |
| Alimony | NA | 12,068 | 11,801 |

Source: US Bureau of the Census, Current Population Reports, *Annual Social and Economic Supplement 2007*, person income table PINC-09.

Notes: 'All Races' includes races not shown separately. Persons 15 years old and older as of March the following year. 'White' and 'Black' as shown are equivalent to 'White alone' and 'Black alone.'

Units: Number of persons in thousands; mean income in dollars.

## Table 7.17: Per Capita Money Income, 1990–2005

|  | Black | White | All Races |
|---|---|---|---|
| **Current Dollars** | | | |
| 1990 | $9,017 | $15,265 | $14,387 |
| 1995 | 10,982 | 18,304 | 17,227 |
| 1999 | 14,362 | 22,451 | 21,239 |
| 2000 | 14,796 | 23,582 | 22,346 |
| 2001 | 14,953 | 24,127 | 22,851 |
| 2002 | 15,441 | 24,142 | 22,794 |
| 2003 | 15,775 | 24,626 | 23,276 |
| 2004 | 16,025 | 25,223 | 23,857 |
| 2005 | 16,874 | 26,496 | 25,036 |
| **Constant Dollars** | | | |
| 1990 | $13,059 | $22,108 | $20,837 |
| 1995 | 13,969 | 23,283 | 21,913 |
| 1999 | 16,824 | 26,299 | 24,879 |
| 2000 | 16,772 | 26,732 | 25,331 |
| 2001 | 16,490 | 26,607 | 25,200 |
| 2002 | 16,762 | 26,207 | 24,744 |
| 2003 | 16,741 | 26,134 | 24,701 |
| 2004 | 16,561 | 26,067 | 24,655 |
| 2005 | 16,874 | 26,496 | 25,036 |

**Source:** US Bureau of the Census, *Statistical Abstract of the United States, 2008*, table 682.

**Notes:** 'All Races' includes other races not shown separately. For 2002 and later, 'White' and 'Black' as shown here are equivalent to 'White alone' and 'Black alone.'
Constant dollars based on 2005.

**Units:** Income in current and constant (2005) dollars.

## Table 7.18: Families Below the Poverty Threshold by Type of Family and Presence of Related Children, 2004–2006

|  | Black | White | All Races |
|---|---|---|---|
| **2004** | | | |
| *Total Families* | *8,908* | *63,227* | *77,019* |
| Families below poverty threshold | 2,034 | 5,315 | 7,854 |
| Married-couple families | 380 | 2,591 | 3,222 |
| Male householder, no wife present | 154 | 435 | 658 |
| Female householder, no husband present | 1,500 | 2,288 | 3,973 |
| *Total families with children under 18 years* | *5,655* | *31,212* | *39,710* |
| Families below poverty threshold | 1,613 | 3,866 | 5,847 |
| Married-couple families | 208 | 1,540 | 1,915 |
| Male householder, no wife present | 99 | 305 | 443 |
| Female householder, no husband present | 1,306 | 2,021 | 3,489 |
| **2005** | | | |
| *Total Families* | *9,051* | *63,414* | *77,418* |
| Families below poverty threshold | 1,997 | 5,068 | 7,657 |
| Married-couple families | 341 | 2,317 | 2,944 |
| Male householder, no wife present | 170 | 439 | 669 |
| Female householder, no husband present | 1,486 | 2,312 | 4,044 |
| *Total families with children under 18 years* | *5,747* | *30,844* | *39,394* |
| Families below poverty threshold | 1,631 | 3,682 | 5,729 |
| Married-couple families | 208 | 1,392 | 1,777 |
| Male householder, no wife present | 123 | 296 | 193 |
| Female householder, no husband present | 1,300 | 1,993 | 3,493 |

*(continued on next page)*

## Table 7.18: Families Below the Poverty Threshold by Type of Family and Presence of Related Children, 2004–2006

|  | Black | White | All Races |
|---|---|---|---|
| **2006** |  |  |  |
| *Total Families* | *9,274* | *64,120* | *78,454* |
| Families below poverty threshold | 2,007 | 5,118 | 7,668 |
| Married-couple families | 346 | 2,278 | 2,910 |
| Male householder, no wife present | 177 | 440 | 671 |
| Female householder, no husband present | 1,484 | 2,400 | 4,087 |
| *Total families with children under 18 years* | *5,813* | *31,140* | *39,780* |
| Families below poverty threshold | 1,653 | 3,773 | 5,822 |
| Married-couple families | 214 | 1,348 | 1,746 |
| Male householder, no wife present | 114 | 308 | 461 |
| Female householder, no husband present | 1,326 | 2,118 | 3,615 |

**Source:** US Bureau of the Census, Current Population Reports, *Annual Social and Economic Supplement 2005*, Poverty tables POV44 and POV45; *2006*, tables POV44 and POV45; *2007*, tables POV44 and POV4.

**Notes:** 'All Races' includes races not shown separately. "White' and 'Black' as shown are equivalent to 'White alone' and 'Black alone.'
Figures shown are for families with income below 100% of the poverty threshold.

**Units:** Number of families in thousands.

## Table 7.19: Families Below the Poverty Threshold, 1980–2006

|  | Black | White | All Races |
|---|---|---|---|
| **Number below the poverty threshold** | | | |
| 1980 | 1,826 | 4,195 | 6,217 |
| 1985 | 1,983 | 4,983 | 7,223 |
| 1990 | 2,193 | 4,622 | 7,098 |
| 1995 | 2,127 | 4,994 | 7,532 |
| 2000 | 1,686 | 4,333 | 6,400 |
| 2001 | 1,829 | 4,579 | 6,813 |
| 2002 | 1,958 | 4,862 | 7,229 |
| 2003 | 1,986 | 5,058 | 7,607 |
| 2004 | 2,035 | 5,293 | 7,835 |
| 2005 | 1,997 | 5,068 | 7,657 |
| 2006 | 2,007 | 5,118 | 7,668 |
| **Percent below the poverty threshold** | | | |
| 1980 | 28.9% | 8.0% | 10.3% |
| 1985 | 28.7 | 9.1 | 11.4 |
| 1990 | 29.3 | 8.1 | 10.7 |
| 1995 | 26.4 | 8.5 | 10.8 |
| 2000 | 19.3 | 7.1 | 8.7 |
| 2001 | 20.7 | 7.4 | 9.2 |
| 2002 | 21.4 | 7.8 | 9.6 |
| 2003 | 22.3 | 8.1 | 10.0 |
| 2004 | 22.8 | 8.4 | 10.2 |
| 2005 | 22.1 | 8.0 | 9.9 |
| 2006 | 21.6 | 8.0 | 9.8 |

Source: US Bureau of the Census, Current Population Reports, *Historical Poverty Tables*, table 4.

Notes: 'All Races' includes races not shown separately. Families as of March of the following year. For 2002 and later, 'White' and 'Black' as shown are equivalent to 'White alone' and 'Black alone.' The 2004 data has been revised to reflect a correction to the weights in the 2005 Annual Social and Economic Supplement.

Units: Number of families below the poverty threshold in thousands; percent of all families.

## Table 7.20: Persons Below the Poverty Threshold, 1980–2006

| | Black | White | All Races |
|---|---|---|---|
| **Number below the poverty threshold** | | | |
| 1980 | 8,579 | 19,699 | 29,272 |
| 1985 | 8,926 | 22,860 | 33,064 |
| 1990 | 9,837 | 22,326 | 33,585 |
| 1995 | 9,872 | 24,423 | 36,425 |
| 2000 | 7,982 | 21,291 | 31,581 |
| 2001 | 8,136 | 22,739 | 32,907 |
| 2002 | 8,602 | 23,466 | 34,570 |
| 2003 | 8,781 | 24,272 | 35,861 |
| 2004 | 9,014 | 25,327 | 37,040 |
| 2005 | 9,168 | 24,872 | 36,950 |
| 2006 | 9,048 | 24,416 | 36,460 |
| **Percent below the poverty threshold** | | | |
| 1980 | 32.5% | 10.2% | 13.0% |
| 1985 | 31.3 | 11.4 | 14.0 |
| 1990 | 31.9 | 10.7 | 13.5 |
| 1995 | 29.3 | 11.2 | 13.8 |
| 2000 | 22.5 | 9.5 | 11.3 |
| 2001 | 22.7 | 9.9 | 11.7 |
| 2002 | 24.1 | 10.2 | 12.1 |
| 2003 | 24.4 | 10.5 | 12.5 |
| 2004 | 24.7 | 10.8 | 12.7 |
| 2005 | 24.9 | 10.6 | 12.6 |
| 2006 | 24.3 | 10.3 | 12.3 |

**Source:** US Bureau of the Census, Current Population Reports: Income, *Poverty, and Health Insurance Coverage in the United States: 2006* (Series P-60-233), table 3.

**Notes:** 'All Races' includes races not shown separately. For 2002 and later, 'White' and 'Black' as shown are equivalent to 'White alone' and 'Black alone.'
The 2004 data has been revised to reflect a correction to the weights in the 2005 Annual Social and Economic Supplement.

**Units:** Number of persons below the poverty threshold in thousands; percent of total persons.

## Table 7.21: Children Below the Poverty Threshold, 1980–2006

|  | Black | White | All Races |
|---|---|---|---|
| **Number below the poverty threshold** | | | |
| 1980 | 3,961 | 7,181 | 11,543 |
| 1985 | 4,157 | 8,253 | 13,010 |
| 1990 | 4,550 | 8,232 | 13,431 |
| 1995 | 4,761 | 8,981 | 14,665 |
| 2000 | 3,581 | 7,307 | 11,587 |
| 2001 | 3,492 | 7,527 | 11,733 |
| 2002 | 3,645 | 7,549 | 12,133 |
| 2003 | 3,877 | 7,985 | 12,866 |
| 2004 | 3,788 | 8,308 | 13,041 |
| 2005 | 3,841 | 8,085 | 12,896 |
| 2006 | 3,777 | 7,908 | 12,827 |
| **Percent below the poverty threshold** | | | |
| 1980 | 42.3% | 13.9% | 18.3% |
| 1985 | 43.6 | 16.2 | 20.7 |
| 1990 | 44.8 | 15.9 | 20.6 |
| 1995 | 41.9 | 16.2 | 20.8 |
| 2000 | 31.2 | 13.1 | 16.2 |
| 2001 | 30.2 | 13.4 | 16.3 |
| 2002 | 32.3 | 13.6 | 16.7 |
| 2003 | 34.1 | 14.3 | 17.6 |
| 2004 | 33.7 | 14.8 | 17.8 |
| 2005 | 34.5 | 14.4 | 17.6 |
| 2006 | 33.4 | 14.1 | 17.4 |

Source:  US Bureau of the Census, Current Population Reports: *Income, Poverty, and Health Insurance Coverage in the United States: 2006*, table B2.

Notes:  'All Races' includes races not shown separately. For 2002 and later, 'White' and 'Black' as shown are equivalent to 'White alone' and 'Black alone.'
The 2004 data has been revised to reflect a correction to the weights in the 2005 Annual Social and Economic Supplement.

Units:  Number of persons under 18 who are below the poverty threshold in thousands; percent of total children.

## Table 7.22: Persons 65 Years Old and Over Below the Poverty Threshold, 1980–2006

|  | Black | White | All Races |
|---|---|---|---|
| **Number below the poverty threshold** | | | |
| 1980 | 783 | 3,042 | 3,871 |
| 1985 | 717 | 2,698 | 3,456 |
| 1990 | 860 | 2,707 | 3,658 |
| 1995 | 629 | 2,572 | 3,318 |
| 2000 | 607 | 2,584 | 3,323 |
| 2001 | 626 | 2,656 | 3,414 |
| 2002 | 680 | 2,739 | 3,576 |
| 2003 | 680 | 2,666 | 3,552 |
| 2004 | 705 | 2,534 | 3,453 |
| 2005 | 701 | 2,700 | 3,603 |
| 2006 | 701 | 2,473 | 3,394 |
| **Percent below the poverty threshold** | | | |
| 1980 | 38.1% | 13.6% | 15.7% |
| 1985 | 31.5 | 11.0 | 12.6 |
| 1990 | 30.7 | 10.1 | 12.2 |
| 1995 | 25.4 | 9.0 | 10.5 |
| 2000 | 21.8 | 8.7 | 9.9 |
| 2001 | 21.9 | 8.9 | 10.1 |
| 2002 | 23.8 | 9.1 | 10.4 |
| 2003 | 23.7 | 8.8 | 10.2 |
| 2004 | 23.8 | 8.3 | 9.8 |
| 2005 | 23.3 | 8.7 | 10.1 |
| 2006 | 22.7 | 7.9 | 9.4 |

Source: US Bureau of the Census, Current Population Reports: *Income, Poverty, and Health Insurance Coverage in the United States: 2006*, table B2.

Notes: 'All Races' includes races not shown separately. For 2002 and later, 'White' and 'Black' as shown are equivalent to 'White alone' and 'Black alone.'
The 2004 data has been revised to reflect a correction to the weights in the 2005 Annual Social and Economic Supplement.

Units: Number of persons 65 or older who are below the poverty threshold in thousands; percent of total persons.

## Table 7.23: Social Assistance and Welfare, 2003

| | Black | White | All Races |
|---|---|---|---|
| **Percent receiving assistance** | | | |
| *Any program* | *33.7%* | *12.3%* | *15.4%* |
| TANF/General Assistance | 3.7 | 0.8 | 1.3 |
| Supplemental Security Income | 4.8 | 1.8 | 2.2 |
| Food stamps | 18.5 | 4.9 | 6.7 |
| Medicaid | 25.1 | 9.7 | 12.0 |
| Housing Assistance | 11.9 | 2.4 | 3.7 |
| Median monthly benefit for families | $259 | $249 | $255 |
| | | | |
| **Median duration of participation, 2001–2003** | | | |
| *Any program* | *7.5* | *7.1* | *7.2* |
| TANF/General Assistance | 6.5 | 4.0 | 4.9 |
| Supplemental Security Income | 11.8 | 15.0 | 15.0 |
| Food stamps | 8.6 | 7.4 | 7.7 |
| Medicaid | 7.9 | 7.6 | 7.6 |
| Housing Assistance | 7.5 | 3.9 | 4.0 |

**Source:** US Bureau of the Census, *Survey of Income and Program Participation, Dynamics of Economic Well-Being: Participation in Government Porgrams, 2001 Through 2003, Who Gets Assistance?* (Series P70-108), tables A-1 to A-8.

**Notes:** 'TANF' indicates Temporary Assistance for Needy Families or General Assistance. Median monthly family benefits are calculated only for recipients of TANF, General Assistance, Supplemental Security Income, and food stamps.

**Units:** Percent of total population; monthly benefit in 2003 dollars; median duration in months.

## Table 7.24: Child Support Payments Agreed to or Awarded to Custodial Parents, 2005

| | Black | White | All Races |
|---|---|---|---|
| *All Custodial Parents* | *3,431* | *9,493* | *13,605* |
| Child support agreed to or awarded | 1,699 | 5,748 | 7,802 |
| Supposed to receive child support | 1,484 | 5,038 | 6,809 |
| Received payments | 1,027 | 4,005 | 5,259 |
| Full Payments | 584 | 2,475 | 3,192 |
| Partial Payments | 443 | 1,530 | 2,068 |
| Did not receive payments | 457 | 1,032 | 1,550 |
| Child support not awarded | 1,731 | 3,745 | 5,803 |
| | | | |
| *All Custodial Mothers* | *3,174* | *7,644* | *11,406* |
| Child support agreed to or awarded | 1,622 | 5,045 | 7,002 |
| Supposed to receive child support | 1,411 | 4,447 | 6,131 |
| Received payments | 975 | 3,568 | 4,754 |
| Full Payments | 552 | 2,221 | 2,900 |
| Partial Payments | 423 | 1,347 | 1,855 |
| Did not receive payments | 436 | 879 | 1,377 |
| Child support not awarded | 1,553 | 2,599 | 4,404 |
| | | | |
| *All Custodial Fathers* | *256* | *1,849* | *2,199* |
| Child support agreed to or awarded | 78 | 703 | 800 |
| Supposed to receive child support | 72 | 590 | 678 |
| Received payments | 52 | 437 | 505 |
| Full Payments | 32 | 254 | 292 |
| Partial Payments | 20 | 183 | 213 |
| Did not receive payments | 21 | 153 | 174 |
| Child support not awarded | 179 | 1,146 | 1,399 |

Source: US Bureau of the Census, Current Population Reports, *Custodial Mothers and Fathers and Their Child Support: 2005*, table 4.

Notes: 'All Races' includes races not shown separately.

Units: Number of parents in thousands.

# Chapter 8

# Special Topics

## Chapter Eight Highlights

This chapter covers important topics not covered elsewhere in this book, including both the most current data available as well as comparisons of the Black population over time. For almost all tables, corresponding data is provided for the total population of the United States as well as for White persons. This allows for easy comparison between groups.

The chapter includes statistics on social security benefits and beneficiaries for the years 1980, 1990, 2000, and 2006 (tables 8.01, 8.02, 8.03, and 8.04, respectively).

The chapter also includes information about housing units, including tenure (table 8.05) and affordability (table 8.06). It also includes statistics geographical mobility (table 8.07), and on farms and farm operators (tables 8.08 and 8.09).

Also of note are statistics on black-owned firms in various industries, which are organized in a variety of ways, including by state (tables 8.12 and 8.17), by type of industry (tables 8.10, 8.13, and 8.17), and by size (tables 8.12 and 8.17).

We have also included a summary of results of the 2006 Consumer Expenditure Survey, which tracks annual spending on many types of goods and services, including food, housing, transportation, and entertainment (tables 8.20 and 8.21).

## Table 8.01: Social Security Benefits and Beneficiaries, 1980

|  | Black | White | All Races |
|---|---|---|---|
| **Beneficiaries** | | | |
| *Total* | *3,576,014* | *31,431,133* | *35,584,955* |
| Retired workers | 1,533,904 | 17,780,617 | 19,562,085 |
| Disabled workers | 432,449 | 2,376,823 | 2,858,680 |
| Wives | 229,177 | 3,147,297 | 3,436,099 |
| Husbands | 3,719 | 36,728 | 41,328 |
| Children | 645,162 | 3,501,249 | 4,606,517 |
| Widowed mothers and fathers | 115,235 | 428,822 | 562,316 |
| Widows (nondisabled) | 288,931 | 3,935,175 | 4,262,607 |
| Widowers (nondisabled) | 2,208 | 17,870 | 20,328 |
| Widows (disabled) | 20,168 | 104,847 | 126,679 |
| Widowers (disabled) | 139 | 747 | 901 |
| Parents | 1,921 | 12,052 | 14,779 |
| Special age-72 beneficiary | 2,986 | 88,098 | 91,808 |
| Wife of special age-72 beneficiary | 15 | 808 | 828 |
| **Average monthly benefit** | | | |
| *Total* | *$236.00* | *$308.60* | *$300.20* |
| Retired workers | 281.60 | 346.90 | 341.40 |
| Disabled workers | 325.30 | 379.70 | 370.70 |
| Wives | 119.00 | 168.30 | 164.20 |
| Husbands | 111.50 | 132.10 | 130.00 |
| Children | 154.00 | 200.00 | 187.60 |
| Widowed mothers and fathers | 196.60 | 261.70 | 246.20 |
| Widows (nondisabled) | 244.80 | 316.90 | 311.00 |
| Widowers (nondisabled) | 210.00 | 243.20 | 239.40 |
| Widows (disabled) | 169.80 | 212.60 | 205.40 |
| Widowers (disabled) | 131.50 | 148.10 | 145.70 |
| Parents | 247.00 | 282.60 | 276.00 |
| Special age-72 beneficiary | 104.90 | 104.90 | 104.90 |
| Wife of special age-72 beneficiary | 52.60 | 52.60 | 52.60 |

**Source:** US Department of Health & Human Services, Social Security Administration, *Social Security Bulletin, Annual Statistical Supplement, 1982*, table 70.

**Notes:** 'All Races' includes other races not shown separately.

**Units:** Number of beneficiaries; average monthly benefit in current dollars.

## Table 8.02: Social Security Benefits and Beneficiaries, 1990

| | Black | White | All Races |
|---|---|---|---|
| **Beneficiaries** | | | |
| *Total* | *3,707,980* | *34,846,200* | *39,814,330* |
| Retired workers | 1,904,140 | 22,287,520 | 24,826,230 |
| Disabled workers | 489,450 | 2,335,560 | 3,011,130 |
| Wives | 187,660 | 3,046,270 | 3,329,830 |
| Husbands | 4,170 | 28,610 | 36,570 |
| Children | 544,780 | 1,745,840 | 3,193,070 |
| Widowed mothers and fathers | 55,290 | 233,640 | 305,080 |
| Widows (nondisabled) | 388,010 | 4,501,160 | 4,963,820 |
| Widowers (nondisabled) | 4,200 | 28,380 | 33,790 |
| Widows (disabled) | 19,060 | 77,510 | 100,150 |
| Widowers (disabled) | 390 | 1,130 | 1,630 |
| Parents | 800 | 4,190 | 5,840 |
| Special age-72 beneficiary | 310 | 6,790 | 7,190 |
| **Average monthly benefit** | | | |
| *Total* | *$443.10* | *$558.60* | *$544.50* |
| Retired workers | 505.80 | 612.60 | 602.60 |
| Disabled workers | 531.70 | 603.00 | 587.00 |
| Wives | 226.20 | 306.80 | 300.10 |
| Husbands | 175.60 | 189.30 | 183.90 |
| Children | NA | NA | NA |
| Widowed mothers and fathers | 350.80 | 432.70 | 409.00 |
| Widows (nondisabled) | 442.40 | 569.10 | 557.70 |
| Widowers (nondisabled) | 384.00 | 417.40 | 411.00 |
| Widows (disabled) | 341.40 | 404.40 | 389.50 |
| Widowers (disabled) | 213.40 | 233.20 | 228.50 |
| Parents | 425.50 | 506.10 | 491.00 |
| Special age-72 beneficiary | 167.50 | 166.80 | 166.80 |

Source:  US Department of Health & Human Services, Social Security Administration, *Social Security Bulletin, Annual Statistical Supplement, 1991*, table 5.

Notes:  'All Races' includes other races not shown separately.

Units:  Number of beneficiaries; average monthly benefit in current dollars.

## Table 8.03: Social Security Benefits and Beneficiaries, 2000

|  | Black | White | All Races |
|---|---|---|---|
| **Beneficiaries** | | | |
| *Total* | *4,622,040* | *38,853,370* | *45,417,470* |
| Retired workers | 2,282,550 | 25,401,010 | 28,505,990 |
| Disabled workers | 868,070 | 3,701,770 | 5,035,840 |
| Wives | 150,600 | 2,662,350 | 2,925,950 |
| Husbands | 5,020 | 23,310 | 36,070 |
| Children | 827,670 | 2,590,050 | 3,810,490 |
| Widowed mothers and fathers | 34,090 | 141,800 | 201,270 |
| Widows (nondisabled) | 406,230 | 4,152,820 | 4,661,540 |
| Widowers (nondisabled) | 5,980 | 29,290 | 37,120 |
| Widows (disabled) | 40,160 | 145,890 | 195,340 |
| Widowers (disabled) | 1,310 | 3,190 | 4,790 |
| Parents | 360 | 1,830 | 3,000 |
| **Average monthly benefit** | | | |
| *Total* | *$635.70* | *$791.50* | *$767.40* |
| Retired workers | 724.20 | 859.90 | 844.60 |
| Disabled workers | 731.40 | 809.30 | 787.00 |
| Wives | 330.30 | 429.30 | 419.20 |
| Husbands | 240.40 | 239.40 | 232.10 |
| Children | 357.80 | 434.50 | 406.30 |
| Widowed mothers and fathers | 508.40 | 633.10 | 593.00 |
| Widows (nondisabled) | 646.90 | 831.40 | 811.80 |
| Widowers (nondisabled) | 585.80 | 614.90 | 606.30 |
| Widows (disabled) | 465.90 | 542.70 | 523.00 |
| Widowers (disabled) | 387.20 | 342.80 | 352.80 |
| Parents | 643.50 | 735.50 | 701.00 |

Source: US Department of Health & Human Services, Social Security Administration, *Social Security Bulletin, Annual Statistical Supplement, 2005*, table 5.A1.

Notes: 'All Races' includes other races not shown separately.

Units: Number of beneficiaries; average monthly benefit in current dollars.

## Table 8.04:  Social Security Benefits and Beneficiaries, 2006

|  | Black | White | All Races |
|---|---|---|---|
| **Beneficiaries** | | | |
| *Total* | *5,045,907* | *40,554,883* | *49,122,624* |
| Retired workers | 2,556,928 | 27,167,053 | 30,976,143 |
| Disabled workers | 1,146,498 | 4,785,617 | 6,806,918 |
| Wives | 128,100 | 2,303,622 | 2,585,092 |
| Husbands | 5,754 | 27,290 | 46,977 |
| Children | 815,079 | 2,554,160 | 4,040,530 |
| Widowed mothers and fathers | 23,013 | 110,485 | 171,453 |
| Widows (nondisabled) | 332,124 | 3,463,191 | 4,225,561 |
| Widowers (nondisabled) | 5,412 | 24,564 | 47,881 |
| Widows (disabled) | 31,365 | 114,437 | 212,063 |
| Widowers (disabled) | 1,437 | 3,491 | 8,115 |
| Parents | 197 | 971 | 1,889 |
| **Average monthly benefit** | | | |
| *Total* | *$813.30* | *$989.70* | *$955.50* |
| Retired workers | 920.30 | 1,065.40 | 1,044.40 |
| Disabled workers | 908.30 | 1,014.80 | 977.70 |
| Wives | 409.60 | 522.70 | 506.30 |
| Husbands | 331.90 | 297.00 | 288.90 |
| Children | 430.00 | 534.70 | 502.80 |
| Widowed mothers and fathers | 651.80 | 813.20 | 756.60 |
| Widows (nondisabled) | 804.70 | 1,032.80 | 1,009.80 |
| Widowers (nondisabled) | 791.50 | 832.40 | 829.10 |
| Widows (disabled) | 554.00 | 647.00 | 637.40 |
| Widowers (disabled) | 467.70 | 426.60 | 455.00 |
| Parents | 858.20 | 918.30 | 892.20 |

**Source:** US Department of Health & Human Services, Social Security Administration, *Social Security Bulletin, Annual Statistical Supplement, 2007*, table 5.A1.

**Notes:** 'All Races' includes other races not shown separately.

**Units:** Number of beneficiaries; average monthly benefit in current dollars.

## Table 8.05:  Occupied Housing Units, by Tenure, 1980–2005

|  | Black Householders | White Householders | All Householders |
|---|---|---|---|
| **1980** | | | |
| All households | 8,382 | 68,810 | 80,390 |
| Owner-occupied | 3,724 | 46,671 | 51,795 |
| Percent of total | 44.4% | 67.8% | 64.4% |
| Renter-occupied | 4,657 | 22,139 | 28,595 |
| **1991** | | | |
| All households | 10,832 | 79,140 | 93,147 |
| Owner-occupied | 4,635 | 53,749 | 59,796 |
| Percent of total | 42.8% | 67.9% | 64.2% |
| Renter-occupied | 6,197 | 25,391 | 33,351 |
| **2001** | | | |
| All households | 13,292 | 85,292 | 106,261 |
| Owner-occupied | 6,318 | 62,465 | 72,265 |
| Percent of total | 47.5% | 73.2% | 68.0% |
| Renter-occupied | 6,974 | 22,826 | 33,996 |
| **2005** | | | |
| All households | 13,447 | 89,449 | 108,871 |
| Owner-occupied | 6,471 | 65,023 | 74,931 |
| Percent of total | 48.1% | 72.7% | 68.8% |
| Renter-occupied | 6,975 | 24,426 | 33,940 |

**Source:** US Bureau of the Census, *Statistical Abstract of the United States, 1999,* table 1214; *2007,* table 955.

**Notes:** 'All Householders' includes householders of other races not shown separately.

**Units:** Number of housing units in thousands; percent of total units.

## Table 8.06: Housing Affordability for Families, 1995 and 2002

| | Black | White | All Races |
|---|---|---|---|
| **1995** | | | |
| **Percent that cannot afford a median-priced home in their region using conventional, fixed-rate, 30-year financing** | | | |
| *All families* | *80.5%* | *47.4%* | *52.2%* |
| Married couples | 62.8 | 39.9 | 42.2 |
| Male householder (no wife present) | 89.6 | 69.2 | 73.2 |
| Female householder (no husband present) | 94.0 | 79.4 | 84.5 |
| **Percent that cannot afford a median-priced home in their region using FHA, fixed-rate, 30-year financing** | | | |
| *All families* | *79.5%* | *46.1%* | *51.0%* |
| Married couples | 60.5 | 38.3 | 40.6 |
| Male householder (no wife present) | 87.1 | 69.6 | 73.2 |
| Female householder (no husband present) | 94.4 | 79.4 | 84.6 |
| **Percent that cannot afford a modestly priced home in their region using conventional, fixed-rate, 30-year financing** | | | |
| *All families* | *72.5%* | *39.6%* | *44.4%* |
| Married couples | 52.4 | 32.2 | 34.2 |
| Male householder (no wife present) | 79.5 | 59.6 | 64.1 |
| Female householder (no husband present) | 88.2 | 72.0 | 77.7 |
| **Percent that cannot afford a modestly priced home in their region using FHA, fixed-rate, 30-year financing** | | | |
| *All families* | *70.9%* | *37.2%* | *42.1%* |
| Married couples | 49.3 | 29.3 | 31.4 |
| Male householder (no wife present) | 81.4 | 58.2 | 62.8 |
| Female householder (no husband present) | 87.5 | 71.3 | 77.0 |

*(continued on next page)*

## Table 8.06: Housing Affordability for Families, 1995 and 2002

|  | Black | White | All Races |
|---|---|---|---|
| **2002** | | | |
| **Percent that cannot afford a median-priced home in their region using conventional, fixed-rate, 30-year financing** | | | |
| *All families* | 79.5% | 46.1% | 51.1% |
| Married couples | 64.2 | 37.3 | 40.2 |
| Male householder (no wife present) | 85.5 | 73.5 | 75.7 |
| Female householder (no husband present) | 92.9 | 80.0 | 84.1 |
| **Percent that cannot afford a modestly priced home in their region using conventional, fixed-rate, 30-year financing** | | | |
| *All families* | 71.7% | 38.8% | 43.6% |
| Married couples | 54.7 | 30.3 | 33.0 |
| Male householder (no wife present) | 77.3 | 64.9 | 66.9 |
| Female householder (no husband present) | 86.9 | 71.1 | 76.2 |

Source:  US Bureau of the Census, Current Housing Reports, *Who Can Afford to Buy A House in 1995?*, tables 2-2 and 3-2; *2002*, tables 2-2 and 3-2.

Notes:  'All Races' includes families of all races.

Units:  Percent of total families as shown.

## Table 8.07: General Mobility, 1999–2000 and 2005–2006

|  | Black | White | All Races |
|---|---|---|---|
| **March 1999–March 2000** | | | |
| *All people* | *34,948* | *221,703* | *270,219* |
| Non-movers | 28,226 | 187,810 | 226,831 |
| *Moved to:* | | | |
| Same county | 4,078 | 18,811 | 24,399 |
| Different county, same state | 1,208 | 7,135 | 8,814 |
| Different state, same region | 807 | 2,992 | 4,062 |
| Different division, same region | 111 | 1,076 | 1,261 |
| Different region | 346 | 2,633 | 3,105 |
| Abroad | 172 | 1,247 | 1,746 |
| **March 2005–March 2006** | | | |
| *All people* | *36,396* | *232,765* | *289,781* |
| Non-movers | 30,032 | 202,607 | 249,945 |
| *Moved to:* | | | |
| Same county | 4,277 | 18,681 | 24,851 |
| Different county, same state | 1,057 | 6,359 | 8,010 |
| Different state, same region | 427 | 1,132 | 1,731 |
| Different division, same region | 209 | 915 | 1,208 |
| Different region | 357 | 2,166 | 2,740 |
| Abroad | 38 | 905 | 1,296 |

**Source:**   US Bureau of the Census, Current Population Survey, *Geographic Mobility: March 1999 to March 2000*, table 2; *March 2005 to March 2006*, table 2.

**Notes:**   'All Races' includes races not shown separately.

**Units:**   Number of persons one year old and over in thousands.

## Table 8.08:  Selected Characteristics of Farms and Farm Operators, 2002

|  | Black farms | All farms |
|---|---|---|
| **Characteristics of farms** | | |
| *Farms and land in farms* | | |
| Number of farms | 29,090 | 2,128,982 |
| Land in farms | 3,355,791 | 938,279,056 |
| Harvested cropland | NA | 302,697,252 |
| *Farms by size* | | |
| 1-9 acres | 2,626 | 179,346 |
| 10-49 acres | 10,607 | 563,772 |
| 50-179 acres | 11,398 | 658,705 |
| 180-499 acres | 3,557 | 388,617 |
| 500 acres or more | 902 | 338,542 |
| *Owned and rented land in farms* | | |
| Owned land in farms | | |
| Farms | 26,488 | 1,979,140 |
| Acres | 2,196,264 | 584,963,623 |
| Rented or leased land in farms | | |
| Farms | 9,896 | 700,846 |
| Acres | 1,159,527 | 353,315,433 |
| *2002 Market value of agricultural products sold* | | |
| Total | $506,881 | $200,646,355 |
| Average per farm | 17,425 | 94,245 |
| Crops (including nursery and greenhouse crops) | 233,710 | 95,151,954 |
| Livestock, poultry and their products | 273,171 | 105,494,401 |
| *Farms by value of sales* | | |
| Less than $1,000 | 8,635 | 430,953 |
| $1,000-$2,499 | 6,359 | 307,368 |
| $2,500-$4,999 | 4,539 | 243,026 |
| $5,000-$9,999 | 3,947 | 246,624 |
| $10,000-$24,999 | 2,953 | 272,333 |
| $25,000-$49,999 | 1,225 | 163,521 |
| $50,000 or more | 1,432 | 465,157 |

*(continued on next page)*

## Table 8.08:  Selected Characteristics of Farms and Farm Operators, 2002

|  | Black farms | All farms |
|---|---|---|
| **Characteristics of farms (continued)** | | |
| *Farms by North American Industry Classification System* | | |
| Oilseed and grain farming (1111) | 2,767 | 37,540,988 |
| Vegetable and melon farming (11112) | 1,377 | 13,145,448 |
| Fruit and tree nut farming (1113) | 703 | 13,489,154 |
| Greenhouse, nursery, and floriculture production (1114) | 288 | 15,065,589 |
| Other crop farming (1119) | 4,854 | 14,548,102 |
| Tobacco farming (11191) | 925 | 1,506,953 |
| Cotton farming (11192) | 408 | 3,789,565 |
| Sugarcane farming, hay farming, and all other crop farming (11193, 11194, 11199) | 3,521 | 8,315,743 |
| Beef cattle ranching and farming (112111) | 15,000 | 19,755,572 |
| Cattle feedlots (112112) | 474 | 22,895,343 |
| Dairy cattle and milk production (11212) | 231 | 22,737,525 |
| Hog and pig farming (1122) | 1,179 | 12,337,959 |
| Poultry and egg production (1123) | 405 | 24,410,930 |
| Sheep and goat farming (1124) | 288 | 445,366 |
| Animal aquaculture and other animal production (1125, 1129) | 1,524 | 4,274,380 |
| **Characteristics of farm operators** | | |
| Total operators | 36,370 | 2,128,982 |
| *Residence* | | |
| On farm operated | 23,832 | 1,680,160 |
| Not on farm operated | 12,538 | 448,822 |
| *Principal occupation* | | |
| Farming | 19,542 | 1,224,246 |
| Other | 16,828 | 904,736 |
| *Days of work off farm* | | |
| None | 17,392 | 962,200 |
| Any | 18,978 | 1,166,782 |
| 1-49 days | 2,344 | 122,248 |
| 50-99 days | 1,447 | 66,306 |
| 100-199 days | 2,527 | 145,880 |
| 200 days or more | 12,660 | 832,348 |

*(continued on next page)*

## Table 8.08: Selected Characteristics of Farms and Farm Operators, 2002

|  | Black farms | All farms |
|---|---|---|
| **Characteristics of farm operators (continued)** | | |
| *Years on present farm* | | |
| 2 years or less | 1,690 | 74,754 |
| 3 or 4 years | 2,976 | 143,599 |
| 5 to 9 years | 7,217 | 374,756 |
| 10 years or more | 24,487 | 1,535,873 |
| Average years on present farm | NA | 20.7 |
| *Age* | | |
| Under 25 years old | 523 | 16,962 |
| 25-34 years old | 1,233 | 106,097 |
| 35-44 years old | 4,263 | 366,306 |
| 45-54 years old | 9,123 | 572,664 |
| 55-64 years old | 9,201 | 509,123 |
| 65 years old and over | 12,027 | 557,830 |
| Average age | 57.8 | 55.3 |
| *Sex* | | |
| Male | 29,631 | 1,891,163 |
| Female | 6,739 | 237,819 |
| *Principal operator is a hired manager* | | |
| Farms | 1,046 | 55,372 |
| Acres | 204,697 | 103,135,293 |

Source:  US Bureau of the Census, 2002 Census of Agriculture, Vol. 1 *Geographic Area Series, Part 51, US Summary and State Data*, tables 2, 9, 47, 50, 52, and 61.

Notes:  'All farms' includes farms owned/operated by persons of all races. Data was collected, by race of operator, with a maximum of 3 operators per farm.

Units:  Number of farms and farm operators by categories shown; land in acres; market value in thousands of dollars.

## Table 8.09: Farms and Operators, by State, 2002

| | Black Operators | | | White Operators | | |
|---|---|---|---|---|---|---|
| | Farms | Operators | Land in Farms | Farms | Operators | Land in Farms |
| *United States* | *30,605* | *36,370* | *3,836,339* | *2,077,656* | *2,966,230* | *883,755,206* |
| Alabama | 2,460 | 2,889 | 294,306 | 42,407 | 57,863 | 8,613,879 |
| Alaska | 1 | 1 | NA | 574 | 825 | 590,627 |
| Arizona | 46 | 52 | 2,636 | 6,950 | 11,110 | 4,846,435 |
| Arkansas | 1,008 | 1,155 | 173,925 | 45,834 | 65,838 | 14,241,472 |
| California | 336 | 388 | 33,688 | 75,166 | 112,321 | 26,791,340 |
| Colorado | 55 | 63 | 6,590 | 31,050 | 48,283 | 30,689,204 |
| Connecticut | 6 | 6 | 2,092 | 4,178 | 6,425 | 354,618 |
| Delaware | 25 | 34 | 1,333 | 2,345 | 3,537 | 535,686 |
| Florida | 1,132 | 1,363 | 92,741 | 42,358 | 60,195 | 10,265,971 |
| Georgia | 2,079 | 2,390 | 290,268 | 47,161 | 63,239 | 10,468,416 |
| Hawaii | 13 | 13 | NA | 2,367 | 3,149 | 1,046,617 |
| Idaho | 9 | 9 | 198 | 24,831 | 37,372 | 11,328,031 |
| Illinois | 67 | 78 | 12,563 | 72,863 | 99,430 | 27,284,004 |
| Indiana | 60 | 69 | 5,336 | 60,129 | 85,055 | 15,041,774 |
| Iowa | 36 | 43 | 9,050 | 90,544 | 124,932 | 31,708,937 |
| Kansas | 155 | 176 | 56,188 | 64,067 | 87,987 | 47,110,383 |
| Kentucky | 710 | 859 | 61,191 | 85,670 | 119,703 | 13,756,749 |
| Louisiana | 1,943 | 2,317 | 237,484 | 25,475 | 35,170 | 7,611,921 |
| Maine | 1 | 1 | NA | 7,163 | 11,051 | 1,357,281 |
| Maryland | 247 | 296 | 16,691 | 11,893 | 17,740 | 2,058,069 |
| Massachusetts | 25 | 36 | 645 | 6,016 | 9,402 | 516,536 |
| Michigan | 192 | 243 | 20,451 | 52,977 | 77,320 | 10,111,573 |
| Minnesota | 20 | 20 | 4,758 | 80,694 | 111,794 | 27,472,772 |
| Mississippi | 5,266 | 6,194 | 606,932 | 37,104 | 50,069 | 10,500,522 |
| Missouri | 259 | 286 | 49,723 | 106,023 | 153,143 | 29,788,866 |
| Montana | 8 | 9 | 5,590 | 27,066 | 40,669 | 55,645,998 |
| Nebraska | 12 | 14 | 2,577 | 49,262 | 69,393 | 45,856,918 |
| Nevada | 13 | 17 | 412 | 2,896 | 4,605 | 5,170,392 |

*(continued on next page)*

## Table 8.09: Farms and Operators, by State, 2002

| | Black Operators | | | White Operators | | |
|---|---|---|---|---|---|---|
| | Farms | Operators | Land in Farms | Farms | Operators | Land in Farms |
| *United States* | *30,605* | *36,370* | *3,836,339* | *2,077,656* | *2,966,230* | *883,755,206* |
| New Hampshire | 3 | 5 | NA | 3,334 | 5,339 | 441,164 |
| New Jersey | 82 | 107 | 4,237 | 9,781 | 14,715 | 796,328 |
| New Mexico | 65 | 69 | 41,522 | 14,732 | 21,219 | 37,459,047 |
| New York | 87 | 111 | 10,917 | 37,026 | 55,896 | 7,637,736 |
| North Carolina | 1,797 | 2,121 | 187,537 | 51,705 | 71,052 | 8,830,220 |
| North Dakota | 7 | 7 | NA | 30,418 | 40,761 | 38,782,289 |
| Ohio | 188 | 211 | 20,197 | 77,387 | 110,563 | 14,536,960 |
| Oklahoma | 889 | 1,096 | 149,825 | 78,451 | 108,877 | 32,453,807 |
| Oregon | 46 | 47 | 4,129 | 39,401 | 62,551 | 16,272,697 |
| Pennsylvania | 93 | 104 | 7,552 | 57,922 | 84,577 | 7,727,960 |
| Rhode Island | 1 | 1 | NA | 857 | 1,263 | 60,873 |
| South Carolina | 1,987 | 2,262 | 216,052 | 22,592 | 30,303 | 4,647,856 |
| South Dakota | 12 | 12 | 17,768 | 31,177 | 43,728 | 40,846,450 |
| Tennessee | 1,117 | 1,266 | 129,776 | 86,268 | 118,922 | 11,556,118 |
| Texas | 6,223 | 7,755 | 808,203 | 221,687 | 317,543 | 128,788,032 |
| Utah | 4 | 4 | 280 | 15,174 | 22,850 | 7,416,128 |
| Vermont | 3 | 3 | 685 | 6,543 | 10,376 | 1,240,975 |
| Virginia | 1,668 | 1,994 | 233,573 | 45,906 | 65,793 | 8,403,996 |
| Washington | 57 | 67 | 3,515 | 35,268 | 53,209 | 12,827,510 |
| West Virginia | 41 | 46 | 4,473 | 20,750 | 28,946 | 3,574,692 |
| Wisconsin | 45 | 55 | 5,720 | 76,928 | 115,193 | 15,717,963 |
| Wyoming | 6 | 6 | 660 | 9,286 | 14,934 | 32,971,414 |

**Source:** US Bureau of the Census, 2002 Census of Agriculture, Vol. 1 *Geographic Area Series, Part 51, US Summary and State Data*, tables 41 and 42.

**Notes:** Data was collected, by race of operator, with a maximum of 3 operators per farm.

**Units:** Number of farms and operators; land in acres.

## Table 8.10: Black-Owned Firms, by Major Industry Group, 1992

| | All Firms | | Firms with Paid Employees | | | |
|---|---|---|---|---|---|---|
| | Firms | Sales & Receipts | Firms | Sales & Receipts | Employees | Annual Payroll |
| *All industries* | *620,912* | *$32,197,361* | *64,478* | *$22,589,676* | *345,193* | *$4,806,624* |
| Agricultural services, forestry and fishing | 9,820 | 265,089 | 1,491 | 159,119 | 3,904 | 45,547 |
| Mining | 490 | 65,621 | 51 | 46,000 | 293 | 6,454 |
| Construction | 43,381 | 2,651,356 | 8,798 | 1,962,727 | 28,545 | 447,362 |
| Manufacturing | 10,469 | 1,319,193 | 1,958 | 1,155,011 | 12,977 | 251,322 |
| Transportation and public utilities | 49,095 | 2,498,102 | 4,072 | 1,305,091 | 20,308 | 308,376 |
| Wholesale trade | 7,550 | 2,944,321 | 1,510 | 2,745,412 | 8,649 | 203,544 |
| Retail trade | 86,840 | 6,967,644 | 12,096 | 5,591,522 | 82,931 | 760,051 |
| Finance, insurance, and real estate | 40,924 | 3,777,171 | 3,194 | 2,771,537 | 17,606 | 380,056 |
| Services | 332,981 | 11,057,136 | 30,081 | 6,773,932 | 169,248 | 2,393,563 |
| Industries not classified | 39,363 | 651,727 | 1,226 | 79,325 | 731 | 10,350 |

**Source:** US Bureau of the Census, 1992 Economic Census, *Survey of Minority-Owned Business Enterprises: Black*, table 1.

**Notes:** 'All firms' includes firms with paid employees and firms with no paid employees. 'Firms with paid employees' indicates firms that file payroll taxes.

**Units:** Number of firms and employees; sales, receipts, and annual payroll in thousands of dollars.

## Table 8.11: Minority-Owned Businesses, 1997

|  | Black | All Minorities | All Firms in US |
|---|---|---|---|
| *All firms* | 823,499 | 3,039,033 | 20,821,935 |
| Sales & receipts | $71,214,662 | $591,259,123 | $18,553,243,047 |
| *Firms with paid employees* | 93,235 | 615,222 | 5,295,152 |
| Sales & receipts | $56,377,860 | $516,979,920 | $17,907,940,321 |
| Employees | 718,341 | 4,514,699 | 103,359,815 |
| Annual payroll | $14,322,312 | $95,528,782 | $2,936,492,940 |

**Source:** US Bureau of the Census, 1997 Economic Census, *Survey of Minority-Owned Business Enterprises*, printed from www.census.gov/epcd/mwb97/us/us.html on July 14, 2006.

**Notes:** 'All firms' includes firms with paid employees and firms with no paid employees. 'Firms with paid employees' indicates firms that file payroll taxes.

**Units:** Number of firms and employees; sales, receipts, and annual payroll in thousands of dollars.

## Table 8.12: Black-Owned Firms, by State, 1997

| | All Firms | | Firms with Paid Employees | | | |
|---|---|---|---|---|---|---|
| | Firms | Sales & Receipts | Firms | Sales & Receipts | Employees | Annual Payroll |
| *United States* | 823,499 | $71,214,662 | 93,235 | $56,377,860 | 718,341 | $14,322,312 |
| Alabama | 19,077 | 1,008,966 | 2,266 | 728,041 | 13,232 | 231,869 |
| Alaska | 876 | 55,713 | 117 | 44,394 | 704 | 13,094 |
| Arizona | 3,582 | 314,497 | 503 | 252,736 | 5,704 | 92,407 |
| Arkansas | 6,721 | 386,958 | 761 | 264,831 | 2,464 | 40,975 |
| California | 79,110 | 6,395,311 | 7,377 | 4,552,255 | 56,252 | 1,081,299 |
| Colorado | 4,926 | 512,868 | 740 | 423,043 | 4,204 | 88,485 |
| Connecticut | 7,251 | 528,164 | 857 | 403,166, | 4,761 | 135,296 |
| Delaware | 2,707 | 184,549 | 322 | 144,443 | 3,450 | 43,258 |
| District of Columbia | 10,909 | 1,334,651 | 1,232 | NA | NA | NA |
| Florida | 59,732 | 4,092,155 | 6,424 | 2,925,260 | 31,035 | 556,186 |
| Georgia | 55,766 | 4,110,716 | 6,073 | 3,111,892 | 40,593 | 741,509 |
| Hawaii | 638 | 34,165 | 168 | 20,562 | 561 | 7,502 |
| Idaho | 164 | 17,535 | 16 | 14,220 | 231 | 7,321 |
| Illinois | 41,244 | 3,913,240 | 3,747 | 3,253,027 | 35,034 | 787,773 |
| Indiana | 11,107 | 1,192,143 | 1,440 | 1,035,570 | 10,775 | 199,604 |
| Iowa | 1,353 | 233,466 | 262 | 216,904 | 1,931 | 41,387 |
| Kansas | 3,396 | 593,636 | 524 | 547,688 | 5,834 | 174,203 |
| Kentucky | 5,629 | 658,535 | 611 | 588,703 | 7,717 | 121,353 |
| Louisiana | 25,782 | 1,917,295 | 3,050 | 1,451,135 | 27,441 | 464,477 |
| Maine | 257 | 28,088 | 36 | 23,600 | 346 | 6,871 |
| Maryland | 47,614 | 3,964,600 | 4,214 | 3,180,637 | 41,755 | 946,386 |
| Massachusetts | 11,834 | 1,013,134 | 1,239 | 804,314 | 8,267 | 188,731 |
| Michigan | 24,954 | 4,623,414 | 2,843 | 4,157,785 | 37,688 | 921,765 |
| Minnesota | 4,024 | 523,126 | 472 | 459,125 | 4,352 | 99,939 |
| Mississippi | 17,617 | 852,824 | 2,205 | 559,182 | 9,773 | 121,522 |
| Missouri | 13,678 | 1,261,398 | 2,142 | 1,060,253 | 14,503 | 252,769 |
| Montana | 62 | NA | 15 | NA | NA | NA |
| Nebraska | 1,565 | 129,219 | 238 | 110,006 | 1,874 | 29,722 |
| Nevada | 2,796 | 225,880 | 344 | 183,015 | 2,344 | 53,820 |

*(continued on next page)*

## Table 8.12: Black-Owned Firms, by State, 1997

| | All Firms | | Firms with Paid Employees | | | |
|---|---|---|---|---|---|---|
| | Firms | Sales & Receipts | Firms | Sales & Receipts | Employees | Annual Payroll |
| *United States* | *823,499* | *$71,214,662* | *93,235* | *$56,377,860* | *718,341* | *$14,322,312* |
| New Hampshire | 326 | 32,351 | 54 | 26,200 | 506 | 11,137 |
| New Jersey | 26,500 | 2,160,441 | 3,236 | 1,580,808 | 16,862 | 375,877 |
| New Mexico | 1,132 | 142,847 | 165 | 130,131 | 1,121 | 20,051 |
| New York | 86,469 | 5,067,265 | 7,822 | 3,445,063 | 45,703 | 1,005,200 |
| North Carolina | 39,901 | 2,299,285 | 5,441 | 1,701,399 | 33,914 | 441,415 |
| North Dakota | 99 | NA | 8 | NA | NA | NA |
| Ohio | 26,970 | 3,946,848 | 3,486 | 3,499,457 | 32,719 | 788,525 |
| Oklahoma | 5,309 | 333,094 | 618 | 259,565 | 4,847 | 77,957 |
| Oregon | 2,219 | 436,156 | 357 | 398,916 | 2,968 | 66,799 |
| Pennsylvania | 19,791 | 1,993,512 | 2,909 | 1,652,223 | 19,979 | 437,813 |
| Rhode Island | 1,269 | 124,434 | 181 | 104,097 | 1,935 | 26,805 |
| South Carolina | 23,216 | 1,408,925 | 3,148 | 1,030,411 | 17,713 | 234,660 |
| South Dakota | 150 | 17,294 | 22 | NA | NA | NA |
| Tennessee | 20,196 | 1,644,529 | 2,730 | 1,276,080 | 17,583 | 334,204 |
| Texas | 60,427 | 6,857,330 | 6,684 | 5,695,691 | 70,904 | 1,469,459 |
| Utah | 440 | 23,005 | 35 | 16,831 | 327 | 5,480 |
| Vermont | 168 | 37,324 | 36 | 35,449 | 341 | 4,481 |
| Virginia | 33,539 | 3,408,165 | 4,956 | 2,878,899 | 46,971 | 905,842 |
| Washington | 5,553 | 504,109 | 893 | 411,968 | 8,321 | 125,629 |
| West Virginia | 1,148 | 87,649 | 129 | 76,923 | 1,018 | 14,203 |
| Wisconsin | 4,848 | 550,114 | 798 | 462,623 | 8,179 | 139,501 |
| Wyoming | 232 | 12,670 | 64 | NA | NA | NA |

**Source:**  US Bureau of the Census, 1997 Economic Census, *Survey of Minority-Owned Business Enterprises: Black*, table 2.

**Notes:**  'All firms' includes firms with paid employees and firms with no paid employees. 'Firms with paid employees' indicates firms that file payroll taxes.

**Units:**  Number of firms and employees; sales, receipts, and annual payroll in thousands of dollars.

## Table 8.13: Black-Owned Firms, by Major Industry Group, 1997

| | All Firms | | Firms with Paid Employees | | | |
| | Firms | Sales & Receipts | Firms | Sales & Receipts | Employees | Annual Payroll |
|---|---|---|---|---|---|---|
| *All industries* | *823,499* | *$71,214,662* | *93,235* | *$56,377,860* | *718,341* | *$14,322,312* |
| Agricultural services, forestry and fishing | 12,464 | 417,169 | 1,356 | 259,649 | 5,457 | 77,198 |
| Mining | 231 | 21,551 | 16 | 12,867 | 186 | 5,319 |
| Construction | 56,508 | 7,712,059 | 12,973 | 6,587,348 | 70,928 | 1,510,252 |
| Manufacturing | 10,447 | 3,682,510 | 1,931 | 3,463,861 | 26,624 | 652,787 |
| Transportation and public utilities | 71,586 | 6,376,645 | 6,184 | 4,252,240 | 47,289 | 909,470 |
| Wholesale trade | 8,120 | 5,818,734 | 2,139 | 5,573,907 | 13,746 | 471,320 |
| Retail trade | 87,568 | 13,803,266 | 14,074 | 12,244,399 | 125,480 | 1,497,111 |
| Finance, insurance, and real estate | 37,934 | 3,088,582 | 4,820 | 2,189,556 | 18,379 | 498,318 |
| Services | 437,646 | 25,925,092 | 43,529 | 19,503,488 | 388,398 | 8,212,775 |
| Industries not classified | 101,128 | 4,369,056 | 6,347 | 2,290,545 | 21,853 | 487,761 |

Source: US Bureau of the Census, 1997 Economic Census, *Survey of Minority-Owned Business Enterprises*, printed from www.census.gov/epcd/mwb97/us/us.html on July 14, 2006.

Notes: 'All firms' includes firms with paid employees and firms with no paid employees. 'Firms with paid employees' indicates firms that file payroll taxes.

Units: Number of firms and employees; sales, receipts, and annual payroll in thousands of dollars.

## Table 8.14: Minority-Owned Businesses, 2002

|  | Black | All Minorities | All Firms in US |
|---|---|---|---|
| *All firms* | 1,197,661 | 19,894,823 | 22,977,164 |
| Sales & receipts | $88,779,041 | $8,303,716,399 | $22,634,870,406 |
| *Firms with paid employees* | 94,585 | 4,712,168 | 5,526,111 |
| Sales & receipts | $65,933,700 | $7,629,211,216 | $21,867,386,411 |
| Employees | 756,697 | 52,209,027 | 110,832,682 |
| Annual payroll | $17,576,171 | $1,548,757,745 | $3,815,069,400 |

**Source:** US Bureau of the Census, 2002 Economic Census, *Survey of Business Owners: Black-Owned Firms, 2002* (SB02-00CS-BLK), table 2.

**Notes:** 'All firms' includes firms with paid employees and firms with no paid employees. 'Firms with paid employees' indicates firms that file payroll taxes.

**Units:** Number of firms and employees; sales, receipts, and annual payroll in thousands of dollars.

## Table 8.15: Black-Owned Firms, by Receipts Size, 2002

| | All Firms | | Firms with Paid Employees | | | |
|---|---|---|---|---|---|---|
| | **Firms** | **Sales & Receipts** | **Firms** | **Sales & Receipts** | **Employees** | **Annual Payroll** |
| *All firms* | *1,197,661* | *$88,779,041* | *94,585* | *$65,933,700* | *756,697* | *$17,576,171* |
| Less than $5,000 | 359,524 | 863,214 | 1,465 | 3,736 | 3,108 | 162,884 |
| $5,000 to $9,999 | 248,976 | 1,688,039 | 2,078 | 14,281 | 743 | 5,948 |
| $10,000 to $24,999 | 294,603 | 4,453,377 | 5,911 | 101,321 | 4,662 | 45,471 |
| $25,000 to $49,999 | 125,278 | 4,283,114 | 9,239 | 341,300 | 10,436 | 102,938 |
| $50,000 to $99,999 | 73,920 | 5,159,069 | 15,427 | 1,122,666 | 25,985 | 325,013 |
| $100,000 to $249,999 | 51,738 | 7,911,531 | 25,010 | 4,093,697 | 77,418 | 1,157,659 |
| $250,000 to $499,999 | 20,916 | 7,257,408 | 15,532 | 5,378,683 | 86,473 | 1,583,195 |
| $500,000 to $999,999 | 11,977 | 8,305,940 | 9,901 | 6,938,500 | 98,773 | 2,219,920 |
| $1,000,000 or more | 10,727 | 48,857,347 | 10,202 | 47,939,516 | 449,098 | 11,973,144 |

Source: US Bureau of the Census, 2002 Economic Census, *Survey of Business Owners: Black-Owned Firms, 2002* (SB02-00CS-BLK), table 6.

Notes: 'All firms' includes firms with paid employees and firms with no paid employees. 'Firms with paid employees' indicates firms that file payroll taxes.

Units: Number of firms and employees; sales, receipts, and annual payroll in thousands of dollars.

## Table 8.16: Black-Owned Firms, by Employment Size, 2002

|  | Firms | Receipts | Employees | Annual Payroll |
|---|---|---|---|---|
| *All firms* | *94,585* | *$65,933,700* | *756,697* | *$17,576,171* |
| No employees | 19,291 | 2,984,958 | NA | 540,489 |
| 1 to 4 employees | 47,028 | 10,702,103 | 96,445 | 2,254,142 |
| 5 to 9 employees | 14,159 | 7,826,592 | 92,584 | 2,136,974 |
| 10 to 19 employees | 7,437 | 7,769,441 | 99,944 | 2,279,426 |
| 20 to 49 employees | 4,414 | 10,911,683 | 133,453 | 3,033,204 |
| 50 to 99 employees | 1,283 | 9,701,158 | 87,549 | 2,156,734 |
| 100 to 499 employees | 882 | 11,199,658 | 162,653 | 3,625,843 |
| 500 employees or more | 91 | 4,838,106 | 84,068 | 1,549,358 |

**Source:** US Bureau of the Census, 2002 Economic Census, *Survey of Business Owners: Black-Owned Firms, 2002* (SB02-00CS-BLK), table 7.

**Units:** Number of firms and employees; sales, receipts, and annual payroll in thousands of dollars.

## Table 8.17: Black-Owned Firms, by State, 2002

| | All Firms | | Firms with Paid Employees | | | |
| | Firms | Sales & Receipts | Firms | Sales & Receipts | Employees | Annual Payroll |
|---|---|---|---|---|---|---|
| *United States* | *1,197,661* | *$88,779,041* | *94,585* | *$65,933,700* | *756,697* | *$17,576,171* |
| Alabama | 28,666 | 1,651,017 | 2,214 | 1,186,833 | 16,367 | 338,065 |
| Alaska | 926 | 80,445 | 102 | 63,459 | 535 | 14,248 |
| Arizona | 6,337 | 535,112 | 636 | 400,483 | 6,581 | 130,574 |
| Arkansas | 8,942 | 441,944 | 689 | 278,845 | 4,440 | 74,171 |
| California | 112,873 | 9,767,066 | 10,046 | 7,090,101 | 67,393 | 1,850,692 |
| Colorado | 7,066 | 758,339 | 794 | 590,973 | 6,060 | 142,604 |
| Connecticut | 10,309 | 723,342 | 731 | 511,316 | 4,184 | 132,407 |
| Delaware | 4,258 | 214,953 | 385 | 130,256 | 2,770 | 38,240 |
| District of Columbia | 12,198 | 1,568,128 | 1,247 | 1,345,015 | 14,130 | 428,953 |
| Florida | 102,079 | 5,728,244 | 7,025 | 3,726,567 | 55,653 | 908,488 |
| Georgia | 90,461 | 5,664,651 | 6,149 | 3,909,083 | 39,106 | 909,070 |
| Hawaii | 817 | 80,778 | 74 | 65,069 | 681 | 18,955 |
| Idaho | 373 | 57,535 | 112 | 50,187 | 391 | 9,958 |
| Illinois | 68,704 | 4,983,941 | 4,223 | 3,910,033 | 38,492 | 1,107,227 |
| Indiana | 14,068 | 1,692,295 | 1,401 | 1,460,656 | 9,851 | 245,769 |
| Iowa | 1,610 | 258,058 | 216 | 230,550 | 1,647 | 46,567 |
| Kansas | 4,468 | 376,367 | 565 | 290,433 | 4,023 | 84,757 |
| Kentucky | 7,592 | 1,106,472 | 631 | 969,866 | 7,737 | 178,091 |
| Louisiana | 40,243 | 1,933,791 | 2,782 | 1,263,307 | 21,193 | 365,497 |
| Maine | 327 | 32,038 | 35 | 24,429 | 199 | 4,144 |
| Maryland | 69,410 | 4,654,696 | 4,399 | 3,320,003 | 39,858 | 1,116,242 |
| Massachusetts | 12,818 | 1,238,959 | 1,241 | 967,096 | 9,257 | 253,608 |
| Michigan | 44,366 | 4,293,679 | 3,112 | 3,592,682 | 32,781 | 866,799 |
| Minnesota | 7,837 | 682,442 | 525 | 550,440 | 4,990 | 183,806 |
| Mississippi | 25,002 | 1,313,636 | 2,005 | 788,830 | 11,239 | 186,607 |
| Missouri | 16,750 | 1,344,628 | 1,998 | 1,060,583 | 16,283 | 315,937 |
| Montana | 220 | 12,367 | NA | NA | NA | NA |
| Nebraska | 2,091 | 140,821 | 251 | 116,176 | 1,526 | 29,622 |

*(continued on next page)*

## Table 8.17: Black-Owned Firms, by State, 2002

| | All Firms | | Firms with Paid Employees | | | |
|---|---|---|---|---|---|---|
| | Firms | Sales & Receipts | Firms | Sales & Receipts | Employees | Annual Payroll |
| *United States* | *1,197,661* | *$88,779,041* | *94,585* | *$65,933,700* | *756,697* | *$17,576,171* |
| Nevada | 4,343 | 433,711 | 454 | 326,506 | 4,321 | 108,742 |
| New Hampshire | 470 | 68,125 | 73 | 53,144 | 888 | 23,041 |
| New Jersey | 36,282 | 3,243,629 | 3,716 | 2,550,803 | 26,473 | 731,799 |
| New Mexico | 1,541 | 255,182 | 174 | 223,453 | 1,018 | 28,657 |
| New York | 129,324 | 7,524,939 | 7,526 | 5,149,602 | 46,079 | 1,235,718 |
| North Carolina | 52,122 | 3,549,176 | 4,857 | 2,623,728 | 37,338 | 677,220 |
| North Dakota | 78 | 13,693 | NA | NA | NA | NA |
| Ohio | 35,658 | 3,600,434 | 3,143 | 2,981,788 | 29,996 | 671,173 |
| Oklahoma | 7,441 | 458,311 | 646 | 336,936 | 4,457 | 88,282 |
| Oregon | 2,222 | 371,029 | 324 | 321,232 | 1,917 | 49,414 |
| Pennsylvania | 24,757 | 2,117,924 | 2,661 | 1,692,371 | 21,333 | 508,254 |
| Rhode Island | NA | NA | NA | NA | NA | NA |
| South Carolina | 28,613 | 1,596,714 | 2,495 | 1,026,533 | 16,158 | 266,341 |
| South Dakota | 122 | 61,187 | 23 | 59,529 | 371 | 19,599 |
| Tennessee | 26,811 | 1,755,025 | 2,075 | 1,232,107 | 18,860 | 352,564 |
| Texas | 88,769 | 6,420,653 | 6,510 | 4,528,274 | 69,411 | 1,350,574 |
| Utah | 649 | 187,990 | 72 | 174,932 | 856 | 19,686 |
| Vermont | 211 | 20,868 | 28 | 18,736 | 178 | 4,088 |
| Virginia | 41,149 | 3,717,859 | 4,595 | 2,990,648 | 39,135 | 1,038,189 |
| Washington | 6,985 | 1,052,997 | 1,138 | 902,330 | 8,585 | 208,801 |
| West Virginia | 1,473 | 98,300 | 121 | 75,776 | 1,289 | 24,828 |
| Wisconsin | 6,685 | 633,444 | 861 | 522,539 | 8,789 | 150,893 |
| Wyoming | 149 | 9,600 | 38 | 7,341 | 108 | 2,456 |

**Source:** US Bureau of the Census, 2002 Economic Census, *Survey of Business Owners: Black-Owned Firms* (SB02-00CS-BLK), table 2.

**Notes:** 'All firms' includes firms with paid employees and firms with no paid employees. 'Firms with paid employees' indicates firms that file payroll taxes.

**Units:** Number of firms and employees; sales, receipts, and annual payroll in thousands of dollars.

## Table 8.18: Black-Owned Firms, by Major Industry Group, 2002

| | All Firms | | Firms with Paid Employees | | | |
|---|---|---|---|---|---|---|
| | **Firms** | **Sales & Receipts** | **Firms** | **Sales & Receipts** | **Employees** | **Annual Payroll** |
| *All industries* | *1,197,661* | *$88,779,041* | *94,585* | *$65,933,700* | *756,697* | *$17,576,171* |
| Agricultural services, forestry and fishing | 3,724 | 230,376 | 349 | 127,441 | 1,842 | 24,829 |
| Mining | 325 | 57,471 | NA | NA | NA | NA |
| Utilities | 508 | 95,876 | 32 | 86,201 | 132 | 7,324 |
| Construction | 75,020 | 9,635,050 | 8,736 | 7,506,982 | 55,145 | 1,718,104 |
| Manufacturing | 10,084 | 4,648,160 | 2,076 | 4,457,455 | 30,583 | 1,021,902 |
| Wholesale trade | 12,498 | 5,648,113 | 1,951 | 5,179,938 | 11,410 | 393,297 |
| Retail trade | 102,123 | 13,586,686 | 8,823 | 11,550,199 | 44,618 | 981,840 |
| Transportation & warehousing | 99,341 | 5,466,549 | 4,742 | 2,180,870 | 27,448 | 561,174 |
| Information | 14,319 | 2,518,049 | 1,392 | 2,299,709 | 14,680 | 689,562 |
| Finance & insurance | 28,324 | 2,821,823 | 3,665 | 2,081,093 | 13,579 | 548,518 |
| Professional, scientific & technical services | 115,765 | 9,397,194 | 11,015 | 7,101,235 | 70,906 | 2,881,641 |
| Health care & social assistance | 245,767 | 11,827,609 | 20,220 | 8,414,713 | 164,135 | 3,495,443 |
| Services | 210,498 | 5,199,718 | 8,646 | 2,113,532 | 32,090 | 574,156 |
| Industries not classified | 1,012 | 115,244 | 1,012 | 115,244 | 860 | 18,891 |

**Source:** US Bureau of the Census, 2002 Economic Census, *Survey of Business Owners: Black-Owned Firms, 2002* (SB02-00CS-BLK), table 2.

**Notes:** 'All firms' includes firms with paid employees and firms with no paid employees. 'Firms with paid employees' indicates firms that file payroll taxes.

**Units:** Number of firms and employees; sales, receipts, and annual payroll in thousands of dollars.

## Table 8.19: Small Business Administration Loans to Minority-Owned Small Businesses, 2000–2006

|  | Black-owned | Total minority |
|---|---|---|
| **2000** | | |
| Number of loans | 2,120 | 11,999 |
| Amount | $388 | $3,634 |
| **2002** | | |
| Number of loans | 2,148 | 14,304 |
| Amount | $419 | $4,228 |
| **2003** | | |
| Number of loans | 3,769 | 20,184 |
| Amount | $399 | $4,215 |
| **2004** | | |
| Number of loans | 4,827 | 25,413 |
| Amount | $481 | $5,144 |
| **2005** | | |
| Number of loans | 6,635 | 29,722 |
| Amount | $627 | $6,132 |
| **2006** | | |
| Number of loans | 7,231 | 33,772 |
| Amount | $693 | $6,606 |

Source: US Census Bureau, *Statistical Abstract of the United States, 2007*, table 745; *2008*, table 742.

Notes: 'Small Businesses' must be independently owned and operated, must not be dominant in their particular industries, and must meet standards set by the Small Business Administration for annual receipts or number of employees.

Units: Number of loans; total amount in millions of dollars.

## Table 8.20: Summary of Results of the 2000 Consumer Expenditure Survey

| | Black consumer units | White consumer units | All consumer units |
|---|---|---|---|
| *Number of consumer units* | *13,230* | *96,137* | *109,367* |
| Average income before taxes | $32,657 | $46,260 | $44,649 |
| Percent homeowners | 46% | 68% | 66% |
| **Average number in consumer unit:** | | | |
| Persons | 2.7 | 2.5 | 2.5 |
| Children under 18 years old | 0.9 | 0.6 | 0.7 |
| Persons 65 and over | 0.2 | 0.3 | 0.3 |
| Earners | 1.3 | 1.4 | 1.4 |
| Vehicles | 1.3 | 2.0 | 1.9 |
| **Average annual expenditures** | | | |
| *Total expenditures* | *$28,152* | *$39,406* | *$38,045* |
| Food | 4,095 | 5,304 | 5,158 |
| Food at home | 2,691 | 3,066 | 3,021 |
| Cereals and bakery products | 393 | 462 | 453 |
| Meats, poultry, fish, and eggs | 909 | 780 | 795 |
| Dairy products | 245 | 336 | 325 |
| Fruits and vegetables | 454 | 530 | 521 |
| Other food at home | 691 | 959 | 927 |
| Food away from home | 1,404 | 2,238 | 2,137 |
| Alcoholic beverages | 211 | 394 | 372 |
| Housing | 9,906 | 12,651 | 12,319 |
| Shelter | 5,678 | 7,312 | 7,114 |
| Owned dwellings | 2,607 | 4,877 | 4,602 |
| Rented dwellings | 2,843 | 1,923 | 2,034 |
| Other lodging | 227 | 512 | 478 |
| Utilities, fuels and public services | 2,571 | 2,478 | 2,489 |
| Household operations | 468 | 714 | 684 |
| Housekeeping supplies | 303 | 507 | 482 |
| Household furnishings and equipment | 887 | 1,640 | 1,549 |
| Apparel and services | 1,695 | 1,878 | 1,856 |

*(continued on next page)*

## Table 8.20: Summary of Results of the 2000 Consumer Expenditure Survey

| | Black consumer units | White consumer units | All consumer units |
|---|---|---|---|
| **Average annual expenditures (continued)** | | | |
| Transportation | $5,214 | $7,721 | $7,417 |
| Vehicle purchases | 2,285 | 3,574 | 3,418 |
| Gasoline and motor oil | 956 | 1,337 | 1,291 |
| Other vehicle expenses | 1,705 | 2,361 | 2,281 |
| Public transportation | 268 | 448 | 427 |
| Health care | 1,107 | 2,198 | 2,066 |
| Entertainment | 1,014 | 1,980 | 1,863 |
| Personal care products and services | 627 | 555 | 564 |
| Reading | 72 | 157 | 146 |
| Education | 383 | 666 | 632 |
| Tobacco products and smoking supplies | 243 | 329 | 319 |
| Miscellaneous | 572 | 804 | 776 |
| Cash contributions | 700 | 1,260 | 1,192 |
| Personal insurance and pensions | 2,313 | 3,510 | 3,365 |
| Life and other personal insurance | 358 | 404 | 399 |
| Pensions and Social Security | 1,955 | 3,105 | 2,966 |

Source:  US Department of Labor, Bureau of Labor Statistics, *Consumer Expenditure Survey, 2000,* table 7.

Notes:  'Consumer units' are defined as either: a) members of a household related by blood, marriage, or adoption, b) a single person living alone or with others, but who is financially independent, or c) two or more people living together who share responsibility for at least 2 of the 3 major types of expenses - food, housing, and other expenses. Students living in university-sponsored housing are also considered separate consumer units. 'All consumer units' includes consumer units of all races.

Units:  Number of consumer units in thousands; average numbers as shown; average annual expenditures in current dollars.

## Table 8.21: Summary of Results of the 2006 Consumer Expenditure Survey

| | Black consumer units | White consumer units | All consumer units |
|---|---|---|---|
| *Number of consumer units* | *14,265* | *100,479* | *118,843* |
| Average income before taxes | $41,142 | $62,661 | $60,533 |
| Age of reference person | 46.2 | 49.2 | 48.7 |
| **Average number in consumer unit:** | | | |
| Persons | 2.6 | 2.4 | 2.5 |
| Children under 18 years old | 0.8 | 0.6 | 0.6 |
| Persons 65 and over | 0.2 | 0.3 | 0.3 |
| Earners | 1.2 | 1.3 | 1.3 |
| Vehicles | 1.3 | 2.0 | 1.9 |
| **Percent of reference units who are:** | | | |
| Homeowners | 49% | 70% | 67% |
| High school graduates (no college degree) | 46 | 35 | 36 |
| College graduates | 49 | 60 | 59 |
| **Average annual expenditures** | | | |
| *Total expenditures* | *$34,583* | $49,994 | *$48,398* |
| Food | 4,530 | 6,289 | 6,111 |
| Food at home | 2,796 | 3,486 | 3,417 |
| Cereals and bakery products | 366 | 455 | 446 |
| Meats, poultry, fish, and eggs | 845 | 782 | 797 |
| Dairy products | 237 | 390 | 368 |
| Fruits and vegetables | 432 | 605 | 592 |
| Other food at home | 916 | 1,254 | 1,212 |
| Food away from home | 1,735 | 2,802 | 2,694 |
| Alcoholic beverages | 210 | 545 | 497 |
| Housing | 12,754 | 16,676 | 16,366 |
| Shelter | 7,378 | 9,791 | 9,673 |
| Owned dwellings | 3,600 | 6,781 | 6,516 |
| Rented dwellings | 3,555 | 2,409 | 2,590 |
| Other lodging | 223 | 600 | 567 |
| Utilities, fuels and public services | 3,461 | 3,395 | 3,397 |
| Household operations | 545 | 1,003 | 948 |
| Housekeeping supplies | 482 | 665 | 640 |
| Household furnishings and equipment | 888 | 1,822 | 1,708 |
| Apparel and services | 1,762 | 1,881 | 1,874 |

*(continued on next page)*

## Table 8.21: Summary of Results of the 2006 Consumer Expenditure Survey

| | Black consumer units | White consumer units | All consumer units |
|---|---|---|---|
| **Average annual expenditures (continued)** | | | |
| Transportation | $6,130 | $8,796 | $8,508 |
| Vehicle purchases | 2,362 | 3,555 | 3,421 |
| Gasoline and motor oil | 1,740 | 2,298 | 2,227 |
| Other vehicle expenses | 1,742 | 2,435 | 2,355 |
| Public transportation | 286 | 508 | 505 |
| Health care | 1,497 | 2,967 | 2,766 |
| Entertainment | 1,172 | 2,564 | 2,376 |
| Personal care products and services | 519 | 587 | 585 |
| Reading | 46 | 128 | 117 |
| Education | 495 | 885 | 888 |
| Tobacco products and smoking supplies | 187 | 353 | 327 |
| Miscellaneous | 544 | 896 | 846 |
| Cash contributions | 1,384 | 1,950 | 1,869 |
| Personal insurance and pensions | 3,354 | 5,478 | 5,270 |
| Life and other personal insurance | 245 | 330 | 322 |
| Pensions and Social Security | 3,109 | 5,148 | 4,948 |

**Source:** US Department of Labor, Bureau of Labor Statistics, *Consumer Expenditure Survey, 2006*, table 2100.

**Notes:** 'Consumer units' are defined as either: a) members of a household related by blood, marriage, or adoption, b) a single person living alone or with others, but who is financially independent, or c) two or more people living together who share responsibility for at least 2 of the 3 major types of expenses - food, housing, and other expenses. Students living in university-sponsored housing are also considered separate consumer units.
'All consumer units' includes consumer units of all races. 'White' includes Native Hawaiian and other Pacific Islander, American Indian or Alaska Native, and approximately 1.2 percent reporting more than one race.

**Units:** Number of consumer units in thousands; average numbers and percentages as shown; average annual expenditures in current dollars.

# Guide to Sources

**Note:** All URLs are valid and accessible as of June 15, 2008. Whenever possible, we have provided a general web address that should still be available when the data sources update, but some sources may move, and the URLs given below may be inaccessible at a later date. Several sources are annual reports and in cases where multiple editions of the report were used, only the most recent edition is cited here. Further details on which editions were used can be found in the **Source** section of individual tables. In addition, several sources are used in multiple chapters. For example, the *Statistical Abstract of the United States* is used as a source throughout this book. In these cases, sources are listed under the most relevant chapter.

# Chapter 1: Demographics & Social Characteristics

*America's Families and Living Arrangements: 2006*, **US Bureau of the Census, Current Population Reports.**

Containing information drawn from the *Annual Social and Economic Supplement*, this report presents a variety of information on marriage and families in the US, including marital status, presence or absence of children, children's custodial arrangements, household and family size, and family types. It also contains breakdowns by a variety of other factors, including race and Hispanic origin, employment, health insurance coverage, poverty status, and educational attainment. Prior to 1999, the report was known as *Marital Status and Living Arrangements*. Accessible at http://www.census.gov/population/www/socdemo/hh-fam.html

*American Community Survey 2006*, **US Bureau of the Census.**

The American Community Survey (ACS) is a major program conducted by the Census Bureau that collects a monthly sample of the entire US population, including information that was previously only collected in the long form of the Decennial Census. Each month, the ACS sends out surveys to approximately three million household units. Currently, the ACS provides data on a statewide and nationwide level, as well as for all cities and counties with populations of at least 65,000. Next year, data will be available for all places with at least 20,000 people, and by 2010, the Census Bureau hopes to provide data for all places, replacing the long form of the Decennial Census. The ACS is already beginning to take precedence over many of the topics covered by the Current Population Survey (CPS) program, due to its much larger sample size and considerable overlap in subject matter. The ACS contains data on population and demographics, as well as labor, unemployment, income, poverty, and a wide variety of other topics. Readers should be cautioned when comparing ACS data to data from other Census programs (such as the CPS), as the groups surveyed may differ. For example, prior to the 2006 edition, the ACS measured only the civilian noninstitutional population. Accessible at http://www.census.gov/acs/www/index.html

*Population Estimates*, **US Bureau of the Census.**

The Census Bureau's Population Estimates program publishes annual estimates of the total population for the nation, states, counties, cities and towns, and other Census-designated places. It also includes data on social and demographic characteristics (such as age, sex, race, and Hispanic origin). The annual estimates are used as input for a variety of calculations and estimates by other programs inside and outside the federal government. Population Estimates data is accessible at the following URLs:

| | |
|---|---|
| **Main page:** | http://www.census.gov/popest/estimates.php |
| **National estimates:** | http://www.census.gov/popest/states/NST-ann-est.html |
| **State estimates:** | http://www.census.gov/popest/states/ |
| **Race and Hispanic origin:** | http://www.census.gov/popest/race.html |
| **Components of change:** | http://www.census.gov/popest/states/NST-comp-chg.html |

*Projections of the Resident Population by Race, Hispanic Origin, and Nativity, Middle Series, 1999 to 2100; and US Interim Projections by Age, Sex, Race, and Hispanic Origin, 2000-2050*, **US Bureau of the Census, Population Projections Division.**

The Census Bureau periodically releases projections for future populations and demographic characteristics, based on current population counts and trends in migration and fertility rates. The 1990 Decennial Census was used to provide projections for 1999 to 2100. In 2004, the Census Bureau released an interim update based on the results of the 2000 Census. Readers should note that none of the projections take into account events that have occurred since their release. Accessible at http://www.census.gov/population/www/projections/natsum.html and http://www.census.gov/ipc/www/usinterimproj, respectively.

*Statistical Abstract of the United States, 2008.* **US Bureau of the Census.**

The *Statistical Abstract* is the summary publication for all the data collected by the Census Bureau, as well as the government's other programs, and collectively presents a thorough profile of the United States and its population, economy, and government. The *Abstract* contains information on just about every possible topic, and is a useful place to start any research project. Each chapter in this book draws some of its information from the *Abstract*. Available at www.census.gov/prod/www/statistical-abstract.html

*Who's Minding the Kids? Child Care Arrangements: Spring 2005*, **US Bureau of the Census, Current Population Reports.**

This CPS report draws from the Survey of Income and Program Participation and is released approximately every 3 years. It contains a wide range of information about child care, including the distribution of care (types of relatives, as well as nonrelatives) and the weekly expenditures on care, both overall and as a percent of the family's income. Accessible at http://www.census.gov/population/www/socdemo/childcare.html

# Chapter 2: Health

*Abortion Surveillance in the United States–2004*, **US Department of Health and Human Services, Centers for Disease Control and Prevention, Morbidity and Mortality Weekly Report.**

This report contains the annual results of the CDC's surveillance of abortions performed (number and rate), as well as characteristics of the women obtaining them. Note that several states do not report abortion data, so the report is based on an incomplete data set. Accessible at http://www.cdc.gov/mmwr/preview/mmwrhtml/ss5609a1.htm

*Births: Final Data for 2005*, **US Department of Health and Human Services, Centers for Disease Control and Prevention, National Center for Health Statistics, National Vital Statistics System.**

This report contains the final (processed) birth statistics for 2005. Released through the CDC's National Vital Statistics Reports, it is accessible at http://www.cdc.gov/nchs/data/nvsr/nvsr56/nvsr56_06.pdf, or through the NCHS at http://www.cdc.gov/nchs/births.htm

*Births: Preliminary Data for 2006*, **US Department of Health and Human Services, Centers for Disease Control and Prevention, National Center for Health Statistics, National Vital Statistics System.**

This report contains the preliminary birth statistics for 2006. Note that this data is considered less reliable than the forthcoming final estimates, and figures may be adjusted in that report. Released through the CDC's National Vital Statistics Reports, it is accessible at http://www.cdc.gov/nchs/data/nvsr/nvsr56/nvsr56_08.pdf, or through the NCHS at http://www.cdc.gov/nchs/births.htm

***Cases of HIV Infection and AIDS in the United States, by Race/Ethnicity, 2000–2004***, US Department of Health and Human Services, Centers for Disease Control, HIV/AIDS Statistics and Surveillance.

This supplement to the annual reports on HIV/AIDS surveillance contains estimates of AIDS cases, including data on how HIV was transmitted and the race/ethnicity of persons with HIV/AIDS. It includes data for the years between 2000 and 2004, and totals dating back to the start of the epidemic. Accessible at http://www.cdc.gov/hiv/topics/surveillance/resources/reports/2006supp_vol12no1/ default.htm, or at the main HIV surveillance page at http://www.cdc.gov/hiv/topics/surveillance/ index.htm

***Deaths: Final Data for 2005***, US Department of Health and Human Services, Centers for Disease Control and Prevention, National Center for Health Statistics, National Vital Statistics System.

This report contains the final (processed) death statistics for 2005. Released through the CDC's National Vital Statistics Reports, it is accessible at http://www.cdc.gov/nchs/data/nvsr/nvsr56/nvsr56_ 10.pdf, or through the NCHS at http://www.cdc.gov/nchs/deaths.htm

***Health, United States, 2007***, US Department of Health and Human Services, Centers for Disease Control and Prevention, National Center for Health Statistics.

*Health, United States* is the annual report published by the CDC's National Center for Health Statistics, and serves as a clearinghouse for the Agency's various data-collection programs. It includes excerpts from the National Health Interview Survey (NHIS), the National Vital Statistics System, and other programs from the National Center for Health Statistics (NCHS), as well as programs outside the CDC that collect data relevant to health. With several hundred pages of data covering a wide range of topics, *Health, United States* should be the first step in any search for health data. In addition, tables in the PDF report include links to Excel spreadsheets, which often include more extensive (and often more current) data than that given in the PDF. Accessible at http://www.cdc.gov/nchs/hus.htm

***Summary Statistics for the US Population: National Health Interview Survey, 2006***, US Department of Health and Human Services, Centers for Disease Control and Prevention, National Center for Health Statistics.

The National Health Interview Survey (NHIS) is the CDC's main source of information on the health of the civilian noninstitutionalized population of the United States. It is an annual survey with a sample size of approximately 35,000 households and 87,500 individuals. This report gives a summary of the overall results of the National Health Interview Survey; several other reports are also available. Accessible at http://www.cdc.gov/nchs/data/series/sr_10/sr10_236.pdf or through the main NHIS page at http://www.cdc.gov/nchs/nhis.htm

***Summary Statistics for US Adults: National Health Interview Survey, 2006***, US Department of Health and Human Services, Centers for Disease Control and Prevention, National Center for Health Statistics.

This report gives a summary of the results of the National Health Interview Survey for questions involving adults at least 18 years of age, and is a part of the larger NHIS. Accessible at http://www. cdc.gov/nchs/data/series/sr_10/sr10_235.pdf or through the main NHIS page at http://www.cdc.gov/ nchs/nhis.htm

***Summary Statistics for US Children: National Health Interview Survey, 2006***, US Department of Health and Human Services, Centers for Disease Control and Prevention, National Center for Health Statistics.

This report gives a summary of the results of the National Health Interview Survey for questions involving children's health, and is a part of the larger NHIS. Accessible at http://www.cdc.gov/nchs/data/ series/sr_10/sr10_234.pdf or through the main NHIS page at http://www.cdc.gov/nchs/nhis.htm

# Chapter 3: Education

*College Enrollment and Work Activity of 2007 High School Graduates*, **US Department of Labor, Bureau of Labor Statistics.**

This report contains labor and unemployment data for students who have graduated from high school in the past year (broken down by college enrollment status), as well as those who have recently dropped out of high school without receiving their diplomas. Data is collected during the Current Population Survey for people 16 to 24 years old. Accessible at http://www.bls.gov/news.release/pdf/hsgec.pdf

*Digest of Education Statistics 2007*, **US Department of Education, National Center for Education Statistics.**

The *Digest of Education Statistics* is the major report from the US Department of Education, and draws from a variety of other reports and data-collection programs. It provides information on all aspects of education in America, from pre-kindergarten through graduate school, with information on schools, enrollments, student social and demographic characteristics, achievement, teachers, educational finance and funding, and more. Accessible at http://nces.ed.gov/programs/digest

*Educational Attainment in the United States, 2007*, **US Bureau of the Census, Current Population Reports.**

This annual report, part of the CPS, tracks Americans' level of educational advancement, providing information based on age, sex, race and Hispanic origin, and a host of other characteristics. The CPS report on educational attainment has been revised and somewhat scaled back for 2007, in part due to the greater role now being played by the ACS, but it remains a useful source of information. Accessible at http://www.census.gov/population/www/socdemo/educ-attn.html

*School Enrollment: Social and Economic Characteristics of Students, October 2006*, **US Bureau of the Census, Current Population Reports.**

The Current Population Survey's annual report on school enrollment provides information on age, grade, race and Hispanic origin, income, enrollment status, and educational attainment, and is part of the CPS' larger efforts to track data on education. Accessible at http://www.census.gov/population/www/socdemo/school.html

# Chapter 4: Government and Elections

*Voting and Registration in the Election of November, 2004*, **US Bureau of the Census, Current Population Reports.**

The official estimates for each presidential and congressional election are contained in this biennial report, which includes information on voter registration and voting, with detailed data on race and Hispanic origin, sex, age, state, income, and educational attainment. Several editions of the report are used for this book. The most recent is accessible at http://www.census.gov/prod/2006pubs/p20-556.pdf. The main page for the reports can be found at http://www.census.gov/population/www/socdemo/voting.html

# Chapter 5: Crime, Law Enforcement & Corrections

*Annual Survey of Jails and Census of Jail Inmates*, **US Department of Justice, Bureau of Justice Statistics.**

The annual jail census presents tables on trend information for the number and rate of jail inmates. Data collected in the survey is used to generate many of the other reports produced by the Bureau of

Justice Statistics. Accessible at http://www.ojp.usdoj.gov/bjs/glance/tables/jailracetab.htm and http://www.ojp.usdoj.gov/bjs/glance/tables/jailrairtab.htm.

**Capital Punishment 2006, US Department of Justice, Bureau of Justice Statistics, Bureau of Justice Statistics.**

This bulletin provides the most current information on prisoners under sentence of death, including time from sentencing to execution and prior legal status. Accessible at http://www.ojp.usdoj.gov/bjs/pub/html/cp/2006/cp06st.htm

**Crime in the United States 2006, US Federal Bureau of Investigation, Uniform Crime Reports Unit.**

*Crime in the United States* is the FBI's annual summary of crime data for the nation, state, county, and city levels. The FBI's Uniform Crime Reports division provides a standardized format for tracking offenses, arrests, and law enforcement personnel, and works with over 17,000 law enforcement agencies to produce the nationwide report. Accessible at http://www.fbi.gov/ucr/cius2006/index.html.

**Criminal Victimization 2005, US Department of Justice, Office of Justice Programs.**

This report provides information on victims of crimes, broken down by type of offense, the time and place the crime was committed, and the characteristics of the victims (including sex, race/Hispanic origin, age, housing tenure, household, and marital status). Accessible at http://www.ojp.usdoj.gov/bjs/pub/pdf/cvus05.pdf

**HIV in Prisons, 2006 and HIV in Prisons and Jails, 2004, US Department of Justice, Bureau of Justice Statistics.**

These reports provide data on the incidence of HIV among prisoners, the number of inmates tested, and deaths from AIDS. The reports are accessible at http://www.ojp.usdoj.gov/bjs/pub/html/hivp/2006/hivp06.htm and http://www.ojp.usdoj.gov/bjs/abstract/hivp04.htm, respectively.

**Homicide Trends in the US, 2007, US Department of Justice, Bureau of Justice Statistics.**

This report details trends for homicides in the United States from 1976-2005, with detailed breakdowns on a variety of characteristics of the victim and perpetrator, as well as circumstances of the crime. Accessible at http://www.ojp.usdoj.gov/bjs/homicide/homtrnd.htm

**Lifetime Likelihood of Victimization, US Department of Justice, Bureau of Justice Statistics.**

This report estimates Americans' likelihood of being victims of crimes, based on race or Hispanic origin, and number of victimizations.

**Prevalence of Imprisonment in the US Population, 1974-2001 and Lifetime Likelihood of Going to State or Federal Prison, March 1997, US Department of Justice, Bureau of Justice Statistics.**

These reports estimate the chances of being incarcerated, as well as the percentage of people ever incarcerated, based on their current age. The most current data is accessible at http://www.ojp.usdoj.gov/bjs/abstract/piusp01.htm

**Prison and Jail Inmates at Midyear 2005, US Department of Justice, Bureau of Justice Statistics.**

This prisoner report contains state-by-state breakdowns of incarceration rates based on race and Hispanic origin. Accessible at http://www.ojp.usdoj.gov/bjs/abstract/pjim05.htm

**Prisoners in 2005, US Department of Justice, Bureau of Justice Statistics.**

The BJS' annual report on prisoners in the United States provides counts and rates for prisoners by state, type of facility, offense category, sex, race, and Hispanic origin. Accessible at http://www.ojp.usdoj.gov/bjs/abstract/p05.htm

**Sourcebook of Criminal Justice Statistics, 2003 and Online, US Department of Justice, Bureau of Justice Statistics.**

The *Sourcebook of Criminal Justice Statistics* collects data from over 200 sources on many topics relating to criminal justice in the United States, including crime statistics, victims, arrests, prisons, sentencing, and public opinion. While the *Sourcebook* began with regular annual editions, since 2003 updates have been added as new data becomes available. Accessible at http://www.albany.edu/sourcebook

# Chapter 6: Labor, Employment & Unemployment

**Employment and Earnings, 2007, US Department of Labor, Bureau of Labor Statistics.**

The major annual report from the CPS on topics relating to labor, employment, and unemployment, *Employment and Earnings* contains information on a wide range of topics, including unemployment rates, employed persons by industry and occupation, weekly earnings, employment status (full-time and part-time), and union affiliation, with further breakdowns based on age, sex, race and Hispanic origin, and educational attainment. The main report is accessible at http://www.bls.gov/cps/cpsa2007.pdf. The CPS' main page at the Bureau of Labor statistics, http://www.bls.gov/cps, contains links to individual tables in this report, and several other useful reports, as well as featuring a tool to create custom tables or download raw data files. Earlier versions of the report were known as the *Handbook of Labor Statistics*.

**Employment and Unemployment in Families by Race and Hispanic or Latino Ethnicity, 2005-2006 Annual Averages, US Department of Labor, Bureau Labor Statistics.**

This is the major report from the Bureau of Labor Statistics concerning employment in families, including data on marital status and presence of children under 18. It is accessible at http://www.bls.gov/news.release/pdf/famee.pdf

**Geographic Profile of Employment and Unemployment, 2003, US Department of Labor, Bureau of Labor Statistics.**

The *Geographic Profile* provides labor information for Census-designated regions and divisions, the 50 states (plus the District of Columbia), 50 major metropolitan areas, and 17 central cities. The full report is accessible at http://www.bls.gov/opub/gp/laugp.htm

**Geographic Profile of Employment and Unemployment, 2006 Annual Averages, US Department of Labor, Bureau of Labor Statistics.**

While the full *Grographic Profile* is released several years after the dates of its data, the program also produces more current preliminary estimates at the statewide level. The statewide estimates are accessible at http://www.bls.gov/lau/ptable14full2006.pdf

**Work at Home in 2004, US Department of Labor, Bureau of Labor Statistics.**

This BLS report presents data on individuals working from home, including information on industry and occupation, the number of hours worked, race and Hispanic origin, sex, marital status, and educational attainment. Accessible at http://www.bls.gov/news.release/pdf/homey.pdf

# Chapter 7: Earnings, Income, Poverty & Wealth

**Annual Social and Economic Supplement 2007, US Bureau of the Census, Current Population Reports.**

The Current Population Survey is a joint program between the Census Bureau's Population division and the Bureau of Labor Statistics. The *Annual Social and Economic Supplement* (ASEC, formerly known as the *March Supplement*) presents much of the data from the Current Population Survey on income for individuals, families, and households, including information on household characteristics, health insurance coverage, and employment status. The detailed ASEC is based on a sample of approximately 76,000 households, and collects much of the same information as the American Community Survey, although the two programs are distinct. Because the ACS collects much of the same data (with a larger sample size), the *Annual Social and Economic Supplement* is losing prominence in favor of the ACS, but it is still one of the Census Bureau's central programs collecting income and demographic data. Data from the *Annual Supplement* is accessible at the following URLs:

**CPS Main Page:** http://www.census.gov/cps
**Person Income:** http://pubdb3.census.gov/macro/032007/perinc/toc.htm
**Family Income:** http://pubdb3.census.gov/macro/032007/faminc/toc.htm
**Household Income:** http://pubdb3.census.gov/macro/032007/hhinc/toc.htm
**Poverty:** http://pubdb3.census.gov/macro/032007/pov/toc.htm
**Health Insurance Coverage:** http://pubdb3.census.gov/macro/032007/health/toc.htm

Data in the *Annual Supplement* has been released under different names in the past, including *Money Income of Households, Families and Persons in the United States*, and *Money Income of Households in the United States*. Some older data can also be found on the CPS' website under 'historical income tables.' Finally, much of the data in the social and demographic tables in Chapter 1 was also drawn from the *Annual Supplement*.

***Custodial Mothers and Fathers and Their Child Support: 2003*, US Bureau of the Census, Current Population Reports.**

This report from the CPS tracks the number of custodial parents receiving child support, and a variety of details about the parents and support. Data is given separately for custodial mothers, custodial fathers, and all custodial parents. Accessible at http://www.census.gov/population/www/socdemo/childcare.html

***Income, Poverty, and Health Insurance Coverage in the United States, 2006*, US Bureau of the Census, Current Population Reports.**

This annual report contains a summary of data on a wide range of measures relating to income, poverty, and health insurance coverage (see the above description for the Annual Social and Economic Supplement). Accessible at http://www.census.gov/prod/2007pubs/p60-233.pdf or through the CPS' main page at http://www.census.gov/cps

***Participation in Government Porgrams, 2001 Through 2003, Who Gets Assistance?*, US Bureau of the Census, Survey of Income and Program Participation.**

The Survey of Income and Program Participation (SIPP) investigates the effectiveness of federal, state, and local government programs by collecting information on income and program participation of individuals and households, including cash and noncash income, taxes, assets, liabilities, and participation in government transfer programs. The SIPP report used in this chapter measured participation in a variety of government aid programs, including the median benefit awarded and duration of program participation. Accessible at http://www.bls.census.gov/sipp/p70s/p70-108.pdf

# Chapter 8: Special Topics

***US Summary and State Data*, US Bureau of the Census, Census of Agriculture, 2002, Vol. 1 Geographic Area Series, Part 51.**

The Census of Agriculture is performed every 5 years, and is comparable in scope for farm and

# Guide to Sources

agricultural data to the Decennial Census for population and demographic data. The Agricultural Census presents a wealth of information on all aspects of farming, and should be considered the authoritative government source on the topic. Data from the 2007 Agricultural Census is still being processed; it will be available in early 2009. Data from the 2002 Census is accessible at http://www.agcensus.usda.gov/Publications/2002/index.asp

**Consumer Expenditure Survey, 2006, US Department of Labor, Bureau of Labor Statistics.**

The Consumer Expenditure Survey is the major BLS program tracking household spending in a variety of areas, including food, housing, apparel, transportation, health care, entertainment, reading, education, and insurance, as well as information on income, household size, housing tenure, and number of vehicles. Accessible at http://www.bls.gov/cex

**Survey of Minority-Owned Business Enterprises: Black-Owned Firms, US Bureau of the Census, Economic Census, 2002.**

The Economic Census is performed every 5 years, and is comparable in scope for business data to the Decennial Census for population and demographic data. The Economic Census presents a wealth of information on all topics related to business, industry, occupations, sales, receipts, employers and employees, taxes, and more, and should be considered the authoritative source on the topic. Data from the 2007 Economic Census is still being processed; results will be available in 2009 and 2010. Data from the 2002 Census is accessible at http://www.census.gov/econ/census02

**Geographic Mobility: March 2005 to March 2006, US Bureau of the Census, Current Population Survey.**

This annual report from the CPS estimates the number of people who have moved in the past year, as well as the type of move (within the same county, or to a different county, state, Census region, or out of the country), with detailed breakdowns by age, sex, and race or Hispanic origin. Accessible at http://www.census.gov/population/www/socdemo/migrate/cps2006.html

**Social Security Bulletin, Annual Statistical Supplement, 2007, US Department of Health & Human Services, Social Security Administration.**

The annual report from the Social Security administration presents information on the number of beneficiaries and benefits paid, with detailed information on type of benefit (including retirees, disabled workers, widows, and widowers) and beneficiary characteristics. Accessible at http://www.socialsecurity.gov/policy/docs/statcomps/supplement/2007

**Who Can Afford to Buy A House in 2002? US Bureau of the Census, Current Housing Reports.**

This report from 2002 measured the percentage of families who could afford a median-priced or modestly-priced house using several different types of mortgages and financing, with detailed breakdowns by marital status and race/Hispanic origin. Accessible at http://www.census.gov/hhes/www/housing/hsgaffrd/hsgaffrd.html

# Glossary

**AGE ADJUSTMENT**

A method of creating an overall rate in order to account for observed differences resulting from different age distributions in populations. The raw rates for each age group are combined (using a weighted average) to produce an overall rate that would apply if the population in question had the same age distribution as a reference population (usually the overall population of the United States).

**AGGRAVATED ASSAULT** *see* **CRIME.**

**AMERICAN COMMUNITY SURVEY**

A monthly sample of the civilian, non-institutionalized population that tracks much of the information previously only measured by the Decennial Census. Currently the ACS provides data on a nationwide and statewide level, as well as for cities and counties with populations over 65,000. For the 2007 edition (available in 2009), ACS coverage will expand to all communities with populations greater than 20,000. By 2010, the Bureau of the Census hopes to use the ACS to track all the information currently collected in the long form of the Decennial Census. *See also* **civilian noninstitutional population.**

**ARSON** *see* **CRIME.**

**AVERAGE** *see* **MEAN, MEDIAN.**

**BED DAY** *see* **DISABILITY DAY.**

**BIRTH** *see* **LIVE BIRTH.**

**BODY MASS INDEX (BMI)**

An estimate of body fat used to determine whether a person is a healthy weight, overweight, obese, or underweight. It is obtained by dividing a person's weight in kilograms by the square of their height in meters ($kg/m^2$). In general, a BMI over 25 is considered overweight, and a BMI over 30 is considered obese.

**BURGLARY** *see* **CRIME.**

**CAUSE OF DEATH**

For the purpose of national mortality statistics, every death is attributed to one underlying condition, based on information reported on the death certificate and utilizing the international rules (International Classifications of Disease) for selecting the underlying cause of death from reported conditions.

**CHRONIC CONDITION** *see* **CONDITION (HEALTH).**

**CIVILIAN LABOR FORCE**

All persons, excluding members of the Armed Forces, who are either employed or unemployed.

**Employed persons** are those persons 16 years old and over who were either a) "at work" – those who did any work at all as paid employees, in their own business or profession, on their own farm, or worked 15 or more hours as unpaid workers on a family farm or in a family business; or b) "with a job but not at work" – those who did not work during the reference period, but had jobs or businesses from which they were temporarily absent due to illness, bad weather, industrial dispute, vacation, or other personal reasons. Excluded from the employed are persons whose only activity consisted of work around the house or volunteer work for religious, charitable, and similar organizations.

Employed persons are classified as either **full-time workers**, those who worked 35 hours or more per week, or **part-time workers**, those who worked less than 35 hours per week.

**Unemployed persons** are those who were neither "at work" nor "with a job, but not at work" *and* who were both looking for work and available to accept a job. Also included as unemployed are persons who are waiting to be called back to a job from which they have been laid off. The unemployed are divided into four groups according to reason for unemployment:

- Job losers (including those who have been laid off)

- Job leavers who have left their job voluntarily

- Re-entrants, who have worked before and are re-entering the labor force

- New entrants to the labor force looking for work

**Discouraged workers**, those who do not have a job and have not been seeking one, not considered to be part of the labor force.

**CIVILIAN NONINSTITUTIONAL POPULATION** *see POPULATION.*

**CIVILIAN POPULATION** *see POPULATION.*

**COLLEGE**

A postsecondary school which offers a general or liberal arts education, usually leading to an associate's, bachelor's, master's, doctoral, or first professional degree. Junior colleges and community colleges are included. *See also **institution of higher education, university**.*

**COMMUNITY HOSPITAL**

All non-federal short-term hospitals, excluding hospital units of institutions, whose services are available to the public. **Short-term hospitals** are those where the average length of stay is less than 30 days.

**CONSUMER EXPENDITURE SURVEY**

A survey of current consumer expenditures, reflecting the buying habits of American consumers. Begun in 1979 and conducted jointly by the US Bureau of Labor Statistics and the US Bureau of the Census, the survey consists of two parts: an interview panel survey in which the expenditures of consumer units are obtained in five interviews conducted every three months, and a diary (or recordkeeping) survey completed by the participating households for two consecutive one-week periods. It should not be confused with the **Consumer Price Index**, which measures the average change in prices of consumer goods and services *See also **consumer unit**.*

### CONSUMER UNIT

An entity used as the basis of the **Consumer Expenditure Survey**. A consumer unit comprises either:

• All the members of a particular household who are related by blood, marriage, adoption, or other legal arrangements;

• A person living alone or sharing a household with others, or living as a roomer in a private home or lodging house or in a permanent living quarters in a hotel or motel, but who is financially independent;

• Two or more persons living together who pool their income to make joint expenditure decisions, and share responsibility for at least two of the three major types of expenses – food, housing, and other expenses.

A consumer unit may or may not be a household. Students living in university housing are usually counted as separate consumer units.

### CRIME

A crime is an action which is prohibited by law. There are two major statistical programs which measure crime in the United States. The first is the **Uniform Crime Reporting** (UCR) program, administered by the FBI. The Bureau receives monthly and annual reports from most police agencies around the country (covering nearly 300 million people in America). These reports contain information on eight major types of crimes (collectively called **serious crime**), which are known to police. Serious crime consists of four **violent crimes**: **murder** and **non-negligent manslaughter** (which includes willful felonious homicides and is based on police investigations rather than determinations of a medical examiner), **forcible rape** (which includes attempted rape), **robbery** (which includes stealing or taking anything of value by force or violence, or by threat of force or violence, and includes attempted robbery), and **aggravated assault** (which includes intent to kill), as well as four **property crimes**: **burglary** (which includes any unlawful entry to commit a felony or theft and includes attempted burglary and burglary followed by larceny), **larceny** (which includes theft of property or articles of value without use of force, violence, or fraud, and excludes embezzlement, con games, forgery, etc.), **motor vehicle theft** (which includes all cases where vehicles are driven away and abandoned, but excludes vehicles taken for temporary use and returned by the taker), and **arson** (which includes any willful or malicious burning or attempt to burn, with or without the intent to defraud, of a dwelling house, public building, motor vehicle, aircraft, or personal property of another).

The second approach to the measurement of crime is through the **National Crime Victimization Survey** (NCVS – formerly known as the National Crime Survey), administered by the Bureau of Justice Statistics. The survey is based on a representative sample of approximately 49,000 households containing 100,000 persons age 12 and over. Although the categories of crime are similar to those used by the FBI in the UCR, the NCVS is based on reports of victimization directly by victims, as opposed to crimes reported to police as in the UCR. As might be imagined, not all crimes are reported or known to police, so NCVS estimates of crime tend to be significantly higher than UCR figures. The NCVS also differs from the UCR in that only crimes whose victims can be interviewed are included (hence there are no homicide statistics), and only victims who are 12 years old or older are counted. The two central concepts in the NCVS are victimization, which is the specific criminal act as it affects a single victim, and a criminal incident, which is a specific criminal act involving one or more victims. Thus, in regard to personal crime there are more victimizations than incidents.

**DEATH** *see* **CAUSE OF DEATH, INFANT MORTALITY.**

**DISABILITY**

The presence of a physical, mental, or other health condition which has lasted six or more months and which limits or prevents a particular type of activity. *See also* **work disability.**

**DISABILITY DAY**

A day on which a person's usual activity is reduced because of illness or injury. There are four types of disability days (which are not mutually exclusive):

a) A **restricted-activity** day, a day on which a person cuts down on his or her usual activities because of illness or an injury.

b) A **bed-disability** day, a day on which a person stays in bed more than half of the daylight hours (or normal waking hours) because of a specific illness or injury. All hospital days are bed-disability days. Bed-disability days may also be work-loss days or school-loss days.

c) A **work-loss day**, a day on which a person did not work at his or her job or business for at least half of his or her normal workday because of a specific illness or injury. Work-loss days are determined only for employed persons.

d) A **school-loss day**, a day on which a child did not attend school for at least half of his or her normal school day because of a specific illness or injury. School-loss days are determined only for children 6 to 16 years of age.

**EMPLOYED PERSONS** *see CIVILIAN LABOR FORCE.*

**EMPLOYMENT STATUS** *see CIVILIAN LABOR FORCE.*

**ENROLLMENT**

The total number of students registered in a given school unit at a given time of year, generally in the fall. *See also **full-time enrollment**, **part-time enrollment**.*

**ETHNICITY** *see RACE*

**FAMILY**

A type of **household** containing two or more persons (including the householder) related by birth, marriage, or adoption living together. All such related persons in one housing unit are considered as members of one family. (For example, if the son or daughter of the family householder and that son's or daughter's spouse and/or children are members of the household, they are all counted as part of the householder's family.) However, non-family members who are not related to the householder (such as a roomer or boarder and his or her spouse, or a resident employee and his or her spouse who are living in), are not counted as family members but as unrelated individuals living in a family household. For Census purposes, a housing unit can contain only one household, and a household can contain only one family.

Families are classified by type according to the sex of the householder and the presence of a spouse and children. The three main types of family households are: **married couples**, in which a husband and wife live together (with or without other persons in the household); **male householder, no wife present**, in which a male householder lives together with other members of his family but without a wife; and **female householder, no husband present**, in which a female householder lives together with other members of her family but without a husband. *See also **household**.*

**FAMILY INCOME** *see INCOME.*

**FARM**

As defined by the Bureau of the Census (and adopted by the Department of Agriculture), a farm is any place from which $1,000 or more of agricultural products were sold, or would have been sold during a given year. Control of the farm may be exercised through ownership or management, or through a lease, rental or cropping arrangement. In the case of landowners who have one or more tenants or renters, the land operated by each is counted as a separate farm. This definition has been in effect since 1974.

**FARMLAND**

All land under the control of a farm operator, including land not actually under cultivation or not used for pasture or grazing. Rent-free land is included as part of a farm only if the operator has sole use of it. Land used for pasture or grazing on a per head basis that is neither owned nor leased by the farm operator is not included except for grazing lands controlled by grazing associations leased on a per acre basis.

## FARM INCOME

Gross farm income comprises cash receipts from farm marketings of crops and livestock, federal government payments made directly to farmers for farm-related activities, rental value of farm homes, value of farm products consumed in farm homes, and other farm related income such as machine hire and custom work.

## FULL-TIME ENROLLMENT

The number of students enrolled in higher education courses with a total credit load equal to at least 75% of the normal full-time course load.

## FULL-TIME WORKERS *see CIVILIAN LABOR FORCE.*

## HATE CRIME

A hate crime, also known as a bias crime, is a criminal offense committed against a person, property, or society that is motivated, in whole or in part, by the offender's bias against a race, religion, disability, sexual orientation, or ethnicity/ national origin.

## HEALTH LIMITATION OF ACTIVITY

A characteristic of persons with chronic conditions. Each person identified as having a chronic condition is classified by the extent to which his or her activities are limited by the condition as follows:

• Persons unable to carry on a **major activity** (the principal activity of a person of his or her age sex group): for persons 1–5 years of age, it refers to ordinary play with other children; for persons 6–16 years of age, it refers to school attendance; for persons 17 years of age and over, it usually refers to a job, housework, or school attendance.

• Persons limited in the amount or kind of major activity performed.

• Persons not limited in major activity, but otherwise limited.

• Persons not limited in activity.

## HEALTH MAINTENANCE ORGANIZATION (HMO)

A prepaid health plan delivering comprehensive care to members through designated providers, having a fixed monthly payment for health care services, and requiring members to be in the plan for a specified period of time (usually one year). HMOs are distinguished by the relationship of the providers to the plan. HMO model types are: **Group** – an HMO that delivers health services through a physician group controlled by the HMO, or an HMO that contracts with one or more independent group practices to provide health services; and **Individual Practice Association (IPA)** – an HMO that contracts directly with physicians in independent practice, and/or contracts with one or more associations of physicians in independent practice, and/or contracts with one or more multispecialty group practices, but is predominantly organized around solo single specialty practices.

**HIGHER EDUCATION** *see INSTITUTION OF HIGHER EDUCATION.*

**HISPANIC ORIGIN**

An aspect of a person's ancestry. The Bureau of the Census in many of its survey asks persons if they are of Hispanic origin. There are four main subcategories of Hispanic origin: Mexican, Puerto Rican, Cuban, and other Hispanic. Hispanic origin is not a racial classification. Persons may be of any race and of Hispanic origin. Hispanic origin is used interchangeably with Spanish and Spanish origin.

**HOSPITAL** *see COMMUNITY HOSPITAL.*

**HOSPITAL DAY**

A hospital day is a night spent in a hospital by a person admitted as an inpatient.

**HOUSEHOLD**

The person or persons occupying a housing unit. There are two main types of households: **family households**, which consist of two or more persons related by birth, marriage, or adoption living together; and **non-family households**, which consist of a person living alone, or together with unrelated individuals. *See also* **householder, family**.

**HOUSEHOLD INCOME** *see INCOME.*

**HOUSEHOLD TYPE** *see HOUSEHOLD.*

**HOUSEHOLDER**

The person in whose name a housing unit is rented or owned.

**HOUSING UNIT**

A house, apartment, mobile home or trailer, group of rooms, or single room occupied as a separate living quarter, or, if vacant, intended for occupancy as a separate living quarter. Separate living quarters are those in which the occupants live and eat separately from any other persons in the building and which have direct access from the outside of the building or through a common hall.

Both occupied and vacant housing units are counted in many surveys; however, recreational vehicles, boats, caves, tents, railroad cars, and the like are only included if they are occupied as someone's usual place of residence. Vacant mobile homes are included if they are intended for occupancy on the site where they stand. Vacant mobile homes on dealers' sales lots, at the factory, or in storage yards are excluded. Vacant units held for seasonal use or migratory labor are also excluded.

*See also* **occupancy status**, t**enure**.

**HOUSING TENURE** *see* **TENURE.**

**INCOME**

The term 'income' has different definitions depending on the context in which it is used. Like many government statistical terms, income can be viewed hierarchically.

**Personal income** is the current income received by persons from all sources, minus their personal contributions for social insurance. Persons include individuals (including owners of unincorporated firms), nonprofit institutions serving individuals, private trust funds, and private non-insured welfare funds. Personal income includes transfers (payments not resulting from current production) from government and business such as Social Security benefits, public assistance, etc., but excludes transfers between persons. Also included are certain non-monetary types of income, chiefly estimated net rental value to owner occupants of their homes, the value of services furnished without payment by financial intermediaries, and food and fuel produced and consumed on farms.

**Disposable personal income** is personal income less personal tax and non-tax payments. It is income available to persons for spending and saving. Personal tax and non-tax payments are tax payments (net of refunds) by persons (excluding contributions for social insurance) that are not chargeable to business expenses, and certain personal payments to general government that are treated like taxes. Personal taxes include income, estate and gift, personal property, and motor vehicle licenses. Non-tax payments include passport fees, fines and penalties, donations, tuition and fees paid to schools and hospitals mainly operated by the government.

**Money income** is a smaller, less inclusive category than personal income. Money income is the sum of the amounts received from wages and salaries, self-employment income (including losses), Social Security, Supplemental Security Income, public assistance, interest, dividends, rents, royalties, estate or trust income, veterans payments, unemployment and workers' compensation payments, private and government retirement and disability pensions, alimony, child support, and any other source of money income which was regularly received. Capital gains or losses and lump sum or one-time payments, such as life insurance settlements, are excluded. Also excluded are non-cash benefits such as food stamps, health benefits, housing subsidies, rent-free housing, and the goods produced and consumed on farms. Money income is reported for households and various household types, as well as for unrelated individuals. It is reported in aggregate, median, mean, and per capita amounts. Money income is also used for determining the poverty status of families and unrelated individuals. Family money income includes only the amount received by all family members 15 years old and over and excludes income received by household members not related to the householder.

### INFANT MORTALITY

The deaths of live-born children who do not reach their first birthday. Infant mortality is usually expressed as a rate per 1,000 live births.

### INSTITUTION OF HIGHER EDUCATION

An institution which offers programs of study beyond the secondary school level terminating in an associate, baccalaureate, or higher degree. *See also* **college**, **university**.

### JAIL

A facility, usually operated by a local law enforcement agency, holding persons detained pending adjudication and/or persons committed after adjudication to a sentence of one year or less. *See also* **prison.**

### LABOR FORCE STATUS *see* **CIVILIAN LABOR FORCE.**

### LARCENY *see* **CRIME.**

### LIMITATION OF ACTIVITY *see* **HEALTH LIMITATION OF ACTIVITY.**

### LIVE BIRTH

The live birth of an infant, defined as the complete expulsion or extraction from its mother of a product of conception, irrespective of the duration of the pregnancy, which, after such separation, breathes or shows any evidence of life such as heartbeat, umbilical cord pulsation, or definite movement of voluntary muscles, whether or not the umbilical cord has been cut or the placenta is attached. Each such birth is considered **live-born.**

### MARITAL STATUS

All persons 15 years of age and older are classified by the Bureau of the Census according to marital status. The Bureau defines two broad categories of marital status: **Single** – all those persons who have never been married (including persons whose marriage has been annulled), and **ever married**, which is composed of the now married, the widowed, and the divorced. **Now married** persons are those who are legally married (as well as some persons who have common law marriages, and some unmarried couples who live together and report their marital status as married), and whose marriage has not ended by widowhood or divorce. The now married are sometimes further subdivided into four categories: married, spouse present; separated; married, spouse absent; and married, spouse absent, other. **Married, spouse present** covers married couples living together. **Separated** includes those persons legally separated or otherwise absent from their spouses because of marital discord (such as persons who have been deserted or who have parted because they no longer want to live together but who have not obtained a divorce). Separated includes persons with a limited divorce. **Married, spouse absent** covers those households where the husband and wife were not counted as members of the same household, or where both husband and wife lived together in group quarters. **Married, spouse absent, other**, includes those married persons whose spouse was not counted as a member of the same household, besides those who are separated. Included are persons whose spouse was employed and living away from home, absent in the armed forces, or was an inmate of an institution. **Widowed** includes widows and widowers, women and men, respectively, whose spouses have died and who have not remarried. **Divorced** includes persons who are legally divorced and have not remarried.

**MARRIED COUPLES** *see* **FAMILY.**

**MARRIED PERSONS** *see* **MARITAL STATUS.**

**MEAN**

The arithmetic average of a set of values. It is derived by dividing the sum of a group of numerical items by the total number of items. Mean income (of a population), for example, is defined as the value obtained by dividing the total or aggregate income by the population. Thus, the mean income for families is obtained by dividing the aggregate of all income reported by persons in families by the total number of families. *See also* **median.**

**MEDIAN**

In general, a value that divides the total range of values into two equal parts. For example, to say that the median money income of families in the United States in 1985 was $27,735 indicates that half of all families had incomes larger than that value, and half had less. The median is less susceptible to distortion by extremely large or small values, and in many situations is preferred over the mean. *See also* **mean.**

**MEDICAID**

A federally-funded but state-administered and operated program which provides medical benefits to certain low-income persons in need of medical care. The program, authorized in 1965 by Title XIX of the Social Security Act, categorically covers participants in the Aid to Families with Dependent Children (AFDC) program, as well as some participants in the Supplemental Security Income (SSI) program, along with others deemed medically needy in each participating state. Each state determines the benefits covered, rates of payment to providers, and methods of administering the program.

**MEDICARE**

A federally-funded nationwide health insurance program providing health insurance protection to people 65 years of age and over, people eligible for social security disability payments for more than two years, and people with end-state renal disease, regardless of income. The program was enacted July 30, 1965, as title XVIII, Health Insurance for the Aged, of the Social Security Act, and became effective on July 1, 1966. It consists of two separate but coordinated programs: hospital insurance (Part A), and supplementary medical insurance (Part B).

**METROPOLITAN AREA**

Roughly, a population concentration of at least 50,000 inhabitants, generally consisting of a central city with a dense population and a surrounding area whose economy is closely linked with the city. The US Office of Budget and Management (OMB) designates which areas are considered metropolitan. The definitions are frequently altered and updated to reflect changes in the population. The most recent definition, **Core-Based Statistical Area (CBSA)**, was adopted in June, 2003. Past categories used the the OMB are **Metropolitan and Micropolitan area, Consolidated Metropolitan Statistical Area (CMSA), Metropolitan Statistical Area (MSA), Primary Metropolitan Statistical Area (PMSA), Standard Consolidated Statistical Areas (SCSA), Standard Metropolitan Statistical Area (SMSA), and New England County Metropolitan Area (NECMA).**

Tables that refer to metropolitan or non-metropolitan areas use the definition that was in effect at the time for the source used. Readers seeking a more detailed explanation should consult the original source or the Office of Budget and Management (www.whitehouse.gov/omb).

**MOBILE HOME** *see HOUSING UNIT.*

**MODESTLY PRICED HOME**

A home that is less expensive than 75% of the owner-occupied homes in that area of residence (often used as a measure of affordability).

**MONEY INCOME** *see INCOME.*

**MURDER** *see CRIME.*

**NATIONAL CRIME VICTIMIZATION SURVEY**

Formerly the **National Crime Survey**, a twice-yearly survey of 49,000 households containing over 100,000 inhabitants 12 years of age and older. Administered by the Bureau of Justice Statistics, the survey measures criminal victimization by surveying victims directly. It differs from the **FBI Uniform Crime Report** (UCR) which is based on crimes reported to police. *See also crime.*

**OCCUPATION**

The kind of work a person does at a job or business. Occupation is reported for a given survey period, or **reference period** (most frequently the week including March 12). If the person was not at work during the reference period, occupation usually refers to the person's most recent job or business. Persons working at more than one job are asked to identify the job at which he or she works the most hours, which is then counted as his or her occupation.

Occupations are classified according to the the federal Office of Management and Budget's Standard Occupational Classification system (SOC).

**OWNER-OCCUPIED HOUSING UNIT** *see* **TENURE.**

**PART-TIME ENROLLMENT**

The number of students enrolled in higher education courses with a total credit load of less than 75% of the normal full-time credit load.

**PART-TIME WORKERS** *see* **CIVILIAN LABOR FORCE.**

**PERSONAL INCOME** *see* **INCOME.**

**POPULATION**

The number of inhabitants of an area. The total population of the United States is the sum of all persons living within the United States, Puerto Rico, Guam, and the US Virgin Islands, plus all members of the Armed Forces living in foreign countries. Other Americans living abroad (e.g., civilian federal employees and dependents of members of the Armed Forces or other federal employees) are not included.

The **resident population** of the United States is the population living within the geographic United States. This includes members of the Armed Forces stationed in the United States and their families, as well as foreigners working or studying here. It excludes foreign military, naval, and diplomatic personnel and their families located here and residing in embassies or similar quarters, as well as Americans living abroad. Resident population is often used as the denominator when calculating birth and death rates, incidence of disease, and other rates.

The **civilian population** is the resident population excluding members of the Armed Forces. However, families of members of the Armed Forces are included.

The **civilian non-institutional population** is the civilian population not residing in institutions. Institutions include correctional institutions; detention homes and training schools for juvenile delinquents; homes for the aged and dependent (e.g., nursing homes and convalescent homes); homes for dependent and neglected children; homes and schools for the mentally and physically handicapped; homes for unwed mothers; psychiatric, tuberculosis, and chronic disease hospitals; and residential treatment centers.

**POVERTY STATUS**

Although the term "poverty" connotes a complex set of economic, social, and psychological conditions, the standard statistical definition provides for only estimates of economic poverty. These are based on money income before taxes and exclude the value of government payments and transfers such as food stamps or Medicare; private transfers, such as health insurance premiums paid by employers; gifts; the depletion of assets; and borrowed money. Thus the term poverty as used by government agencies classifies persons and families in relation to being above or below a specified income level, or **poverty threshold**. Those below this threshold are said to be in poverty, or more accurately, as below the poverty level. Poverty thresholds vary by size of family, number of children, and age of householder, and are updated annually. Poverty status is also determined for unrelated individuals living in households, but not for those living in group quarters nor for persons in the Armed Forces. The poverty threshold is revised each year according to formula based on the **Consumer Price Index**, which measures the average change in prices of consumer goods and services.

**PRISON**

A confinement facility having custodial authority over adults sentenced to confinement for a period of more than one year. Prisons are usually run by state or federal authorities. *See also* **jail.**

**PRIVATE SCHOOL** *see* **SCHOOL.**

**PROPERTY CRIME** *see* **CRIME.**

**PUBLIC SCHOOL** *see* **SCHOOL.**

**RACE**

The Bureau of the Census in many of its surveys (most notably in the decennial censuses of population) asks all persons to identify themselves according to race. The concept of race as used by the Bureau reflects the self-identification of the respondents, and is not meant to denote any clear cut scientific or biological definition.

Although it is often reported with racial categories, **Hispanic origin** is not a racial category. Persons may be of any race and of Hispanic origin. Those who describe themselves as Hispanic (or Mexican, Cuban, Chicano, etc.) in response to a question about race are included by the Bureau in the racial classification, "other." *See also* **Hispanic origin.**

**RAPE** *see* **CRIME.**

**REFERENCE PERSON**

Most frequently, the person who responds to a government survey. Most surveys done by the federal government are based on households and begin by asking the initial respondent the name of the person in whose name the housing unit is owned or rented (this person is designated as the **householder**). Usually the householder is the reference person. Other household members are defined in relation to the householder.

**REGION**

The Bureau of the Census has divided the United States into four regions. This division is the primary geographic subdivision of the nation for statistical reporting purposes. As a result, almost all federal agencies, along with many private data collectors, have adopted the regional subdivision and use it for presenting statistical data. The four regions are the Northeast (Maine, New Hampshire, Vermont, Massachusetts, Rhode Island, Connecticut, New York, New Jersey, Pennsylvania); the Midwest (Ohio, Indiana, Illinois, Michigan, Wisconsin, Minnesota, Iowa, Missouri, North Dakota, South Dakota, Kansas, Nebraska); the South (Delaware, Maryland, District of Columbia, Virginia, West Virginia, North Carolina, South Carolina, Georgia, Florida, Kentucky, Tennessee, Alabama, Mississippi, Arkansas, Louisiana, Oklahoma, Texas); and the West (Montana, Idaho, Colorado, Wyoming, New Mexico, Arizona, Utah, Nevada, Washington, Oregon, California, Alaska, Hawaii). All regional data in this book conforms to these definitions.

**RELATIVE STANDARD ERROR**

A measure of an estimate's reliability derived by dividing the **standard error** by the estimate itself. Estimates with a high relative standard error are considered unreliable, and are frequently not presented in reports.

**RENTER-OCCUPIED HOUSING UNIT** *see* **TENURE.**

**RESIDENT POPULATION** *see* **POPULATION.**

**ROBBERY** *see* **CRIME.**

**RURAL** *see* **URBAN.**

**SCHOOL**

Elementary and secondary schools are divisions of the school system consisting of students in one or more grade groups or other identifiable groups, organized as one unit with one or more teachers giving instruction of a defined type, and housed in a school plant of one or more buildings. More than one school may be housed in one school plant, as in the case where elementary and secondary programs are housed in the same building.

**Regular schools** generally are those which advance a person toward a diploma or degree. They include public and private nursery schools, kindergartens, graded schools, colleges, universities, and professional schools.

**Public schools** are controlled and supported by local, state, or federal government agencies.

**Private schools** are controlled and supported mainly by religious organizations, private persons, or private organizations.

**SCHOOL ENROLLMENT** *see* **ENROLLMENT.**

**SELF-EMPLOYMENT INCOME**

A type of money income which comprises net income (gross receipts minus operating expenses) received by persons from an unincorporated business, profession, and/or from the operation of a farm as a farm owner, tenant, or sharecropper. *See also* **money income.**

**SEPARATED PERSONS** *see MARITAL STATUS.*

**SERIOUS CRIME** *see CRIME.*

**SINGLE-PERSON HOUSEHOLDS** *see HOUSEHOLD.*

**SINGLE PERSONS** *see MARITAL STATUS.*

**STANDARD ERROR**

An estimate of the variation of a statistic, obrained by dividing the standard deviation by the square root of the sample size. See also *relative standard error.*

**SUBURBAN** *see URBAN.*

**TAXES**

Compulsory contributions exacted by a government for public purposes (except employee and employer assessments for retirement and social insurance purposes, which are classified as insurance trust revenue). All tax revenue is classified as general revenue and comprises amounts received (including interest and penalties, but excluding protested amounts and refunds) from all taxes imposed by a government.

**TENURE**

A concept relating to housing units. All occupied housing units are classified as being either owner-occupied or renter-occupied. A housing unit is **owner-occupied** if the owner or co-owner lives in the unit, even if the unit is mortgaged or not fully paid for. All other housing units are considered to be **renter-occupied**, regardless of whether or not cash rent is paid for them by a member of the household. *See also housing unit.*

**UNEMPLOYMENT** *see CIVILIAN LABOR FORCE.*

**UNIFORM CRIME REPORTING (UCR) PROGRAM**

A program administered by the FBI which collects reports from most police agencies in the nation (covering nearly 300 million people in America) on serious crimes known to police (violent crime and property crime), arrests, police officers and related items. The Bureau issues monthly and annual summary reports based on the program. *See also crime.*

**UNIVERSITY**

An institution of higher education consisting of a liberal arts college, a diverse graduate program, and usually two or more professional schools or faculties and empowered to confer degrees in various fields of study. *See also higher education.*

**URBAN**

**Urban, suburban,** and **rural** populations refer, respectively, to people living in the central city of a **metropolitan area**, outside the central city in a metropolitan area, or in a non-metropolitan area. Readers seeking a more detailed explanation, and the definition of metropolitan area that was in effect at the time, should refer to the original source. See also **suburban**, **rural**, **metropolitan area**.

**VICTIMIZATION** *see* **CRIME.**

**VIOLENT CRIME** *see* **CRIME.**

**VOTING-AGE POPULATION**

All persons over the age of 18 (the voting age for federal elections) in a given geographic area comprise the voting-age population. The voting-age population does include a small number of persons who, although of voting age, are not eligible to vote, such as resident aliens, and inmates of institutions. The voting-age population is estimated in even-numbered years by the Bureau of the Census.

**WAGES AND SALARIES**

A type (subgroup) of money income that includes civilian wages and salaries, Armed Forces pay and allowances, piece rate payments, commissions, tips, National Guard or Reserve pay (received for training periods), and cash bonuses before deductions for taxes, pensions, union dues, etc. *See also* **money income.**

**WIDOWED PERSONS** *see* **MARITAL STATUS.**

**WORK DISABILITY**

A health condition which limits the kind or amount of work a person can do, or prevents working at a job. A person is limited in the kind of work he or she can do if the person has a health condition which restricts his or her choice of jobs. A person is limited in amount of work if he or she is not able to work at a full-time (35 hours or more per week) job or business.

**WORK-LOSS DAY** *see* **DISABILITY DAY.**

# Index

Index

doctors, *see health*

Doctoral degrees, *see higher education*

drinking, *see alcohol use*

dropouts, *see schools*

drug use, 2.49

earnings, *see income; civilian labor force*

education, *see higher education; schools*

educational attainment, 1.10, 3.32, 3.34

    college completion, 3.33

    by degree type, 3.34

    labor force status, 6.23

    of mothers, 2.03

    by sex, 3.32

    unemployment, 6.24

    *see also higher education; school and schools*

elected officials, 4.01, 4.02

    by state, 4.02

    members of Congress, 4.19

elections, *see voters and voting*

emotional distress, 2.50

employment, *see civilian labor force*

enrollment in college, *see higher education*

enrollment in school, *see schools*

executions, 5.27, 5.34, 5.35, *see also death penalty*

exercise, *see leisure-time physical activity*

families

    child care expenditures, 1.26

    with children, 1.19–1.22

families *(continued)*

    employment, 6.08

    family income, *see income*

    with female householder, 1.19–1.21

    married couples, 1.19–1.21

    number of, 1.19–1.21

    number of earners, 1.19–1.21

    persons per family, 1.19–1.21

    primary care for preschoolers, 1.25

    poverty status, 7.18, 7.19

    size, 1.19–1.21

    structure, 1.22

family income, *see income*

farms and farming, 8.08, 8.09

    by state, 8.09

feelings of sadness, hopelessness, worthlessness, nervousness, restlessness, 2.50

firearm mortality, 2.25

fertility rates, 2.02, 2.05

fetal mortality, 2.08

firms (business), 8.10–8.18

    by employment size, 8.16

    by industry, 8.10, 8.13, 8.18

    minority-owned, 8.11, 8.14

    by receipts size, 8.15

    by state, 8.12, 8.17

first professional degrees, *see higher education*

forcible rape, *see arrests and arrest rates; crime and crime rates*

foreign-born, *see nativity*

## ORDER FORM

| Title | Qty | Edition | Price | Extended Price | Standing Order | |
|---|---|---|---|---|---|---|
| | | | | | YES | NO |
| **State & Municipal Profiles Series** | | | | | | |
| Almanac of the 50 States 2008 | | Hardcover | $89 | | ☐ | ☐ |
| Almanac of the 50 States 2008 | | Paperback | $79 | | ☐ | ☐ |
| California Cities, Towns & Counties 2008 | | CD | $119 | | ☐ | ☐ |
| | | Paperback | $119 | | ☐ | ☐ |
| Connecticut Municipal Profiles 2008 | | CD | $85 | | ☐ | ☐ |
| | | Paperback | $85 | | ☐ | ☐ |
| Florida Cities, Towns & Counties 2008 | | CD | $119 | | ☐ | ☐ |
| | | Paperback | $119 | | ☐ | ☐ |
| Massachusetts Municipal Profiles 2008 | | CD | $109 | | ☐ | ☐ |
| | | Paperback | $109 | | ☐ | ☐ |
| The New Jersey Municipal Data Book 2008 | | CD | $119 | | ☐ | ☐ |
| | | Paperback | $119 | | ☐ | ☐ |
| North Carolina Cities, Towns & Counties 2008 | | CD | $119 | | ☐ | ☐ |
| | | Paperback | $119 | | ☐ | ☐ |
| **Essential Topics Series** | | | | | | |
| Energy, Transportation & the Environment: A Statistical Sourcebook and Guide to Government Data 2008 | | Paperback | $77 | | ☐ | ☐ |
| **American Profiles Series** | | | | | | |
| Black Americans: A Statistical Sourcebook and Guide to Government Data 2008 | | Paperback | $77 | | ☐ | ☐ |
| Hispanic Americans: A Statistical Sourcebook and Guide to Government Data 2008 | | Paperback | $77 | | ☐ | ☐ |
| Asian Americans: A Statistical Sourcebook and Guide to Government Data 2008 | | Paperback | $77 | | ☐ | ☐ |

Offer and prices valid until 12/31/08

Purchase orders accepted from libraries, government agencies, and educational institutions.
Prepayment required from all other organizations.

| | |
|---|---|
| Order Subtotal | |
| (Required ONLY for shipments to California) CA Sales Tax | |
| Shipping & Handling | |
| Total | |

Please complete the following shipping and billing information. If paying by credit card or PO please call **(877)544-4636** or fax your completed order form to **(877)544-4635**. To pay by check, please mail this form and your payment to the address below.

Information Publications, Inc.
2995 Woodside Rd., Suite 400-182
Woodside, CA 94062

**U.S. Ground Shipping Rates**

| Order Subtotal | Shipping & Handling |
|---|---|
| $0-$89 | $7 |
| $90-$119 | $9 |
| $120-$240 | $14 |
| $241-$400 | $19 |
| $401-$500 | $22 |
| >$500 | Call |

Call for Int'l or Express Shipping Rates

**Shipping Information** (UPS/FedEx tracking number sent via email)

| | | |
|---|---|---|
| Organization Name | | |
| Shipping Contact | | |
| Address (No PO Boxes, please) | | |
| City | State | Zip |
| Email Address (req'd if want tracking #) | Phone # | |

**Payment Information** (mark choice)

| | ☐ **Check** | ☐ **Credit Card**  ☐ Visa  ☐ MC  ☐ AMEX | ☐ **Purchase Order** (attach PO to this form) |
|---|---|---|---|
| | Check # | CC# | PO # |
| | | Exp Date | |

**Credit Card Billing Information**   ☐ Check if same as Shipping Address

| | | |
|---|---|---|
| Name on Credit Card | | |
| Billing Address of Credit Card | | |
| City | State | Zip |
| Signature | | |

2995 WOODSIDE RD., SUITE 400-182
WOODSIDE, CA 94062

WWW.INFORMATIONPUBLICATIONS.COM

TOLL FREE PHONE 877-544-INFO (4636)
TOLL FREE FAX 877-544-4635

• Since 1980, A Trusted Ready Reference Resource for Easy-To-Use Federal, State and Local Information •

## ORDER FORM

| Title | Qty | Edition | Price | Extended Price | Standing Order | |
|---|---|---|---|---|---|---|
| **State & Municipal Profiles Series** | | | | | YES | NO |
| Almanac of the 50 States 2008 | | Hardcover | $89 | | ☐ | ☐ |
| Almanac of the 50 States 2008 | | Paperback | $79 | | ☐ | ☐ |
| California Cities, Towns & Counties 2008 | | CD | $119 | | ☐ | ☐ |
| | | Paperback | $119 | | ☐ | ☐ |
| Connecticut Municipal Profiles 2008 | | CD | $85 | | ☐ | ☐ |
| | | Paperback | $85 | | ☐ | ☐ |
| Florida Cities, Towns & Counties 2008 | | CD | $119 | | ☐ | ☐ |
| | | Paperback | $119 | | ☐ | ☐ |
| Massachusetts Municipal Profiles 2008 | | CD | $109 | | ☐ | ☐ |
| | | Paperback | $109 | | ☐ | ☐ |
| The New Jersey Municipal Data Book 2008 | | CD | $119 | | ☐ | ☐ |
| | | Paperback | $119 | | ☐ | ☐ |
| North Carolina Cities, Towns & Counties 2008 | | CD | $119 | | ☐ | ☐ |
| | | Paperback | $119 | | ☐ | ☐ |
| **Essential Topics Series** | | | | | | |
| Energy, Transportation & the Environment: A Statistical Sourcebook and Guide to Government Data 2008 | | Paperback | $77 | | ☐ | ☐ |
| **American Profiles Series** | | | | | | |
| Black Americans: A Statistical Sourcebook and Guide to Government Data 2008 | | Paperback | $77 | | ☐ | ☐ |
| Hispanic Americans: A Statistical Sourcebook and Guide to Government Data 2008 | | Paperback | $77 | | ☐ | ☐ |
| Asian Americans: A Statistical Sourcebook and Guide to Government Data 2008 | | Paperback | $77 | | ☐ | ☐ |

Offer and prices valid until 12/31/08

Purchase orders accepted from libraries, government agencies, and educational institutions.

Prepayment required from all other organizations.

| | |
|---|---|
| Order Subtotal | _____ |
| (Required ONLY for shipments to California) CA Sales Tax | _____ |
| Shipping & Handling | _____ |
| Total | _____ |

Please complete the following shipping and billing information. If paying by credit card or PO please call **(877)544-4636** or fax your completed order form to **(877)544-4635**. To pay by check, please mail this form and your payment to the address below.

Information Publications, Inc.
2995 Woodside Rd., Suite 400-182
Woodside, CA 94062

**U.S. Ground Shipping Rates**

| Order Subtotal | Shipping & Handling |
|---|---|
| $0-$89 | $7 |
| $90-$119 | $9 |
| $120-$240 | $14 |
| $241-$400 | $19 |
| $401-$500 | $22 |
| >$500 | Call |

Call for Int'l or Express Shipping Rates

**Shipping Information** (UPS/FedEx tracking number sent via email)

| | |
|---|---|
| Organization Name | |
| Shipping Contact | |
| Address (No PO Boxes, please) | |

| City | State | Zip |
|---|---|---|
| | | |

| Email Address (req'd if want tracking #) | Phone # |
|---|---|
| | |

**Payment Information** (mark choice)

| ☐ **Check** | ☐ **Credit Card** ☐ Visa ☐ MC ☐ AMEX | ☐ **Purchase Order** (attach PO to this form) |
|---|---|---|
| Check # | CC# | PO # |
| | Exp Date | |

**Credit Card Billing Information** ☐ Check if same as Shipping Address

| Name on Credit Card | | |
|---|---|---|
| Billing Address of Credit Card | | |

| City | State | Zip |
|---|---|---|
| | | |

| Signature | |
|---|---|

• Since 1980, A Trusted Ready Reference Resource for Easy-To-Use Federal, State and Local Information •